REASON, ETHICS, AND SOCIETY

ephen Darwall • David Gauthier • Joseph Raz
Peter Railton • Laurence Thomas • Shelly
agan • Judith Jarvis Thomson • Thomas
canlon • Jean Hampton • J.B. Schneewind •
tephen Darwall • Joseph Raz • Peter Railton •
aurence Thomas • Laurence Thomas • Shelly
agan • Judith Jarvis Thomson • Thomas
canlon • Jean Hampton • J.B. Schneewind •
tephen Darwall • David Gauthier • Joseph Raz
Peter Railton • Laurence Thomas • Shelly
agan • Judith Jarvis Thomson • Thomas
canlon • Kurt Baier • J.B. Schneewind •
tephen Darwall • Joseph Raz • Peter Railton •
aurence Thomas • Laurence Thomas • Shelly
agan • Judith Jarvis Thomson • Thomas
canlon • Kurt Baier • J.B. Schneewind •
tephen Darwall • David Gauthier • Joseph Raz
Peter Railton • Laurence Thomas • Shelly
agan • Judith Jarvis Thomson • Thomas
canlon • Kurt Baier • J.B. Schneewind •
Stephen Darwall • Joseph Raz • Jean Hampton
Laurence Thomas • Laurence Thomas •
helly Kagan • Judith Jarvis Thomson •
homas Scanlon • Kurt Baier • J.B.
chneewind • Stephen Darwall • David
authier • Joseph Raz • Peter Railton •
urence Thomas • Shelly Kagan • Judith Jarvis
omson • Thomas Scanlon • Kurt Baier •
ephen Darwall • J.B. Schneewind • Joseph
az • Laurence Thomas • Peter Railton •
urence Thomas • Shelly Kagan • Judith Jarvis
omson • Thomas Scanlon • Kurt Baier • J.B.
hneewind • Stephen Darwall • David
uthier • Peter Railton • Laurence Thomas •
elly Kagan • Judith Jarvis Thomson •

REASON, ETHICS, AND SOCIETY

Themes from Kurt Baier, with His Responses

EDITED BY J.B. SCHNEEWIND

Open Court
Chicago and La Salle, Illinois

First printing 1996

Printed and bound in the United States of America.

Library of Congress Cataloging-in-Publication Data

Reason, ethics, and society: themes from Kurt Baier, with his
responses / edited by J. B. Schneewind.
p. cm.
Includes bibliographical references and index.
ISBN 0–8126–9315–9 (alk. paper). — ISBN 0–8126–9316–7 (pbk. : alk. paper)
1. Baier, Kurt—Ethics. 2. Ethics. 3. Social ethics. 4. Social sciences and ethics. I. Baier, Kurt. II. Schneewind. J. B. (Jerome B.), 1930–
BJ354.B353R43 1996
170'.92—dc20 96-11814
CIP

Contents

Preface

Philosophy and philosophers thrive on controversy. The dialectic of assertion, criticism and reply is philosophy's substitute for the laboratory, the controlled sample, and the space probe. Disagreement with what someone has already said is one of the great sources of new philosophical ideas. Thales must have had a predecessor who held that the world was made up of several different kinds of material. Whatever the topic, we all learn to understand it better by seeing the different possible conceptualizations of it, and by weighing the costs and benefits of taking one or another line about it. Strong philosophers participate in existing controversies in ways that alter the terms for a good deal of future disagreement. Kurt Baier is such a philosopher.

The essays in this volume were written by philosophers for whom Baier's work has been significant. Many originated as papers for a conference revolving around the completion of the first part of Baier's *The Rational and the Moral Order.* The conference, organized by Robert Brandom and Richard Gale of the Philosophy Department at the University of Pittsburgh, took place in April 1993. Additional papers were contributed by some who could not attend. Like Baier's work itself, the essays take up questions central to our understanding of rationality, morality, and their relations.

The first paper sketches the development of Baier's work in order to bring out some of the innovations in *The Rational and the Moral Order.* It then locates Baier's general approach in the history of modern moral philosophy, in a way that leads to a Kantian question about the availability to ordinary unphilosophical moral agents of the ethics Baier proposes.

Stephen Darwall's essay also situates Baier's work in relation to a historically important set of problems, those involved in natural law theories and in the development of thought about moral autonomy. Darwall's aim is to question Baier's success in grounding morality in rationality, and to suggest that a Kantian approach is more fruitful.

David Gauthier distinguishes between being rational and being reasonable, in a way that Baier does not, in order to challenge Baier's thesis that reasonable action must involve socially established guidelines. He argues instead that the kind of rationality needed for morality is rooted in the individual, not in society.

Joseph Raz argues against the thesis, important to Baier and many others, that there is a deep distinction between moral considerations justifying action and other kinds of consideration. When we understand the differing ways in which different kinds of goods serve as reasons for action, he thinks, we will realize that there is no such thing as a special moral point of view.

Jean Hampton discusses instrumental reasoning. It is not clear, she argues, that a naturalistic account can be given of the force of the 'ought' in hypothetical imperatives. She traces the bearing of this problem on the work of Baier and a number of other contemporary theorists who claim to be naturalists while invoking instrumental reasoning in their theories of morality.

Peter Railton discusses internalism and externalism in the course of examining Baier's views on 'objective practical reasons'—reasons for action valid even if they do not directly motivate the agent who acknowledges them—in the light of a comparison of them with theoretical reasons—reasons for believing some proposition to be true.

The next three essays relate to Baier's important claim that the applicability of a theory of morality is an important test of its strength. Laurence Thomas considers the motivating force of moral reasons accepted by an agent through examining the problems raised by the psychology of those who sexually abuse children while acknowledging that it is wrong to do so.

The essays by Kagan and by Thomson draw on Baier's unpublished Carus Lectures, which were forerunners of chapter 9 of *The Rational and the Moral Order*. That chapter was unavailable at the time of the conference, but the importance of what it was to cover was already clear. The Carus Lectures gave the commentators ample material to consider, and most of what the Lectures said is retained in the book. Although it is regrettable that they must refer to an unpublished manuscript, the essays raise important questions about Baier's formulations in the book. The essays themselves make quite clear the positions they are considering. I have left standing their references to the Carus Lectures manuscript.

Shelly Kagan considers the common-sense moral distinction between killing and letting die, and challenges Baier's defense of it. Baier himself seems to allow a difference between the prima facie duties involved; Kagan pushes for, and fails to find, an acceptable account of it.

Judith Thomson also considers Baier's views on killing and letting die. In the light of his general theory, she finds them more persuasive than Kagan does, but thinks that they still leave important questions unanswered.

In the final essay Thomas Scanlon turns to a matter central to Baier's enterprise. Can it be shown, against Prichard, that the question, 'Why should I be moral?', is not only important but has a satisfactory answer? Scanlon argues that a satisfactory answer may be forthcoming in something like Baier's terms, but that the question is not as important as Baier thinks it is.

In his comments Baier responds where he thinks that doing so will carry forward the debate on the issues. In doing so he has richly supplemented his book. He modifies some of its positions in the light of criticisms, and he expands on topics, such as the views of Kant on imperatives, which are not as fully discussed in the book. His essay is thus more than a set of *ad hoc* answers to objections. It is a remarkably fresh examination of the issues they raise.

The contributors join the editor in thanking Kurt Baier not only for his thoughtful reflections on their work but for providing so much over the years for everyone interested in moral philosophy to consider. We hope the present volume will help to advance the enterprise.

J. B. SCHNEEWIND

BALTIMORE, FEBRUARY 1996

A Note on References

References to *The Rational and the Moral Order* are indicated throughout by the letters RMO. Baier's earlier book, *The Moral Point of View,* is indicated as MPV. For references to Baier's essays and articles, we use the numbers of the items listed in the complete bibliography of his work to be found at the conclusion of the volume.

Acknowledgments

The Department of Philosophy at the University of Pittsburgh was a munificent host for the conference that initiated this volume. Those who attended are grateful to the Department for planning and supporting it.

My thanks go to Collie Henderson for invaluable assistance in preparing Baier's comments and the bibliography of his work. I am particularly grateful to Natalie Brender, who brought the page references of the contributions into line with the published version of RMO and carried out the many other chores associated with making the manuscript one from which the volume could be published. Thanks also to Kerri Mommer and her staff at Open Court for their expert professional aid.

Baier's Theory of Morality: A Historical Introduction

1

J. B. Schneewind

Kurt Baier's *The Rational and the Moral Order* is the culmination of a lifetime of thought on the problems of moral philosophy. On his way to it Baier has produced a good deal of the most stimulating as well as meticulous work on ethics that the twentieth century has seen. The final result is as complex in its inner structure as it is comprehensive in its aim.

The aim, Baier says, is to solve some of the problems that so far have prevented ethics from being as successful a discipline as (say) logic. At the very beginning of *The Rational and the Moral Order* he expresses distress because it seems that "ethics [is] still only a branch of philosophy, as natural philosophy used to be before it became physics" (RMO, 1). We should be able, he thinks, to obtain "satisfactorily established" solutions to specific moral issues, such as that of whether killing is worse than letting die (RMO, 20). In the final part of his book he tries to show how such solutions can be obtained from the rationally grounded principles he develops. The first part of the book naturally begins with a diagnosis of the issues that prevent us from having a firmly grounded science of morality.

Confining himself to "the nature of morality, its place in ethics as a whole, and its relation to rationality" (RMO, 3), Baier finds three formidable problems. First, are the life according to reason, the good life, and the moral life identical, and, if not, how can all of them be reasonable (RMO, 3)? Second, how can reason be effective in motivating us to action (RMO, 7–16)? Third, what justifies societies in imposing sanctions to prevent moral wrongdoing (RMO, 16–20)? Baier approaches these problems by a thorough examination first of reason and of reasoning about practical matters, then of motivation, deliberation, and agency, and finally of the grounds of practical reasons, both those anchored in the concerns of each individual self and those anchored in the concerns of society.

The position he defends is roughly this. We need not and cannot answer the question "What sort of person should I be?" in order to answer the question "What should I do?" The latter question is fundamental. The answer is to be given by appeal to objective reasons for action, some of which warrant other people interfering in our lives to make sure we act as those reasons direct. The point of these norms is to prevent or adjudicate conflicts among the private interests of different members of society. Everyone is better off if all or almost all direct their actions in compliance with these socially anchored rules. The norms would be pointless if individuals did not have their own aims, but the reasons provided by socially anchored rules overrule reasons of private good, however expansively considered. Individual agents can and must be brought by proper education or training to take socially anchored rules as reasons for limiting their pursuit of their personal ends. Baier refuses the simplifications of utilitarianism, egoism, and Kantianism. No single principle can cover all of morality. But although he thinks there must be a multiplicity of socially anchored reasons, he is no intuitionist. He insists that there must be a statable and defensible method for settling disputes among individuals and for criticizing accepted moral rules. And although, like a pragmatist, he takes it that our starting point consists inescapably of the norms our society has in fact instilled in us, he thinks—quite unpragmatically—that there is a single all-encompassing rational foundation for the method that constitutes the core of the moral point of view.

In *The Rational and the Moral Order* Baier locates many of the main issues of ethical theory in a rich network of distinctions and offers sophisticated arguments for his conclusions. It will help those who examine the work to have some idea of its place in the development of ethical theory generally. I shall try, therefore, to place the work in history—first, in the history of Baier's own development; and second, in the larger history of moral philosophy. I use the second set of historical remarks, but not the first, to develop a critical question about Baier's view.

I

Baier's earliest publication took up several themes that have remained central to his thought. In "Objectivity in Ethics" (Baier 1) he asked what it means to assert or deny that the statements of ethics are objective or subjective, and proposed some ways of settling the issue thus clarified. If 'objective' means 'being like perceived properties such as color or taste', then some ethical statements seem to be objective. When we attend seriously to what such an utterance is about, for instance killing innocent people, we cannot avoid experiencing it as wrong, and we expect others to have the same experience. The experience of wrongness in this case is not under our control, and it is public. It is therefore like experiencing a red apple as red when we look at it under proper conditions. But many ethical statements do not seem to be like that, Baier said, so he proposed a second understanding of 'objective'. When people disagree on something we might hold that one party rather than the other must be right, or we might say it doesn't matter. If the former, we might think we can settle the issue by taking a vote, or we might say that voting is altogether the wrong way to settle it. Ethical statements are objective if we insist on settling disagreements but reject voting as a method. The question whether an adjective refers to an objective quality amounts to the question of the procedures it is proper to use—not simply those we actually use—for settling disputes about its presence. Baier did not think it either necessary or sufficient for the objectivity of moral statements that they concern properties like redness. He suggested that the one aspect of morals—finding out what is right—is not a matter for decision, although the second aspect—doing it—plainly is. But though he thus pointed to the conclusion that moral statements are objective because moral disputes must be settled, and not by voting, he did not offer a full argument for it. Little wonder, seeing how complex that argument turned out to be!

Many English-language philosophers were addressing the issues Baier considered in this paper. The late '40s and the '50s were the period when the hold of logical positivism and its dismissal of moral utterances as nonsense or as noncognitive expressions of emotion[1] were being challenged, often in the name of ordinary language. Baier used appeals to ordinary language as he continued the criticism of emotivism and subjectivism begun in the first paper. He argued, for instance, that the then widely made distinction between descriptive terms said to be used in science and emotive terms said to be central to morality was largely due to linguistic confusion (Baier 3, 203–4). "Descriptions," Baier claimed in a 1952 paper written with Toulmin, "can be as emotive as you please, and are never 'true' or 'false'" (Baier 5, 13). Like many others Baier thought that philosophers should not deviate from or aim to alter the ways we usually talk (Baier 6), but his main interest in considering what we ordinarily say was in bringing out the complex social practices that we all know in knowing the ordinary use of words.

One example Baier gave, in "Decisions and Descriptions" (Baier 3), turned out to be quite significant. Baier there discussed the commitments entailed by various sorts of language-using activity. To assert a proposition, for instance, is to imply one's belief that it is true. Hence it is quite odd to say "Jones is at home but I don't think so" (Baier 3, 182–83). This kind of assertion, which famously perplexed G. E. Moore, figured in a number of Baier's later papers, and it is easy to see why. Concerned with the rationality of morals, he could propose this kind of assertion as displaying an irrationality that was not the same as self-contradiction though just as patently and unquestionably irrational. Moreover it was an irrationality springing from incoherence in what someone—in this case a speaker—was claiming to do. To be a competent speaker of a language entails knowing that to say that P is to imply (in some sense) that the speaker believes or knows that P; so the

Moorean sentence involves a rational incoherence in what the speaker is doing. Could morality involve a form of rationality forced upon us as the only way of avoiding this sort of incoherence in some kind of activity of ours—an activity we cannot rationally give up?

In his 1953 paper "Good Reasons" (Baier 7) Baier gave the rudiments of an argument of this kind against skepticism about reasons for actions. When someone offers a reason for an act, Baier held, she is saying something that requires either agreement or disagreement and cannot be treated either as simply her acceptance of a convention or as a brute fact about her (Baier 7, 4). The practice of giving reasons, that is, brings with it the apparatus of objective truth and falsity. He then tried to show that there is a fact—the painfulness of a course of action—that cannot rationally be denied to be a reason against doing an action. To establish this he argued—against Ryle, among others—that pain is not merely "a sensation of a special sort, which we ordinarily dislike having" (Baier 7, 9). To have a pain is rather to have a sensation that by its very nature grounds rejection. Because of the way we learn and use pain-language, we necessarily treat some act's causing us pain as a reason against doing it. Baier allowed that painfulness yields only an overrideable reason against an action. But even this, he thought, provided enough to show the skeptic that there can be good reasons for or against some action. He rejected the thought that a deductive proof of the existence of good reasons can be found. His claim was that he could show "that anyone denying that a certain fact is a good reason (prima facie and presumptively) against doing something is laying himself open to criticism of a sort just as serious as that he is contradicting himself, namely, that he is irrational" (Baier 7, 7).[2]

In 1953 Baier published a proof of a particular moral judgment (Baier 8), designed to be a counter-example both to emotivist skepticism and to the skepticism that resulted from the objectivist positions of Moore and Ross. The continuing argument was deepened by the important 1954 essay "The Point of View of Morality." Baier's aim there was to show that there is an appropriate method for answering moral questions and thus that moral claims can be verified, though not in ways then considered standard (Baier 11, 104–5).

What makes the question "What shall I do?" into a moral question? That it is asked from the moral point of view, Baier replied, which means that in deliberating one takes into account the moral rules of one's society (Baier 11, 106–7). Distinctively moral rules have various characteristics, such as being backed by moral pressure in one's society and being universally teachable. It follows that it would be absurd to try to make certain types of rules part of a morality—not because such rules are self-contradictory but because they suffer from other, equally evident, irrationalities (Baier 11, 111) such as being self-defeating or not being openly teachable to everyone. The first step in the method of answering moral questions, Baier claimed, is to see if a proposed action contravenes the moral rules. If so, the act is at least prima facie wrong (Baier 11, 119).

This, however, is not all there is to it. The group's morality must itself be open to examination. The social function of moral rules makes it necessary that they be open to criticism. It would thus be absurd for anyone who accepted the need for something to do what moral rules do to deny that criticism of existing mores must be possible. Hence whatever is needed as a basis for such criticism must also be accepted (Baier 11, 119–26). Morality thus expands beyond agents' questions and answers to the judgments of those who criticize particular actions, the statements of a critic of the morality as a whole, and the utterances of a moral reformer. All of these can be reasonable, and no one kind of statement exhausts the moral domain. (Baier 11, 133–35).

II

Plainly by 1954 Baier had in mind the elements of his first book, *The Moral Point of View*, which appeared in 1958. Before discussing it I want to say something about the basic motivation with which Baier approached the problems of moral philosophy. Here I draw on a fascinating autobiographical paper—the only one Baier seems to have written—which is less widely known among philosophers than it deserves to be, perhaps because it was published as part of a symposium on and by Austrian exiles and emigrants.[3]

In "Zeitzeuge"—literally, "Time Witness"—Baier recalled his upbringing in a conservative, nationalistic, religious Austrian family that held itself aloof from politics and that drove him to be liberal, cosmopolitan, and freethinking (Baier 89, 125). A number of his relatives, he continued, particularly those who were more modern and more prosperous than his parents, accepted what was called "healthy anti-Semitism." They thought it important to exclude Jews from certain aspects of social and commercial life, so that medicine and law would not be overrun by them (one would not want one's wife examined by a Jewish doctor). But they rejected what they thought the "excessive anti-Semitism" of vocal extremists around them. Baier described himself as having included healthy anti-Semitism in the vague enlightenment attitude he held at the time. And so he found it all the more shocking to discover, shortly before the Anschluss, that his actual father—he was raised by his mother and a stepfather—was classified by the Nazis as a Jew. "There is, I think, scarcely anything," Baier wrote, "that makes the concept of injustice clearer to one than involuntary membership in a group against which law and public opinion discriminate sharply" (Baier 89, 126).

This moving glimpse into Baier's formation helps us to understand how he was led to some of the recurrent themes of his work. He has persistently held, first, that in thinking about morality there is no place to start except the mores of one's group or society, as one has been educated into them; second, that the mores must not be taken as final, but must be subjected to criticism; and third, that even good people may act in horribly unjust and immoral ways, so that standards of just and decent action must dominate consideration of the virtue of agents.[4]

The autobiography also sheds light on the roots of Baier's lifelong rejection of religious views of philosophical problems and, more important, of life's problems. His inaugural lecture at Canberra, "The Meaning of Life," gave a full account of his outlook on these matters. Published just a year before *The Moral Point of View,* it helps us understand the larger significance of the stress on individual fulfillment that has always been present in Baier's work. He has never accepted either psychological or normative egoism, but he has always taken it for granted that each of us should have the best chance we can of living the best possible life, whatever we may decide that it involves.

Living the best humanly possible life is not for Baier a lowly or unworthy enterprise. Beset with contingencies and the possibility of failure, without any supernatural assurance, it is, he argued in the inaugural lecture, an enterprise worthy of pursuit. Giving one's own life meaning is, moreover, a goal that can be coherently pursued. In the lecture Baier argued that it seems impossible to state the religious understanding of the meaning of life in such a way as to make it both coherent and acceptable. A perfect being, a God, could not coherently have making our lives meaningful as its goal (Baier 13, 21–22). We can, and we can do so by understanding the concepts of personal responsibility and independence in ways that, Baier claimed, are denied us by the religious outlook (Baier 13, 23–24; see also Baier 30, Baier 87).

III

If his autobiography points toward the considerations that brought him to these views, only the philosophy itself can show whether the views are right. Baier's early experience of the politics of exclusion and conflict unquestionably put him in a frame of mind to appreciate the enduring central problems of modern moral philosophy, which I shall outline later. Before turning to that broader history, I should like to try to point out some of the differences between Baier's two main efforts to present a comprehensive moral theory, first in *The Moral Point of View* and now in *The Rational and the Moral Order.*

The main task Baier faces in *The Moral Point of View* is that of justifying social rules of reason. We all start with socially accepted and transmitted beliefs about what is and what is not a reason for acting. Some reasons concern our own good; others concern morality. Morality is constituted by norms designed to apply in cases of conflict of interest (MPV, 190). Socially accepted norms serving this purpose would be mere taboos if not criticizable. They can be criticized from the moral point of view, which is by definition not that of individual interest (MPV, 190) but "that of an independent, unbiased, impartial objective dispassionate disinterested observer"—a "God's eye point of view." (MPV, 201). Rules justifiable from this point of view may conflict with individual rules of reason, justifiable only from the self-interested point of view. If we reason at all concerning our own interest, or concerning what would be a good life for us personally, we are committed to accepting certain rules, such as the rule that requires us to maximize our satisfactions and minimize frustrations. If we did not accept that rule, we would be going counter to the very purpose of reasoning from the personal point of view about what to do. And it is irrational to the point of madness to give up maximizing satisfaction (MPV, 301–3). So there is no real problem about the rational basis for rejecting or accepting what we have learned about self-interested reasons. The problem concerns social rules of reason.

Moral or social rules of reason claim to be superior to rules of self-interest. They must be so if they are to serve the purpose of regulating action when it would be harmful to everyone if everyone acted only from self-interest. But is the claim warranted? It is, says Baier, because when we ask whether moral rules are warranted, we are "looking at the world from the point of view of anyone . . . . We are examining two alternative worlds, one in which moral reasons are always treated by everyone as superior to reasons of self-interest" and one in which the reverse holds. "And we can see," he continues, "that the first world is the better world" since the alternative is a world of Hobbesian nastiness. When I ask what I ought to do, I am asking what course of action is supported by the best reasons, and we have now seen that moral reasons are the best reasons (MPV, 310). And the question, Why should I follow reason? either makes no sense, since asking it is just asking for reasons; or it is asking whether I should deliberate at all, and then the answer is plainly that I should, since deliberation is the most reliable way of getting guidance that pays (MPV, 318–19).

Of course one wants to ask here: who is this "anyone" whose point of view I am supposed to accept? What is "anyone's" standpoint to me? And what is it to find one world better than another? In *The Moral Point of View* the answer to the question of why I should be moral thus seems at the least to be a little hasty. The same cannot be said for the answer given in *The Rational and the Moral Order,* and I do not propose to try to trace its intricacies.

If I understand the argument, Baier is avoiding the appeal, not only to a comparison of worlds (RMO, 123; 131) but also to the "anyone" who takes the God's-eye point of view. His aim is to show that each of us has a self-anchored reason to accept a set of norms that overrules our self-anchored reasons for action in certain cases (RMO, 190–93). Moreover, he tries to show that we all have reason to try to make ourselves into agents whose concern for our own compliance with socially anchored rules is a matter of ever-growing direct personal concern. We have reason not only to follow the norms of morality but to follow with an increasingly good will. And this is all true although we would not be contradicting ourselves if we denied it.

In part 1 of *The Rational and the Moral Order* Baier gives us an account of reason and in particular practical reason that is far more elaborate than anything in *The Moral Point of View.* He also goes into far more detail about the moral psychology behind our ability to comply with socially anchored reasons. It was part of the originality of *The Moral Point of View* that in it Baier appealed, before it was fashionable,[5] and in quite an informal way, to what we now think of as game-theoretical considerations. In *The Rational and the Moral Order* the technicalities of game theory have moved into the core of the argument. If the outcome is a far more illuminating and compelling presentation of the theory, the basic idea is plainly one that has run through the whole of Baier's philosophical career. To be reasonable in practice is not—as Kant mistakenly thought—simply to avoid self-contradiction. It is to avoid a kind of absurdity akin to that. We cannot rationally avoid using reason to guide our quest for a good life, and once embarked on that quest, Baier thinks, we cannot reasonably deny that it would be better for us as well as everyone else to comply with norms that sometimes conflict with the best reasons we have from our private point of view.

IV

I turn now to the task of placing Baier's view in the larger history of modern moral philosophy. To begin with I must cover some ground that is more fully treated in Darwall's paper in the present volume.

The historical antecedents to Baier's theory in the history of the quest for a rational justification of morality are quite clear. As his repeated use of Hobbes as a benchmark shows, his theory centers on the fact that although most of us need or want to live with one another, we always find ourselves coming into conflict with one another. We can no more eliminate our tendency to controversy than we can do without human company. Morality is essentially the solution to the problem of how beings with our unsocially sociable nature can form stable societies. I have echoed Kant's famous phrase, "unsocial sociability," because I think Kant was as much engaged with this general problematic as Hobbes, and Kant's moral theory forms the second benchmark for Baier's own work.

The problems engaging Hobbes, Kant, and Baier first emerged in Hugo Grotius's *On the Law of War and Peace,* published in 1625.[6] Grotius developed a theory of natural law as an answer to skepticism about morality. The fact that he took skepticism seriously differentiated his approach from that of earlier natural law theorists, who did not. He differed from them also in not giving an account of the highest good and in making no appeal to it in his justification of the laws of nature. There would be no agreement, he assumed, on what constitutes the highest good, but he took it that even the skeptic would agree that humans, despite our tendency to controversy, are sociable, and he proceeded to argue that certain specific minimal constraints on behavior are therefore justified.[7] These constraints he called obligatory, and he held that because they are justifiable God will punish those who do not observe them. There are other rational constraints on action, those coming from the agent's own purposes and her need to use appropriate means to achieve them. But advising someone on these matters is not the same as obligating someone to do what is essential for society, and morality, for Grotius, centers on the latter.

Grotian views of morality were developed by Hobbes, Pufendorf, Locke, Thomasius, and many others. Because they held that we have to do what we are obligated to do, they explained obligation as moral necessity, by which they meant a necessity working through the will. To be obligated, on their view, is to be under orders from a superior who backs his orders with threats of punishment. They took God to be the pertinent superior whose command is involved in morality. Because changing one's own ends is obviously not a way of evading God's will, moral obligation binds in a way Kant later called 'categorical'.[8] But because the natural lawyers, Hobbes perhaps aside, were concerned to preserve our responsibility before God, they had difficulty with their explanation of moral necessity. Moral necessity arises from our need to avoid the punishments attached to noncompliance. But if we are necessarily motivated by our perceptions of good and ill, and we know that God's punishments are inescapable, how can we be free to comply or not? Pufendorf suggested that we may be able to comply with moral law out of respect for it as God's will, but because his psychological theory did not give him the resources to explain how this is possible, the concept of obligation continued to pose a problem.

Kant was in important respects a Grotian although he did not try to justify his version of the moral law by arguments of the kind the lawyers used. He held with them that the concept of categorical obligation is the key to resolving the problems posed by our unsocial sociability, but he offered a new account of the concept. The nonpsychological nature of the necessity involved in the moral law enables Kant to explain how certain actions can be necessary although the agent for whom they are so is free to perform them or not. Our awareness of these categorical obligations shows us that we are free agents. Our recognition of the moral necessity of certain actions itself necessarily provides a motive for performance. Sanctions, therefore, are needed neither for defining obligation nor for explaining motives for compliance, and have a role in one part of morality. Kant could thus understandably think he had resolved all the problems in the natural law concept of obligation.[9]

Baier's stress on divergence of interests as well as his agreement with the Grotian theses that we cannot expect agreement on the good life and do not need it for morality all mark him as a Grotian (Carus II, 4). Clearly the Grotian mode of justifying morality raises just those questions about the relations among being reasonable, pursuing one's own good, and being moral that Baier takes as central. Leaving these to Darwall, I shall examine some of the issues that arise for moral psychology. In doing so I relate Baier's views to earlier debates on the subject.

V

Baier wishes to combat skepticism as much as Grotius did. He thinks it central to this endeavor to show that justified norms can affect behavior. More specifically, he aims to show that justified norms can affect our behavior because they have the justification they do. Morality is rational, and we can be motivated by our understanding of its rationality.

To make his case Baier argues that Humeans are wrong in their understanding of what reasons are, and he challenges the claims of internalism that often go with Humean skepticism. He understands internalism to be "the view that, if a fact is a reason for someone to do something, then it necessarily also is a motive for him to do it" (RMO, 90). Internalism, Baier thinks, entails that if some fact does not arouse a motive, then the fact cannot be a reason. To defend his thesis that there is an objective order of reasons for action, he wants to show that internalism concerning practical reason is also wrong.

Baier argues that internalism for cognitive reasons fails since someone can have excellent reasons for believing something and not be moved to believe it (RMO, 90–91). Internalism for practical reason fails because it cannot account adequately for deliberation. There is a two-fold failure. First, we ordinarily think deliberation might lead us to conclude that we ought to do what we now strongly don't want to do. But the internalist must say either that in such cases we have no reason to deliberate, which is absurd, or that we can have reasons to act that don't motivate, which contradicts the thesis (RMO, 10). Second, we normally think that in deliberating we should consider everything that bears on our options. But the internalist must restrict us to considering only what is made pertinent by our existing motives, since nothing else can be a reason. She confines us, that is, to asking what we are already overall inclined to do; but that amounts to a redefinition of 'deliberation', and one we would do well to resist (RMO, 14–16).

As part of his rejection of internalism, Baier rejects Hobbes's definition of the will as simply an appetite or desire in a particular causal relation to action. The will is rather "the ability, or its exercise, to become set on doing what one decides to do (something analogous to Kant's 'Willkür'), and a rational will is the ability, or its exercise, to become set on doing what in one's judgment one has reason, all things considered, to do (something analogous to Kant's 'Wille')" (see RMO, 90). A being with a will must be able to resist her strongest desire in order to act as the objective order of reasons directs. To defend the claim that such an order of reasons can be effective, Baier must explain what is required for someone to be psychologically constituted in this way. He is plainly concerned to avoid Kantian incursions from the noumenal in his account. If there can be what is sometimes called 'agent-causation', it must be explained in naturalistic terms (RMO, 100).

Baier gives the explanation in chapter 3 of *The Rational and the Moral Order*. We must look beyond conscious creatures displaying reflex actions and yielding to irresistible urges, and beyond beings having only one desire at a time, to organisms aware of several desires and able to think about scheduling them for maximal overall gratification (RMO, 104–9). Then we have someone who is not moved by a strongest felt desire. If this being starts to think about what he will want at some later time in order to satisfy the urgent desires he will then feel, he will act from beliefs that are even less directly tied to felt desire. His beliefs may give rise to new desires, and in some cases we may want to point to beliefs rather than desires as causes of his behavior (RMO, 94–97). But although we can now see motivating beliefs, we so far do not have an agent: we have a conscious being whose behavior is simply the outcome of the direction and relative strengths of complex psychic forces (RMO, 105).

To find an agent, someone who can be either master of his desires or their slave, we must find a self and something it can bring to shape the outcome of these forces. We need someone who has preferences about the desires he finds in himself. Moreover he must be so constituted that when he forms the belief that if he does one thing rather than another he will get a preferred outcome, the belief itself must bring it about that he does the one rather than the other. Thus he can stand back from the play of inner forces, evaluate his alternatives, and activate motivational forces that will move him to act as he prefers. Because he brings so much to bear on the outcome, we think of him as a decision maker. He has "at least the beginnings of" a will (RMO, 106).

An agent must have acquired a "standing desire to deliberate" when wrong decisions are probable and costly. When he has this desire, he can mobilize motivations on the right side by directing his attention to the motivating beliefs that will do the trick. What is more, because he can review his preferences, he can come to prefer having some preferences he now does not have; and since his beliefs about how to acquire these may move him, he can be moved by beliefs that do not tie directly into any of his present desires (RMO, 106–8). Presumably if he does this he masters his desires and is free. Baier adds one further point, to bring out the distinction between explanatory and justificatory reasons. I must take a fact to be a reason if it is to be my reason for acting. Thus the fact that I have not reached a joke's punch line may *justify* my continuing to talk, but the justifying fact *explains* why I ramble on only if I believe that it is a reason to do so.

Baier's agent, then, must have multiple desires, preferences about their order, and preferences about having certain preferences. He "has come to have the standing desire to do what he ideally wants . . ." and to deliberate about how to get it. He has the ability to attend to factual beliefs that would move him to satisfy some desires rather than others, and the ability to take these beliefs as reasons for action (RMO, 116). Baier thus explains agency by bringing out what it takes to have a will. And in his summary he quite strikingly stresses the contingency of our possession of such an ability. "If my account of the will is on the right track," he says, "it is a power that depends a great deal on early and persistent training of the right kind . . ." (RMO, 117). On Baier's view if we lack a will, we are slaves of our passions. This amounts to saying that it is a contingent matter whether or not we are free.

VI

Neither Grotius nor Pufendorf nor Kant held this view. But there were philosophers of their period who came close to it. I think we must locate the philosophical ancestry of Baier's moral psychology in their work. The theorists I have in mind—the rationalistic perfectionists, and in particular Malebranche and Leibniz—developed the main seventeenth-century alternative to the natural-law view of morality. They gave the improvement of our inner moral condition an importance beyond that attributed to it by the natural lawyers. Leibniz thought that reason would lead us from self-centered concerns to a direct interest in the good of everyone alike that we would otherwise not have. This is not quite the same as the limited good will Baier thinks we must come to have, but it is close enough to help explain the similarities between the two outlooks. Kant was initially a Wolffian, and he worked out his own views in part through a critique of Leibnizian ethics. Though he accepted the Grotian problematic, he did not wholly abandon the perfectionism of his teachers. I shall sketch only enough of Leibniz's view to explain why I take him to be Baier's forerunner in these matters.

Given Baier's avowed admiration for Hobbes, this is perhaps a surprising suggestion; and I am not insinuating that Baier has wilfully concealed one source of his position. The similarity exists because Baier and Leibniz—unlike Hobbes—have shared views of the importance of inner improvement. They also agree about the constraints on an acceptable moral psychology. Like Baier, Leibniz did not accept any breaks in the causal necessity that orders the universe. His, to be sure, is a spiritual universe, not a crude Hobbesian jumble of atoms and void, but it is a determined one for all that. He rejected Hobbes's account of the will. He sought, as Baier does, a way of explaining action that allows the possibility of not acting from the most strongly felt desire one happens to have. His philosophical ground for imposing this constraint was the same as Baier's. He thought he could show that the differing perfections of things in the universe provide an objective order of reasons for action, that we can come to know this order, and that the knowledge can be effective in guiding practice. Consequently like Baier he is an externalist about practical reason.

I must add an explanation about internalism and externalism. Leibniz's view implies that "if a fact is a reason for someone to do something, then it necessarily also is a motive for him to do it"—that is, it answers to Baier's description of internalism (RMO, 90). But if we take internalism to be a thesis about the meaning of "having a reason," then Leibniz is certainly not an internalist. God necessarily acts for the good in everything he does, but that does not mean God lacks freedom. He is free because it is not *logically* necessary that God should act for the best. It is intelligible to say that God knew the best possible world but did not create it. What is true of God in this respect is true of us. We could meaningfully be said to know what the most reasonable course of action is and yet not be moved to do it.

For Leibniz the necessity of pursuing what appears good to us is hypothetical or moral. It arises from the principle of sufficient reason, not the principle of noncontradiction.[10] This allows us to understand another feature of Leibniz's theory. Baier takes the internalist to start with a knowledge of motives that is independent of knowledge of reasons. Leibniz ties reasons and motives by going in the other direction. If reason shows us a good we had not considered, then we must conclude that we now have a motive for pursuing it. Leibniz is aware that we may not think we have motives to do what we believe best, but his response is clear: "there are insensible inclinations of which we are not aware" (Leibniz 1981, 2.21.41: 194). Perception of good or ill always makes us "lean one way rather than the other," even if we cannot say exactly what we are perceiving. We are often unconscious of our inclinations and penchants, but they move us nonetheless; and reason can show us what they are.

Because of this a priori truth, Leibniz held, we can use reason to control the passions. To do so we must become agents, and not allow ourselves to be moved passively by whatever perception of good we just happen to have. The explanation Leibniz gives of how this is accomplished is uncannily close to Baier's account of agency.

Because desire is necessarily aroused by every belief that a good is available, we could not avoid being moved by a desire if it were the only one we had. Leibniz's metaphysics gives him a priori arguments to show that we never have only one desire. Given that we have more than one, he holds, we can suspend choice by refusing to assent to the prompting of any particular desire. During the time when we suspend action, we can attend to our different desires and see which of them prompts us to the greatest good. When desires are first presented, they are usually confused and indistinct. They can move us even so, but to be moved by such thoughts is precisely to be passive. "[S]ubstances are active only when their perceptions . . . are becoming better developed and more distinct. . ." (Leibniz 1981, 2.21.72: 210). When we attend to ideas we can make them more distinct and thus increase the extent to which in any given matter we are agents. "On this way of looking at things," Leibniz says, "intelligences will differ in how free they are. . ." because they will differ in the extent to which they are active (Leibniz 1981, 2.21.21: 181).

We become agents when, after examination, we consent to a clear and distinct practical idea—to a perception of something as good. Whatever I see most clearly to be the greatest good is what I consent to. If it represents the greatest good actually available to me, there would be an objective reason for me to act to obtain it even had I not been aware of it. If I simply become aware of it, my perception might move me without my attending to it during suspense of judgment. In that case the perception would be the motive that causes my behavior. Once the perception has been cognitively assessed and accepted, it becomes my reason for acting. Leibnizian consenting to a motive is what Baier calls taking a justification as a reason to act.

Leibniz shares Baier's concern about deliberation. For him the question is how we can see to it that we suspend consent and attend to our perceptions. "But how can we ensure that it occurs to us to do this whenever the need arises?" There is a standing disposition to do so, because the will, for Leibniz, is the disposition to move toward the greatest good available. But Leibniz thinks this disposition must be aided by training, by accustoming oneself to thinking in methodical ways, "rising above the hubbub of present impressions. . ." (Leibniz 1981, 2.21.47: 196). Early education is best, but even badly brought up adults can train themselves to think appropriately (Leibniz 1981, 2.21: 187). We cannot directly will to have our will set on something, but we can directly will to put ourselves in a situation that gives us a will with a certain direction (Leibniz 1981, 2.21.24: 182). We can, for instance, remember certain principles that at first are mere words to us; if we attend to them we can make the goods and ills represented in the ideas the words recall vivid enough to move us (Leibniz 1981, 2.21.32: 185–86). Our knowledge of the facts can thus become a tool for managing our desires.

For Leibniz, then, to be an agent is not to interrupt the causal chain with noumenal mystery. It is to be moved without ignorance or error by desires arising from the fullest awareness of all the facts pertaining to one's condition, desires whose motivating force one accepts after attending to the claims of other pulls to action. Agents can justify their actions because on rational grounds they take as reasons the motives that would otherwise be only explanatory causes.

VII

The striking similarity between Baier's moral psychology and Leibniz's brings out a problem with Baier's view that was also raised by critics of Leibnizian ethics. It has to do with an aspect of moral skepticism.

A full reply to moral skepticism must satisfy a requirement that is not so pertinent to replies to skepticism about theoretical knowledge.[11] If morality is to function as an effective means of guiding action, then it must somehow be effective in each moral agent. It must motivate us all alike. And if its motivational power depends on each agent's knowing the reasons for the requirements morality imposes, and not simply the requirements, then a full reply to the moral skeptic must include an account of how awareness of the rationale for morality can be equally available to everyone alike.

The Grotian natural lawyers did not think that everyone alike could have a full grasp of the rationale for the laws of nature. Most people, they thought, could not grasp the complex way in which everyone's compliance with the laws is for the good of everyone alike. They also held that although we need and perhaps also want to live in societies with others, we tend to be dominated by self-interest. Even if we knew exactly how compliance is equally for the benefit of all, we might not care enough to comply in cases where we are called on to make a serious sacrifice.

They sought the solution to the second problem in sanctions, though they were embarrassed by the need to appeal to punishments after death in what should have been a purely rational theory. They had much less to say about how the requirements of morality could be put within the reach of everyone alike. Locke urged frequent preaching to field hands and dairy maids, not being optimistic about their having the leisure and incentive to come to think through the rationale of morality for themselves. Hobbes, who also thought preaching might help, added something else: a method easy enough for anyone to use. Ask yourself, he suggested, if you would like to be treated as you propose to treat someone else; if not, refrain.

The philosophically interesting point about Hobbes's proposed popular method is that it is, to use a term of art, opaque. It does not allow agents to see the real reason for the rightness or wrongness of the acts it enables them to assess. It shows users *what* is required or forbidden, but not *why*. Critics of natural law theory eventually began to object to its implication that most people cannot understand morality well enough to be moved toward compliance by their understanding of its rationale. They developed theories according to which everyone is able to use a method that is transparent, showing the reason for a moral requirement and not only the behavior required.

Of the two main schools of thought working along these lines, the Shaftesburyan sentimentalists are less pertinent to us than the new rationalists, Clarke and his followers. The latter argued for an objective order of reasons, and to explain its universal accessibility tried to show that it was very simple: a matter of a few self-evident axioms, not of the vast metaphysical knowledge of perfections, or of utilities in a ramified social system, as their opponents held. Indeed virtue, or compliance with the self-evident rules or axioms of morality, is on their view good in itself, and is to be followed for that reason, although it is in fact also instrumentally good as promoting public or private happiness.[12] They held also that knowledge of moral truths carries with it a special motivation. As Clarke's follower John Balguy put it, "What is the reason exciting a man to the choice of a virtuous action? I answer, his very approbation of it is itself a sufficient reason, wherever it is not overruled by another more powerful" (Balguy 1734, 81; cf. 50). This motivation is a rational being's response to reason, and consequently arises always and only in connection with acts falling under moral principles.

Balguy spoke of the connection between rational insight and motivation in moral obligation as "internal" and contrasted it with the merely external obligation attaching to ordinary civil law (Balguy 1734, 68).[13] I do not think, however, that Balguy took internalism as a view about language. And Kant himself is as little an internalist as Leibniz is—and as much. For Kant I can understand what it would be to admit that the categorical imperative requires me to do something while not having a feeling that moves me to do it. The tie between recognition of the requirement and the motive is not analytic. That taking something to be required by the categorical imperative carries the motive of respect with it is, moreover, not just an empirically observed fact. It is a synthetically necessary tie, and the unavailability of our motives to introspection makes it no surprise that we do not always know when respect is at work in us.

One of the philosophical motivations for Kant's radical revolution in moral theory was the aim—inspired in him by Rousseau, and perhaps by Crusius as well—of showing how moral knowledge and motivation to act on it are equally available to everyone alike. He took over the Leibnizian idea that the will is the tendency to seek the greatest good and transformed it into the thesis that the will is the tendency to seek the greatest rationality in action. Like Leibniz, he argued that the will works by keeping us from action while it tests our desires to act, and sees which of them can be accepted. But he rejected the Leibnizian belief that the only form of practical rationality is means-ends rationality.[14]

Categorical duties can be known to everyone in part because their consequences are not what ground their binding force. Their inherent rationality does so. Baier says he is Kantian in assigning a categorical status to moral requirements. But in fact he is only partly Kantian. Moral norms overrule personal ends and bind regardless of any actual ends the agent might have, and in that sense they are categorical. But for Baier moral obligations are justifiable as instrumental—instrumental to producing a social order that benefits everyone alike. Consequently, whatever his success in showing that moral obligations have a claim on us regardless of our actual ends, Baier is faced, I believe, with a difficulty in explaining how knowledge of the grounds of obligation can be equally available to everyone alike. I can put it very briefly.

On Baier's view, justifiable norms can affect our actions if we understand their justification. If I am to know the reasons that give rise to the binding nature of my obligations, I must be able to figure out the utilities involved. Kant rejected Leibnizianism in part because he thought most people could not calculate utilities of such complexity. I confess that I could never have come up with the ingenious argument about rational choice that leads Baier to his conclusions. Even after reading the chapter with some care I am far from sure that I understand the argument. And if we add the need to have enough information about how my society works to be sure that it is reasonably equitable in distributing good, the difficulty is severely increased. If there is to be a method of ethics based on this theory, it will have to be an opaque one for me. But then I am not sure what motive I will have, or be able to create in myself, to comply. And Baier does not wish to rely solely on the sanctions that society may rightly impose.

My objection to being confined to an opaque method of ethics is not that nothing like that can work. It can work all too well, in an elitist society where a special group controls affairs. But it makes social criticism difficult. As things are, we are brought up to believe that certain practices and distributions of goods are equitable or fair, and to play fair by respecting the rules. We are also taught how to criticize the rules, appealing to some of them as grounds for claiming that others are out of line. In complying with or criticizing the accepted ways of our society, we think we can appeal to the factors that make actions right or wrong. If all that most of us ever learn in our social upbringing is contingent marks of right and wrong, then we cannot be the rational critics of the mores that Baier thinks we should all be.

Baier regrets that we do not have a science of morality as we now have a science of physics, and that we cannot treat ethics as we treat logic. There are experts in physics and logic who understand the results of work in those fields, and the reasons underlying the results, far better than laypersons ever will. Must any 'scientific ethic' have this kind of implication for the common understanding of morality? Although Baier himself does not welcome it, his way of developing such an ethic seems to lead to that outcome.[15]

Johns Hopkins University

Notes

1. Charles Stevenson was a pragmatist rather than a positivist, but his emotivism was shared by many with positivist roots and commitments.

2. Baier explored Moorean absurdity further in a brief paper on the subject (Baier 9), in which he examined relations among contradicting someone, contradictory remarks, contradictory sentences, contradicting oneself, and self-contradictory remarks.

3. The essay has been translated into English by Elizabeth Hughes Schneewind as "Exiled Reason" and published in *Free Inquiry,* June 1995.

4. See for instance Baier 73, Baier 76, and, more guardedly, Baier 86.

5. Luce and Raiffa's *Games and Decisions,* which made game theory accessible to nonspecialists, was published in 1958, the same year as MPV. Braithwaite's lecture "Theory of Games as a Tool for the Moral Philosopher" was published in 1963.

6. I explain what follows more fully in "Modern Moral Philosophy: From Beginning to End?" (Schneewind 1993b).

7. Grotius did not argue that the skeptic shows her desire for sociability by publishing her arguments—but Shaftesbury did: see his *Essay on the Freedom of Wit and Humour,* in his *Characteristics* (Shaftesbury 1900, 1:61–62), on Hobbes.

8. The lawyers also make compliance the business of others—it is always God's business—not just of the agent. See Baier 24, p. 218, claiming that every version of the will theory of obligation fails; see also SRRM, 219. On this view divine sanctions back obligations concerning others, but there are no sanctions for mere personal imprudence—a point Baier would see as heading in the right direction; see SRRM, 22.

9. See my "Kant and Natural Law Ethics" (1993a).

10. "But choice, however much the will is determined to make it, should not be called absolutely and in the strict sense necessary: a predominance of goods of which one is aware inclines without necessitating, although, all things considered, this inclination is determining and never fails to have its effect" (Leibniz 1981, 2.21.49: 199; cf. 2.21.8: 175).

11. See my "Natural Law, Skepticism and Methods of Ethics" (1991) for a fuller account of much of what follows.

12. See, e.g., John Balguy, *The Foundation of Moral Goodness,* 1728, p. 83.

13. To my knowledge this is the first time these terms were used in this connection.

14. The story is more complex, because I have left out the contribution made by Shaftesbury and Hutcheson to Kant's view. Leibniz rejects the view that one can "divide the mind from its motives, as if . . . the mind had, besides motives, other dispositions to act, by virtue of which it could reject or accept the motives." (Leibniz 1956, 59: Leibniz's fifth paper, sec. 15). Rejecting or accepting motives is exactly what Shaftesbury's moral sentiment, which Kant turned into a rational capacity, was meant to enable the mind to do.

15. This paper was written while I was a Fellow at the Center for Advanced Study in the Behavioral Sciences, in Stanford, California. I am grateful to the Center for the time and support it provided. Special thanks go to Dr. Kathleen Much for her meticulous editorial comments.

Reason, Norm, and Value

2

Stephen Darwall

I. Baier's Problematic

Kurt Baier begins *The Rational and the Moral Order* with a puzzle concerning the relations between the moral, the good, and the rational life.[1] Morality is defensible only if it does not require agents to act contrary to reason. So a first premise is that the moral life must be a rational life or, at least, not an irrational one. But second, practical reason may appear to counsel an agent to lead the good life, one in which her good is maximally realized. Finally, moral requirements are categorical, unconditional on their relation to the agent's good. Together, these three propositions are inconsistent. It can't both be the case that moral demands must have the force of reason and that they are unconditional on the agent's good if practical reason invariably counsels self-interest.[2]

Like some other approaches he rejects (Kantian views, for example), Baier attempts ultimately to avoid the skeptical conclusion that morality is unjustified by denying the second premise. Practical rationality has, he believes, a deep connection to the good, but none so tight as the second premise's rational egoism; considerations of the agent's good are prominent members of the set of practical reasons, but they don't exhaust it. In the first place, an agent may have a better (because more fulfilling) life if his deliberations are sometimes guided by other considerations. Life without love, for example, is empty. But love *includes* acting for others' sakes, guiding oneself by considerations of their, rather than one's own, good. So one can have love in one's life only insofar as one comes to acknowledge the good of other individuals as practical reasons. Baier calls even these reasons "self-anchored," however, because they are grounded in the agent's conception of the good life.[3] This grounding consists in the fact that the agent can realize the good life as she conceives it only if she *treats* the considerations as reasons.[4] Consequently, the agent's good functions in Baier's thought both as a reason for acting ***and*** as a ground for other considerations being reasons as well.

But neither does Baier believe that self-interested and self-anchored considerations together exhaust the class of reasons. For over thirty-five years he has prominently defended the position that morality is, as he now puts it, an "order of reason," which provides a collective solution to the mutually disadvantageous conflict that would result were individuals to be guided solely by their respective self-interested (or even self-anchored) reasons. Everyone does better if everyone treats moral requirements as reasons for action—reasons that are unconditional on whether such action advances the agent's good, and, indeed, that trump both self-interested and self-anchored reasons. Therefore, he argues, moral requirements actually are reasons for action of such overriding weight.

Simplifying greatly, this gives us three categories of reasons, related to the good in three different ways. Self-interested reasons simply *are* considerations of the agent's own good. Self-anchored reasons, we may say, are considerations whereby an agent's regarding them as reasons and guiding herself by them in deliberation (independently of whether others do) tends to advance her good. And moral reasons are considerations of which it is true that everyone's treating them as (overriding) reasons advances everyone's good (including the agent's), while an individual's doing so does not.

The question obviously arises, what explains this complexity? What is it about reasons for acting that explains their relation to the agent's good in these three different ways? Or perhaps more to the point, what is it about considerations related to the agent's good in these ways that makes them reasons? Suppose we start with the thought that an agent's good gives her reasons to act. Our point of departure will then be that an agent has reason to act because doing so will promote her good. The connection to her good is the reason for her to act. Thus far, the reasons are ones of self-interest.

To get to self-anchored reasons, Baier appears to be thinking, we must appreciate that an agent's good is achieved in realizing her "conception of the good life" for her. Now this raises a number of questions in itself. *A person's good* is most naturally understood in relation to the ideas of welfare, benefit, and interest. To advance a person's good is to benefit her. But while the phrase "a person's conception of the good life (for her)" is sometimes used interchangeably with "a person's good," caution is required.[5] For most of us, a conception of the good life will involve ideas of value quite different from benefit. Baier's example of love will serve to make the point. In loving my wife and children, I take them and our relations to have a value different from their benefit to me (or, indeed, to them). Of course, these relations are of great benefit to me, but they are so partly because I see them as valuable in a different way.[6] And my seeing them so is part of what it is for them to figure prominently in my conception of the good life for me. Moreover, my seeing them in this way partly consists in my taking considerations of their good as reasons for me to act, quite independently of such action's relation to my good. Still, even though I conceive of my life's value as involving the value of other people (and our relations) distinct from their instrumental contribution to my welfare, it will nonetheless be true that, since I have such a conception, my own good will be realized only to the extent that this conception is realized (or, at least, insofar as I believe or, perhaps, experience it to be). My own good will be achieved, that is, only if I treat my wife's and children's goods as reasons in themselves. Apparently on these grounds, Baier concludes that such self-anchored considerations are reasons for me to act.

To get to the thought that moral requirements are reasons, Baier asks us to reflect on what things would be like if *everyone's* practical reasoning were exhausted by reasons of self-interest and self-fulfillment. If people were perfectly so guided, they would not fail to have the best lives available to them, insofar as this depended on *their own* individual conduct. Still, everyone's good would be less well achieved than would be the case were everyone to give overriding deliberative weight to sound moral requirements.[7]

An obvious difference between reasons of self-interest, on the one hand, and self-anchored and moral reasons, on the other, is that while the former recommend action on the strength of its relation to the agent's good, the latter do so on grounds held to be reasons because agents' *treating* them as practical reasons, either individually or collectively, advances their goods. To adapt some helpful vocabulary of Parfit's, we may say that Baier appears to extend reasons from the self-interested to the self-anchored on the grounds that self-interested reasons are *individually self-defeating*.[8] Our conceptions of the good life (for ourselves) give importance to various things other than our own welfare, and they (and consequently our own welfare) will be realized only if we express this sense of importance, giving weight in deliberation to considerations other than our own good. Similarly, self-interested and self-anchored reasons (taken together) are apparently *collectively self-defeating*.[9] Were everyone to be guided by them, everyone's good would be less well achieved than would be the case were everyone to take sound moral requirements as overriding reasons to act.

But it may be asked (as Parfit has) why must reasons for acting be neither individually nor collectively self-defeating?[10] Call a theory of practical reasons *good-based* if it holds justification, and hence, justifying reasons, to derive (directly or indirectly) from the good. For all we have so far seen, Baier's theory appears to be good-based in this sense. Unlike rational egoism, which restricts practical reasons to considerations *directly* relating alternative acts to the agent's good, Baier's theory admits both self-anchored and moral reasons. Still, these latter apparently derive their justificatory force for Baier from their *indirect* relation to the good—that is, insofar as individual and collective guidance, respectively, promote it. That is why I call Baier's theory (to this extent) good-based. On the basis of appearances so far, we might say that it is an "indirect" rather than a "direct" good-based theory.

There is, I think, a significant question how a good-based theory of practical reasons can sensibly be other than direct- or act-consequentialist. If the good is the unique source of justification, then why isn't what is relevant to settling what *to do* simply the relation between what the agent *can* then do and the good? Specifically, if the *agent's* own good is the ultimate source of justification for his action, then why isn't rational egoism the correct theory? Granted, rational egoism may be individually self-defeating. Agents may do better if they deliberate on some other basis, guiding themselves in choice by self-anchored considerations independent of (and potentially conflicting with) self-interest. But if this is so, why should we not simply conclude that there is reason for them to (come to) deliberate in this way, and not additionally (as Baier would have us), that the facts to which they would be giving weight thereby become genuine reasons for them to act? If, after all, considerations of others' goods are supposed to earn their way as reasons because acting on them enhances the goodness of *one's* life, then why should we not say that, while one has reason to *treat* these as reasons, only considerations of self-interest are reasons in fact?

The question is analogous to one that direct-consequentialist moral theorists pose to indirect consequentialisms. All can agree that practices in which agents give independent (and perhaps overriding) weight to rules that require suboptimal acts have substantial utility and that such practices should therefore be established and supported. But the direct consequentialist insists that this does not show that acts whose consequences are better than available alternatives, but which are proscribed by optimific rules, are thereby made wrong. If the good is the ultimate source of moral justification, they argue, then what must be true is that an agent should do whatever within his power will maximally promote it, even if the rules society should have, or the deliberative moral reasoning the agent should engage in, would proscribe that very act.

This line of thought should seem even more convincing for a good-based theory of rationality than it may for a moral theory, especially if we suppress the first premise of Baier's puzzle: that moral requirements cannot defensibly demand that agents act contrary to reason. A morality-reasons externalist such as Mill can propose that 'wrong' be reserved for a rule-utilitarian use (where a practice of public proscription would have the best consequences) precisely because he is not concerned to defend the proposition that agents cannot have reason to do what is wrong.[11] When, however, we come to a theory of ultimate justification—to a theory of practical reasons—it should seem more difficult to hold both that the good is the only source of justification and that an action can be most justified—best supported by reasons—although some other action will better promote the good.[12]

Recall the original puzzle. Baier wants to maintain both the first and third propositions: that morality's requirements are defensible only if they have the force of reason and that they are categorical, unconditional on the relation between what they require and the agent's good. If he is to avoid the conclusion that morality is unjustified, therefore, he must reject rational egoism, the second premise. But I have adduced some considerations for thinking that, to the extent that Baier's theory is (agent's) good-based, this may be difficult for him to do. Below I shall explore the possibility that a non-good-based theory can resolve this problem. By way of preparation, however, I want first to describe some important developments in philosophical thinking about the relations between the good, the rational, and the moral that took place at the beginning of the modern period in the seventeenth and eighteenth centuries, developments that provide the context necessary for Baier's problematic and, I shall suggest, philosophical resources for resolving it.

II. Natural Law, Classical and Modern

We should begin with a discussion of the tradition against which so much moral philosophy of the modern period was reacting, the classical tradition of natural law deriving from St. Thomas Aquinas. Most important for our purposes is the fact that this tradition *identified* the rational, the moral, and the good life. Morality or natural law is for Aquinas a formulation of what he calls "eternal law," by which he means God's ideal or archetype for all of nature—"the exemplar of divine wisdom . . . moving all things to their due end."[13] This scheme of final causes also serves to determine every creature's good: "the end of a thing is its perfection. But the perfection of a thing is its good."[14] Individuals realize their respective goods, therefore, only if they function properly in the overall scheme. That is what realizing their respective goods *is*. It follows that it is metaphysically impossible that anyone might do better by departing from forms of cooperation that are collectively best, those dictated by the scheme of final causes making up God's eternal law.

All things are "ruled and measured by the eternal law," but rational beings, because they have "a share of the eternal reason," are subject to law in a different way than nonrational creatures.[15] They are subject to what Aquinas calls "natural law" because, by "the light of natural reason," they can "discern what is good and what is evil."[16] So morality or "natural law," he concludes, "is nothing else than the rational creature's participation of the eternal law."[17]

There is thus no difference between the moral life and the good life. Natural law (morality) directs rational beings to ends inherent in their nature as represented in eternal law, the overall teleological scheme. But such a life is also one in which their good is maximally achieved, since "the end of a thing is its perfection" and "the perfection of a thing is its good." Even later followers like Suarez, who held that what gives this teleological scheme the force of a formally obligating law is its issuing from God's superior will, nonetheless agreed with the central Thomist tenet that eternal law directs agents by ends inherent in their nature, and thus, that the moral life is, of necessity, the good life.

Additionally, there is no space on the classical theory of natural law for the rational to diverge from the moral and the good. The will, for Aquinas, is rational appetite, and "every appetite is only of something good."[18] All reasons for action must therefore be based in the good. But since the agent's good cannot be separated from the perfectionist ideal inherent in his nature as end (eternal law), and since morality is just another representation of that, it follows that the rational, the moral, and the good life are all identical.

Because the classical theory of natural law holds that the good and the moral life necessarily coincide, it effectively rejects the third premise of Baier's puzzle. Morality's requirements are not unconditional on their relation to the agent's good because morality directs us towards the perfection in which our real good consists. But if morality necessarily coincides with the good life, no problem results from accepting the other two premises of Baier's puzzle. It may be the case both that morality is defensible only if its requirements have the force of reason and that the rational life coincides with the good life. Baier's problematic is not a live one for classical natural law.

What underlies the classical tradition's identification of moral and good lives, of course, is a teleological metaphysics of nature. This provides a coincidental basis for normativity and for the good. Inherent in everything, including every human being, is an end, what it *should be*. Normativity is thus already intrinsic to our metaphysical nature. But this end is also our good. There are two important consequences. First, an individual's good is normative for him in a way that that of others cannot be (for him). That his good is *to be sought by him* is guaranteed metaphysically, while the good of others lacks this essential practical relevance. Second, since the good of each is given in the overall teleological scheme, any deep conflict is ruled out. The question, "Should I live my life to achieve my good, or that of others?" cannot gain a foothold.

Once teleological metaphysics is given up, however, as it was increasingly in the early modern period, things begin to look very different. For one thing, when the notion of a person's good is disconnected from an overarching teleological scheme, the possibility of conflict arises. It is thinkable not only that individuals' interests may conflict (perhaps fairly widely), but also that an individual's interests may conflict with those of all (impartially considered), or that they may be best advanced by doing what it would be against her (or everyone's) interest for everyone to do. And the question can now be raised: In such cases what *should* a person do? Should she act for her own good? For the good of all (impartially considered)? Or should she do what it would be in everyone's interest for everyone to do? Moreover, once the agent's good is no longer held to be given as a necessary end inherent in her nature, its having a normative claim on her that the goods of others do not ceases to be dictated by metaphysics.

Changes in these directions are evident in the writings of the so-called modern natural lawyers: Grotius, Pufendorf, Hobbes, Cumberland, and Locke. Consider, for example, Grotius's attempt, right at the outset of the first great work of modern natural law, *On the Law of War and Peace* (1625), to disarm what he takes to be a fundamental skeptical objection to the very existence of natural law. Grotius puts this objection in the mouth of the Academic skeptic, Carneades:

> [F]or reasons of expediency, men imposed upon themselves laws, which vary according to customs, and among the same peoples often undergo changes as times change; moreover that there is no law of nature, because all creatures, men as well as animals, are impelled by nature towards ends advantageous to themselves; that, consequently, there is no justice, or, if such there be, it is supreme folly, since one does violence to his own interests if he consults the advantage of others.[19]

In reply, Grotius argues that since human beings have "an impelling desire for society," it should not be conceded that "every animal is impelled by nature to seek only its own good." Universal laws can be justified as necessary for a social order that is in everyone's interest.[20]

Several themes are notable here. First, it is common ground to Grotius and his skeptical challenger that the good of a person is not to be identified with a Thomistic perfection or the excellent performance of an Aristotelian function. Challenge and response are both formulated with a notion of advantage or good that requires no perfectionist or teleological metaphysical framework and that can easily be accepted by the most mechanistic social scientist.

Second, Grotius accepts the skeptical challenger's implicit claim that natural law's requirements conflict (perhaps frequently) with the good of agents they purport to obligate. Where the classical tradition rejected Baier's third premise (that moral requirements are unconditional on their relation to the agent's good), Grotius and his skeptical challenger both accept it. Indeed, the Carnedean challenge simply amounts to accepting all three of Baier's premises—additionally, that moral requirements are defensible only if they have the force of reason and that reason directs agents to act in their own interest—and then drawing the skeptical conclusion that morality (natural law) is indefensible. Grotius's problematic is thus Baier's: how could there be such a thing as morality (natural law) if its requirements must have the force of reason but nonetheless conflict with the agent's good? Set out in the first systematic work of the modern period, it has been with moral philosophers ever since.

Finally, Grotius's own answer is to argue that moral requirements can be shown to have the force of reason for human beings since humans have "an impelling desire for society" and the social order they make possible is in everyone's interest. He calls this (somewhat misleadingly) an a priori proof of natural law, since it shows how moral requirements are grounded in our "rational and social nature" (Grotius 1925, 42). As social, we naturally seek the good of others as well as our own. Morally required conduct, he seems to saying, will be rational from that point of view.[21]

Grotius hardly developed his solution at any length or in a way his contemporaries could find compelling. His discussion of natural law's foundations is only a brief preliminary to the systematic working out of the normative theory that was his primary preoccupation and greatest contribution. But the foundational issues he first aired had genuine staying power, even if his solution did not. In Locke's *Essays on the Law of Nature*, for example, we find a discussion of the relation between morality and the agent's good obviously inspired by Grotius's presentation of the skeptical challenge.[22] Locke devotes the final essay to a discussion of this challenge, which, like Grotius, he attributes to Carneades, quoting virtually verbatim the passage discussed above (Locke 1954, 205). Locke interprets the challenge less as an objection to natural law than as the positive proposal that "every right and equity [is] determined not by an extraneous law but by each person's own self-interest" (Locke 1954, 205). "Is Every Man's Own Interest The Basis of the Law of Nature?," Locke asks (Locke 1954, 205). He answers resoundingly, "No."

It is because he believes morality to require genuine sacrifice that Locke feels the full force of Grotius's (Baier's) problem. Human interests genuinely conflict, he thinks, because individuals' goods are in some respects economic. "When any man snatches for himself as much as he can, he takes away from another man's heap the amount he adds to his own" (Locke 1954, 211). Were natural law to dictate to each her own interest, it would only confirm this conflict to mutual disadvantage. But morality is the solution to this problem, not part of it. Natural law is "the strongest protection of each man's private property"; its observance secures the property (and thus the good) of each, thereby making it possible for each person *effectively* "to pursue his own advantage" (Locke 1954, 207).

The problem for Locke is how this can be. Morality can secure property, and thus mutual advantage, only if moral requirements somehow give (overriding) reasons to agents to follow them. But Locke actually agrees with the skeptic's rational egoism; the agent's own good is her only source of practical reasons. So how, if morality requires genuine sacrifice, can it provide the appropriate reasons? Locke's solution is to make a distinction between an agent's interest's being "the basis of the law or the ground of obligation," and a morally required act's being in the agent's interest *because* "it is in accordance with the law" (Locke 1954, 215). Locke accepts Baier's third premise in the sense that he denies that moral requirements are hypothetical imperatives, having an obliging force deriving only from the relation the required act has to the agent's ends or good. But he also believes that every morally required act is ultimately for the agent's good, and that this is so because it is morally required. Thus although moral requirements do not themselves provide practical reasons, it is always the case that when a person is morally required to do something, she has conclusive practical reason to comply since *obedience* to natural law is always in her interest. "Our answer to the objector is this," Locke declares: "Utility is not the basis of the law or the ground of obligation, but the consequence of obeying it" (Locke 1954, 215).

Locke's explanation of why it is invariably prudent to act as morally required is unlikely to appeal to his readers these days. Locke is a theological voluntarist. He believes that natural laws are God's commands, and that their obligatory force derives from God's superior authority. God's authoritative command is the source of moral requirement. This, not the agent's interest, is "the basis of the law or the ground of obligation." But while there is for Locke no intrinsic connection between moral obligation and rational motive, God guarantees an extrinsic connection. He recognizes that His creatures face a collective action problem, that if each acts rationally to advance his own happiness this will be mutually disadvantageous. This, indeed, is His reason for commanding natural law and, therefore, for morality's existence. God commands natural law by requiring us to act in ways that are mutually advantageous, but individually suboptimal (abstracting from the benefits of obedience). We know, however, that God does not act vainly, and so could hardly command His creatures to do what they could not rationally choose to do. So we may conclude that He establishes a system of eternal sanctions ensuring it is invariably rational (maximally beneficial) to obey Him. For Locke, the doctrine of eternal delights and torments is the conclusion of something like a transcendental deduction of the very possibility of moral obligation, where morality is conceived in the distinctively modern (Baierian) way as a system of categorical constraints on agents' pursuit of self-interest for mutual advantage, but within the framework of theological voluntarism.

Locke's rational egoism is what leads him to hold that moral requirements, since they concern acts that would be imprudent absent their being required, must somehow be brought into accord with prudence if they are to be justifiable. Now, as we saw, the classical tradition of natural law had what amounted to a metaphysical rationale for holding that an agent's own good is normative for her in a way that the goods of others cannot be. A person's good is her perfection, the realization of her ideal role in God's archetype. And as this end is inherent in her nature, it has necessary practical relevance. Its being the case that she ought to realize her good (perfection) is guaranteed metaphysically. Moreover, no other person's good is related to her in this way. Finally, the possibility of deep conflict between individuals' goods is ruled out by the fact that the good of each consists in realizing their role in the comprehensive archetype.

Locke, of course, rejects the teleological metaphysics necessary to make this picture work. He is a rational egoist because he is a psychological egoist. He thinks it impossible for agents to desire other than their own goods (pleasures), although he does suppose a "present uneasiness" can move agents to a short-run good (or the avoidance of a short-run evil) at long-term cost. A rational human agent is one who takes adequately seriously that "that which is future, will certainly come to be present" and gives no preference in deliberation to present goods and evils over future ones (Locke 1985, 275).

But if my good can conflict with that of others, if I can voluntarily seek either, and if my good is not an end inherent in my nature in a way that that of others is not, what rationale is there for thinking that only my good gives me reasons to act? Indeed, what gives my good whatever normativity it has? If psychological egoism is true, a plausible version of 'ought' implies 'can' presumably rules out the possibility that I ought to seek the goods of others, or of all impartially conceived, when these conflict with my own. But if psychological egoism is false, if I *can* pursue the goods of others as well as my own, then what is the justification for thinking I should pursue my own good whenever these conflict? The good of others is no less good for them than is mine for me. So long as metaphysics does not guarantee that mine is my end and theirs is not mine but theirs, the fact that my good is mine and theirs is theirs is only a fact about who benefits, not about for whom the benefit is normative—about who, that is, is *to seek* it. Apparently, I *can* make *either* my own good or that of others (or all) my end, and so the question remains, which should I?[23]

This line of thought, familiar to students of Sidgwick's *Methods of Ethics*, derives ultimately, I believe, from a contemporary of Locke's, Richard Cumberland, whose *A Treatise of the Law of Nature* was counted, along with the books of Grotius and Pufendorf, as one of the three great seventeenth-century works of natural law.[24] Cumberland holds that we can will to pursue the goods of others no less than we can our own. He accepts the traditional theory of the will as invariably being of the good, but interprets this to mean that we can will anything we judge will promote the *good of any being*, oneself or others. Since, however, we can will either, we face a question which to pursue when they conflict.

In discussing Hobbes on the "right of nature," Cumberland remarks, "there is no doubt, but that Man has a *natural Power*, or *Will*, which he himself may determine to act which way he pleases" (Cumberland 1727, 90). Since the pursuit of any person's good is in our power, the question remains, when these conflict, which *should* we pursue? And about this question, Cumberland remarks, "when we are enquiring into the *Right* of Acting, the *Question* is, 'Which, among those Actions which are in our power, are *lawful*?' Any Answer to the Question, without respect had to *Law*, at least that of *Nature*, is absurd" (Cumberland 1727, 90). As agents who can frame the choice between our own good and that of others when these conflict, we face the question of which we should pursue. If there is an answer to this question, it will lie in a "law of nature," that is, some normative principle concerning what agents should do in situations like that. Nor can we simply assume that our own good has precedence simply because it is ours. The goods of others can be our end no less than our own good can, and they are no less good.

As suggested by his account of the will as capable of aiming only at the goods of self or others, Cumberland conceives of agency and action in purely instrumental terms. Consequently, he takes the question of what an agent should do when promoting her good conflicts with promoting the goods of others, to be the same as the question of which "effect" is better. An end is simply an effect, the idea of which "preconceiv'd in the Mind, first moves a Rational Agent to intend the producing it" (Cumberland 1727, 196). So, he concludes, "*laws*, perfectly fitted to a *Rational* Nature, must both point out the *best End*, and the *most suitable Means* for obtaining it" (Cumberland 1727, 196).

But "best end" cannot simply mean "best for the agent," nor, for that matter, "best for others." It is an assumption of the question Cumberland is asking that one course of action will promote an end better for the agent, another, an end better for others. The question is, in such circumstances, what should a person do? Since he interprets this question as which end (or effect)—a certain amount of good for the agent or a certain amount for others—is *best*, and since he thinks there is no value an effect can have other than the goods of beings realized in it, Cumberland concludes that there is no alternative to understanding the question, what should a person do when goods conflict, to be the same as the question, which course of action will produce the greatest good *for anyone*, i.e., for all on balance. "[S]ince there is no cause why the Happiness of one of these [say, the agent] should be his ultimate End, rather than the Happiness of another should likewise be his ultimate End; we may conclude," Cumberland writes, that "Reason dictates" to no agent "that he should propose to himself his own Happiness only, as his greatest End, but to every one, rather his own in conjunction with the Happiness of others; and this is that *Common Good*, which we contend is to be sought after" (Cumberland 1727, 214).

III. Reason, Norm, and Will

For Cumberland, as for any theory that views agency and action in exclusively instrumental terms, normative questions of practical reason must be understood as questions about the good. The question, "What should I or do I have reason to do?" thus becomes, "What can I do that will have the best effect?" As we've seen, Cumberland argues that this last question is equivalent, not to "What can I do that will maximally promote my good?", but to "What can I do that will maximally promote the good of persons (or of any beings who can have a good), impartially conceived?" But while this has the virtue of avoiding the result that the conflict between an agent's good and the good of all is a walkover in one direction (i.e., that others' goods have no independent justificatory weight), it does so only by creating a walkover in the other. And not just by asserting the substantive normative thesis that agents ought (have reason) to do whatever will maximize benefit, impersonally conceived, but by holding that its being the case that they ought consists in nothing more than that their doing so will have this effect.

But just as it is a genuine normative issue whether an agent should promote her own good or that of others, when these conflict, so likewise is it a genuine normative issue whether, for example, she should promote her own good or that of all, impersonally conceived, when these conflict. This question cannot be formulated, moreover, as one concerning which action will promote her good, or which will promote the good of all. Agreement about these latter is assumed background for the further normative question: the facts about alternative acts' relations to her good and the good of all being as they are, which, in a situation of this kind, should a person choose? An answer to this question cannot take the form of any fact about the good of persons, whether agent-relative or agent-neutral. It must consist, rather, in a proposition about which such facts are weightier reasons for acting—and, implicitly, in a normative principle of practical reason—even if the answer is that in every situation a person should maximize her own good, or that she should maximize the good of all.

If we take such issues seriously, then, we will have disconnected questions of practical reason from questions about the good, at least insofar as these concern welfare. Earlier I suggested that to the extent that Kurt Baier's theory of practical reasons was (agent's) good-based, it would be difficult for him to avoid rational egoism, and thus to vindicate moral reasons. In what remains, I wish to sketch a non-good-based approach to practical reason that began to be formulated in the modern period, one that stressed the connection between practical reason and autonomous agency. In its purest, Kantian form, this approach might be called *principle-based* rather than good-based.

To some extent, what is at issue is the nature of the will. Compare the classical Thomist definition of the will as rational appetite, every appetite being of something (conceived as) good, with Kant's view: "Only a rational being has the power to act *in accordance with his idea* of laws—that is, in accordance with principles—and only so has he a *will* . . . the will is nothing other than practical reason."[25] For Kant, what distinguishes agency or will from other instances of intelligent goal-direction is that actions are undertaken *for reasons* (the agent's reasons), and thus involve determination by the agent's conception of *(justifying) reasons to act.* Implicit in the latter is a conception of normative principle or what Kant calls practical law. In taking there to be reason for me to do something in a given situation, I commit myself to a normative view concerning how someone like me should act in a situation like mine, other things being equal. Suppose, for example, I do something because it is for my good, regarding this as sufficient reason in the situation. I can hardly think relation to my good provides me a reason to act unless I am prepared to think that other agents' goods provide them reasons to act as well. In acting for that reason I commit myself to the principle that agents ought to promote their respective goods, other things being equal. For Kant, will involves the self-presentation, if not also the reality, of autonomy or self-*governance*—determination by a conception of normative principle or law.

Kant was not the first modern writer to think along these lines. Cudworth, Locke, Shaftesbury, Balguy, Clarke, Butler, and Rousseau, in their various ways, were all attempting to work out a notion of autonomous or self-determining will.[26] And, with the exception of Locke, all asserted that agency involves *governance* by a normative conception, by a conception of authoritative principle or law. What's more, one finds in these writers movements towards a Kantian approach to normativity, that being under an 'ought', or there being reasons to act, is something realized *within* autonomous will or practical reasoning, not in any normative reality that might somehow be discovered independently of the exercise of practical reason.[27]

On this picture, the agency necessary for 'ought' involves determination under the idea of reason for acting and thus, implicitly, under the idea of normative principle. Although rational agents of course have desires, they act on these only when they incorporate them into their reasons, and thus, into a principle by which they govern themselves. In taking my own good to give me sufficient reason in a situation, and acting for that reason, I manifest not just a desire for my good, but adherence to a normative principle.

But what reasons are there for me to act? What principles are normative for me? This is the concern expressed in Cumberland's question: when we can promote either our own good or that of others, "Which, among those Actions which are in our power, are *lawful*?" Or the question we put to Cumberland: "What should a person do when she can either promote her own good or that of all, impersonally conceived?" As we then noted, in taking these questions seriously, an autonomous agent is seeking to answer no question about the good, either her own or that of all. Her question is: the facts about the goods of persons being as they are, what should a person do? What relative weight do these facts have as reasons for her to act?

What could constitute an answer to this defining question of autonomous agency? If there is no normative reality that normative propositions might describe more or less accurately with which we might come into epistemic contact, then, Kant concludes, practical normativity can be nothing other than the rational will's capacity to be a law to itself, through its own self-legislation. It must be realized *in* the practical reasoning of an autonomous agent.

This places us in the region of Kant's derivation of the Categorical Imperative. The autonomous agent governs her conduct by principles she can regard as binding on all. There are, of course, states she desires to bring about, but these figure in her practical reasoning only through such principles. Autonomous conduct is *governed* by reasons, and hence by principles; that is what distinguishes it from other intelligent goal-directed, hence from (merely) desire-based, behavior. Since, Kant writes, this "rob[s] the will of every inducement that might arise for it as a consequence of obeying any particular law, nothing is left but the conformity of actions to universal law as such, and this alone must serve the will as its principle" (Ak. 402). But how can this be? How can "conformity of actions to universal law as such" serve the will as its principle? Since there is no normative reality that propositions of universal law correctly describe, there is no way of factoring the autonomous agent's task into two: a "theoretical task" of discovering this reality (and hence the law), and a "practical task" of willing conformity to it.[28] Practical norms are realized nowhere but in practical reasoning, and so in the will, itself. The autonomous agent's only test of what principles she should regard as law, therefore, is what principles she can *will as law*, which she can will to govern the practical reasoning of all agents, and through this, her own. "That is to say," Kant concludes, "I ought never to act except in such a way that I can also will that my maxim should become a universal law. Here bare conformity to universal law as such (without having as its base any law prescribing particular actions) is what serves the will as its principle" (Ak. 402).

It is easy to miss the force of Kant's thought here. The point cannot simply be that it is a necessary condition of any normative principle to which an agent is actually subject that she be able to will it as law in the sense that she be able to *treat* or regard it as law. That condition, important as it is to the Kantian, depends entirely on how the principle figures in the agent's own practical reasoning (perhaps, that she will she act on it whether or not, on the occasion, she wants to); it implies nothing about her will with respect to the practical reasoning of others, so it cannot entail any form of the Categorical Imperative.

Kant believes that the practical law is not given, so autonomous agency cannot have "as its base any law prescribing particular actions" (Ak. 402). It is important to see that Kant rules this out no less than he rules out a desire for any "consequence of obeying any particular law" as the grounding motivation of a free moral agent. Since we are given no stock of normative principles to which we respond as laws (and to whatever degree we seem to be, we can always ask, as autonomous, why we should so regard them), we need a way of determining which principles *to* regard as normative for free rational agents. It is at *this* point that the Categorical Imperative acquires its unique salience for Kant. Able to will freely only under the idea of law, but lacking any given stock of laws to follow, an autonomous agent's only alternative is to regard as normative (for all) only principles he wills that everyone so regard. Only in this way can the idea of law determine conduct "all the way down."

IV. Principle, Good, and Moral Reasons

Unlike good-based theories of practical reason, the Kantian approach is principle based. What makes some consideration a reason to act is not its relation to any value outside of practical reasoning, but its suitability to function as a reason within the principled deliberations of an autonomous agent. In section I, I noted that Baier apparently relies on the facts that self-interested reasons are individually and collectively self-defeating to argue that they do not exhaust the class of practical reasons, and thus to vindicate self-anchored reasons and moral reasons, respectively. An agent whose practical reasoning is restricted to a deliberative basis of self-interest will have a less beneficial life than he would were his conception of practical reasons extended to include self-anchored considerations. And if all agents restrict their practical reasoning to self-interested and self-anchored reasons, they will have less beneficial lives than they would were they to give (overriding) weight in their deliberations to moral reasons. I also there noted Parfit's objection that these facts show, at best, how individuals or groups might be well advised to think about their decisions, but nothing about the correctness of those thoughts. It might be the case that agents should regard, say, the moral 'ought' as overriding reasons, but also that they are not in fact.

This objection is serious, if not devastating, to a theory of practical reasons that is good based, as Baier's often seems to be. If, however, what makes a consideration a reason is its role in the practical reasoning of an autonomous agent, then the gap on which the objection relies may not exist. A principle-based account will doubtless recognize some gaps between how an agent should reason practically and the soundness of her practical thoughts—for example, when good strategic reasons recommend deliberating in an erratic, unpredictable way. But there can be no gap on a principle-based account between its being the case that an ideally autonomous agent would regard a given consideration as a reason and that consideration's actually being a practical reason. Most directly relevant to Baier's case for moral reasons, there can on a Kantian account be no gap between its being the case that an autonomous agent would will that the practical reasoning of all be governed by moral considerations and its being the case that such considerations actually are practical reasons of overriding weight.

Baier rejects the Kantian approach for the following reason:

> The problem with a theory of reason such as the roughly Kantian one we are now considering is that it rejects any connection between reason and such other commonly recognized "ultimate ends." It has therefore cut reason off from those undeniable sources of motivation which, if conceived of as internal to reason, are not embarrassed by the question, "But why go for that?"[29]

This, however, mislocates the Kantian's thought. Acting on principles one can regard as normative is not an ultimate end in the sense of a good to "go for." Rather, governance by (what one can regard as) reasons is the defining project of agents as such and a presupposition of any serious consideration of the question "Why do anything at all?" Of course, governance by principles one can regard as normative is not identical, on its face, to governance by the Categorical Imperative. But if that connection could be made out, it would follow that an autonomous agent is committed to governing herself by the Categorical Imperative, and, therefore, by moral requirements grounded in it. If, as I have argued, a good-based account of practical reasons cannot vindicate moral reasons, and thereby enable Baier to resolve his problematic, perhaps there is some reason to reconsider a principle-based, Kantian approach.

University of Michigan

Notes

1. Baier calls this the "rationality problem." See RMO, 4–7.
2. Baier puts all these points in terms of *lives* that are, respectively, rational,

good, or moral, rather than individual acts. Although for many purposes this difference is quite important, for ours it will not be.

3. "The point of view of one's own good cannot be that of self-anchored reason because it would rule out as acting contrary to reason when, from love or friendship and the like, we are motivated to promote the good of others to our own detriment. I rejected this because for many people (if not all) a life that contains such other-regarding concerns comes closer to a good life as they conceive it than one without such concerns. But, it seems, the point of view of self-anchored reason must not exclude such other-regarding consideration when they direct us in ways that make our lives better" (RMO, 140–41). Also: "a conception of the good life for oneself . . . is the point of view of self-anchored reasons" (RMO, 153).

4. Thus: "self-anchored reason must not exclude such other-regarding consideration when they direct us in ways that make our lives better" (RMO, 141).

5. For example, see Rawls, *A Theory of Justice* (1971), who appears to be the source, for contemporary discussion, of the phrase "a person's conception of the good."

6. I discuss value of this sort, which I call *intersubjective value,* in *Impartial Reason* (1983), 130–67. See also Elizabeth Anderson, *Value in Ethics and Economics* (1993) for an extended discussion of relevant points.

7. This is so, in Baier's view, because the soundness of a moral requirement itself consists in its being the case that it advances everyone's interest for everyone to treat it as an overriding reason for action.

8. *Reasons and Persons* (Parfit 1984), p. 5. This is what Parfit calls "indirect" individual self-defeat.

9. See ibid, 27. More accurately: "indirectly collectively self-defeating".

10. Or just not individually self-defeating? Or just not collectively self-defeating?

11. John Stuart Mill, *Utilitarianism* (1979), p. 47.

12. These remarks hold only *to the extent* that the theory is good-based. There may, of course, be some further desideratum for a theory of reasons, in no tension with its being good-based, that, together with the latter, entails an indirect, non-act-consequentialist theory of reasons. In "Rational Agent, Rational Act" (1986), I argue that David Gauthier's attempt to ground such an indirect theory fails because the only independent rational he provides for indirection is a conception of the relation between reasons and autonomy that is actually in tension with the idea of a good-based theory. More on this, and the relevance to Baier's theory, below.

13. St. Thomas Aquinas, *Summa Theologica,* Q. 93, art. 1, in *Basic Writings of Saint Thomas Aquinas* (1945), 2:763.

14. *Summa Contra Gentiles,* (1945) Vol. 2, bk. 3, chap. 16:26.

15. *Summa Theologica,* Q. 91, art. 3 (1945), 2:750.

16. *Ibid.*

17. *Ibid.*

18. *Summa Theologica,* Q. 8, art. 1 (1945), 2:246.

19. Hugo Grotius, prolegomena to *The Law of War and Peace* (1925), 10–11. Note the similarity between this passage and the challenge of Hobbes's fool in chapter 15 of *Leviathan.*

20. The latter is more a theme of Grotius's earlier *De iure praedae* (1604). On this and on the "modern" elements of Grotius more generally, see Richard Tuck, "The 'modern' theory of natural law" (1987).

21. A second, a posteriori ground for natural law lies in Grotius's notion of the *consentium gentium.* A consensus across nations on a core of law is evidence that it is composed of valid requirements, not because consensus somehow makes it so, but because the consensus is best explained by a "universal cause": a "common sense of mankind" that such laws actually are necessary for a mutually beneficial social order, and ultimately, that they are so in fact.

22. Composed in the 1660's, and deposited in the Lovelace Collection in the Bodleian Library at Oxford, Locke's manuscripts on natural law were first published as *Essays on the Law of Nature,* trans. W. van Leyden (1954). A more recent translation is *Questions concerning the Law of Nature,* trans. Robert Horwitz, Jenny Strauss Clay, and Diskin Clay (1990). Because the van Leyden translation is more familiar, I will refer to it. See the translators' introduction to *Questions,* however, for a critique of some aspects of von Leyden's translation.

There are three manuscripts, which von Leyden labeled A, B, and C. Von Leyden and Horwitz, Clay, and Clay agree that for purposes of establishing a text, C, which is largely an error-ridden copy of A and B, made by Locke's amanuensis, probably around 1681, is useless. (For C's probable date, see Locke 1990, 69.) And they agree that B was composed in 1664, and A, sometime between 1654 and 1664, but probably close to the latter date.

23. Unless, of course, my good is simply defined in terms of what I make my ends.

24. Originally published in Latin as *De Leqibus Naturae Disquisitio Philosophica* in 1672. I will refer to the English translation by John Maxwell (Cumberland 1727).

25. Immanuel Kant, *Groundwork of the Metaphysics of Morals* (1964), 80. Further references will be to page numbers of the Preussische Akademie edition and will be placed parenthetically in the text, e.g., (Ak. 412) for the current passage.

26. These are doubtless not the only examples. Cudworth's views are set forth in his manuscripts on freedom of the will, housed in the British Library. One of these has been published: *A Treatise of Freewill* (Cudworth, 1838). For Locke, see his revised chapter "Of Power" from the second edition of the *Essay.* See also, Anthony Ashley Cooper, the Third Earl of Shaftesbury, "Soliloquy, or Advice to an Author" from *Characteristics;* John Balguy, *Foundations of Moral Goodness;* Samuel Clarke, *A Discourse Concerning the Being and Attributes of God;* Joseph Butler, *Fifteen Sermons Preached at the Rolls Chapel;* and Jean Jacques Rousseau, *The Social Contract.* I discuss Cudworth, Shaftesbury, and Locke in *The British Moralists and the Internal 'Ought': 1640–1740* (Cambridge University Press, 1995).

27. Sometimes they held this view alongside incompatible doctrines. For example, Locke's references to obligation within the context of his discussion of autonomy in the revised "Of Power" in the *Essay* are along these lines, even though his usual view is that obligation consists in the command of a superior authority.

28. These terms come from Baier's MPV, p. 142.

29. RMO, 15.

Individual Reason

3

David Gauthier

1. The title of Kurt Baier's book, *The Rational and the Moral Order,* reveals the problem that I propose to address. Why suppose that the roots of reason and morality are social? I want to propound a very different thesis: that the roots of human morality and society are to be found in reason.

My thesis is not genetic. No doubt the capacities for reasoned, rational, and moral behaviour are developed and actualized only among human beings who are born into and mature in a social context. But the ascription of both reason and rationality to individuals is quite independent of any social context, much less that peculiar social context that Baier characterizes as "an order of reason" (RMO, 51). This is the first claim that I shall endeavor to defend.

And I have a second claim. Rationality is a socially subversive characteristic of individuals. As Rousseau recognized, "reason . . . turns man back upon himself."[2] Rational reflection destroys the bonds that hold traditional forms of human society together. But at the same time it provides the basis for reconstructing those bonds. Baier is right to speak of a society that is "an order of reason," but this order must be created, and its creation presupposes and depends on individual reflective rationality. And this order of reason proves to include some, if not all, of what we traditionally consider morality.

For the present I propose to put morality to one side. It will naturally reenter my argument at the point at which I establish the rationale for "an order of reason"—a rationale that, let me emphasize from the outset, speaks to an individual whose exercise of reason and of rationality are characterized without reference to society. To establish that rationale, I must first sketch an account of reason and rationality, and defend the thesis that their ascription is strictly individualistic.

2.1. I want to distinguish rationality from reason. Baier characterizes reason as "the ability we have when we are fully rational" (RMO, 37) but this seems to me to conflate two very different things. On the one hand there is the capacity that human beings, and perhaps certain other animals, have, to act for reasons. It is this capacity that I propose to identify with reason, and a being can possess it, at least in a rudimentary way, without being rational, or capable of rationality, which I identify with the capacity for assessing reasons. Although rationality will be my main concern, I need first to clarify reason.

If a being acts for reasons, then these reasons must be genuinely explanatory of its actions. As Dretske notes, "The fact that they have a content, the fact that they have a semantic character, must be relevant to the kind of effects they produce" (Dretske 1988, 80). Reasons, then, are representations of some part of the world, as it is or might be. Taking a position akin to Dancy here (Dancy 1993, esp. 13–14), I suppose that an agent who acts for a reason has a representation of some part of the present state of the world, and one or more representations of those parts of the world, each as it would or might be, were she to perform an action that she considers possible for her. We explain the agent's action, then, by reference to the content of some or all of these representations.

I do not suppose that this sort of explanation is possible for all human actions, or for most actions of even the most sophisticated of nonhuman animals, or for any actions at all of most members of the animal realm. Here I see my position as in some ways parallel to that of Gibbard (Gibbard 1990, esp. 56–57), in supposing that there are kinds of motivation, associated with ideas of appetites, drives, and the like, that are evolutionarily prior to motivation in terms of reasons. But Gibbard's contrast is between these prior forms of motivation and normative motivation, and nothing in the account that I have just sketched brings in the idea of being motivated by norms. The causal role played by the content of our representations should not be identified with normative direction. That has yet to enter my account.

Gibbard's contrast is also between kinds of motivation that do not and could not essentially involve language, and motivation that is linguistically infused. Whether semantic representation requires full-blown language is not a matter that I propose to discuss. It seems safe to say that without language, semantic representation must be very limited. My guess is that the ape who finds it impossible to reach the bunch of bananas hanging tantalizingly in the tree (cf. RMO, 37), and then after what we should describe, were the ape human, as pondering the situation, goes and fetches a stick with which he proceeds to knock the bananas out of the tree, has the capacity to form at least some representations of the world as it is and might be, and to be moved by the content of these representations. But a great many representations of the world as it might be are clearly quite impossible without language. And those unoriginal comments are all that I propose to say here about the matter.

I should perhaps note that what I term reason must be distinguished from what Baier terms intelligence. Intelligence, for Baier, is the capacity "to learn by and from experience" (RMO, 39). Now an agent can learn from experience, can have its behavior modified by its experiences, without being motivated by its beliefs, by the semantic content of its representations. To be sure, an agent who has beliefs, and is motivated by their content, must be capable of modifying its beliefs in the light of its experiences. In ascribing beliefs to it, we ascribe to it the capacity to form representations that are caused by what they represent. Such representations are therefore learned from experience. But not all forms of learning, conceived blandly as behavior modification experientially caused, involve belief, and so not all forms of intelligence involve the capacity to act for reasons.

Before proceeding, I should also note that I include believing among those actions that are performed for reasons. Indeed, to ascribe a belief to an agent is to ascribe a representation to her that she holds partly in virtue of its own content. But questions about belief are not directly relevant to my present argument, and I shall therefore leave them to one side.

My brief account of acting for reasons departs from the belief/desire model, Humean if not Hume's, that I have accepted in my earlier writings. The sketch I have just given relates motivation to the agent's beliefs, but makes no mention of her desires. We may, if we like, say that what the agent desires can be determined from her reasons for acting, but this would give desire no independent role to play in the account of acting for reasons. And I have come to think that for motivation by reasons, this is probably right. But I do not want to dismiss desire altogether from a motivational role. Certainly there is room for desire in those kinds of motivation that are evolutionarily prior to acting for reasons. And there is also room for felt desire as among those things that the agent represents to herself in acting for a reason. Roughly, the agent is then moved by the representation of the desire, but not by the desire itself. She takes her desire as, in the situation, providing her with a reason for acting. Two points are important here. The first is simply that an agent may represent herself as having a felt desire without taking herself to have a reason for acting, or without acting or being in any way motivated to act on it. Thus the presence of a felt desire is not in itself sufficient to give an agent, or at least a human agent, a reason for acting. The second is that an agent need not represent herself as having a felt desire to take herself to have a reason for acting, or to act or be motivated to act on some representation or belief. Thus the presence of a felt desire is not necessary to give an agent, or at least a human agent, a reason for acting. Thus I am offering an essentially cognitive account of motivation in acting for reasons.

But I use the term 'cognitive' here with misgivings, since it invites misunderstanding. In particular, I want to distinguish motivational cognitivism from normative cognitivism. To clarify this, I need to make a prior distinction between the capacity to act for a reason—to be moved by the semantic content of one's representations of the world as it is and as it might be, and the very different capacity that I mentioned at the outset—the capacity to assess a reason, to consider the appropriateness of being moved in a certain way by a certain semantic content. The former is a motivational capacity; the latter is a normative capacity that presupposes, but is not fully presupposed by, the motivational capacity. We can imagine an agent who is capable of forming representations about the world as it is and might be, and of being motivated by the content of those representations, and thus an agent who is able to act for reasons, at least in a rudimentary way, but who nevertheless is unable to assess the appropriateness of those reasons. She is unable to consider reflectively whether her actions fit her representations. The ape who pondered the problem of reaching the bananas may well have been exhibiting the motivational capacity to act for a reason while lacking altogether the normative capacity to assess the appropriateness of his reason.

How we should characterize the motivation of an agent who acts for reasons is then a question distinct from how we should characterize the norms, if any, that appropriately govern the agent's assessment of these reasons. I have proposed that an agent who acts for a reason is moved to act by her representations of the world as it is and as it might be. This is motivational cognitivism. But I have so far said nothing about how an agent might assess her representations as reasons. An account of her normative capacity that offers no substantive definition of rationality, and is noncognitive in the way recently proposed by Allan Gibbard (Gibbard 1990, esp. 6–9), might seem to be entirely compatible with a cognitivist account of her motivation. Whether it actually is compatible—whether there are instead links between motivational and normative cognitivism that I have not uncovered—is not a matter that I shall be able to pursue here.

In distinguishing motivational from normative capacity, I have in effect introduced what I take as the distinction between reason and rationality. An agent who has some capacity to act for reasons need not be, even potentially, a rational agent. A rational agent is one who has the capacity to assess her reasons, and to be motivated only by those representations that she takes to be appropriate. In being moved by the semantic content of her representations of the world as it is and might be, an agent may implicitly exhibit a standard of fit between her actions and the world, which we, as rational observers, can elucidate. And we may then be able to ask about the appropriateness of this standard. But she may herself be unable to articulate this standard so that her acceptance of it is not even potentially within her control. And if her standard is thus purely implicit, her actions may not be judged rational or irrational. Only if she is able to articulate the standard of fit between her actions and the world, and to consider whether to conform to it, is our judgment of its appropriateness a basis for considering her actions rational or irrational.

So rationality, as I understand it, is the capacity to assess reasons for acting and of course to be motivated by one's assessment. The rational agent has, as Baier notes, both a reflective and an executive task (cf. RMO, 36). In effect the motivational capacity to act for reasons is extended by rationality, so that it becomes the capacity to act not simply on the content of the agent's representations, and so to fit her actions to her beliefs, but the capacity to act on the agent's assessment of the appropriateness of her actions to the content of her representations, so that she endorses the fit between her actions and her beliefs. This is an expansion of reason, but it seems to me that it must be possible for any agent with a fully developed language. Language makes it possible to represent the fit between action and belief, and we cannot, I think, intelligibly suppose that an agent might be able to represent this fit to herself without being able both to question it and to be motivated by her answer. Language brings normative capacities in its train. Or so I claim, but I have not offered, and within the confines of this paper, I shall not attempt to offer, an argument adequate to support this claim.

2.2. Given the distinction I have drawn between reason and rationality, it should be evident that the question 'why follow reason?' does not arise—we simply are the sort of beings that form motivating representations. But of course the question that Baier asks in the form 'why follow reason?' does seem to arise, since it becomes for me the question 'why follow rationality?', and this is on the face of it a sensible normative issue, arising from reflection, not on the appropriateness of taking particular beliefs as reasons for particular actions, but on the appropriateness of being motivated by assessments of the fit between particular beliefs and particular reasons. But if it is a sensible issue, it is surely not to be answered in quite the way that Baier answers the question 'why follow reason?', and in considering why this is so one aspect of my fundamental disagreement with Baier about the relation of the social and the rational will become apparent.

Baier claims that "there is a substantive answer to 'Why follow reason?' "and it is quite simple: "following reason is the best available way to attain certain very general ends which, at least when we think about it, we all, at least normally, want to attain" (RMO, 50). As an example of these ends, Baier mentions "discovering true rather than false answers to questions about matters that are important to us." Is Baier right? Putting the issue in my terminology, is being rational, or following rationality, the best available way to attain certain important general ends? Baier claims that "It is the best method because it consists in following certain general guidelines made available to us by our culture for the purpose of enabling us to guide ourselves in our attempts to find answers to such important questions" (RMO, 50).

That Baier is thus committed to treating normative assessment as conceptually dependent on the existence of social guidelines for answering questions about what to do, seems clear. He claims that the question 'Why follow reason?' has a substantive answer that makes reference to social guidelines. And if the answer is indeed substantive, then the terms in which it is given—and so the existence of social guidelines—must be part of a substantive account of rationality. No guidelines—no rationality. Consistently with this, Baier further insists that the ape who fetches a stick to enable him to reach the bananas, "cannot be said to be either rational or irrational: he is not a member of an order of reason and so could not . . . take advantage of the socially provided "machinery" needed to reflect in a regimented way about which of the alternative performances open to him is according, which contrary to reason, and then to perform according rather than contrary to it" (RMO, 51). Baier's argument is not that without such guidelines the ape would be doomed to irrationality, but that without such guidelines the ape's performance could not be assessed in terms of rationality. This again is to treat the existence of guidelines for solving problems about what to do as part of a substantive account of rationality.

But can this be right? Consider two cases. Suppose that a culture does not provide such guidelines. Now we might think that it would then be quite impossible for an individual agent to get very far in attaining her important ends, or indeed in achieving anything else, by assessing her reasons for acting and modifying her behavior in the light of her assessment. But surely we should not want to deny that she could engage in this activity, that she could subject her motivating reasons to normative assessment. Sally finds herself disposed to inflict some harm on persons who have insulted her, and so she takes the fact that Peter has insulted her as reason for inflicting some harm on Peter. Reflecting on this, she asks herself whether the fact that Peter has insulted her is indeed a good reason for harming him in return. She can surely ask herself this question with or without social guidelines for answering it. Even if revenge itself is a socially based motive, it need not come with public guidelines. Sally can simply ask herself whether revenge makes sense. It seems to me if an agent asks herself such questions, even if she lacks "publicly available . . . guidelines for solving frequently occurring problems" (RMO, 51), then we should be quite prepared to make such judgments as, 'Her actions were as rational as could be expected given her circumstances'—that is, those circumstances that affect the ways in which she is able to engage in normative assessment.

Suppose now that a culture does provide guidelines of the type that Baier envisages. The existence of these guidelines will surely be an important feature of the circumstances that affect how an agent in that culture is able to engage in normative assessment. We should no doubt be surprised if someone simply ignored available guidelines. But it seems to me that we should neither refuse to assess the person and her actions on the dimension of rationality, nor dogmatically insist that the person and her actions were irrational. To be sure, we should no doubt expect the person to offer some reason for rejecting the standing guidelines. And Baier seems to agree; he says, "We may . . . sometimes be able to discover flaws in these guidelines; in such cases, following reason means suitably departing from them" (RMO, 51). But if rationality can be a matter of departing from guidelines, as well as following them, it is unclear, at least to me, why rationality should be thought to require the guidelines. What matters, surely, is the activity of normative assessment; that this is likely to remain at the most rudimentary level in the absence of cultural guidelines does not make it conceptually dependent upon them.

Should we totally dismiss Baier's insistence on the social roots of rationality? I have argued that it is not a substantive constraint on what counts as normative assessment. Should we perhaps understand it as a proposal that comes from within the practice of normative assessment and seeks to delimit that practice? Perhaps Baier should be understood as claiming that when we reflect on the practice of normative assessment—when we turn normative assessment reflexively on itself—we find no way for an agent to proceed in the absence of guidelines provided by her society. But is this so? Surely Sally can proceed with the question whether taking revenge on Peter makes sense, by considering how taking revenge will affect the attainment of her various ends and objectives. This may not be the only way for Sally to proceed, but it seems a possible way, and one that involves social guidelines contingently rather than necessarily.

What I can salvage from Baier's account of the social roots of reason is that it offers a proposal about how normative assessment should normally be conducted—a proposal that is itself a candidate for being a higher-order social guideline: 'Pay attention to social guidelines in assessing the fit between one's representations and one's actions'. This seems to me the most plausible understanding of the relation between society and rationality, even if it is not Baier's. But then the idea of social roots is a profoundly misleading metaphor. Normative assessment has a typically social character but the practice itself may be understood, although no doubt not effectively conducted, in the absence of social guidelines.

2.3. Underlying Baier's appeal to social guidelines, there seems to me to be a different account of rationality, which does not make it conceptually or even normatively dependent on social guidelines. Baier insists that these guidelines have the purpose of enabling us to answer questions about the best way to attain general and important ends. This surely suggests that he could dispense with them in his account of rationality; being rational just is assessing the fit between one's beliefs and one's actions in relation to attaining such ends. Among them we might plausibly include the agent's well-being and happiness, and also her self-respect and sense of her own worth. Thus it may be supposed that Sally answers her question whether the fact that Peter has insulted her is indeed a good reason for harming him, by determining whether she may expect that harming Peter as a return for having been insulted by him, will contribute to her own well-being and self-respect. No doubt she expects some immediate satisfaction from making him suffer, but she may question the real value of this form of satisfaction, and may think that she would diminish her self-worth by seeking it. She may come then to reject the fact that Peter has insulted her as a reason for revenging herself.

Suppose rationality concerns the fit between actions and ends. Then the answer to the question, 'Why be rational?' might seem evident. To be rational is to assess one's actions in terms of their suitability for attaining one's general ends, and to be guided by one's assessment. And it may then seem that to be rational must be the best way to attain those ends. But this need not be so. It is possible that an agent would do better not to engage in the normative assessment of her reasons for acting, even if such assessment is governed by the fit between her actions and her ends. For it may be that simply acting directly on the basis of one's representations of the world as it is and as it might be, is a better way of securing one's ends than is engaging in the practice of normative assessment and being guided by its outcome. Even if normative assessment leads one to a better fit between the reasons on which one acts and one's ends, the cost of engaging in such assessment may outweigh the benefits of this better fit.

The question 'Why be rational?' is a normative question—a question which puts the practice of normative assessment under normative scrutiny. Perhaps it fails to survive this scrutiny. Certainly it is not always rational to engage in rational assessment. Nevertheless I see no serious reason to doubt that sometimes it makes sense to reflect about the fit between our representations and our actions, and to be guided by our reflection. But should we accept the view that normative assessment, and so rationality, must concern the fit between one's actions and the attainment of "certain very general ends which, at least when we think about it, we all, at least normally, want to attain" (RMO, 50)?

This may seem a very bland characterization, in not specifying any ends. But it does suppose that the appropriate fit between our representations and our actions is to be determined by ends, and that these are ends that everyone, normally, wants to attain. Each of these italicized terms might be questioned. Are there considerations quite independent of ends that affect, or should affect, normative assessment? Are there ends that apply to everyone, or at least to every person in a normal condition, and if there are, are these the only ends that are the concern of rationality? How do we identify a normal condition, and what precisely is its relevance to normative assessment? And should we say that an end applies to a person if and only if she wants, or normally wants, to attain it?

I shall not attempt to answer these questions here. But I shall offer a few comments on them. The idea that the universe is purposively ordered was no doubt more widely shared before evolutionary theory showed how to give nonpurposive explanations of the appearance of purpose. But a person who accepts this idea will no doubt insist on its relevance to normative assessment. Yet it seems to me that he need not say that the purposive order determines ends that everyone normally wants to attain. And even if he does say this, it will not be the fact that there are ends that everyone normally wants to attain, but rather the fact that these ends are determined by or related to the purposive order of the universe, that justifies our appeal to them in our assessments of rationality. And while we may want to reject his views and even insist that nowadays no truly rational person can share them, it seems to me that disqualifying them on conceptual grounds, or on the basis of our account of rationality, would be unsatisfactory.

The idea that there are very general ends that all persons want to attain, has generated considerable philosophical and psychological heat, but not, I think, a comparable amount of light. Even the most apparently vacuous attempts to formulate this claim—for example that all persons want to maximize expected utility, where utility is defined as a measure of their preferences—have invited more dissent than agreement. More substantive formulations—that happiness and only happiness is a good to persons—have fallen pretty heavily out of favor. But if we were to be persuaded that there were general ends that all persons wanted to attain, and that the fit between one's actions and the attainment of these ends was the proper basis of normative assessment, we should surely want to claim that someone who disagreed with us fell short of full rationality, but not that his acceptance of other grounds for normative assessment disqualified him from being judged rational or irrational. As long as he engages in a recognizable practice of assessing the fit between his representations and his actions and modifying his behavior in the light of this assessment, he exhibits not merely the capacity to act for reasons, but the capacity for rationality. We may think he does a poor job, but we must surely agree that what he does a poor job of is normative assessment.

There is a standard objection to the argument that I have been presenting. In order to take someone to be engaging in normative assessment, I must be able to make sense of his activity under that characterization. The objector asks how I do this, except by an appeal to shared standards. Now it is certainly true that if I am to interpret someone merely as acting for a reason, I must be able to see some fit between what I take him to be doing and what I take to be his representations of the world as it is and might be. And it seems to me that if I can do this, and if I can also understand him as a language-user, then there is no further problem in principle with my interpreting some of his behavior as normative assessment. I shall of course have to interpret him not only as fitting his actions to his representations but as considering alternative possibilities of fit, rejecting some, accepting others. But it seems to me that unless I need to appeal to public standards in order to understand his acting for a reason, I do not need to appeal to such standards to understand his assessing possible reasons.

So the objector must claim that interpreting a person's behavior as reasoned requires an appeal to publicly available standards. These need not be standards that I share with the agent, but standards that the agent shares with others in his culture. But this seems to me mistaken. I have already suggested that I can understand the ape's behavior as reasoned, when he fetches a stick to enable himself to reach the bananas. But the ape is not part of a society considered as an order of reason. If there is a problem in understanding the ape's behavior as motivated by reasons, it surely arises from the doubt that he has the capacity to form the representations of the world in order to be motivated by their content. Perhaps then the objector should be taken as claiming that this capacity requires publicly available standards. Then the objection reduces to the more general contention that intentional states can be ascribed only to beings who live in a social order that develops publicly available guidelines for semantic representation. This is too large an issue for me to pretend to resolve in this present paper. So I shall claim only that there is no special objection to the possibility of rationality outside a social order, over and above a more general objection to the possibility of nonsocial intentionality.

Baier claims that "A being's performances cannot be judged rational or irrational until he and his 'fellows' have available to them this sort of apparatus [i.e., guidelines "for solving frequently recurring problems of certain kinds" that society "develops, makes publicly available, tries to improve, and educates its members so as to be able to apply"] for determining what, in a particular situation, it is according and what contrary to reason for a particular individual, whether himself or others to perform" (RMO, 51). I conclude that this is mistaken. We need not look to a being's fellows to determine if its performances can be judged rational or irrational. We need not consider what its society makes available to it. To suppose otherwise is, I think, to confuse social conditions without which, as a matter of fact, a being could exhibit only the most rudimentary and unreflective motivation by reasons, and so would not exhibit rationality, with conditions that are found in the individual, and that determine whether its behavior is motivated by reasons, and if so, whether it exhibits rationality in being able to assess those reasons.

3.1. I want now to turn to the second of my themes—to the claim that rationality is subversive of traditional social order, but affords the basis for the reconstruction of that order. Rationality, as I have characterized it, is a capacity that manifests itself primarily in reflective activity. Sally finds herself being moved by the thought that Peter has insulted her to inflict some harm on him in return; she reflects on whether she is right to be so moved, or whether it makes good sense for her to be so moved. Now there are two quite different ways of parsing this latter thought. Sally might reflect on whether (it makes good sense) (for her to be so moved), or she might reflect on whether (it makes good sense for her) (to be so moved). The second parsing contains a second, implicit pronominal reference, which can be made explicit by saying that Sally reflects on whether it makes good sense for her that she be so moved.

I want to defend the second parsing. That is, I want to claim that in reflecting on one's reasons for acting, the agent considers what makes sense for him, that he do. Of course, he may think that what makes sense for him is simply what makes sense. But he need not think this. He may think that what makes sense, or is rational, makes sense for an agent, so that nothing makes sense sans phrase, and he may have no thoughts about how what makes sense for one agent relates to what makes sense for some other agent. Or in other words, he need not suppose that rationality involves, explicitly or implicitly, universality.

No doubt it would not make sense for me to suppose that I can make this heretical doctrine fully convincing. I shall confine my argument to two points. The first begins from the fact that rationality, as I have characterized it, is a capacity of an agent, exercised in his deciding what to do. And deciding what to do is characteristically deciding what oneself is to do. We do of course speak of someone deciding for another person—"We've decided," the parents announce to their delighted offspring, "that you will go to piano class." But although I shall not try to argue the claim here, deciding for oneself must be the primary mode of decision.

To be sure, to reflect on what it makes sense to do, to consider whether an action would be rational given the world as it is and might be, is not in itself to make a decision. One might then suppose that rationality is exercised only in judging what it makes sense to do. And this might seem to remove the question from the first-person context of decision. But I agree with Baier that rationality has both a reflective and an executive task. The reflective task is to judge what it makes sense for one to do; the executive task is to do what one has judged makes sense. An agent who was not motivated to act on the basis of his reflective judgments of what it makes sense for himself to do, would lack an essential part of the capacity for rationality; he would indeed not be rational as an agent.

So the reflective moment in rationality is exercised in the first-person context of decision. If the agent asks 'What does it make sense to do?' he does not thereby take his reflection out of or beyond that context. The change in focus implicit in stepping back to consider the fit between one's representations and one's actions need not be a change in scope, which may continue to be simply the particular context of first-person decision. The agent may of course consider whether certain actions simply make sense, or make sense for anyone. He may find these questions intelligible, and so be able to move beyond the first-person context, and he may insist on the rationality of doing so. But his insistence is a higher-order judgment about the proper exercise of rationality, and not a necessary feature of the reflective practice constituting that exercise.

It may be possible to defend universality as a feature of good or correct normative assessment. But that is not my concern, which is only to deny that universality is a constitutive feature of normative assessment. Confusion between these two quite different matters, between the higher-order normative issue of what constitutes correct normative assessment, and the constitutive issue of what necessarily characterizes the practice of normative assessment, seems to me to be at the root of many bad arguments about rationality and its implications. Much of this confusion is engendered, I think, by a failure to see that the constitutive features of rationality, or normative assessment, depend in part on the context within which rationality is primarily exercised—the first-person context of deciding what one is to do.

But there is a further confusion that lies behind the insistence that rationality is necessarily universal, which arises from focusing on the rather special context of deciding what one is to believe. This is my second point against the universality of reason. Belief is linked necessarily to truth; to believe is to believe true. And reasons for believing must therefore be reasons for believing-true. Now this link with truth does, I think, establish a form of universality, although to say precisely what is the link between truth and universality would take me far beyond the bounds of this argument. But the link will not be challenged by those who want to defend the thesis that rationality is necessarily universal. My charge is that they recognize that reasons for believing are inherently universal, but mistakenly ascribe this to the requirements of reason rather than to those of belief. And this leads them in effect to suppose that all reasons must share the universality found in reasons for believing, which in effect is to suppose that an analogue to truth can be found as the proper object of all of our actions.

3.2. I want now to return to the first part of my second thesis—that rationality subverts social order. My thought is simply that the agent, in considering what makes sense for him to decide that he will do, is led to assess the accepted practices and institutions that are fundamental to his society, from his own point of view. Indeed he is led to develop an individual point of view. And from this point of view he wants to know why the grounds traditionally offered for conforming to social practices and institutions are reasons for him.

Traditional grounds are not typically couched in individually oriented terms or related to matters of individual concern. Here I am of course making an empirical claim. Human society could have developed as a "cooperative venture for mutual advantage," to employ, as I so often do, Rawls's useful phrase (Rawls 1971, 4). But in fact human societies have not developed in this way. Now I do not want to claim that when an individual begins to reflect on the reasons, if any, that he has to uphold the existing terms of social order, he must come to think simply in terms of his own advantage. Were this so, then the step from rationality to subversion would be a very short one. In any society that is not a cooperative venture for mutual advantage, some persons would come to think that their only reasons for conforming to the social order reflects the power of that order to coerce them into conformity, and this thought is indeed a subversive one. But my claim is much weaker. I do not propose that there are substantive constraints on the direction that must be taken by the reflective assessment of the adequacy of alleged reasons for acting, but only make the observation that, just as traditional human societies have not developed as cooperative ventures for mutual advantage—although in principle they might have—so individual reflection on social order does bring the agent's advantage, broadly and blandly conceived, or perhaps better, the agent's reflectively endorsed concerns, to the fore—although in principle it might not. And of course I want to interpret the democratization that is characteristic of modern societies and constitutive of their legitimacy as the constructive fruit of rational reflection that has subverted earlier grounds of legitimation.

But before turning to construction, I should mention another way in which rationality supports the subversion of the traditional grounds for conforming to the practices and institutions of society. Negatively, these grounds are not based on individual concerns; positively, these grounds typically relate the existing social order to the gods—to the universe, or to aspects of the universe, thought of as supernatural. Again, I do not claim that this is a necessary feature of social order, but only that actual human societies have been thought of as providing a locus or loci for humans to participate in an immanent spirituality, or as ordained to meet human inadequacies by a transcendent spirituality. And it is my claim, which I recognize to be controversial, that rational reflection, directed now towards reasons for believing, leads to the disenchantment of society, the dissolution, if not of the spiritual, at least of the claims of social structures to relate human beings to the spiritual. And what this dissolution leaves in place, or perhaps allows to come to the fore, is the individual agent, with his claims against the social order.

3.3. What I have offered in the last few paragraphs falls far short of a full argument to show that the development of individual rationality is subversive of traditional social order. At best I have pointed to some of the materials from which such an argument might be constructed. But for present purposes this will have to do, since I want to consider—albeit equally briefly and inadequately—the constructive moment that leads me to claim that, rather than looking for the social roots of reason, we need to consider the rational roots of morality and society.

There is nothing original in this claim, which appears fairly clearly in Hobbes (Hobbes 1991, esp. chaps. 13–15). I shall assume familiarity with the main outlines of his argument, and focus on two features of it that seem unsatisfactory, and that must be rethought if it is to serve my purposes. Hobbes argues that each person's overriding endeavor to promote his own conservation would, in the absence of society, lead to behavior inimical to everyone's conservation. And he argues that to meet this problem, reason suggests articles of peace, or laws of nature, that require each person to be willing, provided others are equally willing, to accept certain constraints on his own behavior. These constraints, as expressed in the laws of nature, constitute the moral virtues, and the need to enforce them is the basis of Hobbes's defense of a political order. Now the two features of Hobbes's account that I think are unsatisfactory are his insistence that each person's sole or overriding object of concern must be his own conservation, and, more important for my critique of Baier's account of the relation between reason and morality, his insistence that each individual's rational acceptance of any form of constraint—any diminution of what Hobbes calls the right of nature—depends on the equal acceptance of constraint by others. I think that Baier has accepted something analogous to this second claim of Hobbes in his argument for the rationality of morality, and has taken this as a further ground for thinking of morality as having social roots, so that we can assess a particular agent's behavior as moral or immoral only in terms of standards that must be equally available and justifiable to his fellows.

I want to begin my argument here by eliminating the emphasis on the agent's own conservation. I have supposed that in reflecting on his reasons for acting, an agent will be led to reject those that, albeit sanctioned by tradition or convention, prove not to be congruent with a disenchanted understanding of society and an emphasis on individual concerns. In effect, this will mean the replacement of a single social standard for the evaluation of states of affairs and so of the actions that bring them about, by multiple individual standards. To be sure, the idea of a single standard is no doubt always an ideological facade masking conflict and diversity, and the emphasis on multiple standards ignores the persistence of widespread common evaluations. Nevertheless there is a difference, and one that not only leads, as multiple standards become prevalent, to the weakening of the social fabric as such, but also to those forms of conflict that we have come to identify as generalized Prisoner's Dilemmas, in which persons, each guided by his own normative assessments, are led to interact in ways leading to outcomes that are sub-optimal, in being worse from everyone's perspective than some feasible alternatives. These forms of conflict then are what give rise to Hobbes's problem—each person's endeavor to promote his own concerns, whatever they be, would, in the absence of society, lead to behavior inimical to everyone's concerns. No reference to conservation as an overriding concern is needed.

But if we focus exclusively on the Prisoner's Dilemma structure of much interaction, we are likely to come to think that the remedy, if remedy there be, must be entirely at the social or interpersonal rather than the individual level, since no person can unilaterally alter his behavior to correct for sub-optimality in ways that will not prove individually costly. I want therefore to direct attention to situations which in some ways resemble Prisoner's Dilemmas, but in which sub-optimality results from the behavior and dispositions of a single individual. These situations reveal, in the clearest possible way, the rational roots of morality.

Suppose then a situation with the following simple structure. You have an initial choice between two options, x and y, and I have a subsequent choice, also between two options, v and w. What you judge that it makes sense for you to choose, and indeed what you will choose, depends on your expectation of what I shall subsequently choose. Let us ignore all complications occasioned by probabilistic or indeterminate expectations; either you expect me to choose v, in which case you judge that it makes sense for you to choose x, or you expect me to choose w, in which case you judge that it makes sense for you to choose y. Suppose that I strongly favor (xv) to (yw), so that I judge that it would make sense for me to bring about (xv) rather than (yw), were I able to do so. However, suppose also that I favor (xw) to (xv), so that I judge that, if you were to choose x, it would make sense for me to choose w rather than v, at least ceteris paribus. And of course my actual choice is between v and w.

Let us put flesh on these abstract bones. Your initial choice is whether or not to help me (x) or not (y), and my subsequent choice is whether to help you (v) or not (w). You judge that it makes sense for you to help me if that will elicit my help in return, and you believe that I shall certainly not help you if you do not help me. So if you expect me not to help you (w), you will judge that it makes sense not to help me (y), whereas if you expect me to help you (v) provided you help me (x), you will judge that indeed it makes sense to help me. Now I favor reciprocal assistance (xv) to neither helping (yw), but also I favor not reciprocating (xw) to returning your help (xv), and so judge that if you were to help me (x), it would make sense for me not to reciprocate (v). But if you believe this, and expect me therefore not to reciprocate, you will not help me, and the outcome will be neither helping (yw), although each of us would think it made sense for him to bring about reciprocal assistance (xv) rather than neither helping, if he were to have that choice.

Reflecting on situations such as this, which are by no means uncommon, has led me to the view that insofar as I am rational, then in normal interactions of this kind I shall be disposed to reciprocate. The rationale for my being so disposed is this: (1) If I am believed to be reliably disposed to reciprocate, then I can expect to do better, with respect to any normal range of concerns, than if I am not believed to be so disposed, and (2) it is much more likely that I shall be believed to be reliably disposed to reciprocate, if I am in fact so disposed, than if I am not. (1) is straightforwardly supported by situations such as I have characterized; if you believe me reliably disposed to reciprocate, you will act in ways from which I may expect to benefit; if not, not. (2) is of course an empirical claim about human psychology.

The claim that a rational person will have certain dispositions implies that it is within his power to acquire or develop them. But to have a disposition such as a reliable willingness to reciprocate is in effect to take certain representations as providing one with reasons for acting, and so to be motivated by them. The acquisition or development of dispositions to take representations as reasons is simply part of rationality. The question then is whether a rational agent, simply in virtue of his rationality, must acquire dispositions as specific as a reliable willingness to reciprocate. Note that the argument I have offered for this disposition does not rest on any substantive judgments about the aims or ends that it is rational to pursue. It does not require us to suppose that a rational agent would seek to bring it about that he maximizes his utility, or that his life goes as well as possible, or even that the world goes as well as possible, whether from his point of view or in some allegedly objective manner. It does require us to suppose that he will find himself interacting with other agents capable of reasoned behavior, but it makes no particular claims about their dispositions.

This is a fundamentally important point. The problem of sub-optimality arises for interactions of the following kind: the outcome depends on each person's choice; if each chooses in a way that he judges makes sense ceteris paribus, then the outcome will be such that there is at least one alternative such that each would judge that it made sense to choose that alternative instead, were such a choice available to him. Baier focuses on this problem in the form of the Prisoner's Dilemma, and in this form the solution requires each to act differently, and so to be motivated by considerations over and above, or even instead of, those that would suffice to motivate that action that ceteris paribus would make sense. Since each must act differently, Baier supposes that what is required is a "society-anchored reason," which is "dependent on others also having it, and following it when they have it" (RMO, 190). It is then plausible to think of such reasons as having social roots in a stronger sense than holds for those based (according to Baier) on social guidelines, but which a person has "even if no one else has it or acts on it" (RMO, 190)—"self-anchored reasons" in Baier's terminology. And so even if one rejected Baier's defense of the social roots of self-anchored reasons, one might think that he had identified a further class of moral reasons that, since they hold for one person only if they hold for his fellows, must have social roots.

But Baier has, I think, been misled—just as, I must admit, I have in the past been misled. For suppose that we think of sub-optimality in relation to reciprocal assistance. We first realize that a person who is motivated solely by representations of the possible outcomes he can bring about through his choices will lack the disposition to be reliably willing to reciprocate. Such representations may ceteris paribus suffice to determine what it makes sense for him to do, but in this particular situation exclusive attention to them leads him to ignore the effect of his reasoning on the expectation of his potential beneficiary. Being reliably willing to reciprocate is then manifest in his taking the representation of receiving a benefit, perhaps with the expectation of some return, as motivating the return. This disposition resolves the problem of sub-optimality, and does so regardless of whether it is shared by the other person. Hence it affords the agent with a reason for acting which is strictly independent of others having it and following it when they have it.

Let us now return to situations that have a Prisoner's Dilemma structure. Here an agent reliably disposed to reciprocate will act cooperatively if and only if he expects the other agent also to act cooperatively. Each must of course act in ignorance of what the other actually does; each has only his expectation to guide him. Now it will be rational for an agent to be reliably disposed to reciprocate in PD-type situations if and only if (i) having this disposition affects the expectations of others in ways beneficial to him, and (ii) his own expectations are sufficiently reliable so that he usually cooperates when (enough) others do, and not when (enough) others do not. Unless at least some others were themselves reliably disposed to reciprocate these conditions would not be satisfied. But this is only to say that it is rational for an agent to extend his disposition to reciprocate to PD-type situations only if, among other conditions, there are other persons who are similarly disposed. It does not make the representation that one expects others to cooperate into a socially anchored reason motivating one's reciprocal cooperation.

I have argued that there are moral dispositions, and reasons for acting, that do not require the anchor of society. I do not want to deny that there are further reasons, associated especially with law, that do depend on social institutions, and so might be thought of as socially anchored. Indeed, I try elsewhere to defend the idea that law should be treated as public reason (Gautier 1995). But that is not a matter I can consider in the present context, where my concern is only to show that individual roots can be found that are adequate for both reason and morality.

3.4. I have been defending the thesis that certain fairly specific dispositions are a part of full rationality. What is the status of this thesis? Is it a substantive claim about the constitutive features of rationality, or a normative claim about what dispositions we should accept as rational? Although I am willing to accept that many disagreements about rationality are themselves normative in character, in which theses about normative assessment are themselves being normatively assessed, I do not think all disagreements about rationality have this character. Some are substantive, and if I have made a correct substantive claim, then someone who disagrees would not, or not only, fail fully to exhibit rationality, but would be simply mistaken about what the capacity for rationality includes. But if I have made a correct normative claim, then someone who disagrees need not be mistaken about the capacity for rationality, but would simply fail to exercise it correctly, and thus reach a mistaken normative conclusion. And one might argue that disagreement about the rationality of dispositions is properly a normative matter, on the ground that whether or not it makes sense to be, say, disposed to reciprocate, itself depends on a further normative claim—that it makes sense, or is rational, for different agents to assess possible outcomes, and more generally states of affairs, differently, in considering them as providing reasons for acting. Two particular states of affairs may bear quite differently on different agents, and this difference in bearing may correctly affect each agent's assessment of his reason to choose one rather than the other, should he have that choice. I shall term this the claim that reasons for acting are agent-relative.

Many persons reject this thesis, but I shall confine myself here only to those utilitarians who deny it. They think that states of affairs may be weakly ordered in terms of value, and that this weak ordering, which holds objectively, provides the necessary and sufficient basis of rational choice. Thus they think that if any person who may choose between two states of affairs has reason to act to bring about one rather than the other, every person who may so choose has reason so to act. Were this true, there would be no agent-relative reasons, the sub-optimality problem could not arise in fully rational interaction, and there would be no need for such dispositions as reliable reciprocation. Now some utilitarians, such as G. E. Moore, would be committed to rejecting the sub-optimality problem on the basis of what are represented as substantive theses about reason and value—roughly, that reasons for acting can only depend on values, and values must be strictly objective.[3] Were these the only grounds for rejecting the sub-optimality problem, and with it the rational necessity of such dispositions as reliable reciprocation, then I should be able to represent my argument as a substantive rejoinder to what I regard as patently false claims. But they are not. A utilitarian may quite consistently agree that nothing in the nature of reason and value rules out the possibility that the different bearing of states of affairs on different agents could correctly affect each agent's assessment of his reason to choose one rather than the other, but nevertheless argue that the only reasons that survive correct normative assessment do relate to an objective weak ordering of states of affairs. She would therefore reject the claim that good reasons for acting are agent-relative in a way that gives rise to a sub-optimality problem in interactions among fully rational persons. In my view she would be normatively mistaken, but she would not have committed any conceptual error about rationality.

So I should put my thesis in this way: if there are agent-relative reasons for acting, then dispositions such as reliable reciprocity are rational. And then the rest of my argument is very simple. The dispositions that a rational agent exhibits in meeting the sub-optimality problem are a part, though perhaps not the whole, of our conventional understanding of morality. They are dispositions that, by leading the agent to behave conditionally favorably towards others, invite others to satisfy the condition by behaving in ways favorable to the agent. They comprise the domains of trust and fairness. Thus a part of morality is given a rational foundation, without any appeal beyond the individual agent. And society, considered as the institutional structuring of interactions that constitute a "cooperative venture for mutual advantage," may be given the same foundation. It stands firm as "an order of reason," immune from the subversion that is the fate of more traditional orders. To be sure, social institutions require the tacit agreement of agents in ways that moral dispositions do not. The upshot of the revised Hobbesian argument is to display the individual rationale for the social contract. And so as I claimed at the outset, the roots of human morality and society are to be found in reason.

University of Pittsburgh

Notes

1. I am grateful to All Souls College, Oxford, and the John Simon Guggenheim Memorial Foundation, for support at the time this paper was written.

2. Jean Jacques Rousseau, *Discours sur l'origine . . . de l'inégalité* (1755), in Rousseau 1964: "C'est la raison . . . qui replie l'homme sur lui-même" (p. 156).

3. See Moore (1903), pp. 97–99, 146–48. In the latter passage he argues that to assert that an action is right is to assert that it will produce the greatest possible amount of good; I take this to defend the thesis that reasons for acting can only depend on value. In the former passage he argues that to assert that something is *my* good is to assert that it is absolutely good that I possess it; I take this to defend the thesis that values are strictly objective.

On The Moral Point of View

4

Joseph Raz

I. The Issue

In the years since Kurt Baier made the notion of the moral point of view central to his moral philosophy[1] many moral philosophers have found the idea that morality consists of a set of considerations which form a point of view or which can be seen from a special point of view—not necessarily in the sense that Baier understood it to be so—fruitful and suggestive. This essay offers some inconclusive reflections on the existence and nature of a moral point of view. In particular it argues against one way of conceiving it.

The moral point of view whose existence is my subject is not the common or garden-variety point of view which is manifested whenever one says "morally speaking what you did was not ideal," or "morality demands very high standards of integrity," and the like. The use of such expressions indicates that the speaker believes that in the context of his utterance some considerations can usefully be marked off from others as being moral. Such a belief imports no commitment to the view that

(1) there is a philosophically deep way of dividing considerations into moral and nonmoral such that even though other, context-dependent, uses of the terms are legitimate, it marks the correct, or the significant delineation of morality; or that
(2) moral considerations are a distinct type, distinct either in how we find out about them or in what makes them into considerations with a call on our attention.

The understanding of the moral point of view which I will challenge subscribes to both propositions. But right at the outset we can set aside one context of reference to points of view which, though presupposing the two propositions, is of no interest for the present inquiry. Quite often we refer to a point of view when we want to imply disbelief in the validity of the considerations encompassed by it, or when we wish to remain uncommitted to their validity. In this fashion an atheist may discuss how things are from a Christian point of view, meaning all those considerations that in virtue of their Christian beliefs, Christians believe to be valid. In a similar fashion the amoralist may talk of the moral point of view as encompassing those considerations that those who believe in morality believe to be valid. Adopting the common distinction between morality and beliefs about its content I will use "morality" to refer only to valid considerations. People may have mistaken beliefs about morality. But it makes no sense to say that morality is mistaken.

Acceptance of the two propositions is common to all the philosophically significant reflections on the moral point of view. Kurt Baier and others who think of morality in that way usually add to the two propositions others relating to the comparative weight or stringency of moral considerations. These may be the assertion that

> (3') Whenever moral considerations apply one should follow (or comply with) them regardless of the countervailing nonmoral considerations, unless the moral considerations themselves provide no definite guidance.[2]

An alternative principle which has found favor with some says

> (3") Moral and nonmoral considerations cannot be compared in stringency. When they conflict there is no true judgment of what one should do all things considered. One can only judge what one should do from a moral point of view and what one should do from some other point(s) of view.

Other philosophers suggested various ways in which moral and nonmoral considerations may be discounted against each other. I will discuss no such proposal in detail in this essay. I am assuming, however, that all propositions which entail

> (3) The moral character of a consideration affects the weight or stringency it has when it conflicts with the agent's desire or with other (nonmoral) considerations affecting what the agent ought to do

presuppose that (1) and (2) are true. That is I am assuming that if the moral character, rather than, or as well as, the specific content, of a consideration affects its weight or stringency this is so because moral considerations belong to a special kind of consideration, whose nature affects their stringency.

Possibly, if propositions (1) and (2) are true a decent argument can be put forward that typically the common use of expressions such as "morally speaking" presupposes their truth. But no support for the truth of the two propositions can be derived from the use of these expressions because they are readily explicable without presupposing the two propositions.

We are familiar with a variety of invocations of points of view. Consider but one example. "As a teacher I have to condemn such conduct (say failing to complete your homework), but as a parent I fully understand it (the piano competition your boyfriend participated in yesterday was very important to you both)." In contexts like this, and arguably in all or most others, not much of general theoretical importance can be extracted from the fact that two points of view are contrasted. There is no assumption that they belong to different orders (ontic or metaphysical) of considerations, nor that they differ epistemically. Nor is it assumed that what counts as a parental consideration in this statement cannot consistently be counted as outside the parental perspective in some other context. On some other occasion the same parent can contrast her role as the daughter's mother with her role as her friend both of which are subsumed under the same standpoint in the statement illustrated above.

Many philosophical discussions of ethics either argue for or simply proceed on the assumption that things are otherwise in ethics. They assume that the two propositions are true. There are a variety of reasons for which they may thought to be true, and correspondingly a variety of ways of understanding what is the moral point of view and how it is constituted. I will examine only one way of understanding the moral point of view, an understanding which assumes something like the following: Every person has a nonmoral reason to do whatever either best serves his interests, or contributes to achieving a goal he has, or contributes to making his life successful. Regarding any moral agent, the moral reasons which apply to him do not derive from his interest, goals or well-being. Indeed they may conflict with them. The question of the binding force of morality is the question of how is it that people are bound by considerations which are independent of their goals, interests or well-being.[3]

I will present what seems to me a powerful argument for the distinctness of the moral point of view and then proceed to examine its foundations. The results will be relevant to the assessment of other philosophical doctrines not directly connected with the examination of the issue of the nature of the moral standpoint. In particular they will be relevant to the thesis that there are internal and external reasons for action, and to forms of agent-relativism which depend on it.

II. Preliminaries I: Context-Dependent Standpoints

I will have little to say on the first of the two propositions which characterize belief in a distinctive moral point of view, namely the view that there is a coherent, context-independent way of separating the moral from the nonmoral, on which a correct understanding of morality depends. Undermining the second proposition renders the first less secure. If there is no ontic, metaphysical, or epistemic significance to the distinction between moral and nonmoral considerations, no difference between them which accounts for their call on our attention, then it is less likely that there is a context-independent distinction between them.

It is useful, however, to spend a few brief paragraphs to give a concrete example of how the distinction between the moral and the nonmoral could be context-dependent. Consider the observation: "What I did may have been tactless, but it was not immoral. I'm not saying that it was a moral act. Rather that it was neither moral nor immoral, but merely tactless." Contrast the case of a "merely tactless" act and an action which humiliates. Both hurt others, and both may display an indifference or at least a careless disregard for the feelings of the hurt people. (One can be both tactless and humiliating deliberately. But one need not.) The claim that the tactless act escapes moral judgment depends on its relatively trivial consequences. It may have needlessly hurt other people, but it is not as grave a matter as humiliating them. (Notice that the gravity of humiliation is not in the degree of hurt to the feelings of the humiliated person. It is in the meaning, or symbolic significance of the act).

Contrast this case with the case of Peter and Butrus, who, being senior registrars in their respective hospitals, both apply for a position as consultant at a hospital in the capital of Somalia's most famine-stricken region. Peter has no previous connections with Somalia. His current job is at Guy's in London. He applies for the new job primarily because he wants to help with alleviating the suffering caused by the famine. He is aware that the work experience will help him in his future career. But he would not have taken his decision to go to Somalia for that reason. Butrus, who is currently serving in the same Somali hospital, is also motivated by a desire to alleviate the suffering caused by the famine. He too is aware that the new position will be a promotion and will advance his career. But he is young and relatively new in his current more junior position. Only his justified dissatisfaction with the incompetence of his superiors and its consequences for the victims of the famine makes him apply for promotion at the present time.

Unlike the example of tact and humiliation, in classifying Peter's and Butrus's actions as moral or nonmoral their consequences or symbolic significance play a much lesser role. Peter's act is moral because of a combination of his motivation and of the disruption to his normal life that his action will—if successful—bring about. Had he gone to Somalia for career reasons his action would not have been regarded as moral, in spite of the fact that its consequences for the victims of the famine would have remained the same.[4] To the extent that we feel some ambivalence about calling Butrus's action moral that is because it involves no disruption to his normal life. If successful his life will remain the same, subject to the increased responsibilities he will assume and the greater rewards he will receive. His motivation is not in doubt, nor are the consequences of his actions to famine relief. They may affect our judgment of the morality of his character, but it is less clear that his action itself qualifies because of them as moral. I suppose that different people will feel differently regarding this case, and—more interestingly—that the same person may classify it differently on different occasions depending on the purpose and context of his remarks.

These illustrations do not prove that there is no common basis for all our (correct) classifications of actions or of considerations into moral and nonmoral. That is not their point. Their point is to suggest that we are not compelled by the facts on the surface of our discourse to do so. Their point is to suggest that we are adept at interpreting such classifications as based on classifying principles in ways which change with the context. There may be a unified understanding of what is moral behind them, but on the other hand there may not. This matter cannot be taken for granted. Its outcome is determined by theoretical reflections on the nature of practical reason.

III. Preliminaries II: Relational Goods

Moral considerations bear on the evaluation of character and character traits, emotions and attitudes, people and institutions, and many other factors. To simplify, and in the expectation that the arguments to be explored here are not affected by the simplification, I will proceed on the assumption that the respective natures of the good, values, and reasons for action are the backbone of the case for the existence of a moral point of view.[5] I will further proceed on the basis of a common though not unchallenged assumption about the dependence of reasons for action on values: Only if an action realizes or protects, or is likely to realize or protect, some good, or if it contributes to the realization or protection, or is likely to contribute to the realization or protection, of some good, can there be a reason for its performance, and the fact that it is so related to the good will be (part of) that reason.[6] The assumption is formulated to allow for the possibility of deontic requirements or prohibitions, that is for the possibility that some actions are required or forbidden on grounds independent of how good they are, or of how much good or ill they will or are likely to bring about. I am assuming, however, that deontic requirements apply only to acts which are good,[7] and that deontic prohibitions apply only to actions which are bad. I believe that the conclusions of this paper are not affected by the existence of deontic requirements or prohibitions, even if that condition is rejected. To simplify the presentation of the argument of the essay I sometimes disregard the case of deontic considerations.

The assumption is of a one-way dependence. Reasons, it assumes, are rooted in values. It leaves untouched the question whether all values or goods provide reasons for action, as well as the question, some aspects of which will be at the center of much of what follows, which agents have reason to realize which values.

I will distinguish "relational" and "nonrelational" judgments about goods or values. Nonrelational judgments of value are judgments of the form "X is good (or valuable)," or "something is a good (or valuable) X." Relational judgments of value have the form "X is good (has value) for Y." The variables "X" and "Y" can be replaced with the names or descriptions of objects, events, processes, actions, activities, institutions, animals, functions or roles, ideas, regimes, principles, and many others.

For some pairs, X and Y, the relation of X being good for Y holds true only if having X makes Y good, or better (than it would have been without X). If proportional representation is good for democracy then a democracy (any democratic regime) is a better democracy if it incorporates proportional representation. Similarly, if changing the engine oils every so often is good for the car this is only if a car which is so looked after is (or is likely to be) better (or in better condition) for being so looked after.[8] But this is not always the case. The fact that having a pay increase is good for teachers does not imply that having a pay increase makes teachers into better teachers. It need not even be likely that they will be better teachers (nor of course that they will be better people). Similarly, the fact that getting her much coveted delicacy is good for my cat is not conditional on it making her a better cat (nor on it making her a better pet).[9]

The question arises, what is the significance of this difference? I suggest, though I do not know whether this is a necessary as well as a sufficient condition, that if something can be good for X without making X better then X's good is not merely an instrumental good. It is good in itself. In other words, the fact that I claim that there are things which are good for my cat even though they do not make it into a better cat (nor a better pet, nor a better anything else[10]) indicates that I believe that the good of the cat matters in itself. But saying that the good of the cat matters in itself leaves open the question: matters to whom? Is it simply that it matters to the cat? Or does it matter in a nonrelational way? Is the intrinsic good of the cat simply a good for the cat? Or is it good *tout court,* good *simpliciter,* or perhaps, as people sometimes say, the good of the cat contributes to the good of the world?

The issue concerning the separateness of the moral point of view may be thought to raise the question whether there are nonrelational goods, and of their relation to relational goods. But for this question to stand a chance of capturing the issue about the separateness of the moral point of view a nonrelational good cannot be just a good described or asserted by a true nonrelational value judgment. Clearly there are true nonrelational value judgments. For example, "the computer I am writing on is a good computer" is a true nonrelational value judgment.

Perhaps something is a nonrelational good if there is a true nonrelational value judgment stating that it is a good, which neither presupposes nor entails the truth of a relational value judgment. Thus understood it could be argued that all goods are relational: Many nonrelational judgments of value are either elliptical for relational judgments of value or presuppose them. In those cases in which everything which is or can be good for X makes X better, how good X is matters because it matters to someone who has an interest in X. It also matters because there can be someone who could have or acquire an interest in X, and if he does, what is good for X would matter to him. This can be so either because X is useful to him (e.g., if it is his car) or because he has become fond of X and thus cares about its value or well-being (e.g., if X is his picture collection—which we can assume has no exchange value but is dear to his heart—or to give another example, if X is his cat). The case of beings of whom it is not true that necessarily what is good for them makes them better is even simpler. In their case what is good for them (or their well-being) matters in itself and not merely instrumentally or to those who are attached to them or who are fond of them, etc.; nevertheless what is good for them or for their well-being is, just by being good for them, essentially relational.

The reason this way of understanding relational and nonrelational goods is unsatisfactory is that it always seems possible to invent a fictitious something or someone such that whatever is good is good for it or him, or alternatively to find a real someone or thing for whom whatever is good is good in a fictitious sense. For example, is it good for history if countries have good leaders? Is it good for humanity if the weather is good? Is it good for art if art education is good? Is the world a better world if it has more (morally) good people in it, or if more of the people in it are (morally) good? In some sense the answer to all these questions is in the affirmative. But the fact that we can say things like "the world would be a better place if more people were good" may be a *façon de parler,* a mere way of saying that these things are good *tout court,* or that they are good for people, or for some other unstated subject.

This way of describing the difficulty is itself no more than a *façon de parler*. It merely shows that this way of drawing the distinction between a relational and a nonrelational good does not capture the distinction I am after. Possibly everything which is good or valuable, including what is intrinsically good or valuable, is also good or valuable for someone or something, such that all nonrelational goods are also relational ones. But this can be a merely grammatical fact. Views which regard all goods as relational should not gain plausibility by inventing empty relational judgments of value. "If life is valuable then the world is better for the existence of life," etc.

To get closer to the underlying philosophical issues let me stipulate that a good is relational if and only if it is good solely because it is good for someone, i.e., if it can be stated by a true relational value judgment the reason for which, or explanation of the truth of which, is exhausted on showing that it is good for someone. By way of contrast I will call a good or a value nonrelational if what makes it good is (or depends in part on) something other than that it is good for someone. Naturally, since the same thing can be good in two ways, or for two reasons, the same good can be both a relational and a nonrelational good. Promotion to managing director may be good both for Jane, since it serves her welfare, and for the company, which will get the benefit of her insight and initiative. So it is a relational good twice over. If anything can be nonrelationally good at all then we must allow that it can also be relationally good, i.e., good in a special way to some particular person.

Relational goods should not be confused with instrumental goods. The latter are relational goods, whose value resides in their having valuable consequences (or in the fact that they are likely to have such consequences). Relational goods can be intrinsically valuable. In many people's view a person's wisdom, e.g., is intrinsically but relationally valuable. It is good because it makes one better, or makes one's life a better life. The relation of wisdom to its possessor is constitutive, not causal. Yet wisdom is often valued because of its contribution to the life or personality of its possessors, i.e., relationally.

I have to admit that there is a certain awkwardness in the distinction, and in the way I will handle it in the next section The awkwardness, I believe, is not accidental. Part of the purpose of this essay is to show that the notions of being good *tout court* and of being good for someone are so closely connected that a systematic distinction between relational and nonrelational goods is misleading. But as we are to examine a case for the moral point of view which depends on the distinction, the elucidation I have offered will be helpful in setting it out. A few examples will help in understanding the distinction. A good car is relationally good for its value derives from its value to potential users (and perhaps some others). A good holiday is likewise relationally good, for its goodness lies in its contribution to the well-being of those who have it. If I or my cat has a good life that good is, perhaps, nonrelational. It is true that it is good for me and good for my cat to have a good life. But saying that does not illuminate the notion of a good life.[11] It is at best puzzling to say that the reason it is good to have a good life is that it is good for the person who has it. Clearly having a good life does not make the person whose life it is into a better person (though it may, and—more to the point—only people who are not bad in certain ways can have an altogether good life). What else can one mean by saying that the reason a good life is good is that it is good for those who enjoy it? These rephrasings of the near-tautology that a good life is good add very little to it, other than that in various contexts they can be used to dispel various possible misunderstandings.

Similarly, even those who believe that the world is a better world if the people in it are better people or if they have a better life do not normally regard this as a reason why a good life is valuable. A month's holiday in the mountains is a constitutive component of my life, and if it is good it makes my life better just by making part of it good. But I doubt whether we stand in the same relation to the world. While it makes sense[12] to say that someone wants a good holiday in order to have a good life it seems absurd to suggest that someone desires a good life, for himself or for another, *in order* to make the world into a better world. If this is absurd then the goodness of one's life or personality are nonrelational.

IV. The Thesis and its Argument

The conception of the moral point of view which is at the center of the present inquiry turns on the way in which value relates to reasons for action. We can simplify the principle of the value-dependence of reasons by saying that generally speaking, and subject to exceptions which need not concern us, we only have reason to perform actions which are likely to realize value. Talking of realizing value is jargon. I will use it as a shorthand for doing what is good for, or what prevents something bad happening to, someone whose good matters in itself. This formula requires sensitive unpacking. Take one example: Exercise is good for me. But I must take exercise (in the appropriate way) for it to do me any good. If something is valuable for me then there are various things which can happen or be brought about such that if they do happen I benefit from the good: this may be eating an apple, or listening to music, or watching a film, or repairing a roof, or keeping myself healthy. All such actions are covered by the jargon expression "realizing value." I will also talk of promoting value, or engaging in valuable activities, and use similar expressions all of which require sensitive translation into a range of ordinary verbs to make literal sense. Luckily, for present purposes the details of the unpacking do not matter.

What goods do we have reason to protect or promote, what good activities should we engage in? Is there any reason for anyone other than the being for whom the good is good to realize it? Clearly not everything which is good for someone or something gives rise to reasons for people other than those it is good for. Watering the flowers is sometimes good for them. Having the car serviced every year is good for the engine. But not everyone has reason to water the flowers or to get the car serviced. Other things being equal only those who have an interest in the flowers or the car have a reason to look after their good. Does it follow that, other things being equal, only those with an interest in my well-being have a reason for doing what is good for me?

A simple consideration lends further support to the view that this is indeed so. What is good for one person may well be bad for another person. Assuming that the goods in question are relational goods, one of the people concerned has reason to bring that thing about (since it is good for him) and the other has reason to prevent its coming about (since it is bad for him). It would seem that other people whose interests are not involved have no reason either way. Some people, I believe, have been tempted by such considerations to embrace the view that all reasons are agent-relative, and that they all derive from what is good for the agent or for his life, or from goals which he happens to have. We need not consider that suggestion for the moment. Our immediate interest is in a much weaker, and therefore more plausible, thesis. All that the conception of the moral point of view investigated here has to establish is a certain difference between the way in which one's own good provides reasons for action for oneself and the way nonrelational goods provide reasons for action. To establish that nonrelational goods provide reasons (for everyone) is part of what is required to establish the validity of the moral point of view, as here envisaged. From the moral point of view, one may say, people have reason to protect and promote the good of all, because the good of people is good *simpliciter* and not only good for them. To establish the validity of the moral point of view is to show that people are permitted or required to adopt it either always or if certain conditions are met.

In setting out these points I have followed the common understanding that universal reasons arise either from what is good for everyone or from what is good *simpliciter*. Therefore, if everyone has reason to protect and promote what is good for John, regardless of whether what is good for John is good for everyone, then what is good for John is also good *simpliciter*.[13] Two obvious ways in which moral reasons can be distinct suggest themselves: the values (the moral goods) which give rise to moral reasons may be distinct, or they may be related to moral reasons in a way which is distinct and unlike the usual relations between goods and reasons. These two ways give rise to the two priority theses: The priority of relational goods over nonrelational ones and the priority of relational reasons.

Let us turn first to the thesis of the priority of relational goods. For the purpose of the argument that follows it is convenient to proceed on the basis of a further assumption common to many writers about morality, namely that only considerations related to the character and the well-being of people are moral considerations. Most commonly it is assumed that morality regards the well-being of all human beings and the virtue of their characters as nonrelationally valuable, and thus a source of reasons for action for all human beings.

If the well-being of people is a nonrelational value, then, the claim is, it is also what I will call a *dependent* value. A value is dependent if it is valuable in a certain way, for someone or something, or for a certain reason, only because it is valuable in another way, or for another reason, or for something or someone else. The well-being of people is nonrelationally valuable only because it is relationally valuable, only because it is, tautologically, good for the people whose well-being it is. Dependence can be reciprocal. But in the case of well-being the dependence is all one way. One's well-being is good for one independently of whether it is good for anyone else, or just good *simpliciter*. Individual well-being may be a special good. It is sometimes held to be the one ultimate or supreme good. But the same relationship of one-sided dependence, the claim is, applies to all goods. The normal way to show why it is good *simpliciter* that John shall not be homeless, is that it is good for John not to be homeless. But one can show that it is good for John without presupposing in anyway that it is good in a nonrelational way. It is morally good to assure John of adequate housing only because it is good for John to have adequate housing. It is good for John to have adequate housing not because it is morally important that he should have it. It is good for him since it is a precondition of his having a good life that he should be properly housed. When we think of that good not as a good for him but as a good *simpliciter*, and therefore as a moral good potentially determining moral reasons for everyone, we must acknowledge that the moral good depends on the, to use the common jargon, prudential good. Housing John is good morally only because it is good prudentially. If art is good, good *simpliciter*, that is only because it is good for people, but it is good for people independently of its being good *simpliciter*. If these assumptions are justified we could say that relational values have an ontic (as well as an epistemic) priority over moral ones. That is, moral values, which are nonrelational, depend on relational values, whereas relational values do not (i.e. do not as such, not as a class) depend on moral values. The claim that there is such a one-sided dependence of nonrelational goods on relational ones is the thesis of the priority of relational goods.

The second priority thesis, the priority of relational reasons, follows a parallel line of reasoning. Following the distinction between relational and nonrelational goods, a reason which one has to protect or promote a good because it is good for oneself will be called a relational reason. A reason one has to protect and promote what is good *simpliciter* is a nonrelational reason. The thesis I will call "The priority of relational reasons" holds:

(1) That something is good for the agent is a reason for him to protect or promote that good.
(2) The truth of (1) can be established without presupposing that people have reason to protect and promote nonrelational goods.
(3) The moral point of view, or more generally, the view that people have reason to protect and promote nonrelational goods, presupposes (1).

The vindication of the thesis seems to require no more than pointing out that the fact that something is good for John gives him a reason to bring it about which others do not have. Possibly what is good for John is also good nonrelationally. Even if it is, however, the point that it is good for John stands. Therefore, he has a reason to realize it which is special to him, a reason separate and independent of any reason anybody else may have to realize that good. If owning a house is good for John then that is a reason for him to acquire a house. If his owning a house is a nonrelational good then (from the moral point of view) everyone has a reason to see to it that he owns a house. But his reason differs from theirs, and would exist even if theirs did not. Moreover, given that, by our hypothesis, concern for him explains why other people have reason to provide him with housing it seems plausible that they can have such a reason only if he has an independent, relational reason to do so, for surely no one has reason to act for the good of a (competent) agent unless he has reason to do so himself. This is the thought behind the second priority thesis.

If the realm of morality is the realm of nonrelational values and of the reasons for action they give rise to, the thesis of the priority of relational reasons constitutes an argument for the existence of a moral point of view. That is, it supports the conclusion that agents can recognize and pursue some values without recognizing or pursuing any moral values. This would show that moral values form either epistemically or metaphysically a separate range of considerations which can be validated or established only by special arguments, arguments which go beyond those which convince people of the existence of relational values.

It is implausible to suppose that if there are nonrelational values all of them are moral values. Beauty and understanding the nature of reality are often thought to be examples of nonrelational values which are not moral.

But while this may suggest that the considerations canvassed above should be supplemented with others to establish the distinctness of moral values when contrasted with other nonrelational values, this need not concern us here. Believers in the moral point of view are normally concerned only with the contrast between it and relational values. This contrast will be the focus of our discussion. If it fails then one common and powerful case for a distinct moral point of view fails with it.

V. The Refutation I: The Priority of Relational Goods

The thesis of the priority of relational goods must be rejected if relational goods presuppose nonrelational ones. The crucial case is of intrinsically valuable goods. The good of health, money, adequate temperature, etc. is that they enable people to have a better life. Reading poetry, climbing, skiing, disco-dancing, being with friends, and many other activities make the life of the person engaged in them better. They constitute his life and their goodness makes his life good.[14] These are good for the agent. They are also good *simpliciter* if we assume that everyone has reason to protect and promote whatever is good for any person. But are they good because they are good for their agents, or are they good for their agents because they are good? I will argue that both answers are correct, and therefore that the priority thesis is mistaken in that it denies this reciprocity.

Typical explanations of what is good for agents display a dual structure. It is good for Johnny to play the piano because engaging with music is good, and because he has enough of an ear and physical control to be able to do so by playing the piano. In other words in justifying that anything is good for any agent we show (a) that the thing is good, and (b) that the agent has the ability and the opportunity to have that good. I can think of no other way to account for why what is intrinsically good for some person or other (or for other things whose good matters in itself) is good for them. If this is so then relational goods presuppose nonrelational goods.[15]

The only alternative explanation I know of suggests that what is good for people is for them to have what they want, provided that their wants meet some conditions, a possible example of which is that having what one wants is not self-defeating.[16] This explanation fails because it does not take account of the fact that one can only want something because of a good one believes the thing to have.

Some people reject this point, believing that one can want anything, and not only what appears to one to be good or of value. This equates a desire for something with an urge for it which attacks one. Urges, impulses, cravings, passions and their like are real enough, but it is wrong to take them as the basis for an analysis of wants and desires. (I am using "desires" in the way customary in philosophical writings. Its common use makes it far closer to urges and passions. But when so understood its proper use is far too restricted for it to do its philosophical duty, i.e., in its common use it is false that whenever one acts intentionally one acts because of a desire to do what one does). Unlike urges, most ("philosophical") desires do not have a felt quality. My desire to get in time to a meeting on European democracy starting in an hour's time is typical of instrumental desires, and my desire to read Ivan Klima's new novel is typical of noninstrumental ones. Neither is a felt desire; they arose because of my belief that I have good reasons for both actions, and because something in me responded to these reasons and made me want to act on them.[17] If I do not get to act on them that is most likely to be either because the opportunity did not arise or because when it arose I preferred to act for another reason. Either way I am unlikely to feel frustration or any sense of loss. Of course if I tried to satisfy my desires and failed I may well feel frustrated. But that feeling of frustration is not a result of an unfulfilled desire but of a failed action, and is likely to be acute only if it is due to my clumsiness, thoughtlessness, incompetence, etc.

Of course, we do have urges, etc., to perform certain actions, but normally we do not endorse them, i.e., they do not become our desires unless we find them (and it may be no more than a rationalization) to be backed by reasons. If a force beyond my control propels me to take an action which I see no reason to take, then, regardless of whether I actually take the action or not, it would be misleading to say that I want to take that action. Not infrequently we prefer to satisfy an urge or a craving as a way of ridding ourselves of it. In those cases our reason is that the craving is troublesome and the action which satisfies it will rid us of it. Acting for such reasons is sometimes akratic, but it need not be. Either way it is action for a (good, albeit not necessarily sufficient) reason.[18]

So if I want to count the blades of grass in my garden I do so because I think that this will take my mind off some upsetting event, or because the action has some other good-making property. If I find myself drawn to count blades of grass, but cannot think of any reason for doing so, I would certainly deny that this is a desire of mine.[19] It is a force which seizes me in spite of myself. If I am overcome by it and perform the action, I would be right to say that I could not help it, though in a way it would be an intentional action. All I say is that anyone will recognize this as a pathological case.[20] Contrast it with many normal desires: if I want to have a drink because I think that it tastes good, and am then convinced that this is wrong, then I no longer want to have the drink. No loss, or regret, etc., is involved. The desire—as it were—disappears with the loss of belief in the reason.

The point is reinforced by the fact that there is always a reason for any desire. The statement that one wants to paint potatoes green is incomprehensible, not least to the agent himself, unless there is something in the action, his beliefs about it, or its circumstances and consequences which appears to him to make the action sensible. Not everything can be desired. Only what is seen as in some way good can be.

Some people may concede that one can only desire what one believes one has reason to desire while denying that the reason must be a good which what one desires is believed to possess. They may say that people's reasons for desiring whatever it is that they desire is that they believe that they would still have that desire even if they were completely rational and possessed all the information which might affect having such a desire. Such an attempt to reconcile the existence of reasons for all our desires with the primacy of relational goods fails for the simple reason that we need not desire what we believe to be good for us. I know that going to see good films would be (intrinsically) good for me. Yet I do not desire to see good films (nor bad ones either). I believe that it would be good for me to see good films because that is a valuable activity which it is within my imaginative, emotional, and intellectual capacity to benefit from, that is I am able to understand the films and react to them as one should. Yet I do not want to see films. I am too busy doing other things and have no regrets that films have to be left out of my life. I cannot have everything that it is good for me to have. There are just too many such things for me to have all of them. Therefore there is no point in wanting all of them.

Relational goods, I conclude, presuppose nonrelational ones in that (a) understanding the concept of a relational good requires understanding the notion of nonrelational goods, (b) there are no relational goods unless there are also nonrelational ones, and (c) if anything is intrinsically good for a valuer (and I am assuming that the good of valuers is good in itself) then it is also good *simpliciter*. At the same time, as I indicated above, any intrinsic nonrelational good is also a relational one. Whatever is good *simpliciter* is at least potentially good for some valuer. That is, if it is intrinsically good then it is good for any valuer who can engage with it in the right way. Appreciating art is intrinsically good, and is good for those animals (so far as we know, all of them human) who can appreciate art. And what is instrumentally valuable can be valuable to anyone whose interests or worthwhile goals will be served by it.

For reasons already explained the reciprocity of relational and nonrelational goods is not to be confused with the priority of the nonrelational goods. Nor does this reciprocity establish that values are anthropomorphic. Suppose that unbeknown to us there are Martian, nonhuman, persons who are valuers (in the sense in which we are). They, let us imagine, value many things we know nothing about, or that we do not value. The fact that their judgments of value differ from ours does not establish that they are false. They may be true and if they are true it follows that there are many things of whose value we are unaware. Perhaps we can learn about them and their value, perhaps we can even acquire the ability to engage in them in the right way, as one can be educated to appreciate the beauty of paintings. But even if we cannot, even if those goods are bound to remain beyond the reach of human valuers, we must concede that those things are good, even though not good for us. In relation to such goods our situation is that of a tone-deaf person with regard to music. The tone-deaf must also admit that music is valuable, even though he cannot relate to it.[21]

There remains the fact that since whatever is good is (at least potentially) good for someone there is a logical reciprocal relation between values and valuers, a relation which important though it is, and difficult to unpack and to state adequately as it is, is not one which lends any support to the view that moral value belongs to a special point of view.

VI. The Refutation II: The Priority of Relational Reasons

The argument of the previous section shows that the thesis of the priority of relational goods is mistaken, and therefore the conception of the moral point of view explained in section 4 above is mistaken as well. The distinctness of the moral point of view cannot rely on the contrast between relational and nonrelational goods and reasons and on the priority of the first. The argument does not affect many of the other conceptions of the moral point of view which have been advanced by various writers on morality. For example it does not affect those,[22] like Nietzsche, who are primarily concerned to contrast the aesthetic with the moral point of view.[23] The argument does, of course, affect a whole family of conceptions of morality which directly or indirectly presuppose the primacy of relational goods. For different reasons it also affects most conceptions of morality which focus on a contrast between the moral point of view and that of self-interest. The argument of the previous section was that whatever is good for the agent (and thus in his interest) is also good *simpliciter.* The only condition for what is good to be good for a person is that he is able to take advantage of it, to engage with it in the right way. This suggests[24] that self-interest does not constitute a distinct point of view in any "deep" sense,[25] and that though a person's self-interest can conflict with moral considerations, there is no fundamental conflict between the two.

If the argument of the previous section disposes of the thesis of the priority of relational goods does it not also refute the priority of relational reasons? If what is good is good for any agent who can reach it then the very reason any agent has reason to pursue what is good for him is thereby also a reason to pursue what is good, and vice versa. But this thought leads to an objection to the priority of relational goods, based on the credentials of the priority of relational reasons. I will consider this objection by considering the case for the priority of relational reasons.

Typical examples of moral activities are: going to disaster areas to help victims, giving money to charity, offering shelter to homeless or stranded people, donating a kidney to save someone's life. They are, in other words, cases of providing people with the means or the preconditions for a decent life, rather than being involved with them in intrinsically valuable activities. Perhaps this reflection should be born in mind when we consider below the claim that moral reasons always override conflicting nonmoral ones. But for the moment the relevance of the point is that it reinforces the thought that typically moral reasons depend on prudential ones. The moral agent has reason to engage in moral activities because someone else—the intended beneficiary of his action—has such a reason. But the reason of the moral agent is problematical in the way that the reason the beneficiary has is not. For the moral action—so the argument goes—will (tautologically) benefit its beneficiary, but will not, except accidentally, benefit the moral agent.

It has to be admitted that many ways in which one person can contribute to the well-being of another do not conform to this pattern. People's lives are enriched by playing music together, by sailing together, by reciprocating the love of those who love them, by having parties together, etc. In some respects these are the most profound ways in which people affect each other's lives. In all these cases the goods they are pursuing are shared goods, rather than dependent ones. They are shared for they can only be enjoyed together. The sharing is an essential part of the good. Interestingly we do not tend to regard activities of the kind instanced by my list as moral; at least they are not typical of what we think of when we think of moral activities. So for the sake of the argument it is simplest to put them on one side and concentrate on the typical range of moral actions as illustrated above.

Proceeding, therefore, on the assumption that typical examples of moral action are instrumentally valuable to their intended beneficiaries (providing them with money, shelter, etc.) the question of the reasons the moral agent has to perform them may seem puzzling. Given my contention that what is good is also good for whoever realizes it I am committed to holding that since it is good for John to have housing it is also good for me to give him housing. In other words, I am committed to the view that it is good for anyone who can do so to realize any good *simpliciter*. But is it good for me to provide John with housing in the way it is good for him to have it or to provide it for himself, i.e., instrumentally? Hardly. Special cases aside, doing the morally good thing is good for me in the same way that playing the piano or going to a dance is good for me, i.e, because it is doing something intrinsically good, something worthwhile or worth doing. This makes it clear that such morally good actions are good for the agent in a different way from the way they are good for the recipient, for whom they are instrumentally good. Correspondingly, they furnish the moral agent with reasons which are different from those their beneficiaries may have in the same matter.

This may be the source of a doubt whether moral actions can really be good for the agent. Fundamentally, as we saw, they are actions which are good because they are instrumentally good for some beneficiary. How can that make them intrinsically good for the agent? Let us put on one side mixed cases like teaching. Only if being taught is instrumentally good for the taught, and only because of this, is teaching good for the teacher. But if this condition is satisfied then teaching can readily be understood to be intrinsically good for the teacher since teaching is a challenging, complex activity which can be fulfilling to those engaging in it.[26] Such cases are cases of ordinary valuable activities; teaching is not different in this regard from wind-surfing, except that given that serving another is the intrinsic purpose of the activity it cannot succeed, and therefore cannot be good for the agent, unless it is achieving its purpose, and that means that it cannot be intrinsically good for the teacher unless instrumentally good for the students. But how can the same be true of giving money to charity? Or donating blood? Where are the intrinsically good-making features of such acts which make them, like teaching, not only good for others but for the agent as well?

Maybe we can see here a way to justify the distinctness of the moral point of view. Moral actions are not, just by being morally good, good for their agents. If people have to abide by them this must be for different reasons or on different grounds from those which explain why they have reasons to engage in worthwhile actions which are such that engaging in them is good for the agents.

Promising as this line of thought may appear it leads nowhere. First, it is motivated by concentrating on a very narrow range of moral activities, the "giving money to charity" type of examples. While these are among the typical examples we think of when thinking of moral actions, perhaps even the most typical, they cannot be regarded as exhausting the range of what is commonly believed to be central to morality. Cases of shared goods and mixed cases are regarded as having a moral bearing at least in some contexts. Moreover, according to all plausible accounts of their moral value, the fact that they are shared goods is essential to their moral character, and cannot be dismissed as a mere accidental concomitant of it.

The main reason why the priority of relational reasons is a blind alley is that the puzzle which created the temptation to go down that road in the narrow range of cases we concentrated on is not really a puzzle at all. The apparent puzzle arose by contrasting teaching with giving money to charity. Both are instrumentally valuable to the receiver, but while in the case of teaching we can understand both how it can be intrinsically valuable to the agent and why its value to the agent is conditional on its value to the intended beneficiaries, how could the same be true of giving to charity? What is intrinsically valuable about writing a check?

Thus drawn the contrast between teaching and giving to charity is real enough, but it is not a contrast between the moral and the nonmoral. It is a contrast between the intrinsic good of activities and the intrinsic good of acts, defined by their results,[27] whose value resides in the value of their results. Breaking the world one hundred-meter sprinting record is an example of such an act. Sprinters may enjoy the running, but they need not. Even if they do not the act of breaking the record is worthwhile. Its value is, however, in its result: setting a new world record. Those who achieve it cannot complain that they do not enjoy the activity of racing which led to the result as well. Their reward is in the result.[28] The same is true of giving to charity. There need be no intrinsic value in the activity which constitutes the giving. Writing a check need not be intrinsically rewarding. The value is in the giving to charity, in doing something which is morally good. That is the reward of the agent, just as setting a new record is the reward of the sprinter. The fact that the giving is not morally good unless it is instrumentally good to the needy endows giving to charity with a moral character that breaking the record does not have. But it does not help to show any respect in which moral considerations differ fundamentally from others.

VII. The Question of Stringency

My refutation of the priority of relational goods consisted in showing that whatever is good for someone (whose good counts in itself) is also good *simpliciter.* The refutation of the priority of relational reasons consisted in showing that whatever is good *simpliciter* is also good to anyone who can realize it. Of course, "good" here means "good other things being equal." I am not trying to deny that pursuing a moral good may be against the interests of the agent. All I was arguing, all I had to establish to refute the priority of relational reasons, was that where that is so it is because of various side effects of pursuing that moral good. In as much as it is a moral good it is in the interest of any agent capable of pursuing it to do so.[29] I will conclude by discussing briefly and in a preliminary way the contention that my argument in denying the special character of moral considerations makes their special stringency inexplicable.

Let it be granted that doing volunteer work at a hospital in one's free time can contribute as much to one's well-being as playing golf, or going to the beach. From this point of view moral and nonmoral goods are on a par. But is not the claim that morality is special valid at least in that moral reasons are particularly stringent? Once we understand what it is that makes them so stringent we will understand what constitutes the moral point of view. Perhaps. The first difficulty is in articulating a sense in which moral considerations are more stringent. To start with we must put on one side the possibility that there are absolute moral injunctions (e.g., an absolute prohibition on torture). It is plausible to assume that in some sense of absolute there are such absolute moral prohibitions. But they do not constitute the whole of morality, nor are moral prohibitions the only absolute ones. Arguably there are also nonmoral absolute prohibitions on sex between siblings or with corpses, or on eating human flesh. Some will classify some of these prohibitions as moral. Others will deny that they are absolute. Without full analysis of the notion of an absolute injunction, and of the reasons, if any, for them, all that can be said is that if there are such injunctions it is likely that some of them are nonmoral, and that this is so for any account of morality other than one which stipulates that all absolute injunctions are moral injunctions just in virtue of being absolute. So absolute injunctions are irrelevant to the suggestion that moral considerations have a special kind of stringency. The same considerations show that concepts of guilt and of wrong-doing are not special to morality. They apply to all unjustified violations of absolute prohibitions.

Some people believe that all moral considerations override any and all nonmoral considerations. This claim seems implausible. Assume that there are circumstances in which the only moral considerations which bear on the choice of action relate to human welfare. Assume that such was the case when Jane decided to have a baby. In doing so she changed her situation quite radically. As a lone parent bringing up a baby she had to give up her full-time work for the homeless in order to obtain a better paid and part-time job in the financial sector, and in order to use the rest of her time with her baby. Her decision to have a baby was not motivated by any moral considerations. Nor were there any moral considerations in favor of having the baby, other than that as a healthy caring person she would not be acting irresponsibly in having it. At the time she made her decision there were no moral reasons for Jane to have a baby. On the other hand she had moral reasons to carry on with her work for the homeless, and having the baby put her in a situation in which it would have been immoral (because it would have involved neglecting her baby) to do so. Yet she did no wrong in deciding to have a baby and acting on her decision.

For the purpose of my argument it does not matter whether Jane's job in serving the homeless is morally supererogatory or whether she is discharging her moral duty to the poor in holding to that job. The question is whether moral considerations must be a special class, for otherwise one cannot explain their stringency. The answer is that they are not specially stringent, e.g., some of them are supererogatory. To say that moral *duties* override nonmoral considerations does not help support the suggestion that morality as a whole constitutes a special point of view. Furthermore, it is misleading to think of morality as consisting of either duties or of supererogation. Most moral considerations are in between. Jane's is a case in point. She has a job working for the homeless which she likes and which is well paid. She is making no sacrifice in doing it rather than working for a stock broker. Other things being equal she would rather stay with that job. Other things are not equal. She wants a baby and therefore a part-time job which will pay as well as her full-time job. To achieve that she is willing to sacrifice some job satisfaction. There is nothing here to suggest that she is acting beyond the call of duty in working for the homeless.

The temptation to respond to her example by saying that it does not count for she is acting supererogatorily betrays the powerful grip of the confused picture of morality as particularly stringent that many of us succumb to. Being shown a moral consideration which is not stringent we want to consign it into a ghetto which does not count. In fact it does not belong to that ghetto. It is a typical case of moral consideration. Some will say that it is Jane's way of discharging her imperfect moral obligations to people in need. On that view it is a duty but an imperfect one for she could have discharged that duty some other way. There are, however, various obscurities in the notion of an imperfect duty which make it best to avoid it for the purpose of the present discussion. All that matters is that it exemplifies a moral consideration of a fairly common kind, which is overridden by a nonmoral one, i.e., the good of having a child.

There are countless examples of this kind, i.e., cases in which we make important decisions about our relations with other people which make us less able to conform to moral reasons which apply to us at the time, and where there is no moral reason to act as we do, but where we do no wrong in so doing. That last fact may be seized upon to show that morality permits us not to comply with moral reasons in the situations described, and therefore that they are not really cases of nonmoral reasons overriding moral ones. Rather they are cases of morality overriding itself. But this is sheer confusion. There are no moral reasons which justify not acting on the moral reasons which apply to us at the time, and it is generally the case that we have reason not to put ourselves in a situation in which we will be unable to comply with reasons which apply to us. It follows that Jane has a moral reason not to have a baby. It is true that she is not acting wrongly, not even morally speaking, in deciding to have the baby. But to say this is to say that the moral reasons are overridden, or at least neutralized, by other considerations. And as the only other considerations are nonmoral ones it is they which defeat, or neutralize, the moral reasons applying to her. One is not acting wrongly if one is acting on an undefeated reason, even if that reason is not a moral one, and even if it defeats or neutralizes conflicting moral reasons. Only those who have already established what is here denied, namely that there is an independent deep moral point of view, can expect that in such a situation one would be morally in the wrong, whatever is the true overall verdict about one's action, unless some special moral considerations provide dispensation from adhering to the moral reasons which apply to one.[30]

Accepting, then, that moral considerations are not always overriding, how is one to account for the general intuition that they possess special stringency? One suggestion might be that there is a positive/negative asymmetry in the case of nonmoral reasons for action. Since playing golf is a good thing and since Jules likes playing he has a reason to spend Saturday afternoon playing golf. This means that if he decides to play golf for that reason his action will be intelligible and—assuming that, not unreasonably, he does not believe that he has overriding reasons not to play golf on Saturday—rational. But it does not follow that he has to explain why he did not play golf if he does not play golf. That he did not feel like doing so is a good enough explanation. He does not have to show that he did something at least as worthwhile instead. Moral reasons are not like that. They not only make actions in their pursuit intelligible, and, when they are reasonably not believed to be defeated, rational. They also make every failure to comply with them culpable, unless there is an appropriate justification or excuse, and "I just did not feel like doing so" is neither. On this view the greater stringency of moral considerations lies in the fact that they are both reasons for an action and reasons against its omission, whereas nonmoral reasons are subject to the negative/positive asymmetry, that is they are reasons for an action but not against its omission.

The alleged negative/positive asymmetry is, however, no more than an illusion due to the other-regarding character of all or many typical moral considerations. In fact were Jules to spend the afternoon watching comic strips on TV rather than playing golf he would have shown himself to be a couch-potato. The reason to play golf is also a reason against omitting to play, in the sense that it reflects adversely on the character of the agent's actions if he does not follow it. He proves himself to be weak-willed, self-indulgent, etc. It is in precisely the same way that a failure to comply with moral reasons reflects on the agent, except that in the case of moral failure other people are typically affected, and therefore other people, not necessarily those affected, feel more of a right to pass judgment on the agent, and sometimes they do not stop there, and of course sometimes they are justified. But none of this establishes the special stringency of moral considerations, nor are these factors specific to morality. All we can say is that they are more typical of moral than of nonmoral cases. But nonmoral failures can also be failures towards friends, relations, or associates, triggering outside censure.

The question we are looking into is not whether many moral considerations are among the most weighty or stringent considerations which people face. We are looking for a reason to think that something which makes them moral also makes them weighty or stringent, that being moral gives them stringency, and this is the claim that we failed to substantiate. There could be other interpretations of the nature of moral considerations which will indeed show them to be more stringent than nonmoral considerations. I have to admit that I know of none, and in their absence my tendency to believe that moral considerations do not form a special subclass of nonrelational goods and values is strengthened.[31]

Oxford University

Notes

1. MPV.

2. As might be the case if they are tied or incommensurate, or if they refer the agent to nonmoral considerations.

3. Moral considerations are independent of the interest of the agent when considered as the interest of this agent. They can be affected by it when it is taken to be the interest of one person among many.

4. Humiliating another person is a moral (as opposed to a nonmoral) act regardless of one's motivation or of the impact of the action on the life of the humiliated.

5. This means that I leave unexamined the possibility that moral musts and must nots are at the center of the distinctness of the moral point of view. Such a view is inconsistent with our common understanding of morality which allows that some actions or consequences are morally desirable without being *musts,* and that some of them are supererogatory.

6. In formulating claims and theses I will accentuate the positive. But they should be read to include the negative. That is, the fact that an action is necessary to avoid some ill is also a reason for its performance.

7. This means that they have valuable qualities, though not necessarily that their performance is productive of more good on balance than the performance of any alternative option.

8. Notice here the various formulations which I allow as vindicating the same thesis. Throughout the paper I will resort to simplified linguistic formulae, which have to be sensitively rendered in natural sentences in a context-dependent way.

9. Is it true of all such cases that the fact that X is good for Y implies that X will, or is likely to, make Y's life better? Often, though not always, this is so, but my point here remains unaffected.

10. Though sometimes they make the cat's life better.

11. Other than negatively by excluding the thought that what is good about our life is that it is useful to someone else (though of course it may be that as well).

12. However, see more on this below.

13. For the present argument we need neither assent to nor dissent from the view that what is good for John cannot be good *simpliciter* unless everyone has reason to protect and promote it.

14. Whereas doing a drab job to earn money, though also an activity which makes one's life what it is, is of no intrinsic value and thus does not make the life of the worker better, except that in earning money he obtains the opportunity to do something valuable at some future time.

15. Possibly a third condition has to be met for something to be good for one: it may have to be consistent with one's existing valuable commitments and projects. I did not include it in my list above, for an alternative view is possible, i.e., that what is inconsistent with our current commitments and projects is good for us, other things being equal. But other things are not necessarily equal. This view has the advantage of explaining how one can rationally abandon some of one's current valuable projects and relationships for others. Either way my central claim in the text is unaffected.

16. I.e., provided that having what one wants does not make one regret having it and having wanted it.

17. It could have been that I realized, or believed, that the reasons for the action are such that even when the reasons against performing it are taken into account it would be irrational not to perform it. At the other extreme I may conceive the desire to perform it because of its good points, even if, given the reasons against it, performing it would be irrational. But most commonly it is neither of these. The reasons which make me desire to perform an action are simply those reasons for it which I respond to, whereas others leave me relatively cold.

18. Some expressive actions are an interesting borderline case. I kick the table in frustration, or walk up and down. Do I do so to relieve tension (conforming to the pattern I described of satisfying an urge to get rid of it)? Perhaps, but I am also expressing my exasperation, anger, or what not, and the fact that an action has expressive meaning is a reason to perform it when such expression is appropriate.

19. Cissy: What are you doing? Smut: I am counting its (the sheep's) hairs. Cissy: Why? Smut: To know how many it has. (Greenaway's film *Drowning by Numbers*).

20. The best analysis of such cases is provided by H. Frankfurt in *The Importance of What We Care About* (1988).

21. Furthermore, just as the tone-deaf person has reasons to respect goods which he cannot engage with, because he has reason to respect other people, so do we have reason to respect "Martian-only goods" to the extent that we have reasons to respect Martians. But this is a long and involved story.

22. Given that clearly not all nonrelational goods are moral ones, the argument of the previous section in itself does not establish that agents who act in pursuit of

relational goods must be pursuing moral goods. That was not its aim. Its aim was to deny that the distinction serves to establish the existence of a special moral point of view. That aim should not be confused with the "optimistic thesis" that all agents necessarily pursue moral goods, to which I do not subscribe, partly because I can see no great grounds for optimism, and partly because it itself presupposes the view here challenged, i.e., that the distinction between the moral and nonmoral is of deep importance.

23. Note, however, that the aesthetic may constitute a separate point of view even though morality does not. It is possible that aesthetic properties possess special features which mark them off from any other evaluative properties. That may show that they form a class on their own, and—depending on the nature of their separateness—that the aesthetic constitutes a distinctive point of view. That would leave morality indistinguishable from all other values, excepting aesthetic ones, and therefore would be consistent with the nonexistence of a moral point of view.

24. And I have argued to that effect in *The Morality of Freedom* (1988), chap. 12, and in "Facing Up" (1989). My comments on self-interest (as well as on what is good for a person) are too brief to take account of nuance in our use of these concepts. My comments are true of a minimal use of these notions. But often they are used in a way that suggests not only that the good is within one's ability, but also that one has an opportunity to use it, that there is no greater good one can have, the having of which is inconsistent with having the good under consideration, and that having that good would fit well within the general pattern of one's life. More important is the fact that we say of things that they are in someone's self-interest almost entirely when they are instrumentally good for him. I am not discussing such additional features as they do not affect the argument of this essay.

25. Cf. my remarks on points of view at the beginning of the essay.

26. It is also an occasion for establishing relationships with other people—other teachers and the pupils. But I am disregarding this aspect of the example as it merely brings out the fact that teaching is also a shared good. Perhaps surgery is a purer case here as in many hospitals surgeons have little to do with their patients—though they strike up relationships with other staff. It is important to remember that real life examples are hardly ever pure.

27. I have in mind here the distinction between acts and activities drawn by von Wright in *Norm and Action* (1963). See also A. J. P. Kenny, *Action, Emotion, and Will* (1963).

28. Since the result is intrinsic to the act (you cannot break the world record without setting a new one) the intrinsic value of the result makes the act itself intrinsically worthwhile.

29. And—special cases aside—it does not matter whether the agent does so because he is aware of its "moral character," though whether what is good is good for an agent only if he pursues the goal because he thinks it to be good is a separate issue. See my discussion of it in *Practical Reasons and Norms* (1990), 180–82. For a more extensive discussion see Scheffler, *Human Morality* (1992).

30. As Charles Larmore pointed out to me, my view denies the existence of justified immoralities, i.e., cases in which one takes the right or best (or at least a permissible) action which is nonetheless morally wrong for one to take. That is, on my view we may quite naturally say things like that in contexts in which the action taken is right because the nonmoral reasons for it defeat the moral reasons against it. But "moral" and "nonmoral" are used in a context-dependent way, without assuming any theoretical significance. What the position here advocated assumes is that there are no interesting dilemmas or difficult practical problems of this kind.

31. I am grateful to Bonnie Kent, Charles Larmore, and Richard Moran for helpful comments on a draft of this essay.

On Instrumental Rationality

5

Jean Hampton

The instrumental conception of reason is a popular and pervasive theory of reason not only in contemporary philosophy, but also in law and the social sciences generally. Many theorists regard it not only as descriptively accurate but also as the only conception of reason that explains the prescriptive force of rational directives in a way that is acceptable to the naturalist. However in this essay, I want to argue that it cannot serve as a theory of reason acceptable to the naturalist, for two reasons. First, the authority of instrumental reasons rests on the same conception of objective normative authority that is supposed to make objective moral reasons scientifically unacceptable. And second, the motivational force of the instrumental prescriptions of reason can only be explained in the same (apparently) nonnatural way as the motivational force of moral prescriptions. If these arguments are right, and the instrumental theory of reason is no more acceptable to a naturalist than any moral theory of reason, then insofar as the authority of science rests on the fact that its methods incorporate this conception of reason, science itself is just as nonnatural an enterprise as morality. And if science, given its commitments, is just as unscientific as morality, then to use Mackie's phrase, naturalists are the "companions in guilt" of any moral theorist.

I. Instrumental Theories of Reason

Consider the following definition of an instrumental theory, which has been developed so as to be neutral between descriptive and normative forms of the instrumental theory:

(1) An action is rational to the extent that an agent believes it furthers the attainment of an end; *and*

(2) The process of reasoning involves the determination of means to achieve ends, in a way described by the theory. (I will say, henceforth, that using reason to determine the extent to which an action is a means to an end is an *instrumental* use of reason); *and*

(3) An agent's ends are in no way fixed by reason operating noninstrumentally; i.e., what makes them our ends is something other than instrumental reason.

In this essay I will consider as instrumental all and only theories that accept these three theses, since this is how I believe most philosophers have traditionally conceived of instrumental theories of reason.[1] Note that all three theses are consistent with what might be called the "manifesto" of the instrumental approach to reason articulated by Hume, namely that "Reason is, and ought only to be, the slave of the passions" (Hume 1978, 2.3.3: 415). However, as we shall discuss, a theory of reason is appropriately understood as instrumental even if reason is thought to serve something other than the passions (e.g., God, or the interests of society), and thus, even if it does so by doing something other than maximizing the satisfaction of ends set by passions. Accordingly, many theories that are quite different from Hume's qualify as instrumental on this definition.

I have been deliberately vague in defining thesis 1. Not all means to ends are rational; one must choose "effective" or "appropriate" means. Particular instrumental theories specify whether a means to an end must, in order to be rationally acceptable, be the "best" means given available information, or the "best" given perfect information, or simply "effective" (albeit perhaps not best) as established by certain criteria. Note also that the theory of instrumental rationality, as I am defining it, is not the same as "being prudent," which is commonly understood as performing actions to achieve long-term, rather than mere short term, ends. There is nothing in instrumental rationality which would mandate us to prefer long-term ends over short-term ends—indeed, any such mandate would appear to involve a determination of our "proper ends" by reason, and thus be a violation of thesis 3.

Thesis 3 is the hallmark of the instrumental theory, the thesis that Hume and other proponents of the instrumental theory spend most time defending. Note that thesis 3 is formulated so as to allow the possibility that reason can set goals by functioning instrumentally. However, as I will discuss shortly, there are some instrumental theorists, most notably Hume, who reject even this possibility, maintaining that reason cannot set instrumental goals. Note that thesis 3 is about what is *inside* us, and thus addresses the nature of a human being's mental reasoning. A theory of reason that only evaluated behavior, and was unconcerned with any "interior" issue of human operation, would say nothing about how we should understand either the source of our preferences, or (for that matter) the explanation for our actions, even if they are, from a behavioral standpoint, entirely rational. Such a behavioral theory would say, "no matter how human beings actually think, choose, or operate, they can only be considered rational when their behavior conforms to those norms which this theory takes to define rationality." But this means it cannot incorporate the third thesis of the instrumental theory, and because it cannot, it is not instrumental in the sense that most theorists in the philosophical tradition have understood that position. For similar reasons, an instrumental theory as I have defined it cannot be merely "predictive," i.e., one that (merely) models the kind of consistent choice behavior that we would expect to see from a rational agent (which could be a human being, a firm, even an animal), with the aim of predicting future behavior.[2] Such a theory says nothing about what actually does (or should) go on in the head of the person prior to acting.

So a theory of reason that accepts the three features above is not a behavioral or predictive theory, but rather what I will call a descriptive or normative theory of *reasoning*, one that describes or prescribes the interior mental processes (or reasoning) that a rational agent engages in prior to acting.[3]

Insofar as instrumental theories are species of theories of reasoning, they can be developed along different levels. Such theories, whether descriptive or normative, come in two basic varieties. They can define the reasoning procedure upon which we actually operate (or ought to operate) when we decide how to behave; or they can define the meta-reasoning we use (or ought to use) to *select* operational procedures for deciding how to behave. Theorists such as H. A. Simon[4] have argued for a theory that defines reasoning at both levels. Simon and others have argued that because we are subject to constraints when we reason—in particular, constraints on information-gathering (e.g., limited access, high costs of obtaining, etc.), and constraints on computational ability (e.g., intellectual disabilities, the costs of taxing or intellectual work)—we often rely, when we are making decisions, not on reason itself (and in particular, not on the expected utility calculation) but rather on shorthand rules and procedures. When we use such rules, they say we are "satisficing" in light of our "bounded rationality." So they understand the correct theory of reason to describe or prescribe the "meta reason" that approves or disapproves operational reasoning procedures that, given the constraints on human reasoning, are unlikely to be identical to meta reason itself.[5] This meta reason is, in some sense, what reason really is; by portraying it we show how we calculate (or ought to calculate) when we select among various satisficing procedures that, we hope, will tend, over the long term, to yield the same results as the impossibly hard calculations demanded by reason, explaining why they have been selected and used by us.

Theories of reasoning can also differ in what they take the cognitive level of their descriptive analysis to be. They might take themselves to be describing the deliberation procedure that human beings do or should *consciously* follow when they are appropriately said to be reasoning. Or they might take rationality to be a less conscious, less deliberative affair, something more analogous to Chomskian "deep grammar," the structure of which is not consciously in view as we engage in it. How "unconscious" a theory of reason can be and still count as a theory of reasoning is an interesting question. Little discussion of this issue of the proper depth of mental analysis of rationality appears in the literature; I know of only one theorist to have pursued it.[6]

Most theorists, including Hume, treat their theories of reasoning as describing and prescribing the conscious mode of operation human beings do or should follow. However, Kurt Baier is among those who see the instrumental theory as both an operational and a meta-decision procedure, evaluating not only particular decisions, but also rules or procedures for making these instrumental judgments. Baier says in chapter 1 of his book *The Rational and the Moral Order* (RMO, 50ff.) that reason consists in a set of "guidelines" that enable us to "guide ourselves" in our attempts to attain our ends. Baier argues that these guidelines are social phenomena "made available to us by our culture" so that we can guide ourselves toward attaining our ends; but he notes that these guidelines can be "flawed," and "in such cases, following reason means suitably departing from them" (RMO, 51). So by understanding instrumental reason not only as an operating procedure but also as a meta-reasoning procedure, Baier is able to develop the theory along social rather than individualistic lines: that is, he conceives of the operating procedures we follow as reasoners not as private and internally wired, but as instrumentally defined by society. Indeed, Baier maintains that it is because the guidelines of rationality are social that we can have so much faith in them. Granted, he writes,

> these publicly available guidelines are not themselves the (infallible) guidelines for attaining these important ends, but merely what a culture has worked out to be the closest attainable approximation to them it could produce. But their generality, their public availability, and their widespread employment and revision, generation after generation, gives them a high likelihood that more errors have been eliminated than any single individual among us could eliminate by his own efforts, and therefore are normally our best bet. Of course, a detached comparison between the methods of different cultures may yield still better results. This seems to me the sound basis of the widespread conviction that reason is tied to universality (RMO, 51).

Readers are right, however, to detect an air of paradox in this passage. It cannot be the case that instrumental reason is *entirely* a social matter, otherwise the comparison of different culture's guidelines to see which yields "better results" could not take place.[7] To resolve the air of paradox, Baier can say that (only) the operational procedures of reason are products of a culture; the meta-procedure for formulating, assessing, and modifying the operational guidelines transcends culture (it is, after all, what we use to evaluate the effectiveness of different cultural guidelines) and thus must be universally available to all human beings as part of their human nature. So were Baier to specify the details of the process of reasoning that characterizes instrumental deliberation, those details would likely be different at the two levels; at the operational level, specification of the reasoning process would make reference to culturally defined guidelines; whereas at the meta-level the guidelines could not be culturally defined. Baier says much about the former, and very little about the latter.[8]

Finally, instrumental theories can differ in the ways they take reason to function as an instrument. Even if reason is only a servant, there is more than one way in which it can be a servant.

The most commonly recognized form of reason's servitude is means-end reasoning, and the specification of this form of reasoning is the hallmark of instrumental theories of reason. Hobbes's position is typical in this regard: although Baier accuses Hobbes of rejecting the idea that there is any regimentation in our instrumental reasoning (RMO, chap.1), in fact Hobbes is very concerned to show that instrumental reasoning has a specific structure, involving the "apt imposing of names" of objects and strict adherence to logical rules of inference.[9] Indeed, his *Leviathan* is a kind of massive exercise in instrumental reasoning, which is supposed to demonstrate to all that self-preservation requires the creation of an absolute sovereign and the eschewal of certain actions that, although promotive of glory, will lead to a state of war and a short, miserable life. Subsequent instrumental theorists from Hume to the present day have developed various portrayals of the structure of means-end reasoning.

However there is another task that an instrumental theory might assign to reason and still remain instrumental: that of discovering (but not defining) what our ends of action are. This means that an instrumental theory of reason could specify *two* different kinds of reasoning procedures. Let me distinguish, following Nagel,[10] between "motivated" ends, which are ends desired as a means to satisfying a further end; and "unmotivated" or "intrinsic" ends, that is, ends desired for their own sake, and not as a means to some further end. A theory of instrumental reason can specify a reasoning procedure for identifying each type of end: first, a procedure that determines causes of desired effects for the identification of motivated ends; and second, a procedure for discovering (albeit not defining) what one's intrinsic ends really are. As long as the theory assigns to something other than reason the task of setting the intrinsic ends of human life, thesis 3 is satisfied, and the theory can remain instrumental even while granting reason the role of discovering these ends. If we invoke Hume's servant analogy, we can say either that reason's servitude can involve obeying orders from the master (e.g., our desires, or our God) to take efficient means to achieving the end(s) set by the master; or it can also involve, at least on occasion, finding out who its master really is.

Because neither Hobbes nor Hume thinks that the objects of our desires are particularly difficult to determine, neither grants to reason the task of helping us to see exactly what it is that we want in life. Most likely this is because each of them takes it for granted that the goals established by desires or passions are sufficiently transparent that the agent would find it unnecessary to use reason to help identify those goals.[11] So when Hobbes characterizes the deliberative process someone would use in order to make up his mind about what to do, he says:

> When in the mind of man, Appetites and Aversions, Hopes, and Feares, concerning one and the same thing, arise alternately; and divers good and evill consequences of the doing, or omitting the thing propounded, come successively into our thoughts; so that sometimes we have an Appetite to it; sometimes an Aversion from it; sometimes Hope to be able to do it; sometimes Despaire, or Feare to attempt it; the whole summe of Desires, Aversions, Hopes and Fears, continued till the thing be either done, or thought impossible, is that we call DELIBERATION. (Hobbes 1991, 6.29.28)

This passage is not about cause-and-effect reasoning; it is about deciding what to do when one has conflicting desires, either for unmotivated ends, or for motivated ends (driven by different desires for unmotivated ends). When we decide which end to pursue, Hobbes proposes that our deliberation does not in any real sense involve reasoning, but is rather the phenomenological weighing up of the strengths of these competing desires, which will proceed until the action is performed or until any action becomes impossible. Reason therefore plays *no* role in the process of selecting the desire that will prevail, and deliberation is merely a process in which the stronger desire finally manifests itself.

But we ought to wonder whether Hobbesian and Humean instrumental theorists should be so optimistic about the transparency of the unmotivated ends of human action. Contemporary instrumental theorists have been prepared to admit that our strongest desire-defined ends are not always clear to us. For example, David Gauthier insists that, in order to be genuinely ours, the ends we pursue must be from "considered" preferences. Although he does not describe this process of "consideration," it seems plausible to construe it as a kind of reasoning procedure, akin, perhaps, to Richard Brandt's "cognitive psychotherapy"[13]—a reasoning process that helps us to determine our "true" unmotivated ends. Similarly, Bernard Williams describes a form of deliberation involving one's imagination, whose function is the appraisal of old (unmotivated) desires and the generation of new ones:

> [An agent] may think he has reason to promote some development because he has not exercised his imagination enough about what it would be like if it came about. In his unaided deliberative reason, or encouraged by the persuasions of others, he may come to have a more concrete sense of what would be involved [if he had some object] and lose his desire for it, just as, positively, the imagination can create new possibilities and new desires. (Williams 1991, 105)

Because Williams, Brandt, and Gauthier fail to structure precisely their "desire discovery" procedures, it is unclear how different any of them finally is from Hobbes's unregimented "strongest desire manifestation" process, which Hobbes does not regard as a form of reasoning.[14] But because these modern theorists at least suggest the outlines of a reasoning procedure for discovering (but not defining) intrinsic ends, they can be understood to define reason's servitude broadly, to include not merely finding means to ends, but also discovery of the content of those ends.[15]

Williams suggests that there are other forms of deliberative reasoning, all of which could fit into a (suitably broad) conception of instrumental reasoning, "such as, thinking how the satisfaction of elements in [an agent's subjective motivational set] can be combined, e.g. by time-ordering; where there is some irresoluble conflict among the elements of S, considering which one attaches most weight to (which, importantly, does not imply that there is some one commodity of which they provide varying amounts); or, again, finding constitutive solutions, such as deciding what would make for an entertaining evening, granted that one wants entertainment" (Williams 1991, 104).

However, as my definition of the instrumental approach to reason presupposes, the deliberation process most often associated with the instrumental conception of reason, and the one recognized by all variants of this theory, is means-end reasoning, resulting in a hypothetical imperative. Hence, in appraising the motivational plausibility of the instrumental theory, I will focus on this form of reasoning, and this type of imperative.

II. The Advantages of the Instrumental Approach to Reason

In contrast to these variants of the instrumental approach to reason, noninstrumental theorists present reason not as a tool designed solely either to achieve or to discover the ends of our actions, but as something which, in addition to its instrumental functioning, quite literally, defines ends of action. For these theorists, reason *is* the master. There is more than one way of explaining its masterly role: one can say, following Plato, that reason is the *source* of ends of action, supplying to us the rightful content of our goals in life. Or one can say, following Kant, that reason is that which constrains what it is that we desire to pursue, so that desires propose the content of our goals in life and reason permits or excludes pursuit of these proposed goals (making reason a kind of limiting condition).[16] Those who believe in the existence of a distinctive kind of moral reasoning, by which we come to recognize or determine moral norms authoritative over our action, will generally embrace either a Platonic or Kantian conception of reason. Neither theory denies that reason has an instrumental role, but each insists that it also has a (direct or indirect) role in determining our ends, and that it provides the motivation to pursue the ends it determines. Hence, such theories of reason are generally the foundation of objective theories of morality.

There are two reasons why philosophers have been troubled by the idea that reason has either kind of noninstrumental role. First, the authority of any noninstrumental directives of reason is difficult to understand. What special "sight" or access to normative reality can we realistically ascribe to human reason, such that it can tell us our ends in life? How does a scientific world view permit us to believe that there are unmotivated ends which we are rationally compelled to pursue? Science, after all, does not recognize such objects or properties with inherent prescriptive power, which seem to be too "queer" (to use Mackie's word) given the strictures of science, for us to believe in them (Mackie 1977). Moreover, no scientific description of human beings has identified a rational capacity within us that can determine these objects, respond to their inherent prescriptivity, and motivate action in compliance with their requirements. For those who are committed to a naturalistic account of human beings—and such people usually consider themselves "scientific realists"—these ideas are too fantastic to be believed.[17] Naturalists strongly prefer the instrumental approach to reason, which appears capable of development along entirely naturalist lines, without reference to strange prescriptive objects or human capacities. Indeed, even the *normative* version of the instrumental theory seems to be able to explain the force and strictures of its rational directives in a way that is scientifically acceptable, given that rational imperatives seem to be reducible to beliefs and desires,[18] both of which are (arguably) allowed by, or reducible to, entirely natural phenomena. Hence the normative form of the instrumental theory of reason seems preferable to any noninstrumental normative theory because the former seems capable of being developed as a normative theory even while presupposing only naturalist foundations.

The other problem facing those who say reason can function noninstrumentally concerns motivation. Most theorists share Baier's view that whereas the question "Why be moral?" is deeply troubling, the question "Why be rational?" is not.[19] Yet if reason is understood to operate noninstrumentally, it becomes so expansive, and its directives so wide-ranging and divergent from interests the individual is readily able to recognize, that the issue of behaving rationally, when rationality is defined like *that*, is now a real one (RMO, 16). Baier and others therefore believe Kant has gone down the wrong conceptual road; on their view, the normative form of the instrumental account of reason is the clear superior to the noninstrumental view, given that it appears capable of development in a way that avoids this motivational problem.

In this essay, I will challenge both the idea that the normative form of the instrumental conception of reason is acceptable to the naturalist, and the claim that only this theory is motivationally plausible. Stripped of naturalist credentials, the instrumental conception of reason, and the Hobbesian moral contractarianism built upon it, will no longer look like the compelling alternative to noninstrumental theories of reason and the moral theories they generate.

III. Instrumental Reason and the Psychology of Action

Instrumental theories of reason can be descriptive or normative. Both types of theory understand thesis 3 descriptively, so that a normative instrumental theory does not say that we *ought* to establish ends of action using something other than reason, but only that we *do* operate so that our ends of action are set by something other than reason. But these types of theory disagree about whether theses 1 and 2 describe how we actually operate or how we ideally operate. Descriptive instrumental theories say that, as a matter of fact, when human beings engage in reasoning, they do so in an instrumental way (either at the operational or the meta level), so that, in our definition of the instrumental approach to reason, the details of thesis 2 set out the kind of mental functioning characteristic of members of our species. On the other hand, normative theories of reason are about how we *ought* to reason (at either the operational or the meta level); and their development of thesis 2 specifies the details of the ideal (albeit not always the actual) way to reason.

However, normative instrumental theories can differ in how they explain the nature of the authoritative and motivational force of their imperatives. The difference between these forms of the normative instrumental approach is critically important to the evaluation of the viability of normative instrumentalism generally, and yet these differences have not been noticed or appreciated in the literature. This is because conventional wisdom has it that there is nothing mysterious or especially troubling about the force of hypothetical imperatives issued by instrumental reason, in contrast to categorical imperatives, whose force is far from clear. The appeal, within hypothetical imperatives, to desires seems to make them motivationally unproblematic, without the inexplicable "magic" that Philippa Foot and others say supporters of categorical imperatives have clothed them in (Foot 1978, 167). But I shall now argue that the force of an 'ought' in a hypothetical imperative is just as puzzling as the force of the 'ought' in a categorical imperative.

J. L. Mackie probably speaks for most philosophers when he explains the force of a hypothetical imperative as follows:

> 'If you want to do X, do Y' (or 'You ought to do Y') will be a hypothetical imperative if it is based on the supposed fact that Y is, in the circumstances, the only (or the best) available means to X, that is, on a causal relation between Y and X. The reason for doing Y lies in its causal connection with the desired end, X; *the oughtness is contingent upon the desire.* (Mackie 1977, 28; my emphasis)

But what *exactly* does it mean to say that the "oughtness" in a hypothetical imperative is in some way a function of the desire predicated by the imperative?

Most philosophers have not realized that this question about hypothetical imperatives needs answering. Consider the way Kant distinguishes between hypothetical and categorical imperatives; the former issue directives that are rational insofar as they achieve the satisfaction of some desire, whereas the latter issue directives that are taken to be authoritative no matter what our desires are. Whereas we are supposed to act on categorical imperatives (simply) because they are right or authoritative, Kant says that we act on hypothetical imperatives because their directives are a way to satisfy one or more desires that we have. This way of understanding the difference between them makes the hypothetical imperatives seem, from both a justificational and motivational standpoint, straightforward; and this is what philosophers such as Foot and Mackie have assumed.

But on closer examination, the contingency of the directives of a hypothetical imperative on a certain desire does not, by itself, explain why we *ought* to follow the directive. While it is surely true that the 'ought' statement in a hypothetical imperative should be withdrawn if the action that has been directed is not effective in satisfying an agent's desire, or if the agent does not have the desire (McDowell 1978, 13), nonetheless, if the agent has the desire and the action is effective, that ought statement "holds." But what does it mean to say this? Or to put it another way, how does this hypothetical imperative give the agent a reason for action that is different from the desire assumed by the imperative?

Moreover, how does the hypothetical imperative motivate us, by virtue of the fact that it gives us this reason? Consider that action from a desire, and action from an imperative whose directives are contingent on a desire, are not the same. Nor is the appeal to the desire assumed in a hypothetical imperative sufficient to explain an agent's motivation to follow the imperative; unreflective action motivated by a desire is different, after all, from reflective, rational action upon a hypothetical imperative assuming that desire.

These questions about the force of hypothetical imperatives can be answered in quite different ways, by theories that offer quite different accounts of the normativity of hypothetical imperatives. All these theories, however, sharply distinguish between what I call the *authority* and the *motivational efficacy* of hypothetical imperatives and the reasons they give us. Consider that the question "Why should I be rational?" can have two different meanings: it can be a way of asking for the justification of the instrumental reason I am being given, in which case I am asking about the authority of that reason over me. Or it can be a way of asking about what motivation I have to do that which is assumed to be a justified, and hence, authoritative reason. I will say that a reason generated by a hypothetical imperative is authoritative if it dictates an instrumentally effective way to act in the circumstances (where this reason may, or may not, override any other competing reasons in these circumstances—it can be a reason for us even if it is not a decisive reason to act in the circumstances). However, dictating the best action is not necessarily motivating that action. I will say that a reason generated by a hypothetical imperative is motivationally efficacious if it can, by itself, move us to act as it directs (albeit, perhaps with insufficient force to effect the action it directs).

Just because we know we have an authoritative instrumental reason to do some action x, it doesn't follow that this reason is motivationally efficacious. Alas, philosophers have persistently assumed that it is. To see why that assumption if false, consider once again Bernard Williams' popular and plausible account of what makes something a reason for action (Williams 1981, 101–13). In order for an agent to have a reason for acting, according to Williams, there must be a deliberative connection between the reason's directives for action, and an agent's motives (Williams 1981, 104). Williams calls such reasons "internal," and he denies that there can be any "external" reasons for action, i.e., reasons that do not have this deliberative connection with our motives. Note, however, that this distinction between 'internal' and 'external' reasons concerns the issue of what it is that makes something a reason for action, and not the issue of whether or not a reason is also a motive.

Hence Williams puts forward a variant of what I call *justificational internalism,* which is the view that an agent has a reason to x if and only if x-ing is connected, via deliberation (i.e., deliberation correctly performed) with an internal feature of the agent. It is opposed by *justificational externalism,* which is the view that an agent has a reason to x if and only if x-ing can be connected, via deliberation, with some aspect of the world which need not be, and sometimes is not, an internal feature of the agent. But justificational internalism, by itself, takes no stand on the issue of whether reasons are also motives. Hence one can be a justificational internalist and a motivational externalist, denying that the reasons we have (by virtue of their deliberative connection with certain of our internal features) must also be motives themselves.[20]

So justificational internalism does not imply motivational internalism. This means that if a theorist wants to insist that a motivational effect from a (believed) reason is in some way usual or even inevitable, he must provide an argument to this effect—justificational internalism does not, by itself, provide any argument at all with respect to the motivational efficacy of reasons.

There are two general ways of constructing such an argument. First, one can put forward a variant of a *motivationally externalist* argument: on this view, a reason does not, by itself, motivate action. Hence if, after coming to the conclusion that she has a reason to x, an agent finds herself motivated to do x, that must be because of some inner (but contingent) psychological process causally effected by the deliberation that has produced the motivation. The reason *by itself* is not motivational. Second, one can put forward a *motivational internalist* argument: on this view, a reason is something that can, by itself, generate a motivational force (although it is a further issue whether that motivational force is sufficient to produce the action in the circumstances). It is, in some way, "intrinsically" motivational. On this view, to know that one has a reason to x is also to feel motivated (at least to some degree) to do x.

An account of the "force" of a hypothetical imperative will consist of one of these theses about a reason's motivation, along with a view of the nature of the authority of that reason. There are a number of such accounts. In this section I will describe the four accounts I take to be most promising.

First, there is what I will call the *Kantian* account—i.e., the Kantian account of the normativity of *instrumental* reason; I am not referring to Kant's larger, noninstrumental conception of rationality. Kant is famous for the view that when we act morally we are acting on reason, and he contrasts such moral action with action that is (merely) caused by desires. This rhetoric, however, obscures the fact that he also recognizes a nonmoral component of reason, from which we act when we are motivated by hypothetical imperatives. And a careful look at his account of the force of hypothetical imperatives shows he believes that we are motivated to follow them *not* by the desires assumed by such imperatives, but by *reason*—that is, by the instrumental (and not the moral) component of reason. Although predicated on a desire, Kant maintains that hypothetical imperatives "present the *practical necessity* of a possible action as a means to achieving something else which one desires" (Kant 1959, 33). This "necessity" is the substance of the authority of the imperatives, and it is *in virtue of that authority* that it has motivational effect on the agent: "Whoever wills the end, so far as *rea-*

son has decisive influence on his action, wills also the indispensably necessary means to it that lie in his power" (Kant 1959, 34). I have emphasized the phrase that shows that Kant believes, when we act from a hypothetical imperative, that it is not desire but (instrumental) reason that moves us, just as, when we act morally, it is not desire but reason (in this case, moral reason, not instrumental reason) that moves us, by virtue of its authority. (That is, these imperatives command us with "practical necessity.") And while Kant is aware that many human beings resist the means they ought to take to achieve their ends, his position is that in virtue of the fact that we *ought* to will means appropriate to our ends, we will do so for as long as "reason has decisive influence" on our actions.

Kant also puts the same point in another way:

> [I]t is an analytic proposition that if I must also fully will the effect, I also will the action necessary to produce it. For it is one and the same thing to conceive of something as an effect which is in a certain way possible through me and to conceive myself as acting in this way. (Kant 1959, 35)

There are two ways of interpreting the idea that this proposition is analytic: First, it could be a kind of psychological thesis, to the effect that, in fact, one cannot desire the end without desiring the means to it. So interpreted, the proposition is highly implausible: not only does introspection seem to controvert it, more importantly, it is a psychological thesis that would make irrational action impossible. That is, it would have us say about any agent who appeared to violate instrumental rationality that in fact he had not, because insofar as he wasn't motivated to pursue the best means to an end, he didn't desire the end either. A position that implies that human beings never violate instrumental rationality seems experientially invalidated! One must not argue too enthusiastically for the correctness of a normative thesis, lest one make it impossible for human beings to act contrary to it.

Second, Kant's proposition can be interpreted as (merely) normative, and this interpretation fits with the view of the force of instrumental directives which I have just sketched on the basis of other passages in Kant's writing. On this interpretation, the analytic proposition is a kind of principle of "practical logic," analogous to other principles of logic (like, say, DeMorgan's law) which people can violate, but which they ought not to violate. So although in fact there are agents who desire the end, but not the means to the end, this principle says that they ought not to do so, and will be condemned as irrational to the extent that they do so. The principle is analytic in the way any other logical principle (which human beings are also capable of violating) is analytic, and it is both authoritative over action, and motivational by virtue of that authority.

If we accept this second interpretation, then on the basis of this and previous passages, we can summarize the Kantian position on the force of hypothetical imperatives as follows: When a rational agent acts on a hypothetical imperative, she is not motivated to do so by the desire assumed in the imperative, but by the authority of the imperative (or alternatively the authority or "rightness" of the reason to action given by the imperative), so that the imperative is motivationally efficacious *by virtue of its authority*.[21]

So defined, the Kantian position is really a *family* of positions, and not a single view, for there are a number of ways of elaborating the idea that, to be rational, a person who acts from a hypothetical imperative is motivated by the authority of that imperative. For example, one can hold that the authority of hypothetical imperatives is *directly* motivational, in a way analogous to the direct motivational efficacy of the authority of a (moral) categorical imperative. Alternatively, one can hold that the authority of these imperatives motivates us indirectly, e.g., by having an effect on our psychological structure such that a desire to do what the imperative directs is created.[22] Kant's view with respect to moral reasons is generally the former, but occasionally he suggests the latter.[23] The only difference between the two positions concerns how the authority of the imperative affects our motivational structure: rather than taking it to be able to generate a motive directly, the second position understands the imperative to cause a desire, which in turn provides us with the motive. But both positions assume that the imperative's authority can have an effect on our psychology, and thus both preserve what is fundamental to the Kantian view, namely, the idea that our motivation to follow the imperative is derived from the authority of the imperative, so that we are appropriately said to be acting *for the sake of* the reason given us in the imperative.[24]

There can also be different Kantian positions concerning whether or not the authority of a hypothetical imperative always has motivational efficacy. One might argue, for example, that it always does, in virtue of the fact that the motivational effects of such authority are (in some sense) necessary. Or one can argue (only) that it sometimes does, so that these motivational effects of the authority are likely but neither inevitable nor necessary. And in situations where authority does have motivational effects, one can maintain, for example, that they always are, even if at times they do not succeed in effecting action. Alternatively, one can maintain that while they always have some motivational force, that force may not be sufficient to motivate us to act on its directives in all circumstances. And one can maintain (as Kant did in the case of moral reasons) that the authority of these reasons is always sufficient to yield *some* motivation (albeit, perhaps, not enough to generate the action).

The second position on instrumental reason understands the prescriptive force of a hypothetical imperative as involving only one component, namely, normative authority. On this view, an imperative is authoritative, but *never*, by virtue of that authority, also motivationally efficacious. That is, it gives us reasons for action, but those reasons cannot directly motivate us. They can, at best, be motivationally efficacious indirectly, e.g. by causing the activation in us of certain desires (or any other motivationally efficacious psychological material) that motivate us to act as it directs; they cannot motivate us to act by themselves by virtue of their authority. Whereas Kantian instrumental reasons have what I will call "authoritative motivational force," this view attributes to instrumental reasons (at most) what I will call "causal motivational force." In virtue of the way in which Mill distinguished the "correctness" of a moral imperative from the motivation we have to follow that imperative, I am calling this position *Millian*, even though I am describing a position on the nature of instrumental reason, not moral reason. Mill distinguishes between authority and motivational efficacy in the context of presenting his moral theory in *Utilitarianism*. In chapter 2, after setting out his principle of utility, Mill insists that we should not mistake the (compelling) meaning of a moral principle with the *motive* one might have to obey it.[25] In chapter 3, he goes on to explore the motives we might have for following this principle, concluding that they are largely the feelings of conscience of those who have been raised to have them, and in chapter 4, entitled "How Proved" he embarks upon the task of constructing a proof to establish that only *this* principle constitutes all of morality. But that proof (which generations of students know is problematic) is *not*, for Mill, the source of our motive to follow the principle, nor do our motives justify the principle as the correct standard of moral action. So Mill sharply distinguishes what *gets* us to be moral, from the content and compelling force of morality. A Millian position on instrumental reason distinguishes, in the same way, between what gets us to follow the directives of instrumental reason, and the authority of instrumental reason.

The Millian position would license criticism of people who fail to act rationally in virtue of the way in which they do not act on the reasons supplied by instrumental rationality, even though their motivational structure is such that they have no capacity for doing so. Whereas the Kantian position is a thorough-going form of motivational internalism, i.e., the view that to know that x ought to be done is to have a motive to do x, the Millian position embraces a form of motivational externalism, denying that it follows from knowing that I ought to do x that I have a motive to do x.[26] So although both the Kantian and the Millian positions insist that to know one ought to do x is to have a reason to do x, they differ in the positions they take on whether these reasons are motivationally efficacious. Note, however, that on the Millian view, instrumental reasons are still "internal" in Williams' justificational sense, even though they are motivationally inefficacious, by virtue of the fact that they are deliberatively connected to motives.

The third position on instrumental reasons, which I call *Humean*, agrees that cause-and-effect information can at most be only indirectly involved in getting us to act, by causing in us the development of desires to perform the instrumentally effective action. On this view, reasoning establishes causal connections between ends and means, which have been worked out using logic and causal reasoning (both of which are understood to be components of theoretical reason). And this cause-and-effect information is often (but not always) only indirectly involved in getting us to act, by causing in us the development of desires to perform the instrumentally effective action; it cannot effect action by itself. This position is explicitly argued for by Hume himself:

> [R]eason, in a strict and philosophical sense, can have an influence on our conduct only after two ways: Either when it excites a passion by informing us of the existence of something which is a proper object of it; or when it discovers the connexion of causes and effects, so as to afford us a means of exerting any passion." (Hume 1978, 3.1.1: 459)

But in this passage Hume is saying not only that reason cannot move us to action *alone*, without any help from desires at all, but more importantly that it has a (merely) causal effect on action, and no motivational effect by virtue of any (supposed) authority over action.

However, what is striking about the Humean conception is that it also says that instrumental reason has no authority over our actions![27] Consider Hume's (famous) remarks in book 2:

> 'Tis not contrary to reason to prefer the destruction of the whole world to the scratching of my finger. 'Tis not contrary to reason for me to chuse my total ruin, to prevent the least uneasiness of an *Indian* or person wholly unknown to me. 'Tis as little contrary to reason to prefer even my own acknowleg'd lesser good to my greater, and have a more ardent affection for the former than the latter. A trivial good may, from certain circumstances, produce a desire superior to what arises from the greatest and most valuable enjoyment; nor is there any thing more extraordinary in this, than in mechanics to see one pound weight raise up a hundred by the advantage of its situation. (Hume 1978, 2.3.3: 416)

Note Hume's contention that one is not being irrational in preferring an "acknowledg'd lesser good" to a "greater" good. The meaning of these terms is somewhat obscure: in order for the phrase in which they occur to make sense, there must be some way that we can judge one good "greater" than another, apart from the strength of our preferences for either one. An appeal to instrumental reason gives us a way to make such a judgment. Suppose going to the dentist is a means to avoiding pain in the long term. Suppose further that an agent prefers avoiding long-term pain to spending an afternoon reading. Because going to the dentist is a means to the more preferred end, it is a greater good than spending the afternoon reading. And yet it makes perfect sense to imagine this agent saying that she prefers spending the afternoon reading to going to the dentist. Hume's position would be that *because* spending the afternoon reading is what one prefers to do, it is "not against reason" to do so. Our desires are not only the sole motivational force within us but also the only force within us that can "tell us what to do." And desires can act upon us in a way that causes us to do something other than the course of action consistent with reason's information—e.g., when it fails to cause within us a desire to perform the means that is sufficiently strong to counteract an opposing desire. (Remember Hume's mechanics metaphor: sometimes a pound weight can raise up a hundred by the advantage of its situation.)

Of course there can be some psychological process within us that is usually initiated by reason's instrumental deliberation, eventuating in a desire to do that which one has instrumental reason to do. In Hume's words:

> [R]eason, in a strict and philosophical sense, can have an influence on our conduct only after two ways: Either when it excites a passion by informing us of the existence of something which is a proper object of it; or when it discovers the connexion of causes and effects, so as to afford us a means of exerting any passion. (Hume 1978, 3.1.1: 459)

In the latter case, reason has an "influence on our conduct" (perhaps it operates along the lines of what Hume calls a "general rule"), but note that this influence does *not* come about by virtue of its authority over our action. And its causal effect on the development of motives in us is a contingent phenomenon, derailed in certain circumstances. "Men often act knowingly against their interest: For which reason the view of the greatest possible good does not always influence them" (Hume 1978, 2.3.4: 418). So while we can act "against reason" in the sense that we can fail to act according to its information, we cannot act against its (motivationally efficacious) authority over our action, because such authority doesn't exist. Again, to quote Hume:

> [A]ctions do not derive their merit from a conformity to reason, nor their blame from a contrariety to it; and it proves the same truth more *indirectly*, by shewing us, that as reason can never immediately prevent or produce any action by contradicting or approving of it, it cannot be the source of the distinction betwixt moral good and evil. . . . Actions can be laudable or blameable; but they cannot be reasonable or unreasonable. (Hume 1978, 3.1.1: 458)

Compare Hume's remarks on character and action in which he once again insists that actions cannot be judged as rational or irrational:

> Reason is the discovery of truth or falsehood. Truth or falsehood consists in an agreement or disagreement either to the *real* relations of ideas, or to *real* existence or matter of fact. Whatever, therefore, is not susceptible of this agreement or disagreement, is incapable of being true or false, and can never be an object of our reason. Now 'tis evident our passions, volitions, and actions, are not susceptible of any such agreement or disagreement; being original facts and realities, compleat in themselves, and implying no reference to other passions, volition and actions. 'Tis impossible, therefore, they can be pronounced either true or false, and be either contrary or conformable to reason. (Hume 1978, 3.1.1: 458)

So for Hume, it is, strictly speaking, incorrect to call an action irrational, even if that action fails to achieve the stated aim of the agent.[28]

At the deepest level, Hume's position should be understood as a view of what reason *is*: whereas philosophers such as Wollaston and Clarke considered it to be a normative faculty with both authority and motivational efficacy over our actions, for Hume, reason is a purely informational faculty, working out relations of ideas and causal connections. Although he accepts that this information might play a causal role in the creation of a motive to perform a means to a desired end given the psychological processes of the human mind (and book II is full of accounts of psychological processes generating various passions), he rejects completely the idea that it has any normative authority over action, or any capacity to move us by virtue of that supposed authority.

Contrast the Humean view with the Kantian and Millian conceptions of rational imperatives, both of which assume that reason can have normative authority. On the Kantian or Millian views, if you say about someone: "he ought to do y to achieve x in the circumstances," you are invoking what you take to be an objective norm to criticize him. I call this the "instrumental norm" which directs us to pursue those objects and perform those actions that will be the most effective means to a desired end. For the Kantian or Millian instrumentalist, to say that "reason has authority over us" is really to say that *this instrumental norm* has authority over us.[29] But Hume rejects the idea that there is such an objective authoritative norm. For Hume, acting on a hypothetical imperative does not involve accepting (or being motivated by) the authority of such a norm, but instead involves being caused to act in this way by a process that is affected by both one's desires and the information about how to satisfy them supplied by reason. That information, in conjunction with one's desires, might have the "feel" of an authoritative, natural norm, but in reality, one is being directed by a conjunction of entirely natural (and scientifically recognized) forces. And when those forces fail to direct us, Hume insists that we do not violate any authoritative code of reason applying to action—because no such code exists.

There is a fourth view of the force of hypothetical imperatives, suggested by the work of Alan Gibbard,[30] which one might consider a "naturalized" version of the Kantian view. Whereas the Humean view tries to purge from its theory of reason the problematic idea of normative authority altogether, this fourth view accepts that reason has such authority, but then attempts to explain it naturalistically by appeal to human psychology, and its biological origins. Consider an example of such an explanation: Suppose we have evolved as creatures who have the cognitive capacity to formulate imperatives that we take to be authoritative with respect to our behavior; on this view, normative thinking is a natural part of our mental activity. Suppose it is also true that we have evolved such that normatively authoritative imperatives have motivational effects on our behavior that cannot be assimilated or reduced to the motivations provided by desires. In that case it would be true that these imperatives have a motivational effect on us *by virtue of their felt authority*—where this motivation is distinct from other (recognized) forms of motivation, and yet natural for all that. And we can explain the presence of this motivational effect in terms of the survival advantage it would have given our forebears.

We have no proof of this or any similar speculative story. Note, however, that if such a story is right, it could be used to explain the motivational force of categorical imperatives just as much as hypothetical imperatives, and thus could be used to vindicate the motivational plausibility of noninstrumental conceptions of reason, every bit as much as the Kantian version of the instrumental conception.

So are any of these four positions successful? I will argue that although the latter three do not posit objective norms of reason and reject the idea that there is any motivational forces deriving from the (supposed) objective authority of rational imperatives, none of these positions succeeds as a theory of *reason*. The only theory that succeeds as a theory of reason is the Kantian position, which, as we shall see, is manifestly unsatisfactory from a naturalist standpoint.

IV. The Kantian View

The problem with any of the variants of the Kantian view is that by postulating the idea that a reason's motivational efficacy is necessary by virtue of its authority, all of them accept both a conception of objective normative authority, and an account of motivation by virtue of this authority, neither of which is acceptable to a naturalist. Not only is the idea of objective normative authority nonnatural, even more troubling to the naturalist is the idea that such an authority can move us to act. Whether or not the authority of the hypothetical imperative is taken to motivate action directly, or via some psychological intermediary such as a desire, all variants of the Kantian view take it that *this authority* can get us to perform the mandated action; and this kind of causal efficacy is neither recognized nor studied by science since the (objective) normative authority doing the causing is neither recognized nor studied by science. Indeed, Kant himself accepts this, and strives, in his *Critique of Pure Reason* and in subsequent works on moral theory, to develop a defense of the nonnatural motivational efficacy of this authority. As I've noted, the instrumental theory has been popular with naturalists and social scientists generally, because it seems not only a highly plausible answer to the question "Why be rational?" but also one that is acceptable to naturalists insofar as it does not appear to rely on some kind of "magical" force which human beings are supposed to have the capacity to sense and be motivated by. But the Kantian explanation of the motivational efficacy of a hypothetical imperative by virtue of its authority makes it just as magical as any categorical imperative. However contingent the hypothetical 'ought' is on a desire, it is still *not* the same as a desire; to say, therefore, that its objective normative authority is what moves us to act rationally is to analyze the "prescriptive force" of hypothetical imperatives such that it is identical to the prescriptive force of categorical imperatives. If naturalists reject the plausibility of this analysis for categorical imperatives, they must do so for hypothetical imperatives.

V. The Humean View

To discuss the Humean position I will employ a thought experiment which I have introduced elsewhere.[31] Suppose there is a person who (as a matter of fact) only acts on his occurrent motives, and knows this fact about himself. Such a person is unlike the notorious semi-moral agents criticized by Hobbes and Hume: Whereas Hobbes's "foole" (Hobbes 1991, chap.15) or Hume's "knave" (Hume 1975, 9.2: 282–83) believes "I should do that action which I can establish, using instrumental reason, it is in my interest to perform," this individual, whom I will call a "curmudgeon," believes "I will [not I should] only do that action which is prompted in me by the strongest occurrent motive." Note that whereas the fool's and knave's remark is a prescriptive principle setting out what counts as legitimate reasons for action, the curmudgeon's remark has no prescriptive overtones (he is not saying that he ought only to act on occurrent motives) but is merely setting out what he takes to be an accurate descriptive statement about how and why he behaves as he does.

Given their statement, the fool and the knave believe that they can have reason on occasion to perform actions for which they need have no immediate occurrent motive if and when these actions will causally effect states of affairs leading to the satisfaction of desires or preferences that they have. However, the curmudgeon will believe no such thing: if he, say, has no occurrent motive to go to the dentist, he will not go, even if he knows that such a visit would enable him to satisfy highly important self-regarding desires. A Kantian might contend that, were the curmudgeon to know such a thing, this knowledge would produce in him an occurrent motive to go to the dentist; but in order to illuminate aspects of the Humean view on instrumental reason, I will assume, as this view insists, that knowing that one has an instrumental reason is not sufficient to give one a motive to follow its directives. So the curmudgeon is someone who can know that he has a desire for x, and that y is a means to x, but will not, as a consequence of this knowledge, always have an occurrent motive to do y. And when he does not, he will not do y.

Now suppose you saw this curmudgeon refusing to do y even though he admitted to wanting x, and you issued a hypothetical imperative to him to the effect that he ought to do y to achieve x. If, as a Humean instrumental theorist would insist, you took your hypothetical "imperative" to be merely a statement of a causal connection between an action and an outcome you believe to be desired by the agent, then if he ignores you after you have uttered it, you would merely shrug and turn away. After all, you would believe you could give him neither a reason nor a motive for acting otherwise. But if you would mean your hypothetical imperative to be a real *imperative* and not merely a statement of the causal facts, you would charge him with making a *mistake* if he didn't follow it, calling him 'wrong' or 'irrational'. ("He *ought* to do y; he's irrational not to do it," you would insist.) But to respond to him this way is to attribute to him an authoritative reason for action despite the fact that he refuses to recognize it, and to take yourself to be warranted to do so by virtue of the fact that you believe this reason applies to him whether he likes it or not.

So in essence you are maintaining that, no matter the peculiar psychological or social facts that explain his curmudgeonly behavior, he *necessarily* has a reason to do y in order to achieve x in these circumstances—a reason which, at the moment, he does not recognize. Or to put it another way, when you say that he ought to do y to achieve his desired end x, then you believe, given that he wants x, and y is the means to x, that it follows (necessarily) that he has a reason to do y. But this means you are judging him—and criticizing him—using a norm that you are assuming to be objectively authoritative (albeit perhaps not motivational by virtue of that authority), in just the way moral theorists take their moral norms to be valid. And as I said above, you are really appealing to the objective authority of what I have called the Instrumental Norm: "Act so as to perform the most effective means to a desired end." This norm is implicit in the fool's and knave's account of how they determine what action to perform, and it is the norm that you are using to attribute a certain reason for action to the curmudgeon, a reason which you believe he has necessarily, no matter his views about what actions he should, or will, take. If you believe—despite his disclaimers—that he is capable of acting from this norm, you are adopting the Kantian position on instrumental reason, attributing motivational efficacy to this authoritative instrumental norm. On the other hand, if you doubt its motivational efficacy, then you are embracing the Millian position, accepting the norm's authority, but admitting its motivational inadequacy in the circumstances. In either case, you will believe that, no matter his occurrent motives, he has a reason to do y.

But the Humean instrumental theorist has no room for this instrumental norm in his theory, because such a norm permits us to do what the Humean says is impermissible, namely, criticize actions as irrational. Accordingly, a Humean's hypothetical "imperatives" are merely assertions of causal connections, which in *no* sense give "reasons" for an agent to act. There is nothing either authoritative or motivationally efficacious about the Humean's hypothetical imperatives. And a Humean (curmudgeon-like) agent only follows them if, as it happens, the agent has a preexisting motive to perform y, or if the agent is affected by the assertion such that she develops a motive to do y. In this latter case, the force of the 'ought' is explainable in terms of contingent psychological human responses.

The problem with such a theory of reason is that it can never convict someone of acting irrationally! Those who hear the imperative and don't perform y *make no mistake* when they don't perform y. There are two ways in which the notion of mistaken action is lost on the Humean view.

First, many theorists, including Kant, will maintain that in order properly to be said to have made a mistake, we must not only have done something that we ought not to have done, but must also have been capable of performing the better action. Or in other words, we must have a reason to perform the better action, and that reason must also be motivationally internal—i.e., capable of functioning as an occurrent motive. But on Hume's view, we do whatever it is that our desires dictate, and can do no other. Thus if, as Hume maintains, we can act only on our desires, and we have no desire to perform that action which is a means to our end, then we are not capable of performing it, and thus cannot be criticized along Kantian lines as wrong or mistaken when we fail to perform it.

Philosophers who subscribe to the Millian position on the nature of hypothetical imperatives, will believe this is too strong a condition. They will believe that even in a situation where a person could not have done otherwise, criticism of his actions as irrational is still appropriate for as long as such criticism is interpreted as "external." According to this second position on what it means to call action mistaken, we can admit that a person may have no occurrent motive to perform the instrumentally mandated action, but nonetheless attribute to him (as Mill would do) a (justified) reason to perform that action if, as a matter of fact, he desires some end, and it is true that this action is a means to achieving that end. Our criticism of him as irrational would be based on this reason, which would function as a standard by which to measure his conduct, albeit a standard which, we would admit, he has no way to meet, given the facts of his psychology. But the Humean position on hypothetical imperatives precludes even the Millian external type of criticism. As I noted in the development of the Humean view, it denies the idea that our determination of the best means to an end has any authority over us, and thus denies that instrumental reflection gives us a reason to act. This determination might have a *causal* effect on us, such that, as a matter of (psychological) fact, we develop a desire to do that which is the best means to our ends. But the rational information about means to ends is not *itself* a reason for action. That is, when we determine that x is a means to y, not only is such information not, by itself, motivationally efficacious; more importantly, it isn't even authoritative. So someone who fails to act so as to achieve his ends, in a situation where he has no desire to perform the actions required to achieve those ends, does nothing wrong. This person quite literally *has no reason* to perform x to achieve y. And if he has no reason to do so, then he makes no mistake by not doing so. He violates no standards of action; and indeed, that's the point of this Humean view—*there are no standards of action.* Thus he cannot be criticized as irrationally mistaken.

Of course he can still be criticized, albeit not as irrational. Hume sanctions all sorts of criticisms in his discussion of natural vices, and the criticism of imprudence (i.e., behaving in a way that is advantageous in the short-term but not in the long-term) might be thought to apply to at least some of the curmudgeonly people I am describing. However, not only is imprudent action not the same as instrumentally irrational action (for example, some imprudent actions can nonetheless be instrumentally rational, in virtue of the fact that they satisfy short-term goals), more importantly, calling someone imprudent is *not* calling her mistaken. When, according to Hume, we criticize someone as vicious in some way, we are projecting on to her a property that is created from our displeasure at her actions, occasioned in us after sympathetic identification with her and/or others, where this projection is governed in certain ways by conventional rules generated by our society.[32] But upon reflection, we must admit that this criticism is a function of how her actions strike us. It does not mean that, by her lights, she made any mistake. And even if our criticism of her as (in some way) vicious is supposed to mean that she violated some (external) ideal, it is nonetheless a "projected" criticism that is based on certain emotions experienced by (many but not all) on-lookers as they contemplate her behavior, and not a criticism of her behavior as irrational or in some way a mistake (given her motives).

So Hume's theory destroys the idea that people ever act irrationally, given that, on his view, action is based upon the strongest motivational force, and the "imperatives" of reason have no authority over, or motivational effect on, our actions. The Humean position must be that human beings can only act ***nonrationally***, since reason is neither the standard nor the motivation (by virtue of being the standard) of human action. Of course the Humean view admits that instrumental assertions, coupled with our preferences, might play a causal role in our performance of an action. But these assertions amount merely to psychologically efficacious ways of talking, and not normative prescriptions setting out what we *ought* to do if we wish not to be among those whose behavior violates the standards of reason. Any persistent tendency to interpret them in this latter way would have to be explainable by the Humean via some sort of Mackie-like "error theory" (which would credit us with a natural propensity toward such an interpretation, even while showing that it cannot be true).

But remarkably, this means that the Humean view is actually inconsistent with the instrumental theory of reason as I have defined it above! In particular, it violates thesis 1, i.e., that "an action is rational to the extent that it furthers the attainment of an end." The inclusion of that thesis in the definition of the instrumental approach is inescapable; for how could one endorse a version of instrumental theory of reason but not criticize, for example, the man that wanted to cure his tuberculosis but refused to take the medicine that would do it, or the woman who wanted a college B.A. but refused to work to pass any of her classes? To say, as Hume does in the *Treatise*, that "actions do not derive their merit from a conformity to reason, nor their blame from a contrariety to it" (Hume 1978, 3.1.1: 458), is to refuse to allow reason to have *any* critical impact on human behavior at all. Yet isn't this exactly the position one is taking when one says, as Hume does, that reason only has a theoretical role? Ironically, that position is inconsistent with the instrumental theory of reason, understood as involving a certain kind of rational criticism of behavior, that is standardly attributed to Hume![33]

VI. The Millian View

Insofar as the Millian incorporates the Kantian conception of reason's authority, it is immediately problematic for the naturalist, who will object to the idea that such authority is real, whether or not that authority is taken to be motivationally efficacious. Hence the Millian understanding of the prescriptive force of hypothetical imperatives would introduce the kind of nonnatural elements into that position to which naturalists have objected in other moral theories.

Nonetheless, for those willing to be more flexible about what they take to be 'natural', the Millian position might seem to be plausible, and indeed, a nice compromise between Kantian and Humean positions on reason, insofar as it combines a classic (and, for many, attractive) position on the nature of reasons with a natural theory of motivation.

But I shall now argue that this view is implausible precisely because of its naturalist motivational theory. For a Kantian, acting on the authority of an imperative is being moved to act by the reason given us by the imperative. Or alternatively, the imperative's reason is that *for the sake of which* we act. In contrast, if a hypothetical imperative is a mere causal lever to action, it causes action, but not insofar as it gives us a reason. Its causal efficacy has to do with other features it possesses; e.g., its rhetorical power, or its power on one's memory or aesthetic sense, and is not created by the (bare) idea (which may or may not be in our heads) that there is something for the sake of which we must act.

Consider the following examples of a hypothetical imperative that acts to effect action solely as a lever. First, there is Sally, who has a nasty sore throat. You tell her that she should go to the doctor to cure it. After hearing your imperative, Sally starts thinking about how much she dislikes the offices of the doctors she has seen in the past, then starts thinking about her present doctor, then starts reflecting on the fact that her present doctor has been successful with his investments, and then develops a desire to see him so that she can get him to give her investment advice. Your hypothetical imperative was causally efficacious in generating a motive in Sally to see the doctor. But it is not true that she acted from the reason given her by the hypothetical imperative. That is, your imperative did not give Sally a reason, which, by virtue of its authority, created a motive in her to go to the doctor. Instead, the words you uttered conjured up ideas that initiated a line of thought which, as it happens (and it could have happened otherwise) eventuated in the generation of a desire to perform the action your imperative directed.

Second, consider a (science-fiction) example of a tyrant who, whenever he gave hypothetical imperatives to his subjects, also gave these subjects injections of a serum that resulted in their developing a motive to perform the action prescribed by the imperative. Suppose that one subject, Tom, hated shots, and to avoid getting injected, would immediately develop a motive to do the action directed whenever he heard the tyrant issuing a hypothetical imperative (through some kind of Pavlovian response). In this case, the tyrant's imperative is directly responsible for Tom's motive, and yet it is not responsible for it *in the way* that would allow us to say that Tom's behavior was rational by virtue of the fact that he acted "from" the reason given him by the imperative.

Third, consider Rolf the dog, who has been trained to run to his meal dish to get his dinner whenever he hears the phrase, "Rolf, if you want dinner you must go to your meal dish." Rolf does not run to the meal dish because he is moved by the reason in the imperative—Rolf can't act from reasons. Instead he runs to the dish because there is something about the imperative other than its reason for action that causally effects his action.

So, to say that, on the Millian view, a hypothetical imperative can only effect us as a lever, is to say that *all* imperatives affect *all* of us in the way that Sally, or Tom, or Rolf the dog were effected by the imperatives given them. The Millian view precludes the idea that we can ever act *from* a hypothetical imperative, or *on* the reason given us by the imperative. But this means that, like the Humean position, the Millian view destroys the idea that we can ever act rationally or irrationally, and instead makes all action *nonrational.* Unlike the Humean view, it does so not because it says that there are no reasons for action, but because it insists that there is *nothing* that we can do *for a reason.* This is a subtle point: a person who acts rationally, as a result of your hypothetical imperative directed to her, will say that she is motivated *by* the reason in that imperative to do what she does; she does not say (or mean) that something about your articulation of the imperative (other than its giving you a reason) has (contingently) causally effected her motivational structure to effect a motive to act as the reason directed. In order to capture the idea that we can act rationally and irrationally, a theory of the normative force of instrumental reason must grant that hypothetical imperatives generate reasons for action that are, by themselves, motivationally efficacious, and not mere causal levers that usually (but contingently) have effect on our psychology.

Certain readers will wish mightily to resist this conclusion. Surely, they will insist, there is some way to see the hypothetical imperative as causal, and yet preserve the idea that we can act from it such that we are rational (or against it, such that we are irrational). But I would ask them how that imperative can be causal *in the right way* unless its causality works via the (authoritative) reason it gives us. If it is causally efficacious in any other way, then when we act as it directs we will merely be acting in accordance with that imperative, something that even an animal can do. Our action will be merely (fortuitously) according to reason, and not truly *rational.*

The grain of truth in the Millian position is that we can have a reason that doesn't move us, insofar as we aren't aware of it, or don't understand it. We should not want to deny the reality of nonrationality, manifested by people who don't act rationally because they don't know what rationality demands. But an adequate theory of reason, i.e., one that preserves the idea that we can act rationally and irrationally, must preserve the idea that we can (and should) act from (and not merely according to) reasons.[34] The only theory of reason that preserves this idea is the Kantian theory. Ironically, the theory that has the least plausible answer to the question "Why be rational?" is, thus far, the most plausible as an instrumental theory of reason.

VII. The Gibbard View

The fourth, "Gibbardian," view of the force of hypothetical imperatives recognizes that there is a difference between an imperative's effecting us as a causal lever, and its effecting us by virtue of its authority, and agrees with the Kantian position that to understand rational action, we must accept the latter rather than the former account. However, the Gibbardian position tries to naturalize the motivationally efficacious authority of these imperatives, understanding it as something "in the brain"—generating a distinct kind of motivational effect that has evolved within us. This new naturalist position doesn't banish normativity from reason, but rather tries to "tame" it by naturalizing it.

I will argue, however, that this position still fails to capture the way in which we normally think about rational and irrational action. Consider that this position makes the normative authority of instrumental rationality a contingent feature of human biology, which may not be shared by all humans, and which may not persist as our evolution continues. On this view, different biologies are capable of producing different "instrumental rationalities"; means/end reasoning of the sort we are used to commending cannot be regarded as uniquely and objectively *right.*

Yet we *do* consider it uniquely and objectively right. Although it is common for people to believe that there are different conceptions of morality with different psycho-social origins, it is not common for anyone, and certainly not common for philosophers, to recognize the possibility that there can be different rationalities with different psycho-social origins. A Gibbardian might explain this "prejudice" in favor of the instrumental conception as an inevitable part of the wiring of human beings insofar as members of our species could only have survived if they embraced it. But there are three reasons why this explanation won't suffice to explain our "prejudice."

First, any claim that there is some biological "inevitability" to our being instrumental reasoners is dubious. The survival of virtually every species on the planet is not contingent upon its members thinking in this way (and many survive quite nicely without "thinking" at all). So why should we believe that the survival of our species has depended upon its acceptance? Indeed, we have empirical evidence that it has *not* depended upon it: If instrumental reasoning is an inevitable part of human wiring, why do so many human beings behave, at least sometimes, contrary to its dictates? To explain irrationality, Gibbard has to acknowledge that human brains are complicated, and contain structures that generate behavior at odds with instrumental rationality. Since these (well-entrenched) structures are also a product of evolution, and by hypothesis, contributory to human survival, they would seem to be every bit as important to human functioning as instrumental reason. Note that the temptation to say that they aren't because they aren't the *right* kinds of functioning has to be resisted by the Gibbardian; there is no objective biologically independent conception of rightness to which the Gibbardian can appeal to justify instrumental reasoning. The most this theorist can say is that many people (who regard themselves as "right-thinking") will regard this kind of thinking as "right," by virtue of their psychology and the way it has been affected by their social milieu, but their sense of its rightness cannot be, by itself, an argument for the claim that instrumental reasoning is more important to the survival of the species than other forms of mental processing. Indeed, exactly what features of human beings have been contributory to the survival of the species seems to be more a matter of speculation than anything else, for how can any theory that purports to answer this question be empirically tested?

So someone who violated instrumental reasoning could claim that Gibbard's view does not license any criticism of her, insofar as her reasoning and behavior is just as much a product of her brain, and reflects the evolution of human beings, every bit as much as instrumental reasoning and behavior. Note also that the reality of extensive irrationality among the human population precludes Gibbard from arguing that those who violate the counsels of instrumental reason should not be included as members of the community of rational persons; that would be to exclude virtually all of the human species! But even if such people were unusual, such exclusion is not licensed by biology: biologists do not exclude creatures from membership in a species simply because they display unusual features. Indeed, those features may be potentially important for the species' future survival if the environment selects for them.

To see the second reason for the failure of Gibbard's position, let us put aside, for a moment, the preceding arguments, and suppose that Gibbard is able to define some minimal amount of instrumental rationality, which by hypothesis has been necessary for the survival value of the human species. Even granting Gibbard so much, however, does not allow him to salvage the idea that instrumental reasoning is more than just a kind of reasoning that (merely) "seems" right for some people. In particular, it does not give him grounds for commending those who possess at least this minimal amount of rationality or for criticizing those who do not. Members of this latter group would presumably be biologically different from the rest of us, but we could not consider them "wrong," or their wiring "defective" without treating the instrumental norm generating these evaluations as objective. We might "dislike" their wiring insofar as it differs from our wiring, but there is nothing in the naturalist's world that would permit us to conclude that our wiring is objectively *better* than theirs (we might *think* ours is better, but there is no objective value "out there" upon which our thinking can be based). Moreover, even if it were true that by virtue of our wiring we have superior survival value, *that* fact doesn't make our wiring intrinsically better—the naturalist who repudiates objective normative authority cannot consider survival of a species an objective value by which to measure the traits of individual members of the species.

Third, and most important, even if our species' survival were contingent on the acceptance of instrumental reasoning, the fact that a certain kind of (normative) reasoning is necessary for a species' survival given the contingent circumstances of its environment as it evolves does not make it *right*. The Gibbardian story can, perhaps, explain the *felt* authority of the instrumental norm, but it can never explain how or why this norm "really is" authoritative. Or in other words, the Gibbardian view can say that most of us may think it is authoritative because (for evolutionary reasons) we feel it to be so; but it can never say that we feel it to be so because it *is* so. Hence, there is a kind of Mackie-like error theory implicit in this account; it grants that people take the normative prescriptions of instrumental reason to be "objectively right," and not just a function of how they are made, and it grants that people act on them by virtue of their objective normative authority, but it must deny that there is any such objective authority, and maintain that we mistakenly confuse the "feel" of the authority of these imperatives for this (unreal) objective authority.

But such an error theory is really a kind of skeptical position on practical reason analogous to moral skepticism. Compare Gilbert Harman's position on moral thinking (Harman 1977, chap.1). Suppose we see boys pouring gasoline on a cat and we say "That is wrong." Harman's explanation of our evaluation is that we (merely) *think* it is wrong, where our having this thought can be explained by reference to natural facts about us (e.g., our biology, or psychology, or social influences). But there is no natural property of "wrongness" to which we are responding when we make that evaluation. The Gibbardian position on the nature of instrumental reason is essentially the same: this position explains our evaluations of actions as instrumentally rational or irrational by pointing to the way our brains work, but we do not think that our brains work this way because we are responding to something about actions that "really" makes them rational or irrational.

VIII. Conclusion

It is a testament to the free ride that the instrumental theory has enjoyed from philosophers in the modern era that hypothetical imperatives were thought to be straightforwardly motivational. But the upshot of the preceding arguments is that an 'ought' is an 'ought'. And if we want to interpret instrumental oughts as prescriptive statements that apply to action and which we can act *from* (and not merely in conformity with), we must accept a Kantian account of the authoritative and motivational force of hypothetical imperatives.

So naturalism exacts a high price from us: it robs us not only of the objective normative authority of moral imperatives, but of *any* imperative, even imperatives of instrumental reason. For many, the price will be too high. Moral skeptics claim to have no difficulty dismissing the idea that there is objective moral authority. But dismissing the idea that there is objective rational authority is much harder. Faced with a curmudgeon, we would believe he should be called irrational not because (given the way our brains work) we cannot help but do so, but because he *is* so—which is why we cannot help but consider him so. Even those creatures who are incapable of instrumentally rational action can still have their actions judged by the instrumental norm; we understand how to apply that norm, and outside the philosophical study few of us behave as if we think its application is (merely) a function of an evolutionarily contingent cognitive structure.

If the Kantian account is the only one that salvages the idea that instrumental thinking yields authoritative reasons, then its account of the authority and motivation of instrumental imperatives exactly parallels the traditional account of the authority and motivational force of noninstrumental imperatives. Hypothetical imperatives turn out to be no more, and no less, mysterious than categorical imperatives. However, having said this, let me note that none of the preceding arguments for this conclusion has challenged the idea that the justification of hypothetical imperatives is on sounder ground than the justification of categorical imperatives. That may be so, and if it is, then hypothetical imperatives are to be preferred because of their sounder justificational basis. My point has simply been that they are not to be preferred on metaphysical or motivational grounds, since the authority and motivational efficacy of instrumental reasons in terms of their authority is no different than the authority and the motivational efficacy of noninstrumental (e.g., moral) reasons in terms of their noninstrumental (e.g., moral) authority.

University of Arizona

Notes

1. I believe, however, that the term 'instrumental' is sometimes used more broadly, e.g., as a theory which only involves thesis 1 and 2, but not thesis 3. I will

not explore broader uses of the term here, since the inclusion of thesis 3 is fairly standard in recent philosophical discussions of the instrumental theory.

2. For a nice discussion of this point, see Robert Sugden, "Rational Choice: A Survey of Contributions from Economics and Philosophy" (1991), 751–85.

3. Given that economists standardly describe expected utility theory as a predictive theory of human behavior, on that interpretation, it cannot be considered an instrumental theory of reason. See my "The Failure of Expected Utility Theory as a Theory of Reason" (1994).

4. See H. A. Simon, "A Behavioral Model of Rational Choice" (1955); and "Rational Choice and the Structure of the Environment" (1956). But it is not clear that Simon himself would accept my distinction between levels of analysis, and no such distinction appears in his work.

5. Still, must I *know* that these shorthand rules are utility maximizing in the circumstances and use them for this reason in order to be rational? Or is it enough that my actions merely accord with these rules, even if I don't understand them to be utility maximizing in light of constraints? Just as with morality, the rationality of an agent may depend upon more than just the conformity of her actions with certain normative standards.

6. That theorist is Alan Nelson, who first proposed the issue to me. See his "Are Economic Kinds Natural?" (1990). Nelson suggests the grammatical analogy, and also proposes that "humans might have evolved specialized neurological structures that compute what the efficient courses of need-satisfying action are" and if this is correct, he notes "there is a sense in which human minds or brains actually unconsciously compute utility maxima" (p. 131). But it is not clear to me the extent to which any nonconscious computation can count as *reasoning*, given that our conception of reasoning assumes it to be a conscious, deliberative affair.

7. To quote Putnam, "the 'standards' accepted by a culture or subculture, either explicitly or implicitly, cannot *define* what reason is, even in context, because they *presuppose* reason (reasonableness) for their interpretation." From Putnam's "Why Reason Can't Be Naturalized" (1983), 234.

8. Sometimes Baier suggests that it might be possible to define the meta-level process of reasoning instrumentally. However, this idea is circular; in order to define the instrumental reasoning process instrumentally, one must already have in hand the instrumental reasoning procedure one is attempting to define. I discuss this elsewhere, e.g., in my "The Failure of Expected Utility Theory as a Theory of Reason" (1994).

9. See part I of Hobbes's *Leviathan* and his *De Corpore*.

10. See Thomas Nagel, *The Possibility of Altruism* (1970).

11. For a paper that criticizes this assumption in Hobbes's theory, see Paul Hurley, "The Many Appetites of Thomas Hobbes" (1990).

12. See Gauthier's *Morals by Agreement* (1986), chap. 2.

13. See Brandt's *A Theory of the Right and the Good* (1979).

14. Baier points out that there is virtually no regimentation in Brandt's proce-

dure, a fact that might lead us to wonder why it ought to be considered a "procedure" at all. See RMO, chap. 1.

15. Whether or not such an "end discovery" reasoning procedure should be recognized is related to the issue of whether or not we should consider desires as, in themselves, reasons for action. Some theorists, such as Bond, deny that they should be so considered (see Edward J. Bond, *Reasons and Value* [1983]). Bernard Williams says, in contrast, that "Desiring to do something is of course a reason for doing it" (1985, 19). However I would presume Williams means that we should consider desires as reasons only if they have been approved by the imaginative reasoning procedure he describes, since otherwise they might be deviant, misinformed, or ill-considered, and hence not "justified" in the way we think reasons for action are supposed to be. For Williams' views on the way in which reasons must be justified, see Williams 1991.

16. For a discussion of Kant's view of morality as a constraint on what we pursue in life see Barbara Herman, "Obligation and Performance" (1993), 178–79.

17. For one well-known discussion of the ontological commitments science seems to require of us, see W. V. Quine, "Facts of the Matter" (1977).

18. See Gilbert Harman, "Human Flourishing, Ethics and Liberty" (1983), 319.

19. See Baier's Carus Lectures, Lecture I, "The Moral Order," p. 4.

20. Jonathan Dancy also notes the way in which William's internal/external distinction comes apart from a more traditional motivational way of making that distinction. See Dancy, *Moral Reasons* (1993), appendix 1: 253–57.

21. It is the constant reference to the *necessity* of willing the means to a desired end that persuades me Kant is not taking the view (suggested to me by J. B. Schneewind) that when we desire the end in fact (as it happens) we also desire the means (so that if we fail to perform the means to the end we are divided against ourselves). There can be no necessity to the formation of desires.

22. Kant suggests this idea himself in the section "The Incentives of Pure Practical Reason," chap. 3 of his *Critique of Practical Reason* (1956), 74–92.

23. He suggests it in the *Critique of Practical Reason,* in "The Incentives of Pure Practical Reason." See, for example, p. 82, where he seems to assume that the only way to explain how reason could be motivational is to credit it with the power to effect a desire in us to do the moral action. But note that this view still credits reason with the causal power to create a motive, even if it doesn't credit it with the power to directly motivate.

24. If one holds the former view, one might argue that while it is possible for the authority of imperatives to work indirectly, it is better if it does not; i.e., it is better if we act directly from the reasons we have for acting. In contrast, one could maintain that reason does not demand that in all circumstances our motivation to follow its directives must come from its authority rather than, say, from our desires. For a defense of this latter view, see the work of Joseph Raz, especially his *Practical Norms and Reasons* (1990), and the concluding postscript to the second edition.

25. J. S. Mill, *Utilitarianism* (1972), 17. For a useful discussion of Mill's position, see Christine Korsgaard "Skepticism About Practical Reason" (1986).

26. For further discussion of how Motivational Internalism and Externalism are different from Justificational Internalism and Externalism, see David Brink, *Moral Realism and the Foundations of Ethics* (1989), 38 and Jean Hampton, *A Theory of Reasons* (unpublished manuscript), chap. 1.

27. For discussions on Hume's position on reason, I am greatly indebted to Tom Christiano and Don Garrett.

28. While he notes that we sometimes call a passion irrational, strictly speaking it is the false judgment attending the passion that is irrational, and not the passion itself. See Hume 1978, 2.3.3:416.

29. Note that the authority of this instrumental norm has to be understood noninstrumentally; because it is the foundation of the idea that we ought to act on means appropriate to the achievement of our ends, it cannot itself be defended consequentially. Thus, understood as an imperative, it is categorical and not hypothetical (a delightful bit of irony in this story).

30. See Alan Gibbard's *Wise Choices, Apt Feelings* (1990).

31. See Hampton, "Rethinking Reason" (1992).

32. The importance of conventional rules determining the content of natural virtues and vices is an implication of Hume's discussion in Hume 1978, 3.3.1:581–82.

33. However, note that it would seem one could be a curmudgeon not only about reasons for action, but also about reasons for belief, that is, resisting belief in (and in no way motivated to believe) that which (according to the imperatives of theoretical reason) one has reason to believe. What can Hume say to such a curmudgeon? Why should there be norms that are authoritative over belief, when, according to Hume, there are no norms that are authoritative over action? I believe Hume seriously considers that there may not be authoritative theoretical norms either, which explains why he resorts so often to psychologizing talk in book 1 of the *Treatise*.

34. I would suggest that this means Bernard Williams really defends a Kantian notion of reasons for action. Although Williams took his paper to be a defense of *Humean* understandings of reason and morality, Christine Korsgaard points out that, absent the addition of a substantive argument that rules the Kantian position out, Williams's defense of internal reasons is as much a defense of Kant's conception of reasons, as it is of Hume's. See Korsgaard 1986. But I am pointing out here that, in fact, since Hume's own position obviates the idea that there are reasons for action, and the Millian position is clearly externalist, Williams can only be defending a Kantian position on the *nature* of reasons for action, even if he has a Humean view of what the substance of those reasons can be.

In Search of Nonsubjective Reasons[1]

6

Peter Railton

Introduction

Might there be reasons that are other than subjective? This is hardly a clear question, since there are so many respects in which reasons have been claimed to be subjective and, therefore, in which they might turn out to be something else—something *more,* as philosophers characteristically tend to look at it.[2]

Multiple terminologies have figured in discussions of reasons. Philosophers speak not only of subjective vs. objective reasons, but of practical vs. theoretical, hypothetical vs. categorical, internal vs. external, relative vs. absolute, agent-centered vs. agent-neutral, warranting vs. explaining, justifying vs. exciting, and so on. As someone who has never found himself entirely confident even with the unadorned terms 'reason' and 'rationality', I find this profusion daunting. Yet even so, when I survey the profusion I cannot help thinking that it might not yet be lush enough. That is, I am less inclined to think that these are distinctions without differences than that there may yet be differences without distinctions—differences not best illuminated by existing dichotomies.

So I have chosen the expression 'nonsubjective reason' to give a name to my inquiry, hoping thereby to suggest the broad direction in which I'd like to look. Perhaps the expression is sufficiently ungainly that no one has already appropriated it for another, more definite use. My question is, roughly, whether agents can be seen as having deliberative grounds for action that constitute genuine reasons for them to act, and yet are substantially independent of their particular desires or contingent personal goals.[3] (A more definite idea of what nonsubjectivity involves—e.g., of what this "independence" might come to—will await our consideration of possible examples.)

As a self-confessed insecure speaker of the language of reasons, I can hardly expect the reader willingly to follow my lead through this uncertain territory. Instead, I will take Kurt Baier's *The Rational and the Moral Order* along as a guide. For Baier, too, as I understand him, is in search of nonsubjective reasons. It will not, of course, be his fault if I go astray.

A Parallel with Theoretical Reason

Let me begin as Baier begins, by taking the domain of "cognitive" (or "theoretical") reasons as the most promising place to start if one is looking for something nonsubjective in reasons.[4] Widely recognized fundamental norms for regulating or assessing belief—"Apportion belief to the evidence," "Avoid self-contradiction," "Distrust nonrandom samples," and so on—give no role to one's particular desires or personal goals. We think of agents, ourselves included, as having good reasons to follow these norms even when not doing so would be more expedient or gratifying to personal ambition.

To be sure, Baier cautions, we must distinguish among the various things we call reasons for belief. Claims about the *reasons why* a person holds a certain belief, which are (or purport to be) explanatory, must be distinguished from claims about his or her reasons to hold it, which are (or purport to be) justificatory.[5]

Baier's search for nonsubjective reasons focuses on the latter, justificatory reasons to believe. But among these he makes a further distinction. Some justifications for belief are *pragmatic* in character. They concern the whole array of possible advantages or disadvantages that might attach to the acquisition or possession of certain beliefs—e.g., holding certain beliefs rather than others can reduce one's anxiety, streamline one's thinking, increase one's acceptability in the choicer social circles, or even improve one's chances of survival after cancer surgery. The other sort of justification distinguished by Baier is the *epistemic*. Epistemic justifications involve a more restricted class of considerations, such as the amount or kind of evidence available, the reliability of certain procedures, logical relations among propositions, etc. The sort of justification they produce for belief is linked in the first instance to such notions as warrant or truth, and only secondarily, if at all, to any personal advantage or usefulness unrelated to these. Along with Baier, we will look to these "epistemic cognitive reasons" for nonsubjective reasons that might serve as a model for the practical realm.

Motivational Internalism: An Obstacle to the Parallel?

One might think that, precisely because epistemic cognitive reasons seem to be characterized independently of the agent's desires or personal goals, they cannot serve as an appropriate model for nonsubjective *practical* reasons. Baier defines "Internalism" as the view that "if a fact is a reason for someone to do something, then it necessarily is also a motive for him to do it" (RMO, 90).[6] Since practical reasons are usually defined as reasons to act, and since action requires motivation, it has been popular among philosophers to insist that practical reasons applicable to an agent must meet an "Internalist" criterion. Theoretical or cognitive reasons, by contrast, are held to be reasons for *belief* rather than action, and the conventional view here is just the opposite, according to Baier: "Few philosophers, if any, would (I think) seriously question the claim that Internalism does not hold for [epistemic] cognitive reasons" (RMO, 90).

In light of this seemingly fundamental difference in their domain of application and associated relation to motivation, can we expect that epistemic cognitive reasons afford a parallel that might help us to understand the possibility of nonsubjective practical reasons? Must we, if the parallel is to hold, seek practical reasons that afford no motive for action?

Fortunately not. In the first place, it is not so obvious that one cannot speak of epistemic cognitive reasons as having something like "motivational force" for the agent. When I acknowledge some piece of information I had heretofore disregarded to be relevant evidence, this exerts a kind of pressure on me either to take the information into account or to explain why not. The point therefore is not the absence in theoretical reason of something akin to "motivational force," but rather its seeming independence from any particular desires or personal goals I might have—any desires or goals contingent or exogenous from an epistemic point of view. If I come to believe that certain information affords telling evidence, this *ipso facto* exerts force on my beliefs, even if this is decidedly not seen by me as favorable to my wants or goals. The very fact that many of us contrive so frequently to rationalize away or avert our attention from evidence that threatens to conflict with our current beliefs is testimony to this "motivational force."

In the second place, Baier is seeking to establish the parallel among (what he calls) *directive* reasons, reasons that support an 'ought' applicable to an individual in the context of deliberation. We sometimes use the term 'reason' in either practical or theoretical contexts without intending anything directive. One might for example hear a mathematician say, "Although I thought at the time that this theorem could be proved by known methods, there actually was a very good reason for doubting this—Derwent's result could not be extended to the infinite case." Perhaps neither she nor anyone else in the mathematical community was at all close at the time to grasping this limitation of Derwent's result; indeed, perhaps prevailing expert opinion went the other way. The force of her saying that there was such a reason is more acontextual: this consideration was there all along, waiting to be discovered. The pieces were there, so to speak, but no one saw how they fit together. Such a judgment, though expressed in the language of 'reasons to believe', is evaluative, but not necessarily directive: it would have been mathematically correct, and more fortunate from a mathematical point of view, to have believed that the theorem could not be proved by known methods—even if that was not what seemed most credible at the time.

Let us, then, concentrate on directive reasons and their characteristic features. Baier notes that "directive reasons apply only where we have a measure of control" (RMO, 89), and therefore they take into account what is accessible or feasible for an agent. In the case of reasons for action, what is accessible or feasible will depend not only upon one's state of information and mental capacities, but also upon one's practical capacities, including motivational capacities. If we are to find directive nonsubjective practical reasons, then, it would not be enough simply to identify some state of affairs that would be better or more fortunate from a moral or prudential point of view; we must also show that the state of affairs is one that could motivationally engage the agent.

We can see Baier as seeking, not practical reasons without motivational force, but rather, practical reasons that are—like the epistemic cognitive reasons just considered—effective in influencing agents in ways that do not depend upon the agents' particular, contingent desires or goals. In short, motivating but nonsubjective reasons.

Now this might seem to be a most puzzling prospect in the case of action. On the dominant, neo-Humean view, reason possesses no motivational force of its own, and depends upon desires or personal goals to provide all impetus for action. Indeed, Baier identifies a "motivation problem" for his view:

> The problem is, in the first place, how . . . reason can motivate us at all and in the second place how, as seems to happen sometimes, reason can move us to do something it requires us to do even when our most intense desire is to do something else. (RMO, 116)

This problem looks daunting, especially since Baier appears to agree with the neo-Humean at least in rejecting any special rational motivational faculty:

> [W]e need not think that the motivating power of reasons is either dependent entirely on that of our desires—that reason is and ought to be only the slave of the passions—or else is a faculty that has its own kind of motivation peculiar to it but capable of conflicting with and of overpowering the motivation of our desires. (RMO, 116)

Desires motivate. That seems clear enough. But if reason neither draws upon the motivating power of desire nor has any capacity to produce motivations of its own that can compete on the plane (or planes) of desire, how might it enter into the business of motivation at all?

Puzzling as it is, Baier's "motivation problem" can, I believe, be solved for the case of belief, though this ultimately will involve following a path somewhat different from Baier's. But before our paths part, we must confront another apparent obstacle to any attempt to pursue a parallel between cognitive and practical reasons, and then try to come to an understanding of Baier's principal example of a nonsubjective reason, the case of John.

Belief and the Will: Another Obstacle?

Traditionally, philosophers have worried that any seeming parallel between belief and action will give out at just the point where the idea of *directive* reasons comes into play. Belief is a state, not an action, and though most of us would say that a person can decide to act, it is considerably more controversial whether a person can decide to believe.[7] It therefore is unclear whether we can speak of directive cognitive reasons, since their existence would appear to presuppose some measure of willful control over belief (compare RMO, 89).

An example. Sitting down to a much-delayed meal, I hear the telephone ring yet again. "What a nuisance!" I think. The unwelcome belief that the phone is once more ringing comes to me unbidden, spontaneously. I can decide, now, to answer or ignore the phone. Could I equally decide, now, to believe that the phone isn't ringing after all? Not decide to *pretend* it isn't or to act as if it weren't, but genuinely to *believe* of that very phone that it is not now ringing, despite the apparent noise. One cannot, it is said, believe at will. Of course, if I had earlier, willfully, unplugged the phone, and (while keeping this in mind) now heard this same ringing noise, I would not believe it to be the phone. So I can willfully *undertake a course of action* that will have the predictable result that I come to hold a certain belief. But this is not belief at will. It is action at will, which, among other things, creates evidence for belief.

Now one can also undertake to change one's beliefs in ways that do not necessarily involve creating evidence. I could reshape my beliefs in various nonevidential (as well as evidential) ways by hiring a hypnotist or joining a commune or becoming Associate Dean for Financial Affairs. But these steps, too, are matters of undertaking a course of action which predictably will change belief, not examples of belief at will. Though it might be true that "When the need is strong enough, there are those who will believe anything" (Lobel 1980, 16), this presumably is due to more indirect and insidious belief-shaping mechanisms than direct, deliberate resolution about what to believe.

Yet this is too fast. It would seem that sometimes we do in fact engage in a process of deciding-what-to-believe that stands to belief in very much the same relation as deciding-how-to-act stands to action. Indeed, we use the same expression for both: making up one's mind. Think of oneself as a juror, listening to the testimony of a string of witnesses. It is hardly out of place to describe this process as deciding whom to believe or what to believe, and how much. Is that just an *ex post facto* reinterpretation of a spontaneous process? One certainly does find oneself "spontaneously" thinking that a certain individual is trustworthy or that a particular claim is credible. But these spontaneous thoughts, one knows, often reflect one's preconceptions and suggestibilities. So one doesn't always rush to embrace them. This second-guessing of "spontaneous" beliefs might or might not wholly remove their initial attraction, but certainly it does sometimes lead us to distance ourselves from them.

Listening to a charge of loan-sharking and extortion against a well-respected member of the community and mainstay of the Gilbert and Sullivan Society, I might find that I am quite unable to shed altogether my long-standing image of Mr. Crocker as a dignified gentleman who would never get involved in this sordid business. But after reviewing the testimony, I might nonetheless decide that the prosecution's case against Crocker provides evidence beyond any reasonable doubt that this image, even if it retains some grip on me, is wrong. In this process of "making up one's mind," agents appear to subject *themselves* to a directive epistemic 'ought' much akin to the formation of an intention or resolution to act.[8]

To be sure, this sort of direct "control" over one's doxastic states is not a control which one represents to oneself as a triumph of sheer will—one sees it instead as, e.g., willfully forcing oneself to face up to the evidence. But there is no need, in order to make a case for directive *epistemic* reasons, to locate a form of control over belief that represents itself as epistemically arbitrary. Rather, we must locate a belief-shaping process in the individual worthy of being called epistemic deliberation and resolve, and seen by the individual himself as such.

Perhaps we can best understand this idea of making up one's mind—willfully if need be—in the face of "spontaneous" convictions by introducing a certain structure or hierarchy into the description of one's beliefs. For example, at some level in my psyche, my newly acquired conviction that Crocker has been shown guilty beyond a reasonable doubt simply jostles uncomfortably alongside long-standing conviction that he just isn't that sort. But at a higher level, I have resolved not to grant equal epistemic authority to these two convictions. Directive epistemic reasons, if there are such things, perhaps should be seen as normative for this "degree to which I hold *p* to be warranted" rather than for a quasi-phenomenological state of belief or conviction. One's higher-order epistemic attitudes of this kind seem sufficiently responsive to one's deliberative assessment of evidence and relevance to underwrite the possibility of a genuinely normative epistemology equipped with directive reasons. And that is sufficient, at least relative to the present set of concerns, to allow our parallel between epistemic and practical reason to proceed.[9]

John

Like Voltaire, Baier turns to a question of paternity in order to afford an instance of belief despite evidence.[10] In Baier's example (RMO, 90f.), an individual, John, has a virtually unshakable belief that Jack is his son.[11] We can readily guess the reasons *why* he has this peculiarly strong belief, but the question is whether he has adequate reason to do so. In particular, does he have adequate epistemic reason?

Not as Baier sets out the example. For John possesses information about his own blood type, his wife's, and Jack's, which conclusively establishes—given general biological principles also known to John—that Jack could not be his son. And John is not aware of any independent epistemic reasons to doubt the blood-typing or the relevant parts of genetics, nor is he aware of any genuine possibility that other, compelling epistemic reasons will emerge for believing that Jack is his son. Indeed, the information John possesses is of a kind that he "would perhaps in other cases acknowledge to be conclusive evidence." But not in *this* case. John "is not now moved or to any degree motivated to believe [that he is not Jack's father]" (RMO, 91). Isn't this a case, Baier asks, in which we'd say that John, despite his lack of motivation, nonetheless has a directive—even conclusive—epistemic reason to believe that he is not Jack's father? And, if so, then aren't we in effect saying that there exist nonsubjective reasons, at least in the domain of theoretical reasons?

Yet the example as described thus far would need filling out to sustain so strong a conclusion. To see this, let's reverse direction temporarily and consider practical reason as an analogue for theoretical.

Someone who maintains the broadly internalist thesis that all *practical* reasons are grounded in desire need not deny that someone can possess a reason to *F* without desiring at all to do *F*. Consider the case of Evelyn.

Evelyn is a sales representative, new to the job. She is attending a convention and is scheduled to take Rick to lunch on Wednesday, the second day of the gathering. Rick, she has heard, is a blowhard, vulgar, and generally an embarrassment to be around. But he is also chief purchaser for one of the key firms with which Evelyn's company does business. On the first night of the convention she catches sight of a man holding forth to a small group in the lobby, slightly drunk and half-draping himself over an obviously reluctant young woman whom Evelyn correctly guesses to be his subordinate. Walking quickly past, Evelyn catches a glimpse of his nametag. It's Rick, all right. Her heart sinks. She realizes that she has not the least desire ever to be in the same room with this man, much less to take him to lunch. Wednesday morning comes and finds her—not a religious woman—ardently praying that some natural disaster will intervene. Still, we might say, Evelyn has a very strong reason to keep her appointment despite her powerful aversion to doing so. Does this show the existence of nonsubjective reasons?

That would be an exaggerated response to the case. Evelyn almost certainly has many less vividly present but nonetheless fundamental desires—to prove her "professionalism," to succeed at her work, to support her family, etc.—that would be less well satisfied were she to refuse to meet with Rick and fail to close the deal with his firm. Her reason to lunch with Rick has a firm subjective, internal connection with these desires, even if the thought of time spent with Rick now thoroughly repels her.

To return to Baier's example, John would have to be a very unusual person not to have other fundamental, if now less vivid, desires that would be ill-served by his continuing unresponsiveness to the evidence about Jack's paternity. Virtually everyone cares about possessing knowledge (or at least about not being grossly in error) in matters of great importance to themselves, and perhaps especially about not being (or being seen to be) self-deluding. Moreover John, like many, seems to have an underlying, strong interest in identifying and aiding those who are his actual "blood relatives," primitive as this notion might be. But if so, then continuing to devote himself to Jack is not to the purpose. Indeed, this purpose might better be served by John's facing up to the truth about Jack.[12] Such desires and concerns, even if pallid and abstract in comparison to his concrete passion about Jack's paternity, would still provide some basis for saying that John does after all have a (subjective, internal) motive that would favor squaring his beliefs with the evidence. For Baier's case to work as he intends, we must convince ourselves that John is not overlooking such concerns, but rather is wholly devoid of them, and this is none too easy a thing to do. Indeed, as we will see, to show that someone is wholly uninterested in the truth of his beliefs would involve a good deal more than merely showing him to be atypical.

Of course, we must be careful to avoid a trivialization of the notion of "desire." The expression 'desire' or 'desire-based motive' is sometimes used so broadly that it is a priori that whenever anyone is moved to voluntary action this shows that he acted from desire. "Do you still feel bad about accepting Mirko's invitation to take his seat on the last plane out of the city? Well, it *is* true that someone with Mirko's family background will be tortured and killed if caught, while you as a member of the press would almost certainly be protected. But you needn't worry—he wouldn't have offered you the seat if that weren't what he most desired to do." This undemanding use of 'desire', conflating desire with something more generic, such as preference, does figure in some common-sense contexts, even though common sense also distinguishes in other contexts between acts done from desire and acts done from duty.

But even this undemanding usage need not trivialize our discussion altogether, once we notice that it need not presuppose that the desire's attributes are exogenous to deliberation.[13] That is, this usage leaves open questions about the origins of desire, and therefore leaves open a space for moral or rational motivation: character or conscience or "reason" could be seen as operating by giving rise to desires (that would not otherwise be present) in the agent when he comes to believe that a certain course of action is appropriate or required.[14]

What John Can Know

Let us assume for the sake of the example that John is a most singular person and in fact possesses no independent desire to know the truth (or be undeceived, or devote primary resources to biological kin, etc.) that could supply a self-standing motivation to come to see that, according to evidence he accepts, he cannot be Jack's father. Can we still say, despite this lack of motivation, that John faces a directive epistemic 'ought' to believe the truth about Jack's paternity? We now have come far enough to face another difficulty in filling out Baier's example.

There is a suggestion in Baier's text that, although John possesses the relevant evidence, he is *incapable* of fully grasping its bearing on his beliefs about Jack's parentage. Coming to terms with this suggestion will, I think, eventually take us to the heart of the matter.

As we have noted, Baier concludes his initial discussion of John's case with the observation that, although John possesses evidence that affords a conclusive epistemic reason to believe that Jack is not his son, John "is not now moved or to any degree motivated to believe it" (RMO, 91). Yet Baier also adds what appears to be a significant qualification:

> Of course, this does not show that one can believe something to be a fact and to [sic] believe that fact to be a conclusive reason for one to believe some other fact and yet not be motivated to believe that other fact. (RMO, 91)

Apparently, Baier suspects that while one can *possess* what amounts to a conclusive epistemic reason without having any "motivation to believe," it would be problematic to claim that one could *recognize* this reason for what it is while remaining wholly unmoved.

That seems right. So the question arises: Why might this be? To answer this question, we will need to smooth out a seeming wrinkle in Baier's discussion.

Baier introduces John's case in order to explore the possibility of (what I have been calling) nonsubjective reasons. Let us distinguish between John's subjective condition in the motivational sense—his desires and personal goals—and his subjective condition in the epistemic sense—his evidence, cognitive capacities, etc. Because we are seeking an epistemic reason that would be a *directive* reason for John, we must pay attention to his subjective epistemic condition: a directive reason for *X* to believe that *p* would be, we have supposed, a reason for someone with *X's* evidence, cognitive capacities, etc. Yet Baier claims that in contexts of deliberation epistemic reasons are (unlike practical reasons) "universal in scope." Thus, "the fact that this lump [of sugar] is a cube is a reason *for everyone* to believe the same thing, namely, that it has twelve edges" (RMO, 127).

This would appear to suggest that every epistemic deliberator, regardless of epistemic situation or capacity, has a directive epistemic reason for believing all geometric truths. Thus we could say directively that Homer ought to have believed in the consistency of non-Euclidean geometry. This, it seems to me, would violate any plausible form of the idea that directive reasons are governed by the principle that 'ought' implies 'can'. I propose to ignore this seeming wrinkle in Baier's view, and assume that the sorts of epistemic reasons to which Baier attributes "universal scope" are *non*directive reasons, while directive epistemic reasons (as we have been supposing all along they must) depend upon what is doxastically possible for an agent.

This would restore a certain parallelism with directive practical reasons, while creating no new difficulties for what Baier wants to say about the case of John. For John is in an excellent epistemic position to come to believe that Jack is not his son: (i) John believes the information about blood groups; (ii) John does not believe any "other facts which he regards as weightier cognitive reasons" on the other side; (iii) John understands the bearing of the blood-typing information on questions of this kind, and would "in other cases acknowledge it to be conclusive evidence"; (iv) John has (we safely assume) ordinary inferential powers, and the reasoning involved in drawing the conclusion that Jack is not his son is not complex; (v) John is *de se* aware that the information in question applies to him; and finally, (vi) John's attention certainly could be drawn to the question of what to believe about Jack's paternity. Let us assume that (i)–(vi) suffice to establish that John would meet any appropriate constraints of doxastic availability on the application of a directive epistemic reason to infer that Jack is not his son.

What about John's famous resistance to such a belief? If we are to have a serviceable parallel with the practical case, then we must assume that John meets any appropriate constraints of *psychological feasibility.* His strong resistance to changing his belief about Jack's paternity does not constitute a definitive psychological block. Thus even if John initially finds it "utterly preposterous" that he is not Jack's father, and even if in the end he might find that he cannot wholly shake his initial conviction on this matter, still, he could nonetheless change his higher-order epistemic attitudes and come to regard 'I am not Jack's father' as much better warranted than its denial, given his total evidence.

Finally, let us assume that Baier is right in claiming that there is in the epistemic case a socially developed system of "objective guidelines" (see Baier's chapters 5 and 6) which would license John to draw the conclusion about his paternity, however unwanted it might be. Put another way: we collectively embrace certain guidelines for belief-formation and hold them to be nonsubjectively normative—we are prepared to apply them to individuals who lack "subjective" motivation.

At last, then, we seem to have all the pieces in place in order to speak (in Baier's terms) of John as under a conclusive, directive epistemic reason to believe that he is not Jack's father, despite his apparent lack of any desire to do so. Do we therefore have the sought-after model in the epistemic realm of how directive practical reasons might be nonsubjective?

John Is Stubborn, But Is He Cussed?

That depends. To which sort of subjectively disinclined practical agent does Baier address himself?

Baier believes that, in the case of practical reason, a "cussed" or "perverse" individual "may believe or know that [he] is acting contrary to the dispositive reason but [he] may not regret it" (RMO, 115). Such a person seems able cheerily to accept that a certain course of action is such that he is under a rational, all-things-considered, directive practical 'ought' to follow it, and yet also to feel not the least tinge of a motive to pursue it. The sought-after model in the domain of epistemic reasons therefore would have to exhibit the possibility of a similar perversity or cussedness (*mutatis mutandis*) on the part of epistemic agents.

However, this would appear to be just the step that Baier was unwilling to take in John's case. As we noted, he stopped shy of insisting that

> one can believe something to be a fact and to [sic] believe that fact to be a conclusive reason for one to believe a certain other fact and yet not be motivated to believe that other fact. (RMO, 91)

Therefore, while there is a sense in which John is aware of a conclusive reason for denying his parenthood but is not moved by it—the blood-group information is dispositive—there is another sense in which he is not, since he does not *recognize* the blood-group information to be dispositive in this case. As things stand, therefore, he does not appear to be cussedly thumbing his nose at a reason he himself admits to be dispositive, all things considered (compare RMO, 115).

Baier aims to win us away from Internalism about practical reasons by noting that we do not boggle at non-Internal reasons in the epistemic case. But the example of John makes it clear that we need to bring to light a distinction *within* Internalism, between existence and judgment Internalism.[15] It is one thing to deny that the *existence* of a reason for *A* to *F* presupposes that *A* somehow be motivated to *F;* it is another to claim that *A* could sincerely *judge* that he has a reason to *F*—especially, perhaps, a conclusive reason—without thereby experiencing any motivation to comply.[16] John's case would seem to violate existence Internalism only: he is said to be under a directive, dispositive epistemic reason yet not to be in any way motivated to conform his beliefs to it. He is not said to judge that he is under such a reason. But the cussed practical agent violates judgment Internalism as well: he sincerely judges himself to be under a directive, dispositive reason without feeling any motivation to comply (RMO,115) or compunction about noncompliance (RMO, 116).

Should we, then, improve the parallel between John and the cussed practical agent by simply stipulating that John, too, is cussed—he makes the judgment that he has a conclusive epistemic reason to believe that he is not Jack's father, though this judgment is motivationally inert for him?[17] Interestingly, the crux of the whole issue is that it is doubtful whether we are free to make this stipulation. Is it intelligible for someone fully and occurrently to understand and to believe without qualm both of the following propositions, while having them and their mutual relevance vividly before his mind and without any deflection of attention?

(a) I am Jack's father.

(b) I possess, and am entirely, properly convinced of, conclusive evidence that I am not Jack's father.

Goals in Believing vs. Constitutive Principles of Belief

We have come very close—if not all the way—to what has become known as "Moore's paradox." Moore noticed the seeming untenability of sincerely asserting '*p,* but I believe otherwise'.[18] Why is this seemingly untenable?

One possible explanation would attribute the untenability to a distinguishing characteristic of *belief* as a propositional attitude. There is nothing paradoxical about '*p,* but I pretend otherwise' or '*p,* but suppose otherwise for the sake of discussion' or even '*p,* but I feel in my bones that somehow it can't be so.' It is in some sense partly *constitutive* of the particular propositional attitude of belief that it represents itself as "actually getting things right" and does not merely represent its object "as if" true.[19] Unlike pretending or supposing or various other propositional attitudes, belief is said to "aim at" truth and to "miss its target" if its propositional object is false. A supposition or pretense does not have this target, and *a fortiori* does not miss it if the proposition being supposed or pretended to be true is in fact false.

Now Baier himself might appear to be moving in the direction of this thought when he writes that there are

> certain very general ends which, at least when we think about it, we all, at least normally, want to attain, such as discovering true rather than false answers to questions about matters that are important to us. (RMO, 50)

Moreover, he thinks that truth is "[o]ur normal aim" in the context of belief-formation (RMO, 79), and that truth-in-belief is in general a "universally appealing and unassailable" cognitive goal (RMO, 120).

However, Baier also urges that in rational agents other goals sometimes regulate belief-formation:

> [T]here can be conflicts between epistemic and pragmatic cognitive reasons, that is, truth-based and advantage-based reasons to believe, in which the latter could conceivably defeat the former. . . . Even a seemingly "ultimate" ground such as truth may have to give way, either because there is another even "more ultimate" ground or, alternatively, something that tells us when truth is outranked or rightly set aside and by what. (RMO, 119–20)[20]

To understand the issues before us, we will need to get clearer about what talk of truth as a "target" or "normal aim" of belief might amount to. In particular, we will need to underscore the difference between seeing the relation of belief to truth as teleological, in the way Baier does, as opposed to constitutive, as I will urge.

First, to speak of truth as the "*normal* aim" of belief (my emphasis) is ambiguous: one might mean the *usual* aim of belief, or its *normative* (or *regulative*) aim. The former leaves open the possibility of beliefs that do not even purport to "get things right," and thus suggests that forming beliefs in this way would simply be unusual, perhaps in the way that it would be unusual to "set aside" information about people's notions of propriety in deciding how to dress. But if the role of truth in belief is genuinely constitutive, to self-consciously "set aside" the aim of truth in forming certain beliefs would not be eccentric or foolish—it would be impossible. The propositional attitudes involved, whatever they might be—faith, hope, pretense, acceptance, etc.—would not be belief.

Second, talk of truth as a "target" or "cognitive goal" in belief is also ambiguous: we might mean that belief is (merely) *instrumentally* directed at the goal of coming to possess truths, or that the goal of truthfulness is somehow *intrinsic* to the attitude of belief itself. According to the constitutive conception of the relation of belief to truth, belief is not an independent means that we harness to the goal of collecting truths. One might, for example, be able to enlarge one's stock of true beliefs through the motivational or heuristic effects of believing some falsehood *f*. This would not, however, afford (what Baier earlier distinguished as) an epistemic cognitive reason for belief that *f*; it affords instead (what he calls) a practical cognitive reason for being an *f*-believer even if *f* is not actually true. Practical cognitive reasons are instrumental reasons that treat belief simply as if it were "the success-crowned effort of pursuing some end" (RMO, 119). Yet it would be difficult to sustain this picture as the whole story about the relation of belief to truth. For then we would wonder why an individual epistemic agent who treated belief in this instrumental way might have to hide from herself such merely instrumental reasons for believing that *f* in order to bring herself successfully to believe it. (Contrast here the ease and lack of indirection involved if the agent seeks simply to *suppose* or *accept* that *f* for its heuristic or motivational value.) If belief "aims at" truth, it does so "locally" and intrinsically, so to speak, not "globally" and instrumentally. According to the constitutivist doctrine, then, holding a proposition to be actually true in response to its actual truth—and not to be merely a part of a thought-system useful for the goal of identifying truths—is part of the *price of admission* to the specific propositional attitude of belief with respect to that proposition.[21]

Which of these ambiguous readings of "normal aim" does Baier intend? The passages cited above certainly seem to suggest an instrumental rather than constitutive conception of the relation of belief to truth. Further evidence can be found in his brief account of how he would explain Moore's paradox. Baier uses Moore's paradox as a paradigm of a certain kind of irrationality—the irrationality of acting in a self-defeating way.

> To assert that one does not believe what one has just asserted [as in "Moore's paradox"] is to discredit oneself as an asserter and so defeats an important purpose of serious assertion, namely, to be believed by one's interlocutor. But it is absurd to do (in this case, *say*) something which so obviously defeats one's purpose in doing (saying) it that no normal adult can fail to see it. (RMO, 42)

Certainly, it might be difficult to see what assertoric purpose could be advanced by uttering '*p*, but I don't believe it'. But such a purported assertion is more than pragmatically self-defeating; we seem unable to say what *state of mind* such an assertion could accurately express.

An example might help. Suppose you are about to board a commuter flight with a companion you know to be a nervous flyer. The two of you are engaged in an animated, gossipy conversation. You know that he, like other nervous flyers, is especially anxious about flying in smaller aircraft. You also know that he is quite comfortable traveling by train. Let *p* be the proposition: "Commuter flights on smaller aircraft are very safe in comparison with rail travel." You believe that *p*. You believe that your companion does not, though you think he should. You also believe that the English sentence 'Commuter flights on smaller aircraft are very safe in comparison with rail travel' expresses *p*, and that your companion understands English. The normal thing to do in such a situation would be to utter this sentence to your companion. Yet you know that this would be self-defeating. Such an utterance would not bring your companion to believe that *p*, but would instead simply awaken a train of anxieties that have been, for now, forgotten by him in the lively conversation. Indeed, anyone with the least experience of anxiety—any "normal adult"?—could see that this utterance would "obviously be self-defeating" in this context.[22] Yet there is nothing paradoxical about this situation, or unfathomable about your—or his—state of mind.

Note that we could not replicate Moore's paradox fully even by "integrating" these two states of mind in one agent, thereby internalizing this sort of potential pragmatic self-defeat. Perhaps you are the one who suffers flight anxiety, and who is trying to keep his mind off the entire subject of airline safety by engaging your companion in lively conversation or reading a spy novel. You do in fact believe that commuter airplanes are as safe as trains, but you also realize that this sort of statistic has no purchase at all on your phobia when you are aboard a plane taxiing to the runway. For you to bring this belief consciously to mind would trigger anxiety, not keep it down. Fortunately, we humans seem to have self-protective psychological mechanisms that (at least sometimes) enable us to compartmentalize our thought enough to avoid bringing such self-defeating reassurances to consciousness. Your state of mind is surely complex—you believe that *p*, yet in some general way recognize the need to keep p from view at moments like this. For all that, however, your state of mind is familiar enough, and not opaque to us even if it must be less than fully transparent to you for now.

To capture the genuine absurdity revealed in Moore's paradox, we need a nonpragmatic, noninstrumental explanation of what has gone awry. Simply put, once we have convinced ourselves that our interlocutor is attempting to engage in sincere assertion, and moreover is not uttering '*p*, but I believe otherwise' as a fanciful way of saying something like "*p*, but I still have to pinch myself to prove I'm not just dreaming" or "*p*, but it hasn't really sunk in," we would be at a loss to say what state of mind he might be in. The paradoxical utterance violates our understanding of what it is to assert and to believe (unqualifiedly, paradigmatically). A similar kind of difficulty would attach to understanding what state of mind could accurately be expressed as 'I recognize that p is unquestionably refuted, but I unqualifiedly believe it'.[23]

As we noted earlier, it would be a misrepresentation of the constitutive relationship between belief and truth to think of this connection as depending upon the agent's possession of an *independent* desire to get at the truth, a desire toward the satisfaction of which belief is instrumental. Even if agents typically have such a desire, no such desire need be cited in our constitutivist explanation of the paradox. And we were led to suppose that John himself lacks it.

The Master Argument

Perhaps by traveling a somewhat different path, employing a constitutivist as opposed to instrumentalist account of the relation between belief and truth, we have nonetheless reached the destination Baier sought. Ahead of schedule, one might say. For Baier's argument gave us motivation that depends upon "normal" (though still contingent) desires, and the constitutivist approach is independent even of these. The "aim" of truth for belief exerts its shaping effect on belief-formation not by drawing upon a contingent belief-forming purpose or by adding a new element to compete on the plane of desire, but by providing an element in the essential framework for any rational deliberation about what to *believe*. Unlike one's imaginings or supposings, one must represent one's beliefs to oneself as responsive to the truth and to evidence.[24]

We therefore seem to have arrived at a position in which it is possible to give a nonmysterious solution to Baier's "motivation problem," which earlier seemed so baffling. Recall that the problem is to explain how reason could motivate us—even in spite of our strong desires—without its power to do so deriving either from other desires we happen to have or from some peculiar, rational motivational faculty. On the constitutivist account, the motivational efficacy of deeming something to be evidence follows from the nature of the attitude of belief itself: necessarily, someone who *believes* that *p* will be epistemically "moved" when she judges that she has conclusive reason to believe *not-p;* this is so even if she lacks any independent "desire for truth" to which Humean reason is supposedly a slave, or any non-Humean, motivationally potent "Faculty of Reason." In this sense, the regulative connection between belief and truth (or rather, between belief and what-one-takes-to-be-truth-or-to-be-evidence-thereof) is "nonsubjective" or (more awkwardly) "external" or (even?) "categorical."

Yet at the same time this regulative connection seems "hypothetical" or "internal" for any given agent. For it depends upon whether the agent holds the particular cognitive attitude of *belief* toward *p*. If the agent were merely imagining or supposing or accepting that *p,* then making a judgment of conclusive epistemic reason against *p* would not be necessarily motivating or normative for her. Moreover, the norms that regulate these other propositional attitudes permit responsiveness to (what one recognizes to be) subjective desire or purpose in ways that belief does not. One can, for example, pretend or imagine that *p* is true precisely because that is what one desires to do, and do so openly in the face of overwhelming evidence against *p*. Indeed, it might not be possible to *pretend* or *imagine* that *p* if one thinks *p* obviously true. Similarly, one can accept that *p* (roughly, decide to proceed in actual deliberation *as if p* were true) for various instrumental reasons, including the "epistemic" purpose of facilitating the formation of true beliefs in the long run, in full recognition of *p*'s falsity. So, for any given proposition, there is no "necessary aim" of epistemic agents—only the norms or goals that are constitutive of the particular attitude that the agent happens to hold toward that proposition. One can imagine, for example, an agent who initially believes that *p*, but who confronts increasingly hard-to-deny evidence against *p*, and who therefore shifts gradually from belief to acceptance that *p* for instrumental reasons, or merely "on faith." There would be no necessary absurdity or irrationality either in this transition or in self-consciously occupying its resultant cognitive state.

However, one might at this point usher in a *Master Argument*. Even though it clearly is rationally possible for an agent to eschew belief (in favor of some other propositional attitude) with respect to some propositions, it might be impossible to be rational if one eschewed belief altogether. The "nonoptionality" of belief would be demonstrated by showing that both practical and theoretical reason constitutively involve belief. Deliberation about *belief* is, after all, the very subject matter of theoretical reason. To search for regulative principles for other propositional attitudes would simply be to change the subject. And practical reason is concerned not merely with action as such, but with deliberation about how to act. Practical deliberation, as ordinarily understood, requires belief, which, paired with desire or other aims, plays an ineliminable role in guiding choice. So, without belief, we would at best have (what would seem both to the agent and to us as) a pretense or a simulation of deliberation. Suppositions, imaginings, and pretendings can all play a role in deliberation, but very different roles from belief.

If we were to grant that belief is an essential component of both theoretical and practical rationality, then any constitutive "aim" of belief would therefore be partly constitutive of *being rational* itself. We then could strengthen our argument by locating a kind of nonsubjectivity—the "nonoptionality" of truth as an "aim" of agents—in the very concept of being rational. This would yield a Master Argument that could dispense altogether with contingency—e.g., the contingency of being, relative to some propositions, a believer. We could guarantee that genuinely rational agents would, necessarily, possess whatever "aims" belief might have. And that would take us the final step in reaching Baier's goal of discovering nonsubjective reasons that solve (or, rather, escape) the "motivation problem."

Qualifications

The Master Argument, and the constitutivist account of belief it deploys, are a bit too neat for my taste. First, the account sets a rather high standard for belief. To be a believer one need not only represent the world, but also represent one's representation as responsive to the world in a certain way. This "raising of the bar" would seem to rule out the attribution of belief to infants and primates, for example. Perhaps one should refrain from attributing full-fledged belief to such individuals. One does, for example, hear it said that infants do not distinguish what *is* the case from what they *want* to be the case.[25] Still, such a high threshold for belief would unsettle various intuitive views, and might, as we will see, interact unfortunately with the normative relevance of the Master Argument for *Homo sapiens.*

A second qualification is complementary to the first. The Master Argument treats full-fledged belief as conceptually rich and articulated. But even so, it is in other respects very simple as an account of belief. Believing typically comes in degrees, and seldom is all-or-nothing. Moreover, if there is anything fully worthy of the name "belief state," it is a bundle of things. Belief is commonsensically thought to involve a fine-grained representational capacity as well as mental and behavioral dispositions (in appropriate contexts) to use these fine-grained representations to infer, assert, deliberate, and choose, all the while being subject to various kinds of pressures for internal coherence. Moreover, belief involves a constellation of attitudes concerning what one holds oneself accountable for, credits oneself with authority about, and so on. Looking around us, we observe wholehearted belief, where (virtually) all of the elements in the bundle are fully present,[26] but also ambivalence, "bare belief," partial belief, and other varieties of belief-flavored epistemic commitment. We have already found it necessary to introduce second-order epistemic attitudes in order to suggest how belief might have the "freedom" necessary to be a domain of normative self-regulation. Further, questions of belief ascription inevitably bring in holistic considerations that take us beyond the sorts of evidence already discussed. In the case of the incredulous juror, we saw something of belief's multiple, layered nature, and its potential for delamination. Were John to come to see the relevance of the blood-group information, he might be in, or move into, a number of possible doxastic states or mixtures thereof. How best to describe this seems to me to call for much more subtlety than my discussion has thus far exhibited.

We must, after all, be careful to state the constitutive relation structurally and symmetrically. Schematically, John believes that *p* (that Jack is his biological son), but also believes that *q, r, s,* etc. (that he, Jack, and Jack's mother have certain blood types, that the blood-typing is reliable, etc.), which (we have supposed) together afford an all-things-considered conclusive epistemic reason—in Baier's sense, a "dispositive reason"—for believing that *not-p*. As we have noted, there is thus far nothing problematic about our description of John. An epistemic agent can hold conclusive evidence against one of his own beliefs but fail to see its bearing or import. So, let *x* be the proposition that *q, r, s,* etc. together afford conclusive reason to believe that *not-p*. What appears to be untenable—no matter what John's desires—is that John himself occurrently and with full awareness believe *all of x, p, q, r, s,* etc. One or more of these beliefs must, it seems, be given up or kept from simultaneous self-awareness. But the constitutive relationship does nothing to single out *p* as the culprit. It is a structural or coherence condition only.[27] Therefore, what John directively ought to do about his belief in Jack's parentage is unresolved, even given the Master Argument.

Indeed, the truism that belief "aims at" truth, part of the foundation of the Master Argument, does not enable us to say much about the role of truth in normative epistemology. If all that mattered in belief were truth, then one could aim at this very effectively by aiming to believe only tautologies—they are bound to be true. But informativeness, systematicity, explanatoriness, simplicity, generality, fruitfulness, usefulness in guiding deliberation under uncertainty—all of these seem important in rational belief-formation. The truism relating belief to truth does not tell us how we are to trade off informativeness (e.g.) against evidence of truth, or even how we are to think about such trade-offs, except to say that they must somehow be compatible with the truism relating belief and truth.[28]

As a third qualification on the Master Argument, we should note that there is a special obstacle to drawing the conclusion that we have arrived at a directive epistemic 'ought' applicable to John. A structural principle of *incompatibility* is not itself (at least, not yet) a normative principle.[29] Consider John after the conclusive bearing of the evidence has been brought to his attention. It might be tempting to think that the structural principle should be read as follows: Either John will remove the incompatibility from among his beliefs or he will be, to that extent, *irrational* in his beliefs. Now the structural principle does imply that if John is rational in his beliefs, then he will not simultaneously and with full awareness believe all of *x, p, q, r, s,* etc. But recall that the constitutive principle relating belief to truth formulates a precondition for the very state of *belief* itself: someone who cannot see the bearing of the truth of a proposition *P*, or of a conclusive disproof of *P*, on the character or tenability of her attitude toward *P* is not an *irrational* believer-that-*P*, but someone who is not a believer-that-*P* at all. Thus we do not have a principle that gives a norm of rational belief, but rather a precondition of rational and irrational belief alike.

Note, however, that this precondition nonetheless makes room for a distinction between rational and irrational belief. A willingness on the part of the epistemic agent to admit the relevance of evidence to his beliefs is compatible with quite bizarre views on his part about what constitutes relevant evidence, or with unreasonably strong or weak responses on his part to whatever he does count as evidence, or with serious negligence on his part in attending to the need for evidence, or to other strains or inconsistencies in his beliefs. These would all be forms of irrationality, or, at least, defects in rational belief-formation. So normative distinctions in belief-formation can be sustained. But the present point is that the structural principle is a precondition for the application of epistemic norms, not itself a principle of normative epistemology.

Is this distinction merely verbal? Here is a recipe for turning preconditions of a normative discourse into what certainly look like directive 'ought' statements. If 'ought' implies 'can', then, contraposing, 'cannot' implies 'ought not'. If anything worthy of the name *belief* cannot violate the constitutive principle, then regardless of an agent's particular goals or desires, he cannot be under a directive epistemic 'ought' that would violate the constitutive principle.

In John's case, for example, if he *ought* to believe with full awareness that *x, q, r, s,* etc., then it cannot be the case that he also ought to believe with full awareness that *p,* even if this is what he most wants in the world. We therefore do find statements involving a directive epistemic 'ought' which, owing to the constitutive relationship, enjoy a kind of nonsubjectivity or externality. However, such statements clearly reside *within* the realm of epistemic 'ought's and cannot be used to support a detachable, directive 'ought' where none existed before.

This conclusion follows from some very general philosophical considerations. The connection between belief and truth is, according to the argument, truistic, conceptual, perhaps "analytic." An epistemic 'ought' directively applicable to a given individual, on the other hand, would be substantive, "synthetic." It would, in effect, involve a claim that a certain reason exists for an individual, prescribing some possibilities and proscribing others. We can see this by noting that the constitutive principle is quite compatible with an *error theory* about the whole domain of belief-attribution among humans. Some philosophers have argued that, given the nature of belief, psychology might show—perhaps already has shown—that *Homo sapiens* dramatically fail to meet all the conditions for belief-attribution. This might be because of incoherences lurking in the notion of belief itself, or it might be because humans lack certain characteristics necessary to exemplify that notion. Such claims have been controversial to say the least, and it is not any part of my goal here to defend them.[30] I merely wish to note that, if intelligible, these claims raise the possibility that no directive epistemic 'ought's apply to us, despite the truth of the constitutive principle. (Indeed, one might appeal to the constitutive principle in explaining the conditions on belief-attribution that *Homo sapiens* cannot meet.) The principle tells us something about what it would involve to be a believer, but not whether we are believers. It cannot, therefore, create a directive epistemic 'ought' on its own.

More locally—and quite independently of blanket skepticism about belief—when we consider any particular proposition *P*, the constitutive principle will have normative relevance only if what is at stake is *belief* that *P*. Other propositional attitudes have different constitutive principles. Think of Pascal's Wager, as viewed by a benevolent God aware—as I suppose she would have to be—of the constitutive principle. According to this principle, a belief must represent itself as responsive to truth (or evidence of truth), not sheer interest. But Pascal's Wager trades precisely on interest rather than evidence—our interest in avoiding the pain of eternal damnation should it turn out that God exists. If God is benevolent, she presumably would not wish to see either eternal damnation or active self-deception for mortals who are doing their best with *belief*. After all, they can't help it if belief aims at truth. So for those humans who have no ground other than Pascal's Wager on which to make the case for divine existence, a benevolent God would settle for their acceptance of her existence as an act of faith—she would not also demand that they actually believe it.[31]

Conclusion

Following Baier's lead, we turned from practical to theoretical reason in search of a model of nonsubjective yet directive reasons, reasons that would be applicable to an agent regardless of his particular desires or personal goals. This led us, still following Baier, to fix on the regulative role of truth in belief as a paradigm. We have seen that Baier gives his own account of the "unassailability" of truth as "the aim" of belief, but we found this explanation wanting because it offered only instrumental grounds that depended at bottom on (merely) "usual" human goals, and thus fell short of securing the sought-after nonsubjectivity or accounting for the absence of epistemically "cussed" individuals. Baier's account of Moore's paradox came closer to identifying a "nonoptional" constraint, but once again was instrumental in character and failed to account for the difficulty of identifying the state of mind involved. So we parted company with Baier long enough to recognize the *constitutive* character of the connection between truth and belief, though we continued to share with Baier the goal of locating nonsubjective reasons. Happily, the constitutive connection appears to have an independence from any subjective desires or goals of precisely the sort that Baier sought. Thanks to the Master Argument, we even were able to develop this independence into a kind of rational "nonoptionality."

But unhappily for Baier's project, the very security of the constitutive relationship makes it unsuitable as a model for deriving substantive, directive 'ought's of the kind that Baier seeks. For the connection is conceptual. It can tell us whether a given attitude toward some proposition P is a belief, but it cannot tell us—even when extended by the Master Argument—whether we ought to have it. In the end we cannot, without invoking further and more substantive premises, tell John what he ought to believe about Jack's paternity.

This point might seem unsatisfyingly technical. And perhaps it places more weight on (something very like) the analytic/synthetic distinction than it can bear. Suppose we were to insist that there is not enough philosophical heft in the distinction between meaning and doctrine, or form and substance, to pose an immovable barrier to using the conceptual connection between belief and truth as a model for substantive nonsubjective practical reasons. Perhaps one can say nothing more than that it is a matter of how obvious or hard-to-deny certain claims are. So let us ask whether we can find a constitutive principle for action with the same obviousness as the constitutive principle connecting belief and truth.

Philosophers fond of a certain elegant symmetry have been drawn to the view that, just as belief constitutively "aims at" The True, so does action constitutively "aim at" The Good. To deliberatively resolve to act, on such a view, is to represent the end of one's action to oneself as Good. Isn't *that* obvious?

Well, how hard would it be to deny? Not so very hard. After all, we can ask: *What sort* of good is in question? Which or whose? The agent's good? Everyone's good? Impersonal good? Moral good? Aesthetic good? Epistemic good? We didn't seem to have quite this embarrassment of choice in the case of truth. Truth is One. But Good? Each time we plump for one notion of good to fill out the constitutive principle, we seem to sacrifice the principle's obviousness: it does not seem *constitutive* of acting, or of desire, or of having an end, that one "aim at" (or represent one's acts, or desires, or ends, as conducive to) one's own good, or everyone's good, or impersonal good, or moral good, in particular. There is no evident parallel to Moore's paradox here. Nothing is initially unintelligible about my supposing that I am deliberating and acting—that I possess and pursue identifiable desires or ends in light of my beliefs—even if I self-consciously pay heed only to a goal not on this list.

Now a defender of the view that action constitutively aims at the Good would no doubt claim, following Moore himself, that this talk of various "goods" is spurious. There is but one Good, and all these other goods are mere applications of that notion. "Personal good" could only be that which it is Good that I do or receive; "aesthetic good" could only be that which it is Good that I appreciate; and so on. If this view could be sustained, it would indeed afford the parallel needed to the constitutive role of truth in belief. (It would carry us just as far—which, given the argument of this paper, is not far enough—in the direction of nonsubjective directive practical 'ought's.)

But Baier, as I understand him, rejects this view of Good and the parallel it would afford. Instead, he offers his own candidate for filling the constitutive bill. He suggests that action aims, not at a particular substantive goal, but rather at realizing "a conception of the good life for oneself free of . . . internal flaws" (RMO, 144). There certainly is a sense in which having an end involves representing something to oneself in a favorable light. Yet as Baier himself notes, his own candidate appears plausible only once we have restricted attention to (what he calls) "self-anchored reasons," and there is no apparent rational necessity about an agent's restricting her deliberation to the "self-anchored," or even taking this as part of her goal in a given action. Moreover, a conception of a good life free of internal flaws seems too conceptually rich, temporally extended, and ambitious in its demands of coherence to be anything that an agent *must* act on in order to be a possessor of ends or a performer of acts at all.[32] It hardly seems paradoxical for someone self-consciously to act on the basis of desires that he would deny to be part of a conception of the good life for him, free of internal flaws.

Is there another, less exclusionary or demanding—and therefore harder-to-deny—candidate for a constitutive principle of action? And, importantly for Baier's overall project, could this principle serve to underwrite morality? Consideration of these questions is beyond the scope of the present paper, but a certain dialectic seems inevitable. The more plainly a principle is truistic or hard-to-deny (such as the belief-truth connection), the less evident that anything like morality as a way of life could follow from it. This we can say without recourse to an analytic/synthetic distinction. For morality asks nontrivial things of us, and among the many alternate lives that strike us as not altogether without attraction we find notable variation in the role played by morality. Any seeming truism that could be shown to have so powerful an implication as that we should follow the demands of morality in our lives, whatever our fondest desires, would quickly lose its status as a seeming truism.

Baier observes that it does not appear to be a simple mistake to seek reasons to be moral, or even to ask what can be said in favor of a life we would identify as "rational" (RMO, 50). These are for Baier substantive questions, not to be dismissed with the invocation of a phrase or a concept. Surely, this is right. If what we seek is an understanding of the components or commitments of the discourse of theoretical or practical reason, then truistic, hard-to-deny, constitutive relations will afford us essential insight. If what we seek is an answer to the question "What to think?" or "What to do?" or (to use Baier's own well-chosen phrase) "What to make of our lives?" then we must engage in a broader and more controversial sort of discussion. That we have good reason, all things considered, to be moral might be the truth, but it is unlikely to be a truism, scarcely intelligible to deny. If it is hard to deny, that will be in a different and ultimately more important sense—the sense in which human needs, interests, circumstances, meanings, and commitments are hard to deny.

University of Michigan

Notes

1. Portions of this paper have been presented at the University of Colorado, the University of Toronto, Michigan State University, the University of Illinois at Chicago, and the University of Notre Dame. I am grateful to those present, and especially to my fellow participants in the "Baierfest" at the University of Pittsburgh, for comments and criticisms. My colleagues at the University of Michigan—in particular Stephen Darwall, William K. Frankena, Allan Gibbard, and David Velleman—have furnished much helpful conversation. In correspondence, Christian Piller provided searching comments, and Kurt Baier proved, as always, both personally gracious and philosophically penetrating. I am especially grateful to Baier for allowing me to see his unpublished Carus Lectures and portions of the manuscript of his book, *The Rational and the Moral Order.*

2. Is there a possibility that they might turn out to be something less—might there be no reasons at all? That question will briefly be considered in the concluding sections of this paper.

3. The reasons in question are *pro tanto,* not necessarily conclusive. In what follows, I will omit this qualification when speaking of reasons not assumed to be conclusive. I have included 'personal goals' as well as 'desires' in this characterization of nonsubjective reasons out of respect for the common-sense usage in which not all individual aims are called 'desires'. But common sense is equivocal about this, and I will sometimes below just speak of desires. See below for some further, equally irresolute discussion.

4. I prefer the term 'theoretical' to Baier's term 'cognitive' because the latter carries the suggestion that practical reasons are in some sense essentially not cognitive reasons. However, I will use both terms interchangeably in what follows.

5. To be sure, we can cite an explanatory reason as part of a justification: "Why does he think that Enfeld received money from Gus?"—"Because he was there and saw it." Indeed, on some views of normative epistemology, explanatory reasons have the central role in justification. Such views need not, however, think that the *concept* of a justificatory reason simply reduces to that of an explanatory reason. It is enough if some explanations are justifications.

6. 'Internalism' with a capital 'I' will be used herein to designate this particular view, as glossed by Baier. When written below with a small 'i', 'internalism' will be used more generically. A notable feature of Baier's gloss is that he refers broadly to

motivation rather than specifically to *desire,* even though this latter category has been of special interest to internalists. At various points in what follows we will find it important to distinguish desire from other sources of motivation, and this will somewhat complicate the presentation.

7. Richard Gale, in particular, urged me to take this question to heart.

8. Arnold Lobel, *Fables* (1980), 16.

9. For a considerably stronger view about the relation of deciding to believe and deciding to act, see J. David Velleman, *Practical Reflection* (1989).

10. Baier, too, is concerned to argue that there is room for appropriate kinds of voluntary action in the regulation of belief: "We may not always believe what corresponds most closely to what is recommended by what we believe we have the best reason to believe, but we can work on it." (RMO, 90) Also see the entry "Faith," in Voltaire's *Philosophical Dictionary. Plus ca change,* . . .

11. Biological son, that is. Hereafter, this qualification will be understood.

12. This is by no means to endorse any diminution of John's interest in Jack on the basis of Jack's paternity. What is at issue is simply whether John has a particular desire (defensible or not) that might better be served by responding more appropriately to the evidence about Jack.

13. Cf. Thomas Nagel on "motivated desire," in *The Possibility of Altruism* (1970).

14. However, this undemanding usage often occurs in the company of another thought, which does threaten to trivialize our discussion, namely, the thought that whenever someone does what he desires (in the undemanding sense), he is acting "only for the sake of satisfying his own desires." On this view, when Mirko yields his place on the last plane he is doing so for the sake of self-gratification, nothing more. This view is not to my mind commonsensical, but rather a proto-philosophical effort to debunk common-sense thought. It confuses a truism about desire—that it matters to us whether our own desires are met—with a substantive thesis about what we desire. Far from being a feature of the "Humean model," this substantive thesis is one Hume specifically warned us to avoid.

15. This distinction is due to Stephen Darwall. See his *Impartial Reason* (1983) for discussion.

16. Put in third-person form, whenever *A* judges that there is a directive reason for *X* to *F, A* is in some (perhaps hypothetical or indirect) way motivated in favor of *X's F*-ing.

17. Baier does make a similar stipulation in the case of the cussed *practical* agent: "[S]uch a person may also believe on some occasion that he has requiring reason, *other things equal,* to do a certain thing and *no overruling reason not to do it,* yet intend, without any regret, not to follow this unopposed requiring reason. But then he is not to any degree motivated to follow that reason. . . . Of course, this inference is sound only if he is not prevented and does not act in the grip of desire. To clinch the point at issue here, we can simply postulate that we are speaking only of such occasions. For our question concerns only the conceptual possibility (not

the probability or frequency) of someone's acknowledging that he has a practical reason to do something and is yet not motivated in the least to act in accordance with it." (RMO, 117; his emphasis) Whether one actually can "postulate" this conceptual possibility in the practical case is not the issue here. Rather, the issue is whether, since Baier believes one can, this same sort of conceptual possibility can be "postulated" in the case of epistemic reasons.

18. Baier himself discusses Moore's paradox briefly (RMO, 41–42), though we will see below that he gives it a different explanation from the one I will be suggesting here.

19. For related discussion, see my "Truth, Reason, and the Regulation of Belief," *Philosophical Issues* (forthcoming). David Velleman pursues a similar line of thought, though toward a different conclusion, in "The Possibility of Practical Reason" (unpublished). Since writing this I have learned from Baier that he discusses further the relation of truth to belief in his early paper "Decisions and Descriptions" (Baier 3). Herein I will confine my discussion to *The Rational and the Moral Order.*

20. During the ellipsis in this passage, Baier writes: "[N]evertheless, truth is not dethroned as the ground of cognitive reasons just because there are (or at any rate may be) special cases in which its claim on us is superseded by another." (RMO, 119–20) Although I will try in what follows to explain why truth is indeed an ultimate and un-"dethronable" ground of belief, I will not claim that this shows that truth as a ground can be "superseded" or "set aside" as a "target" in belief.

21. For further discussion of some ramifications of this doctrine for epistemology, again see Railton, "Truth, Reason, and the Regulation of Belief."

22. Is 'p, but I believe otherwise' pragmatically self-defeating in *all* contexts, and therefore in principle different from the self-defeating remark about aircraft safety? If the question really is one of *pragmatic* self-defeat, then the answer must be no. One can certainly imagine contexts in which one's aim is to make a remark that will flummox one's listeners, or (sincerely and truthfully) bring them to believe that one is deeply confused.

23. Once again, we need to distinguish one's "sense of conviction" from one's higher-order epistemic commitments. I might find myself with unshakable faith that *p*, even though I recognize that *not-p* is demonstrably the implication of evidence I cannot dispute. What is most relevant in the present context is not whether one can overcome faith, but whether, insofar as belief rather than faith is at issue, one could fully recognize conclusive evidence against *p* while finding that this had no doxastic "motivational" effect—even if no more than the effect of inducing a defensive reaction.

24. This does not entail, of course, that one's beliefs must actually *be* responsive to truth or evidence.

25. Although I myself have never quite understood this claim, perhaps it could be seen as reflecting an infant's lack of the conceptual or linguistic resources to generate the self-representations necessary to distinguish belief as a propositional atti-

tude from wishing or wanting.

26. At least, we observe this if the bundle is wholly (or very nearly) coherent and actually realizable by *Homo sapiens*. Some skeptics about belief have, notoriously, doubted this. Anti-skeptics have replied that no claim about what is present in the bundle could possibly be so compelling that, were we to find that typical *Homo sapiens* fail to realize it, we would feel compelled to adopt skepticism about belief rather than skepticism about the claim concerning what is in the bundle.

Considerations such as these raise questions about bald claims concerning "constitutive principles" or "conceptual truths." By and large, I've been inclined to think that we do well in philosophy not to hang a great deal on such bald claims. Here, however, I am investigating the prospects of a strategy—potentially friendly to Baier's project, though different from his in modality—which seems best presented via the notion of a constitutive principle.

27. In the example, John is said to have no current information that would place *q, r, s,* etc. in doubt. But perhaps he should take the "unbelievability" of *not-p* as grounds enough for throwing *q, r, s,* etc., into doubt, no matter what else the current evidence holds.

Let us also set aside the related concern that we simply cannot fully characterize what it is for an agent to *recognize* that *q, r, s,* etc., afford dispositive reason to believe *not-p* by attributing to the agent belief in another proposition *x*. This characterization could launch a painful regress. We can, however, allow the "*x*-proposition" to stand in for such recognition in the present setting without untoward consequences for the present point.

These two points are but different ways of suggesting how problematic the notion of a genuinely conclusive—dispositive—epistemic reason is.

28. An example of the invocation of such a truism is to be found in Michael Friedman's criticism of theories of confirmation that give a central role to various values in theory choice without suggesting how they might be compatible with the "aim" of truth. See his "Truth and Confirmation" (1979).

29. I am grateful here to Shelly Kagan for raising a related question about an earlier version of this paper.

30. If the Master Argument holds water, then it would follow from this sort of skepticism about belief that humans also are not rational beings. There would be a silver lining: We would never have to suffer the indignity of considering reasons to believe this sort of error theory!

31. Less theologically, some philosophers have argued that the proper stance of scientists toward their theories is acceptance rather than belief. See Bas van Fraassen, *The Scientific Image* (1980).

32. For example, Baier writes: "[O]ur construction of a conception of the good life for ourselves is an attempt to imagine what sort of life would fulfill us, what ultimate aims that would involve and how we can go about attaining them." (RMO, 152–53)

The Grip of Immorality: Child Abuse and Moral Failure

7

Laurence Thomas

If seeing is a matter of believing, believing is certainly not always a matter of doing. Far too often people fail to do what they know that they should do. It seems, in fact, that people can simply be in the grip of wrongdoing: they have the cognitive recognition that they are doing what is morally wrong, but this has little or no motivational import in their lives. Those who commit child sexual abuse are regarded as a paradigm example of individuals who are in the grip of immorality.[1] In general child sexual abuse is quite unlike many other moral wrongs, including murder, in that rarely does anyone attempt to justify such abuse by appeal to nobler ends. For example, many people are prepared to say that if the only way Hitler could have been stopped is by murder, then they would have been prepared to murder him. With rare exception, it is manifestly clear to (the nonambivalent) child sexual abusers that child sexual abuse is morally wrong, and that they cannot possibility justify their action by an appeal to nobler ends. For contrast, I note here a difference between child sexual abuse and child physical abuse. To be sure, there are manifestly clear cases of physical abuse alone. It suffices to point out, however, that although we are prepared to allow that a person could fail to realize or fully appreciate that the punishment which is being meted out to a child is too harsh, we are not prepared to allow that an adult could fail to realize that her or his behavior towards a child is sexual. In these remarks, I am merely distinguishing between sexual child abuse and physical child abuse rather than maintaining that one is worse than the other. But the generally salient feature of child sexual abuse is the reason why I have focused specifically upon child sexual abuse rather than child physical abuse generally.

A further difference worth mentioning is that whereas we can often make sense of how people are moved to do many wrongs, including murder, without thereby excusing the person, child sexual abuse often astounds in this regard; for it seems to require an unimaginable insensitivity to the pain that is being caused to a manifestly innocent human being, as I take any infant or very young child to be. Not only that, while not all victims of child abuse become child abusers themselves, the percentage of abusers who themselves have been abused is extremely high. Again, it seems unimaginable that a person could cause a manifestly innocent human being the pain of sexual abuse when, in the past, the very person causing the pain had to endure such grotesque harm himself. In view of these considerations, one might suppose that if anyone is in the grip of immorality, it is the child abuser who was also a victim of such abuse. In a most poignant way, then, the sexually abused child sexual abuser (SACSA), illustrates the possibility of knowing the good and doing the bad, where doing the bad is a matter of being in the grip of immorality. So to be more precise: My focus in this essay shall be adults who were victims of child sexual abuse and who unambiguously take themselves to have been egregiously wronged morally but who nonetheless go on to sexually abuse children—their own children, in particular. And I am assuming that because such individuals unambiguously take themselves to have been morally wronged, it is unambiguously clear to them that their own acts of child abuse are wrong. This specificity clearly limits the scope of what I hope to explain in this essay. There are child abusers who do not abuse their own children; and there are child abusers who are ambivalent about the wrongfulness of such behavior. The arguments of this essay shall not address such individuals. Just so, the philosophical and moral significance of the project is not affected at all, since the issue of knowing the good and doing the bad still arises in a most poignant way for the class of individuals I wish to consider.

Perhaps child abuse can be subsumed under the phenomenon of weakness of will, and there is no need to deny that here. Even so, I trust that all will agree that child abuse deserves special attention. Precisely what needs explaining, surely, is how a person could be tempted to do such a thing. For, clearly, child abuse cannot be modeled on the order of the temptation to tell a lie for the sake of advancing one's interest or the temptation to satisfy one's taste buds with a food item that is inimical to one's health. These things may be morally wrong or contrary to one's self-interest, but neither the behavior nor the desire that gives rise to it would be regarded as warped. And it is the profound warpedness of the child sexual abuser's sexual desire that seems so unimaginable to us. How could a person come to have such a desire? How could a person act on it?

In what follows, I want to offer an answer to these two questions. My aim is to explain how sexual abuse could occur in the lives of those who themselves have been a victim sexual abuse. Needless to say, I want neither to justify nor excuse their behavior.

At this juncture one may naturally ask: How does Kurt Baier's work bear upon the objective of this essay? Well, the answer is quite simple. A satisfactory theory of morality must come to terms with people whose lives are in the grip of wrong doing; and with regard to the objective of this essay, I believe that some of the resources for doing so are to be found in Kurt Baier's work *The Rational and the Moral Order.* So, by examining the case of sexually abused child sexual abusers, I shall be concerned to extend rather than to criticize his views. Of course, whether Kurt Baier shall find this preferable to being criticized depends on where, in the end, my extension of his views places him. One can, after all, be uncomfortable with what is clearly meant as a friendly employment of one's views. However, I have no reason to suspect that Baier shall have occasion to worry in this regard. What is more, if my extension of his views is satisfactory, then there is a greater affinity between the writings, or at least the present philosophical thought, of Kurt Baier and Annette Baier than many, perhaps even they themselves, might be inclined to suppose. I shall not argue the case here though.

I begin by collecting several of the main claims from Baier's work which are the springboard for my argument.

I

There are four claims in *The Rational and the Moral Order* to which I should like to draw attention. They are as follows:

1. Reason is a social concept.
2. There can be unsatisfactory preferences, meaning that their satisfaction does not guarantee fulfillment.
3. A conception of the good life can be sound or unsound.
4. Consistency in life does not entail a rational life.

Regarding claim 2, a brief clarificatory remark is in order. Baier's actual word is 'tastes' instead of 'preferences'. As far as I can see, though, what he says regarding tastes applies *tout court* to preferences; and in general he does have plenty to say about preferences. Also, I shall use 'preferences' and 'aims' interchangeably throughout.

At times, I think that Kurt Baier himself does not appreciate just how radical these four claims make him out to be. While, on the one hand, Baier maintains that the notion of reasonableness cannot be understood in the absence of a social context (claim 1); he denies, on the other, that anything counts as reasonableness, just so long as it satisfies the formal constraints of rationality—consistency, transitivity, and the like (claims 2–4). This distinguishes Kurt Baier's latest work from the writings of David Gauthier who in *Morals by Agreement* (1986) maintains that one's preferences are reasonable, whatever they might be, including cutting off one's own finger, just so long as they satisfy the formal conditions of rationality. This would also seem to distinguish Baier from the recent writings of John Rawls who in *Political Liberalism* (1993) likewise has difficulty with the possibility of there being a conception of the good that is not reducible without remainder to the preferences of persons. With Rawls's idea of overlapping consensus, the good turns out to be very nearly the bare minimum that people can agree upon, taking their preference structure as given. By contrast, one might have thought that in *A Theory of Justice* (1971) Rawls sought to give a normative backdrop against which the preferences of persons could be assessed as reasonable or unreasonable; for in that work (especially part 3), human psychology seems to have been very much a guiding force in Rawls's thought.

Part of the significant contribution to moral philosophy of Kurt Baier's thought, as it has been developed in *The Rational and the Moral Order,* is the recognition that there is a social conception of reasonableness that goes beyond the formal constraints of rationality. On the one hand, a person's preferences can be quite appropriate or inappropriate, though not required by or in violation of the constraints of rationality. On the other, there is an indissoluble connection between the preferences that turn out to be reasonable and the character of the social context in which individuals find themselves. Thus, on Baier's view, it is reasonable to have (and unreasonable not to have) a preference for limited altruistic moral principles in a society in which very nearly everyone else has such a preference; and it is reasonable to have (and unreasonable not to have) a preference for an essentially egoistic preference structure in a society in which very nearly everyone else has such a preference. So, if I understand Baier's position correctly, the Good (limited altruism) and the Bad (egoism) are self-perpetuating; for in a morally good society, it will always be reasonable for people to have preferences that, in fact, turn out to sustain that society as a morally good society; whereas in a morally bad society, it will always be reasonable for people to have preferences that, in fact, sustain that society as a morally bad one. A good society begets good citizens; a bad society begets bad ones.

It may be objected that Baier is mistaken, because there is an asymmetry between the Good and the Bad in that while a non-good social context will, indeed, perpetuate itself, a good one will not, since a good social context provides a very fertile environment for doing what is bad. After all, it is far easier to commit theft, say, in a social environment where in general this is not expected, and few precautions against theft are taken, than it is in a social environment in which it is understood that everything must be kept under lock and key because otherwise it will be stolen. Well, I believe that Baier is right, though I cannot argue the case at length here. Suffice it to say that one needs to be mindful of the nature of human beings and the ways in which dispositions are reinforced by the environment. In a morally good environment, a morally good disposition is reinforced—not weakened. This is true whether we have one individual or one + N individuals, regardless of the size of N. To suppose otherwise, as with game-theoretic considerations, is to assume a much more pliable conception of the self than is warranted by human psychology.

In any case, Baier's position—that it is reasonable to have (and unreasonable not to have) a preference for limited altruistic moral principles in a society in which very nearly everyone else has such a preference—underscores the significance which he attaches to the social reality in which humans find themselves. For Baier does not hold that this or that set of preferences is reasonable to have because, counterfactually, they would have been chosen by persons in this or that context. Rather, his position is that if all the aspects of a morally good society (family, school, the legal system, and so on) are operating as they should, then as a matter of fact it will be reasonable to have (and unreasonable not to have) a preference for limited altruism. Notice that on this conception of morality, immoral behavior turns out to be far less numinous. Many hold that rationality—as manifested in a Rawlsian original position, or as the conclusion of Gauthier-type bargaining, or in a Kantian categorical imperative—has a claim upon our acting morally. If true, then nothing turns out to be more mysterious than that immorality abounds. Of course, one can always save moral face by noting that the extent to which immorality abounds shows just how irrational people are. But it goes without saying that this move serves only to persuade the already convinced. By contrast, what is absolutely remarkable about the recent development in Baier's moral thought is that it actually allows for a nonmysterious answer to why there is immoral behavior, namely that not all has gone as it should have gone in a person's social development. This could mean either that the society itself is basically immoral or that some fundamental aspect of social development is misdirected, although society itself is basically moral. The latter can occur either at the societal level (for instance, a widespread practice in elementary school could have deleterious effects upon the developing moral children) or at the individual level, with varying degrees of frequency.

Now, although Baier does not introduce the idea of a warped preference structure, many things he does say suggest it. For with claim 2, he allows that the fulfillment of preferences does not guarantee satisfaction. And he is certainly committed to the idea that preferences which satisfy the formal conditions of rationality may nonetheless be unreasonable. Any account of unreasonableness must allow that the notion admits of degrees. A warped preference structure, then, represents an extreme form of unreasonableness that bespeaks a deficiency of the self. Whether or not fulfillment generates satisfaction, only a person who is deficient would have or seek the fulfillment of warped preferences. In any society, some preferences will not just be unreasonable: they will be warped. The notion of the warped as a moral category is helpful.

I hold that if moral philosophy is to be meaningful in the world in which we live, it shall have to make sense of that world, including the immorality that occurs within it. The problem of immorality cannot be swept under the rug of rationality. In this sense, *The Rational and the Moral Order* is a breakthrough. In the sections which follow I shall return to the problem with which I opened this essay, namely that of sexually abused child sexual abusers. I hope that the discussion which follows is an illustration of the progress that can be made when moral philosophers wrestle with the reality of things that have gone wrong in society. Child abuse can occur in any society, including a basically moral one. But, taking my cue from Baier, at least as I have interpreted him, if child abuse occurs in a basically moral society, then something has gone wrong at an individual level. If some progress can be made in explaining what has gone wrong, then a measure of credence will have been lent to the novel approach which Baier has put forth in *The Rational and the Moral Order.* In the final section, I shall return to Baier's work; for a problem that arises in discussing sexually abused child sexual abusers (SACSAs) is foreshadowed by his theory. Presumably, no explanation of child sexual abuse will justify such behavior. However, there is the issue of whether such an explanation turns out to excuse in any way. In returning to Baier's work, I take up this matter.

II

As I have remarked, if there are any who most starkly illustrate the possibility of knowing the good and doing the bad, it is adults who were victims of child sexual abuse and who take themselves to have been egregiously wronged but who nonetheless go on to sexually abuse children, especially their own children. My focus will be child sexual abuse which occurs in the scope of the immediate family, and which is committed by a parent (or parental surrogate) against a child, where a two-parent model is assumed. I am thus interested in child sexual abuse involving a betrayal of the child's trust in its parents. An adult friend of the family who regularly visits is not, on that account alone, a parental surrogate, especially if the child has loving parents. Accordingly, unless either or both parents know about it and do nothing, sexual abuse by such a friend will not involve a betrayal of the child's trust in its parents, but the family friend, instead. Thus, I take trust of parents (or parental surrogates) to be absolutely foundational. A final qualification is that I am here interested in cases of sustained child abuse. This is not because I take a single instance to be insignificant, as there is no such thing as insignificant child sexual abuse, but because there are important patterns of behavior that are most salient in cases of sustained child abuse. What is more, a single instance does not make a pattern.

To simplify matters, I shall assume throughout that the adult perpetrator is a male—the father figure, and that the other adult in the family is a female—the mother figure. This is meant neither to offend men nor to deny that women are capable of the abominable behavior of child sexual abuse. Rather, the simplifying assumption accords well with the general pattern in Western culture, and so provides a suitably non-sexist explanation for the pattern of gender reference that I shall use. I shall further assume that the abuse occurs in the home, and that the victim is a child who is very early on in the formative stages of his development.

With the kind of sexual child abuse cases I am considering, one understandably asks: How could a person so clearly recognize the profound wrong here, and yet commit it? How in this instance could the moral truth fail to motivate? To answer this question it will be most helpful to look at the failure of reason to motivate in a quite different context, where the failure does not give rise to wrongdoing. Although an individual is generally open to criticism for failing to act in accordance with reason this need not be so. Victims of rape are most instructive in this regard.

It is well-known that immediately following the tragedy of rape, a victim—say, Naomi—may feel especially uncomfortable with being supportively hugged or, for that matter, merely supportively touched by her close males friends—say, Richard and James—though the three of them have been longstanding friends for years and there have been many physical (but nonsexual) displays of affection between her and them. The problem here need not be that Naomi harbors deep and unconscious suspicions concerning the motives of her close male friends because at heart she believes that no male is above suspicion. Nor need it be that the victim no longer wishes to continue interacting with her close male friends in the affectionate manner that has long since been characteristic of their relationship—for she does. Rather, she finds that much to her dismay she cannot do so without experiencing great emotional pain; and this she laments. By her very own lights, her physical distancing is at odds with the way in which she believes that she should be acting given her rational assessment of things thoroughly grounded in her experience with Richard and James. Hence, we have a clear case where two very secure beliefs—namely that Richard and James are longstanding close friends of hers; and that these males are not in any way would-be-rapists—fail to have the motivational import they should have in terms of social interaction. (Though while I have self-consciously cast the victim as female, we do not have a gender-linked phenomenon here. It is all too obvious, I trust, that a male victim of male rape could also experience quite parallel difficulties with men.)

It is perhaps tempting to suppose that Naomi's not wanting to be touched by Richard and James can be straightaway explained by the phenomenon of associative pain, as I shall say. She was raped by a man; Richard and James are men; and that association is simply too painful for her. Richard and James just have the misfortune of being in the wrong gender category. Well, though I hardly want to deny either the reality of associative pain, or that it can have great force, nevertheless I want to resist the view that associative pain suffices as an explanation for Naomi's reaction to Richard and James, where the idea is that their being an instance of the very category of which her rapist is an instance, namely the category of males, suffices to cause her pain.

Consider. Suppose that a Jew or a black is called a "kike" or "nigger" by a group of white non-Jews. While that person—call her Rebecca—could be pained by the presence of all such whites, it is perfectly possible that she is capable of distinguishing between white non-Jews who despise people like her and white non-Jews who do not, especially if some of her best friends are white non-Jews. We do expect people to be able to distinguish between the good and the bad among an ethnic group, especially when they have deep friendships among members of that group, as Rebecca does. Accordingly, we would not for a moment expect her to regard all of her white non-Jewish friends as being as morally base as those who hurled the ethnic slur at her, citing associative pain as an explanation. Even without this example the argument from associative pain, pure and simple, is problematic. For suppose that Naomi knows that both Richard and James are homosexual men in their thirties, and that they have been self-identified as homosexuals since their teenage years. Well, it is obvious that they cannot be readily associated with men who rape women—not by Naomi or anyone else who knows them. Whatever anyone might mean in talking about the way men generally treat women, homosexual men will not be quite what they have in mind. I do not suppose, however, that it is only in the case of homosexual men that, as an explanation, associative pain misses the mark.

The problem with the argument from associative pain is that it does not make sense of Naomi's reaction to James and Richard, because it fails to explain why she is not moved by a substantial and quite evident difference precisely where there is one. After all, it is James and Richard. They are not just any two men; nor are they place-holders for every male who turns out to be sympathetic to the plight of women. They are her dear friends about whom she harbors no suspicions. Thus, to explain her reaction to them by calling attention to the reasonableness of such a reaction towards men in general, by way of associative pain, is rather like explaining that the reason why one will not lend $100 to a longstanding friend is that one does not lend money to strangers. There can be very good reasons for not lending $100 to a longstanding friend; but the mere fact that one does not lend money to strangers cannot be one of them. To be sure, an explanation can equally apply to both the particular and the general. Suppose that $100 is all the money that the person has to her name. Where we must be careful, though, is in supposing that a general explanation applies to all particular cases. Precisely what we want to understand in the Naomi case is why associative pain operates with respect to Richard and James; and that requires an explanation other than an appeal to associative pain.

I assume, then, that we want to be able to make sense of Naomi's not wanting to be touched by her dear friends Richard and James without letting associative pain be either the sole or primary explanation. We want an explanation that does two things. For one thing, Naomi's response in this instance should turn out to be perfectly understandable and not in anyway open to criticism. For another, it should nonetheless turn out that she does not act in accordance with reason, in that her behavior with her male friends Richard and James does not accord with her own rational assessment of them, as given by her experience with them. I shall attempt such an explanation in what follows.

Definitive of rape, I believe, is a certain kind of psychological scar, which is that of suffering a profound sense of diminished personal agency.[2] The idea of a sense of personal agency is absolutely central to being an adult, and at least partially captures the force of 'my' in 'my body'.[3] I shall understand this notion to mean the sense that one has a great deal of control over things that happen to one's body in the course of social interaction with others. To have a sense of personal agency is to have the conviction that, well beyond cases of sheer bodily harm, there are things which a person ought not, and so will not, do to or with one's body, or observe one's doing with one's body, without one's consent. Accordingly, the notion of a sense of personal agency is a normative one. Children are born without a sense of personal agency, but acquire it under favorable conditions in their adult familial environment.

Under favorable conditions, children begin life with rudimentary bodily care being routinely performed on their behalf by others. Then the effort of children to perform routine bodily care is overseen by others, with occasional assistance being offered. Then there is mere monitoring with admonishments. Finally, of course, children are left to do such things on their own, even though it may be necessary to order them to do so. The fourteen-year-old is told to take a shower, not given one. As normal and as ordinary as it may seem for parents to let their child have complete control over the cleaning of its own body, the fact of the matter is that by doing so parents underwrite their child's sense of personal agency. Parents thereby establish that there are boundaries which not even an individual's provider should cross. If all goes well, these boundaries are respected by others from one social context to the next. Naturally, this serves to reinforce the child's sense of personal agency, with the result that the child reaches adulthood with a well-developed sense of personal agency, one that continues to be affirmed if all goes well. If all goes well, these boundaries are so respected that we may take our sense of personal agency for granted. But that which we take for granted can be of major importance.

Needless to say, being able to trust others is crucial to the flowering of a well-developed sense of personal agency. It is not just that parents no longer bathe their fourteen-year-old, but that the teenager can trust his parents not to do so; for he believes that they will not bathe him or monitor him as he attends to other bodily functions, although they could impose upon him in this way with impunity. The same holds for the teenager's belief with respect to others, albeit to varying degrees of stringency. That having a sense of personal agency involves trust supports the observation that a sense of personal agency is normative in character, since trust is, itself, a normative notion.

The very trauma of rape can be located in the pain that comes when one's sense of personal agency has been radically diminished, which entails that the person's trust has been profoundly violated. For though rape is an act of violence, the pain of rape is not conceptually tied to having suffered bodily injury such as a broken arm or leg. One need not endure a single physical scar. Because of the spiritual and personal significance attached to the sex act when it is freely engaged in, the act is in many ways the ultimate expression of personal agency, which makes consent of paramount importance.[4] *Thus, with rape what happens is that the proper normative structure of one's environment shifts against one at a most fundamental level in that one's consent has been made irrelevant regarding one's experiencing the act of sex, something for which there can be neither excuse nor normative justification.* To be sure, there are a multitude of ways in which people can be harmed, which do not admit of excuse or justification either, including ways involving one's body. But only with the act of sex is the difference between the morally good and the morally bad so indissolubly tied to consent alone, where the mere absence of consent qualitatively changes the experience for the worse. Consequently, the act of rape shakes the victim's sense of personal agency at its very core, regardless of how well-developed that sense might be. Rape inevitably does so momentarily; sometimes it does so permanently. These things are true whether the victim is female or male.

Now, when a person's sense of personal agency is shaken at its very core, the individual suffers a radical diminution of the self, as a result of which the person has enormous emotional difficulty making assessments that presuppose a confidence in her ability either to distinguish adequately the good from the bad or to appreciate adequately the resources that remain well within control, the two being related of course. Thus, what has been severely truncated is the person's sense of her powers of effective assessment, as we might say. Accordingly, the innocent can seem threatening and otherwise mundane tasks in life can seem overwhelming. For the issue is not about performing tasks per se, but responding to the reality that the *proper* normative structure of one's environment has been torn asunder at a most profound level. The issue is about being effective in a context where that is so. Repairing the rent in the *proper* normative structure of a life is not like repairing the damage done to a building that is quite salvageable. That is a matter of performing a finite series of relatively well-defined tasks: mortar here; brick there; and so on. There is no issue as to whether the mortar and bricks will behave as they are supposed to behave; whereas precisely the issue with a rape victim is whether she has any reason, given the experience of rape, to believe that people, especially men, will again behave as they ought to.

Herein lies the cognitive dimension that comes with having a severely diminished sense of personal agency as it involves rape. Beliefs fail to have their cognitive import because one has such a severely truncated sense of one's powers of effective assessment, owing to the fissure in the *proper* normative structure of one's environment. The sense that one's powers of effective assessment have been so severely impaired is fundamentally different from experiencing associative pain. Suppose a parent lost her child to a vicious bulldog attack. Understandably, seeing any bulldog might very well result in considerable associative pain. Yet, there need not ever be any question of her powers of effective assessment having been diminished.

Needless to say, it is because of the personal and spiritual significance that is attached to the sex act that rape so radically diminishes a person's sense of personal agency. Most other acts regarding the body do not begin to have the same timbre of spiritual and personal significance as the sex act. To be sure, most of us would certainly resent it if others took it upon themselves to force us to take a shower. But suppose that forcing us to take a shower is all they did, and we were absolutely convinced that they had no intentions of doing anything else—not even observing us; hence, the shower is entirely private. It is very unlikely that we would feel the same sense of violation that is occasioned by rape. This is because, as things stand in Western culture, very little spiritual and personal significance is attached to showering alone. Of course, consent remains important because, after all, it is one's body. However, there is no reason to hold that we regard everything that we do with our body as having the same level of significance. Thus, if there were such a mode of behavior, called pure (as opposed to wicked) hydromania, which we could straightforwardly recognize as such, it is difficult imagine people fearing a pure hydromaniac, however annoying they might find the individual's interruption of their lives.

So, the problem with Richard and James for Naomi is not just that they are men, for men do differ quite substantially among one another, but that the rape so impaired her sense of her powers of effective assessment that *what she truly believes about them, her knowledge that they are trustworthy, fails to yield* the usual confidence accompanying feelings and behavior that has been par for the course. Her beliefs about them fail to have the appropriate cognitive import. And that distinguishes her reaction towards them from her reaction towards men in general, since her behavior towards men in general is not at odds with a like set of beliefs. Indeed, her reaction towards Richard and James helps her to appreciate just how deeply her sense of personal agency has been wounded; since she, too, would have thought that what distinguished them from most other men is that her confidence in them (Richard and James) could have been shaken only by similar wrongful behavior on their part.

It goes without saying that not all victims of rape need have had a well-developed sense of personal agency in the first place, as an abused female child could be raped years later as an adult female. But for those whose good fortune did include a well-developed sense of personal agency, and assuming a single instance of such victimization, then one imagines that with support from loved ones and friends homeostasis will be achieved: the person's sense of personal agency will be restored and the person will be able to get on with her life, interacting with friends as she normally would. Naomi will once again be able to enjoy affectionate (but nonsexual) touches and hugs from Richard and James. Constant victimization, on the other hand, can make recovery next to impossible, notwithstanding the fact that the person had a well-developed sense of personal agency before the victimization began. Again, some people recover from traumatic experiences more easily than others. All by itself, however, this truth hardly tells against the pain of those who do not. That is, the fact that there are some whose sense of personal agency is not much diminished by the traumatic experience of rape or not much diminished for long is hardly a reason to doubt that anyone's sense of personal agency is diminished to a considerable degree, nor is it reason not to take as quite understandable the occurrence of a considerably diminished sense of personal agency in the face of such an experience. That would be like maintaining the absurd view that parents are generally irrelevant to the flourishing of children on the strength of the truth that some children go on to flourish without the support of their parents.

Rather than dwell on the preceding points, I want to turn to the case of adults who were abused as children. But let me conclude this section, by reminding the reader of the extraordinary observation revealed to us by our discussion of rape, namely this: Owing to a diminished sense of personal agency resulting from the trauma of rape, a person's deeply and justifiably held favorable beliefs regarding social interaction with another may fail to have the cognitive import that they would otherwise have, meaning that the person is unable to interact with the other in ways that are appropriate given her beliefs about the other. This can happen because the person's powers of effective assessment have been radically truncated owing to the deep fissure in the proper normative structure of her environment.

III

As I remarked in the preceding section, children do not begin life with a well-developed sense of personal agency. They acquire it if all goes well. But not all need go well. And that is what I want to focus on with respect to the aim of being a morally good person. It will be recalled that my aim is to make some sense of how sexually abused child sexual abusers—that is those who were themselves victims of sustained child abuse—are in the grip of immorality.

Let me begin by stating the obvious:[5] sexually abused child sexual abusers are individuals who as children were constantly terrorized in their adult familial environment. They were helpless and unable to protect themselves against the violation to their person to which they were regularly subjected, and to which they regularly submitted out of fear of being significantly harmed in some way. Further, we have the very important phenomenon that I shall refer to as the condition of social silence in the home:[6] (a) the family member who abuses speaks of the abuse to no one; (b) out of fear, the abused child does not speak of it to anyone; and (c) often owing to fear as well, the other adult family who is aware of the abuse does not acknowledge it to the abused, to say nothing of preventing it.

In some ways, condition (c) can be seen as the most controversial. How can a child have the belief that the other adult knows, when the abuse occurs in secret and no mention is made of it? Let me answer this question indirectly with the following observation. Insofar as a child has the secure belief that it is loved by its parents, this will not be because of their words as such; for by the time words alone are capable of playing an affirming role in the life of the child, the child had better believe that it is loved by its parents or it is already too late. It is through a wealth of nonverbal behavior that the child comes to have the secure conviction that it is loved by its parents. The words of affection that come later build upon the foundation that is already in place. This suggests, then, that the child is an absolutely marvelous monitor of nonverbal behavior, at least the nonverbal behavior of those it encounters frequently and regularly. And if this is so, then the adult who is aware of sexual abuse but does nothing about it will most surely give herself away through her nonverbal behavior.[7]

I want now to make several general observations regarding the adult child sexual abuser who was a victim of sustained child abuse. The first thing to note regarding child abuse is that abuse constitutes a most profound betrayal of the child's trust in his parents. Moreover, it radically ruptures the trust-building conditions necessary for a child to have a healthy sense of trust in others. This betrayal is two-fold. On the one hand, there is the abuser's betrayal of the child's trust; on the other, the child's trust is betrayed by the failure of the other adult who is aware of the abuse to acknowledge it or seek to prevent it. For in a healthy familial environment children naturally look to adults in that environment to protect them from harm and to address their fears. Child sexual abuse constitutes a profound betrayal of trust at the most foundational level, at the very nexus of the child's utter dependence on the parental figures for both physical and psychological well-being.

The second thing to note is that the child's sensibilities with respect to the intimate are warped. The child's first and ongoing encounter with the sexual experience is completely devoid of trust and mutual consent. This ongoing encounter is, instead, a paradigm instance of submitting to the power of another *out of fear* and remaining silent about the matter *out of fear.* While the actual physical aspects of the sexual behavior may be warped, I am here focusing upon the emotional aspects. A first and ongoing sexual encounter under these circumstances almost invariably results in a highly morally objectionable erotic emotional configuration being aligned with the sexual act: exercising brazen power over the other, who is generally helpless, becomes a definitive aspect of the erotic for the sexually abused. I should mention, in passing, that a warped erotic emotional configuration regarding the sex act need not be morally objectionable, at least not in any strong sense. Suppose a person strongly associates the sex act with exquisite gustatory satisfaction; and so caviar, pâté, or some such thing is a prerequisite for complete sexual satisfaction. This would be very strange, indeed; however, the person could hardly be criticized on moral grounds. By contrast, I take it that when a person's erotic emotional configuration is such that exercising brazen power over a helpless person is definitive of the erotic we have a different level of moral concern altogether, one that is of the utmost gravity.

Although I have drawn attention to the role of fear of power in explaining the child's submission, I do not mean to downplay the complexity that arises from the child's wanting to please the adult perpetrator, at least initially. There is no incompatibility here. Fear and the desire for approval often operate together. No doubt part of the explanation for the feelings of guilt which many victims of child abuse experience is owing to their sense of having acted out of love to some extent. What must be borne in mind, though, is that the child's desire to please is an extant general desire that the perpetrator exploits rather than an extant content-specific desire to please by being the object's of the parent's sexual desire. Submitting to sexual advances in the hopes of pleasing is different in every way from being the first to initiate sexual advances in the hopes of pleasing.

The last thing I want to note is that child sexual abuse invariably impairs, in a monumental way, the child's realization of a well-developed sense of personal agency. The child may eventually be allowed to shower and to eliminate waste in private, and so the child will have some sense that there are limits to what others can do to or with her or his body without its consent. But there will have been a rupture in the child's sense of personal agency that is located in the very area of life the spiritual and personal significance of which makes consent absolutely of paramount importance. Accordingly, the sexually abused child will not have an experiential basis for the proper normative structure that pertains to having control over its body. This marks the fundamental difference between a sexually abused child and a child who has been raised in an entirely loving and protective environment. For the latter, there is no incongruity at all between what he learns about how persons should be related to others sexually and his own childhood experiences with others, his parents in particular. The normative experiences he has regarding the matter correspond with the proper normative story that he learns.

By contrast, the normative experiences of the victim of sustained child sexual abuse is quite at odds with the corresponding proper normative story that she learns regarding the body. What is more, that incongruity is occasioned by, of all people, one whom she naturally wants to trust and receive both affection and protection from. Of extraordinary significance, then, is that there is a gulf—a moral gulf, in fact—between the proper normative story that the abused child learns and his corresponding normative experiences.

IV

We are now in a position to make some sense of how it is that a person could be a sexually abused child sexual abuser, although the person unambiguously takes this to be a horrendous wrong. Drawing upon the preceding section, I begin by succinctly stating two psychological profile features (PPF) of a SACSA. PPF 1: Owing to having been sexually abused as a child, he has a morally warped erotic emotional configuration, which was emblazoned upon him in a state of innocence, where the brazen exercise of power over the helpless is definitive of the erotic for him. PPF 2: The development of his sense of personal agency has been severely impaired, the significance of this being that his powers of effective assessment are profoundly undermined; for although he has been told the proper normative story concerning the bodies of persons being their own, and so his body being his own, his actual normative experiences regarding the matter have been incongruous with that story. I shall discuss each of these in turn.

At the outset, it should be noted that while a SACSA yields to the felt pull of the sexual desire, this is by no means unique to him. The felt pull of the sexual desire can be extraordinary, felling the most psychologically whole of individuals known to have extraordinary resolve—individuals whose sense of personal agency has never been so much as even marred. People have yielded to this pull notwithstanding the indisputable claims of morality, as in the case of fidelity, or notwithstanding the indisputable claims of rationality, as when owing to the risk of AIDS or pregnancy it is most rational to refrain from sexual intercourse. So, a SACSA is by no means unique in yielding to the felt pull of the sexual desire when this is at odds with reason, as given by morality or rationality. The difference is that in the instances just mentioned the failure to act in accordance with reason does not lead to the object of one's sexual desire being psychologically harmed; whereas this is precisely what is true when a SACSA fails to act in accordance with reason. This brings us to PPF 1: his erotic emotional configuration, especially the conditions under which he acquired it.

As repulsive as we might find such persons, we must bear in mind that a sexually abused child sexual abuser did not as a matter of choice come to have the morally warped erotic emotional configuration which I have described. Nor can it be said of him that he is culpable (in the Aristotelian sense) for not having properly attended to some untoward consequence of his behavior. A person could not, at least not at the outset, be more innocent of having a more morally fulsome kind of desire. What is more, while a SACSA may recognize and sufficiently appreciate the character of his erotic desire early on, it may turn out, often enough, that this recognition and appreciation does not come about until his sexual desire has been awakened in full force. In any event, a SACSA cannot be characterized as an individual who knows, from the very start, that he has a morally warped emotional configuration. I have mentioned these points because, even when a person's erotic configuration is quite morally acceptable, contending with the awakening of sexual desire can be very difficult. We can be very much caught off guard, never suspecting that this or that form of interaction would result in our being so erotically aroused. And as everyone is well aware, the sexual desire once awakened by the act of sex (or a sufficiently aroused approximation) is not readily returned to a dormant state. Invariably, most people will find a way to give expression to it. No doubt this is part of the insight to be gained from the Garden of Eden story. The truth of the matter is that to be human is to be in the grip of sexual desire. A SACSA has absolutely no immunity with regard to these matters. However, owing to the immoral structure of his erotic emotional configuration, acquired through no fault of his own, a SACSA is in the grip of an immoral sexual desire.

I turn now to PPF 2: the impairment of powers of effective assessment, on account of having a profoundly truncated sense of personal agency, all of which is a result of the incongruity between the normative story he learns about the bodies of persons being their own and his actual normative experiences. I begin with an example.

Suppose that time and time again a person—call her Sally—had been told that she was extremely talented; but, alas, she was never given any responsibilities that corresponded to the talent that she was said to have; hence, she has no actual successes to her credit. It is one thing to be passed over every now and then, it is quite another for this to be the pattern of one's life. In Sally's case, we would have a systematic incongruity between what she had been told regarding her talents and her lived experiences. So, nothing would be more surprising than that she actually had any confidence in herself at all; for over the long run, there simply can be no substitute for the experience of success in having the conviction that one is capable of doing things.[8] The moral of this story, needless to say, is that there are beliefs about the self which are secured, not by the story that we are told, but by our having the corresponding lived experiences.

When it comes to a person's body, the proper normative story, clearly, is that it is her or his own, it being of the importance that another must be given consent in order to do certain things to or with one's body. But surely this belief cannot be secured in a person's life simply by being told that story. For it will be remembered that at the outset of life, it is quite proper that a child has the most rudimentary bodily care performed on its behalf by others without its consent. Thus, if things go as they should, *one normative story replaces another, along with the concomitant normative experiences.* The victim of child sexual abuse does not enjoy this moral good fortune. Specifically, at a most fundamental level, the moral importance of consent is not grounded in its lived experiences. The victim of child abuse learns that consent is important; but instead of having the experience of its importance systematically confirmed in its life, the victim experiences just the opposite.

As both David Hume and Bishop Butler saw clearly, in large measure moral knowledge consists in being able to extrapolate properly from our own experiences to the other. Anyone who has enjoyed the richness of being deeply trusted by another for any length of time can appreciate its affirming qualities, whether in her own life or the life of another. A person who has not enjoyed such trust cannot really grasp its affirming qualities by extrapolating from a life of not having been trusted. For while trust is the absence of distrust, it is not merely the absence of that, in the way that light just is the absence of darkness. Nothing more; nothing less. Accordingly, one cannot expect a person who has never enjoyed being deeply trusted by another to be moved by the goodness of trust in the way that a person who has enjoyed such trust will be, though the former may have some cognitive appreciation for the good of trust. Likewise, the importance of consent in terms of involvement with another's body is not revealed to those for whom that importance was not secured in the formative stages of their lives.

I remarked in section II that only with the act of sex is the difference between the morally good and the morally bad so indissolubly tied to consent alone, where the mere absence of consent qualitatively changes the experience for the worse. As a child, a SACSA is told of the importance of consent, but endures a pattern of experiences that very nearly insures that what is told to him regarding consent will not have the requisite uptake in his life. Just as a person can see that distrust is bad and yet not enjoy the affirming qualities of trust, the child who has been a victim of sexual abuse can appreciate that the absence of consent is bad without being able to grasp fully the significance of consent. Nothing else so sharply and unambiguously marks the difference between morally good and morally bad sex; and the fact that nothing else so marks the difference can be most difficult to appreciate, if at the most formative stage in one's life one's own consent has been rendered irrelevant; for then one is simply without a self-grounded vantage point from which to appreciate, by way of extrapolation, the significance of consent in the lives of others. As one can readily see, this gives us a very powerful explanation for how a SACSA can know the good and do the bad with respect to sexually abusing a child. If Hume and Butler are right, at any rate, then a most important factor in our not harming others is that, based upon our own experiences, we truly have an appreciation, at the affective level, for the negative impact that our actions would have upon others; and the appreciation at that affective level serves to stay our hand. When it comes to the importance of consent regarding the sexual activity, a SACSA is terribly impoverished with respect to having such an appreciation.

Our powers of effective assessment can be diminished, if only momentarily, or they may not be sufficiently realized in the first place. In the Naomi story, Naomi's realized powers of effective assessment were diminished. In the case of victims of child sexual abuse, however, the victim's powers of effective assessment have been prevented from being realized in the person's life, owing to the profound incongruity between the normative story which the victim is told and the victim's actual normative experiences. The victim knows the truth regarding the importance of consent, but that truth fails to have the proper normative pull in his life. That is, the cognitive import of a firmly held belief is lacking. And this, it will be remembered, was the case with Naomi. The child can no more fully grasp the importance of consent by reflecting upon how his life has been harmed than can a child with loving parents fully grasp the horror of child abuse by reflecting upon the good that he, but not an abused child, has enjoyed.

In sum, then, we can say that a sexually abused child sexual abuser is an individual who, on account of having been systematically abused sexually, is in the grip of a warped erotic emotional configuration, where the exercise of brazen power over the helpless is definitive of the erotic, and whose powers of effective assessment regarding the importance of consent in the context of the sex act have been severely impaired, owing also to the abuse. And so we have an explanation for how it is possible for, of all people, an adult victim of child sexual abuse to know the good and yet commit the bad of abusing children.

I should like to conclude this section with two observations. The account that I have offered of how a SACSA could know the good and yet be in the grip of the bad underscores the extent to which we, as human beings, are quintessentially social creatures. For if I have argued soundly, then there are fundamentally important instances when our moral knowledge can have the desired hold upon our lives only if we have had the right sorts of experiences in our lives. Just as the pain of rape cannot be appreciated from afar on merely a cognitive plane, neither can the importance of consent be so appreciated. These things cannot be appreciated from afar any more than the importance of love and friendship can. What is particularly interesting in the case at hand is the fact that the moral quality of the parent-child relationship can bear so directly upon the quality of the moral life that an adult lives. This is a moral truth that moral philosophy has not yet learned to take seriously enough. For insofar as a person lacking in moral appreciation at the affective level should come to have a sufficient appreciation of the good, it is most unlikely that some argument, however sound, will occasion such appreciation.[9]

The second observation which I should like to make concerns a presupposition of this essay with which some might take issue. I have presupposed that there is a fairly sharp divide in our erotic life, with children being on one side and adults being on the other. It might be objected that this divide is not true to the facts. I realize that some readily take offense at the very thought that children might in any way be the object of the least erotic feelings on the part of an adult. Still, it is worth considering this possibility for argument's sake if only to see that it is not as threatening as it might appear to be.

Suppose, then, as some might be inclined to think, that the erotic is a characteristic part of life and even children are often seen in an erotic light, however mild and passive that may be. It nonetheless remains true if we are fortunate that there are very firm boundaries which we are not in the least tempted to cross. It is true enough that we do recognize when the little girl or boy next door will grow up to be an absolutely stunning-looking adult, who will be pursued by just about any and every adult with a heartbeat. What is more, such recognitions, and the expressions of them, may very well bespeak a measure of eroticism on our part toward the children in question. But not even for a moment need any such recognition pass over into an active erotic desire for the child or a desire of this sort to which we would ever yield; for we have neither the relevant warped emotional configuration with respect to the erotic nor a diminished sense of personal agency. Thus, if we are fortunate, either our erotic desire never has the child as its object or, if in some evanescent form our erotic desire does, our intact sense of personal agency owing to the absence of abuse in our lives insures that this particular erotic desire never matures in any way that would give rise to temptation on our part.

As I have said, some might take offense at the very idea that, among morally decent people, a child might in any way be seen in an erotic light. But this line of thought was worth pursuing if only to show that even if this concession is made, the result is not a society that is placed on the brink of child abuse. For part of what moral maturity involves is acknowledging boundaries and not nursing desires which in their evanescent form are morally innocuous, but which in their mature form are morally fulsome. It is one thing to be green with envy, as we say; it is quite another to be riddled with envy. It is one thing to acknowledge that another's spouse is quite physically attractive; it is quite another to develop a salacious attitude toward that spouse.

V

With the account before us of how a sexually abused child sexual abuser could know the good and yet be in the grip of the bad, I turn now to an issue that must be directly dealt with. My aim in this essay, of course, has been to explain how those who have been victims of child sexual abuse could go on to commit this horror against their own family members—not to justify or excuse the behavior of these individuals. While it is manifestly clear, I trust, that I have not done the former, it might seem that, in the end, the explanation which I have offered does excuse their behavior, and that, needless to say, would render the account extremely problematic. Fortunately, I have done no such thing. For I have not argued that once a morally warped erotic emotional configuration, at whatever level of manifestation, has a grip upon our lives, then that grip cannot be loosened or eliminated entirely. That is surely false. Nor have I argued that it is not possible for a person to recover sufficiently from having a diminished, impaired sense of personal agency during childhood and the accompanying loss in powers of effective assessment. There are some things that can be done. And this observation brings me back to the work of Kurt Baier.

As I have observed, Baier is committed to the view that the reasonable is a function of the social context of persons. And one of the things that clearly distinguishes him from many is that he is prepared to say that even nonmoral preferences are reasonable in a social context that is utterly riddled with immorality. Thus, for him, the moral tenor of society bears directly upon the quality of the moral life that its members can be reasonably expected to live, as given by the preferences which they will reasonably come to have in that society. Well, as is characteristic of *The Rational and the Moral Order*, a seemingly innocuous claim is more radical than one might have initially suspected.

For it is possible for a society to embrace, at the very deepest levels, a conception of the good person, for all or some of its members, that is partially mistaken in a fundamental way. When that happens, not only will people be held up to an improper ideal by others in such instances, which is bad enough, but people will often hold themselves up to that ideal even at the risk of distorting or denying the reality of their own experiences. A very stark example in this regard is perhaps the ideal of the male as soldier.[10] Real men, so the ideal goes, just are those who, even at the still formative age of 18, are capable of going into war witnessing and committing death after death without being in the least bit traumatized, and then returning home and picking up their lives where they had left off. A hero's welcome or two is supposed to take care of any sense of minor trauma or psychological disorientation that might have taken hold. But there is no such thing as witnessing death after death without its taking an extraordinary psychological toll upon one. Arguably, embracing this ideal of the male soldier exacts a heavy price upon the male psyche. All the same, as long as this continues to be the widely held view of men, it is reasonable that people expect men to behave this way; more to the point, it is reasonable enough that men often put themselves through psychological contortions in order to measure up to this ideal, lest they should appear to be less than real men in both their own eyes and the eyes of others, women and men alike. To the extent that this conception of real men is mistaken, society is part of the problem regarding the self-identity of males.

Well, there is no problem in Western culture with acknowledging the wrong of child sexual abuse—nearly everyone thinks that it is wrong, and is prepared to say so at a moment's notice. The problem is this: (a) society does not take seriously the ontogenesis of a morally warped erotic emotional configuration and the impairment that sexual abuse can cause to a person's sense of personal agency and powers of effective assessment; (b) society does not fully accept the fact that this morally warped erotic emotional configuration is not something that one can just discard upon becoming aware of it, for it does not yet fully appreciate the phenomenon of a diminished sense of personal agency, as only recently has society begun to appreciate this in the rape of women; accordingly, (c) the very admission that one has a morally warped erotic emotional configuration invites scorn and utter condemnation. What would be much better is that such an admission was seen as an opportunity by friends and family to insure that the person receives the necessary moral and psychological care. The idea here is not to make the abuser an object of sympathy, but rather to respond to the reality of the abuser himself having been a victim of sexual abuse. For a SACSA, it must be remembered, had a morally warped erotic emotional configuration emblazoned upon his life while he was in a state of manifest innocence. Thus, it is not through any wrongdoing of his own that he came to have this configuration. Nor is this configuration dissolved or held in check simply by punishment or the threat of punishment.

Some sort of psychological help is essential. It may be possible to alter the morally warped erotic emotional configuration or, at the very minimum, enable the person to refrain from acting on it. Perhaps the person's diminished sense of self need only be adequately restored. The aim of society, surely, should be to prevent anyone from ever committing the very first act of child abuse, or anything beyond that. But if, from the very way in which society will react, it is more reasonable to hide that one has a morally warped erotic emotional configuration than to admit to it, then society itself is part of the problem.

As I noted in my explication of Baier's views (section II), if rationality has such a claim to our acting morally, then nothing turns out to be more mysterious than that immorality abounds. Now, to be sure, the logic of immorality hardly entails that society must be part of the problem. On the other hand, no small advance in the theoretical character of our moral thought has been made when the very structure of our moral theories are alive to this possibility. Interestingly, Hume's moral theory was quite alive to it; and *The Rational and the Moral Order* shows Hume's influence. Accordingly, I suspect that numerous admirers of Hume from various quarters would be proud of the man called Kurt Baier.

Syracuse University

Notes

1. In writing this paper, I have benefitted from the comments and criticisms of far too many individuals to name. However, I should especially like to mention the extensive written comments which I received from Julia Driver, Elizabeth Hegeman, and Michael Stocker. Versions of this essay were read at Queens College (Kingston, Toronto), Mt. Holyoke College, Rochester Institute of Technology, and Georgia State University. Ms. Davis at Queens College was my commentator. The discussion of associative pain, and the distinction which I draw with respect to it, owes much to her searching comments.

For inspiration in taking on the subject of this essay, I am profoundly indebted to Gary Watson's searching essay "Responsibility and the Limits of Evil," (1987). For a discussion of some of the important issues surrounding moral responsibility and having been a victim of child abuse, see the John Martin Fischer and Mark Ravizza Fischer, introduction to *Perspectives on Moral Responsibility* (1993). See, also, John Christman, "Autonomy and Personal History," (1991), which I believe rightly points in the direction that we need to go in order to sort out these issues. Human beings are more historically bound than is often realized, and thus are not as plastic as philosophical discussions often suppose. The question, of course, is how much weight do we give to a person's history. Well, the answer, surely, has to be that it depends on the content of the history.

2. See Judith Lewis Herman, *Trauma and Recovery: The Aftermath of Violence—from Domestic Abuse to Political Terror* (1992). It is perhaps natural to think of a sense of personal agency as being the same thing as a sense of autonomy, as Herman herself does. I would like not to if only because it seems that quite nonautonomous settings, such as prisons and hospitals, can be more or less respecting of a

person's sense of personal agency. Or, it seems that extremely authoritarian parents can nonetheless be quite conducive to a child's having a sense of personal agency, though not autonomy. The two seem related, though; for it is hard to imagine a very autonomous being with an utterly crippled sense of personal agency.

3. Recall Judith Jarvis Thomson's wonderful essay, "A Defense of Abortion (1971), where the idea that it is a pregnant woman's body—that she can rightly say "This is my body!"—has considerable force in the argument.

4. It is rightly observed that in a sexist society, the importance of consent on the part of women is diminished, as women are often portrayed as little girls or seen as desirable if they so conduct themselves. I am not in this essay offering a critique of sexist society. But if I were, several things should be observed. First, while girls are the object of child sexual abuse, boys are too; and the sexual abuse of boys cannot, in any way, be seen as part and parcel of the idea that women are but little girls. Second, notwithstanding the grip of sexism, not all men rape or commit child sexual abuse, or even come close to doing these things. Even in a sexist society, some men take consent on the part of women quite seriously. So, postulating the existence of sexism will yet leave much to be explained. Third, the idea that women are desirable if they act as little girls is formally different from its being the case that little girls are desirable. Sexual desire is generally very description-sensitive. Otherwise, in a sexist society it would not matter whether the so-called beautiful woman is forward in her intelligence or not; yet, it matters mightily. She is threatening if she is forward in manner, but not if she is demure in manner, though that is the only difference between them. There are numerous men who have been loving fathers to their daughters, though these men believe that it is ordained by the heavens that women should be subordinate to men. These men would be horrified to learn that their sexual attitude towards adult women in any way bespeaks a sexual preference for girls. And rightly so. For an erotic preference for adult women who are subordinate, though certainly wrong, is neither identical to nor entails an erotic preference for little girls. On the other hand, I do not mean to deny that there is any relevance whatsoever between the preference of men for women who are girl-like and sexual abuse. After all, some thing can be quite relevant to another, without being either necessary or sufficient for it. Kurt Baier's very impressive example is candlelight. Though quite relevant to a romantic atmosphere, candlelight is neither necessary nor sufficient for having a romantic atmosphere.

5. The account of child abuse which follows owes much to the following authors: Frank W. Putnam, *Diagnosis and Treatment of Multiple Personality Disorder* (1989); Colin A. Ross, *Multiple Personality Disorder: Diagnosis, Clinical Features, and Treatment* (1989); Frederique Gruyer, et al., *La Violence Impensable* (1991). Among the many factors that contribute to multiple personality disorder, being abused as a child is a most prominent one. Ross points out that for abused children, multiple personality disorder is a creative strategy for coping with and surviving the assault—a creative strategy that goes wrong as the child enters adulthood (pp. 10–11, 76).

6. I owe the formulation of this condition to Gruyer. He writes: "Or, l'enfant abusé a de nombreuses raisons de se taire: en premier lieu, il est soumis a la loi du silence qui regne dans sa famille, it vit sous la constrainte, si ce n'est 'sous terreur"' (p. 57).

7. But for nonverbal behavior, the phenomenon of flirting among human beings could not take place. Based upon a split second's worth of observation on X's part of Y's behavior, X will usually rightly distinguish a) Y's look of sexual interest in X from b) X just being in Y's line of vision and c) Y finding X's attire or physical features to be odd, hence the gaze. The failure to appreciate the role of nonverbal behavior in social interaction has resulted in an impoverished understanding of the moral life. I have discussed the philosophical significance of nonverbal behavior in "Evil and the Concept of a Human Person" (1995).

8. I am indebted here to Robert W. White, *Ego and Reality in Psychoanalytic Theory* (1963). See chap. 3 for his account of the concept of affectance motivation.

9. The remarks in this paragraph draw upon three essays of mine: "Doing Justice to Egoism," (1989); "Moral Deference," (1992); and "The Reality of the Moral Self," (1993).

10. I am indebted here to the illuminating discussion in Herman 1992. pp. 20–32.

Baier on Killing and Letting Die

8

Shelly Kagan

Friends of ordinary, common-sense morality believe in the intrinsic moral relevance of the distinction between killing and letting die. They believe, in particular, that killing is worse than letting die. Armed with this claim, those friends of ordinary morality who are "simple-minded" go on to argue for bold and striking prohibitions. They might hold, for example, that active euthanasia is always impermissible, involving, as it does, the killing of an innocent person.

Kurt Baier is a friend of ordinary morality, and so he thinks that common-sense morality is sound as far as the basic principle goes: killing is indeed worse than letting die. But unlike some, Baier is a sophisticated rather than a simple-minded friend. He believes, for example, that in at least some cases active euthanasia is permissible. More generally, he thinks that in any number of controversial cases involving killing and letting die it is not at all a simple or straightforward matter to determine what it is morally correct to do. We cannot, in particular, derive the conclusion that a given act is forbidden from the mere fact that it would involve killing.

I myself am not among the friends of ordinary morality. As a consequentialist, I deny the intrinsic moral relevance of the distinction between killing and letting die. Accordingly, while I applaud Baier's determination to resist drawing simple-minded conclusions from his belief that killing is intrinsically worse than letting die, I think he errs in granting the distinction any intrinsic moral significance at all.

Nonetheless, it must be admitted that the distinction between killing and letting die is one that possesses a considerable significance from the intuitive point of view. As far as our ordinary moral intuitions are concerned, it seems quite plausible to hold that killing is indeed morally worse than letting die. I believe, however, that in this matter (as in many others regarding ordinary morality) our intuitions are not to be trusted. The question rather is whether sound arguments can be offered on behalf of the relevance of the distinction. I think that the answer is no, and I have argued this point elsewhere.[1] But Baier has new arguments, and given the intuitive appeal of the distinction, it behooves us to examine them carefully.[2]

Baier's main argument for the claim that killing is worse than letting die is really quite simple. He believes that a sound morality will include a prima facie duty not to kill, but will contain no similar prima facie duty not to let die. If he is right about this, it does seem reasonable to conclude that killing really is worse per se than letting die. So the question becomes this: why does Baier think that a sound morality will contain the one duty but not the other?

Baier's main argument relies, in effect, on two premises, and he argues at some length for the first of them, that is, the claim that a sound morality will contain a prima facie duty not to kill. His argument for this claim draws on a number of interesting views about the justification of moral guidelines and the concept of a prima facie duty. Unfortunately, these are complex matters, and so I cannot examine the details of Baier's argument here. (*Very* roughly, the idea is that killings tend to be morally objectionable, enough so that it makes sense to introduce a defeasible prohibition against their performance.) Perhaps, however, it will suffice for our limited purposes if we simply grant Baier this first premise: a sound morality will contain a prima facie duty not to kill. This allows us to focus on what I believe is the crucial issue, namely, Baier's assertion that a sound morality will *not* contain a prima facie duty not to let die. Oddly, and unfortunately, Baier has much less to say about the defense of this second premise.

On the face of it, it seems to me, we would expect a sound morality to *include* a prima facie duty not to let die. After all, as Baier himself recognizes, it is not just acts of killing that tend to be morally objectionable; acts of letting die are often morally objectionable as well, enough so that it does make sense to introduce a general moral guideline against letting die. But Baier thinks that in a sound morality this guideline will not take the form of a prima facie *duty*. Rather, it will be at a lesser level of "stringency." Unlike the guideline concerning killing, which will be at the "nonoptional" level of stringency (hence the appropriateness of speaking of a "duty," albeit a prima facie one), the guideline concerning letting die will be at the "optional" level of stringency. Thus, special circumstances aside, there will be no duty not to let die—not even a prima facie one.

But why this difference? Why shouldn't the guideline concerning letting die be at the same "nonoptional" level of stringency as the guideline concerning killing? Why not have a prima facie duty not to let die? Baier raises this question himself, and replies as follows:

> The answer is that there is, as we have seen, adequate reason to make it a general prima facie *duty* not to kill, but there is no such reason for such a duty to save lives. For no conflict would be generated by the belief that all who have an opportunity to kill a certain person, also had and discharged a duty not to kill her, but there may and often would be such a conflict and a lot of waste if all of

> us who have an opportunity to save a person's life, thought they had and attempted to discharge a duty to save it. If she is to survive, *all* of us who have an opportunity to kill her *must not* do so, but there is no comparable necessity for all of us who have this opportunity, to save her. (III, 7–8)[3]

It is not altogether clear to me exactly what Baier has in mind in this passage. I can think of two possible interpretations of his argument. The first emphasizes the difference in necessity identified in the last sentence quoted: The guideline that opposes killing must take the form of a duty—Baier is arguing—since if any given person is to survive it is necessary that *all* of us refrain from killing that person. In contrast, Baier observes, there is no similar necessity that all of us *save* any given person in need (it would suffice, for example, if one person provides the necessary aid). Accordingly, there is no comparable need for a "nonoptional" duty to save lives.

If this *argument from necessity,* as we might call it, is indeed what Baier has in mind, then it seems to me that he has been misled by his decision to cast the discussion in terms of whether or not there is a prima facie duty to *save* lives. The point at issue, after all, was whether or not a sound morality would contain a prima facie duty not to *let die.* Yet even if we assume that the argument from necessity can successfully establish that there will be no duty to save, nothing in that argument shows that there will *not* be a duty not to let die. For although it is true that there is no need for all of us to *save* any given person in need, it is nonetheless also true that all of us must refrain from *letting the person die.* Just as we don't get the desired outcome (the given person alive) if a single one of us kills her, we similarly don't get the desired outcome if a single one of us lets her die. (I assume here, obviously, that if you let someone die, the upshot is that they end up dead; no death, no letting die.)

Thus, if the necessity of all of us refraining from killing explains why the guideline concerning killing should take the form of a (prima facie) duty not to kill, then similarly, from the necessity of all of us refraining from letting die it seems to follow—for all that Baier has shown—that the guideline concerning letting die should take the form of a (prima facie) duty as well. But this leaves killing and letting die on the same footing—both opposed by prima facie duties. And this in turn completely undermines Baier's main argument for the conclusion that killing is worse than letting die.

(It may seem puzzling how there could be a prima facie duty not to let die in the absence of a prima facie duty to save. But the explanation lies in the very fact to which Baier was drawing our attention. Logically speaking, there is no necessity that all of us take positive, active steps to save any given person in need; if others are already taking adequate steps, this will only result in a waste of effort and resources. All that is required is that one take positive action when others are *not* taking adequate steps. What is required, then, is not a prima facie duty to "save" per se, but rather a prima facie duty to "save when necessary.")

Perhaps, however, I misconstrue Baier's position when I interpret it in terms of the argument from necessity. The passage I have quoted suggests a second possible reading when it warns of the possibility of "conflict" if all who had the opportunity to save a person's life attempted to do so. Similarly, in a later, but related passage, Baier warns of the danger of "confusion and mutual interference" if all those in a position to help tried to do so themselves (III, 8). Perhaps, then, Baier has in mind an argument of this sort: If everyone takes himself to have a duty not to kill, and attempts to fulfill this duty, all is well: there is no danger that the various attempts will interfere with each other, resulting somehow in the unwanted death. In contrast—Baier may be suggesting—if everyone takes himself to have a duty to save, and attempts to fulfill this duty, there is a nonnegligible chance that the various uncoordinated attempts will interfere with each other, and the ultimate result might well be a tragic failure to save the person in question from death. Accordingly, there should not be so much as a prima facie duty to save.

Like the argument from necessity, this new argument mistakenly focuses on the implications of a prima facie duty to save. As we have seen, however, if Baier is to defend the claim that killing is worse than letting die, the relevant question is whether or not a sound morality would contain a prima facie duty not to *let die*—and the absence of a duty to save does not suffice to settle this point. Unlike the argument from necessity, however, this *argument from interference* (as we might dub it) retains a certain amount of plausibility even when we appropriately redirect our attention to the guideline concerning letting die. For Baier might still suggest that if everyone takes himself to have a duty not to let die, and attempts to fulfill this duty, there remains a nonnegligible chance that the various uncoordinated attempts will interfere with each other, sometimes resulting in a failure to save the person in need.

I think it must be admitted that the possibility of such interference cannot be ruled out. (Logically, of course, if everyone *succeeds* in fulfilling a duty not to let die, then the person will be saved. But if we focus instead on the effects of *promulgating* such a guideline, then the most we can be certain of is that people will *attempt* to fulfill the duty, and now the possibility of interference with tragic results cannot be dismissed.) It is, I take it, an empirical question to what extent such deadly interference will arise. (Similarly, it is, strictly, an empirical question whether everyone's attempting to fulfill a duty not to *kill* will result in deadly interference. But this possibility seems sufficiently unlikely to be put aside.)

For myself, I am inclined to think that it would be a mistake to expect very much by way of deadly interference if people attempted to act on a prima facie duty not to let die. Once again, the key is to bear in mind that a duty not to let die does not entail a duty to *save* per se. That is, in situations where others are already taking adequate steps to save those in need, there is no requirement to make positive "saving" efforts oneself. So in such cases, at the very least, the danger of interference seems to me to be minimal. And for those cases where more than one individual must be involved if adequate aid is to be provided, I suspect that good will and a modicum of intelligence can generate sufficient coordination to minimize the likelihood of deadly interference between the various attempts to help. (I might also note that in an appallingly callous world such as ours, the tragic fact is that no one at all comes to the aid of most of those in need, so concern about the dangers of interference seems grossly misplaced. But this is perhaps unfair to Baier, who would certainly condemn current practices as well.)

Still, I see no reason to assume that such undesirable interference would disappear altogether. Does this then suffice to show that a sound morality would not contain a prima facie duty not to let die? I don't see why it should. All moral guidelines involve risks—of misinterpretation, misexecution, and other forms of misuse. I see no reason to think that the danger of interference is sufficiently great to rule out a prima facie duty not to let die. Of course, if we could anticipate a significant amount of such deadly interference, that would be another matter. But once we are careful to avoid being confused by the irrelevant implications of a duty to save per se—that is, a duty to save whether one's efforts are needed or not—it seems likely that the interference generated by a prima facie duty not to let die would be insignificant. At any rate, Baier gives us no reason to think otherwise.

So the argument from interference fares no better than the argument from necessity. On neither interpretation has Baier given us adequate reason to believe that a sound morality will *not* contain a prima facie duty not to let die. But this means that Baier has failed to establish the crucial second premise of his main argument. Even if we grant the first premise of that argument—that a sound morality will contain a prima facie duty not to kill—absent a better defense for the claim that such a morality will *lack* a prima facie duty not to let die, Baier has no ground for concluding that killing is worse than letting die.

Now the passage we have been examining represents Baier's chief and most explicit attempt to defend his claim that a sound morality would lack a prima facie duty not to let die. There is, however, a later passage, which seems to me to point in the direction of a further, distinct argument for this claim. So we need to consider that as well.

After having argued (to his own satisfaction) that the *general* guideline concerning letting die will not take the form of a (prima facie) duty, Baier goes on to suggest that there will nonetheless be various *special duties* to save—that is, duties that will apply only to specific classes of people, or only in certain specific circumstances. Baier reviews several examples of such special duties, including the duty to rescue those in danger, obligations to the incompetent, special role-based obligations, and the like. Finally, after considering the question of how much of our resources we must give to those who lack the necessities of life, Baier concludes that these cases, especially the last, show "beyond reasonable doubt" that

> letting die is not wrong per se but only undesirable, though seriously so. One reason for this is that in these cases, we are even less able to say clearly what a person who is not a member of certain special classes would have to do to discharge a duty not to let die. But since duty (and wrong) imply the highest degree of stringency, namely, non-optionality, which in turn implies the justifiability of coercive social intervention when someone fails to do his duty, we cannot justifiably regard something as a duty concerning which it is seldom or never possible to say whether a person has or has not done it. (III, 10)

Baier's view seems to be that there cannot be a prima facie duty not to let die, for were there such a duty it would often be difficult or impossible to say what constituted fulfilling that duty. (Obviously enough, Baier thinks it unjustified to have a duty where it is difficult or impossible to tell what constitutes discharging it. I propose to grant this principle to Baier, without passing judgment on the adequacy of the particular grounds he offers for it.) But is it really true that we are unable to say clearly what would discharge a duty not to let die?

I am tempted by a trivial answer: what constitutes fully meeting the duty not to let die is not letting anyone die. From the logical point of view, it seems, there is no particular difficulty at all in saying what would discharge a duty not to let die.

Perhaps this is too quick. For the following "logical" difficulty does still remain. Suppose that two people need my aid, but I can only save one—either one. Suppose further that I do save one of them, and the other dies. Did I completely discharge my duty not to let die? Well, did I let the second person die? If we could not answer this question, then I suppose there *would* be a kind of built in vagueness surrounding a duty not to let die. There are, however, at least two possible answers available to us. First, we might say that I have not let the second person die, since "letting die" entails ability to save, and I lack the ability to save the second person if all my resources were used saving the first. I don't myself incline toward this answer (if the cases are completely symmetrical, it still seems true that I might have saved the second, by picking *her,* even though I couldn't save both). But there is a second possible answer: I did let the second person die, but there is a perfectly adequate justification for my doing so, to wit, I was saving someone else, and couldn't save both. (Appeal to this fact would function something like the way an appeal to self-defense does with regard to the duty not to kill: I do kill the person, but am justified in doing so.) I incline toward the second answer, but whichever one we pick, the fact remains that there is no intrinsic difficulty in saying what constitutes discharging a duty not to let die.

Presumably none of this will satisfy Baier. I imagine that Baier will readily concede the trivial point that one discharges the duty not to let die by not letting anyone die. But what then is the difficulty? I take it that it is something like this. Baier thinks we would face special *epistemic* difficulties, that is, difficulties in *telling* whether a given act meets the duty, or whether a given person has fully met the duty. It would be "seldom or never possible" to *know* whether a person had discharged the duty not to let die. That, I take it, is Baier's claim. But why does he think it's true?

Recall that Baier makes this claim after having discussed several kinds of cases involving special duties to save. These cases, he suggests, are what establish the point that letting die is not wrong per se—"the last case even more than the first three." The obvious suggestion, therefore, is that some of the "difficult moral questions" raised in that earlier discussion, especially the questions raised regarding the last type of case, will point to and establish the particular epistemic difficulties that Baier has in mind.

Now, as I have noted, the last of the four types of case that Baier discusses involves saving the lives of those who are dying for lack of the necessities of life. Baier believes that those of us with a more adequate supply of resources do sometimes have a prima facie duty to share them. But he thinks that there is a limit to this duty—a limit to the amount that we must sacrifice. How much, then, must we give? This, Baier apparently believes, is a difficult and obscure matter; and he goes on to raise a number of questions related to it.

All of this suggests the following picture. Baier believes that we have a morally justified *option* to do less than all the good that we are capable of doing; we need not make sacrifices when the cost to ourselves would be too great.[4] But how much, exactly, do we have to do? This is—Baier is suggesting—an inherently obscure matter. Yet any duty not to let die would necessarily inherit this obscurity: if we cannot say exactly how much we have to do, then often we would be unable to tell whether or not we had adequately fulfilled a duty not to let die. So if—as we are assuming—a moral guideline cannot take the form of a duty if it would be difficult or impossible to tell whether that duty had been discharged, there can be no duty not to let die.

If this is indeed the argument that Baier has in mind, then it seems to me that three replies are called for. First, why should we assume that a sound morality will contain options at all? It should be noted that, even if Baier is right and there is an intrinsic moral difference between killing and letting die, it still might be the case that a sound morality would grant no options whatsoever. (That is to say, we might be morally required to do all the good that we can—*within* the limits imposed by our various duties not to kill, not to lie, and so forth.) But if there are no options, then the source of the epistemic difficulty supposedly facing the duty not to let die is eliminated, and Baier's argument fails. So why think that there *are* options?

Unfortunately, this is not a claim that Baier ever tries to defend. Rather, he pretty much seems to assume, without argument, that options will indeed be generated by his general approach. I must say, however, that I find it far from obvious that he is right about this. In point of fact, I am inclined to think that given Baier's general views about the justification of moral guidelines, a more plausible conclusion would be that a sound morality would *lack* options. But to pursue this point would take us rather far afield, and so I think I had better let it go.

Suppose we assume then, with Baier, that options will be included in any sound morality. We will still need to know—and this is my second point—whether these options merely cover cases of letting die (as Baier clearly assumes) or will, instead, extend to cases of killing as well. That is, if there are options, why not an option to *kill*, when the cost of not killing is too high? But if there were options of this second sort as well, then the duty not to kill would face the same epistemic difficulties as face the duty not to let die. Perhaps then there can be neither a duty not to kill nor a duty not to let die. Or perhaps the epistemic difficulties can be somehow overcome in both cases, permitting both kinds of prima facie duties. Either way, however, symmetry would be retained with regard to the guidelines concerning killing and letting die, and so Baier's main argument would be undermined.

Once more, I can only remark that I see nothing in Baier's general approach to support the assumption, implicit in his discussion, that a sound morality would contain options with regard to letting die, but none with regard to killing. But here too, establishing this claim would take us rather far afield, and so I do not intend to press the point further.

Accordingly, let us assume with Baier that a sound morality would contain options, and that these options would apply only to cases of letting die (or, more generally, only to cases of allowing harm). It is still important to note—and this is my final point—that a prima facie duty not to let die would face epistemic difficulties only if we assume that it is obscure just *how much* a person has to do, by way of aiding others. Baier fears that were there a duty not to let die it would inherit obscurity from the intrinsic vagueness surrounding the relevant options. But why believe that the relevant options *would* be obscure in this way?

Now I certainly agree that it is obscure under common-sense moral views just how much is enough. The extent of our options under ordinary morality is a disconcertingly vague matter. But so what? We could easily invent options that draw the relevant lines more sharply. By Baier's own lights, it seems to me, this is presumably exactly what we should do. The relevant question, after all, concerns the nature of the guidelines to be included within a *sound* morality—and even if we assume, with Baier, that a sound morality would include options, it is difficult to believe that a sound morality would include options whose extent is epistemically vague and obscure. But if the appropriate options were to draw the relevant lines sharply, then it would no longer be unclear just how much one would have to do to meet a duty not to let die. In short, once we free the options of their unwarranted obscurity, we similarly rescue the duty not to let die from its alleged epistemic difficulties. And this means, of course, that Baier remains without adequate ground for his claim that a sound morality would lack a prima facie duty not to let die.

I conclude, therefore, that Baier's main argument fails. He has given us no good reason to believe that a sound morality would contain a prima facie duty not to kill, but lack a similar duty not to let die. Accordingly, he has given us no good reason to believe that killing is intrinsically worse than letting die.

This is, of course, disappointing news for the friends of ordinary morality, who must, it seems, look elsewhere if they are to find an adequate defense for the principle that killing is worse than letting die. On the other hand, for me and my fellow consequentialists this negative result is a reassuring one. For as I have said, I believe that the distinction between killing and letting die lacks any intrinsic moral significance.

Suppose, however, that Baier were right, and a sound morality would indeed include a duty not to kill, but lack a duty not to let die. This would, I have conceded, establish one sort of per se difference between killing and letting die, and it would seem reasonable to mark this difference by saying—as Baier wants to say—that killing is per se worse than letting die. Still, caution would be appropriate when drawing inferences from this principle.

This is, in fact, a point which Baier himself is at pains to establish. As Baier notes, the fact—let us suppose him to have shown it to be a fact—that killing is worse than letting die "is not as morally decisive as is generally thought" (III, 11). (It is the recognition of this that marks Baier as a sophisticated rather than a simple-minded friend of ordinary morality.) Basically, Baier's point is this: at best, all that has been shown is that there is a difference between killing and letting die at the level of prima facie duties. But the move from prima facie duties to duties *all things considered* is not necessarily simple or straightforward. What it is right or wrong to do in a determinate case will depend on a number of facts about that case, and the mere fact that one alternative is a killing and the other a letting die does not suffice to show that the first alternative is forbidden all things considered.

Baier illustrates this point with a discussion of euthanasia. In at least some cases, Baier thinks, if a person's life is no longer worth living, and if, recognizing this, she asks to be killed, it is permissible to kill her—despite the prima facie duty not to kill.

Of course in some ways cases of voluntary euthanasia are unusually easy (not that this in any way threatens Baier's point): the choice that we face is between killing a person and letting that very same person die, and—what's more—even the person to be killed is requesting that we kill her. What about cases where we must choose between killing one person and letting someone *else* die, where the person to be killed does not want to be killed? Here too Baier thinks that in at least some such cases it is permissible to kill, for example, when we kill an aggressor, so as to save his victim's life.

Thus, as a sophisticated friend of ordinary morality, Baier recognizes a number of cases in which it is permissible to kill, even though the alternative merely involves letting die. Nonetheless, there are cases at which Baier would draw the line—cases where, he thinks, we must let die rather than kill—and he discusses one of them in some detail. By drawing the line in this way, Baier reveals the extent to which he remains a *friend* of ordinary morality. Yet it seems to me that Baier's conclusions here are problematic, and do not follow from the substantive position for which he has argued.

Baier imagines a case in which Anne will die within a few days unless she gets a heart transplant, and Bill will die within a few *months* unless he gets a kidney transplant. Suppose the only relevant alternatives are these: the doctor can kill Bill, and then transplant his heart into Anne, or he can let Anne die, and then transplant her kidneys into Bill. (Let us imagine as well that either operation will be successful, and that there are no other relevant consequences of either choice.) Baier affirms—and here, I think, he speaks on behalf of all friends of ordinary morality—that the doctor must let Anne die, rather than kill Bill.

Why is this? Why isn't it permissible to kill Bill instead? (Suppose we flip a coin, and Bill loses.) Here is Baier's initial explanation:

> Is it because killing is worse than letting die? Surely not. The reason is, rather, that a physician may not discharge his duty to save one of his patient's life if it involves violating the general duty not to kill anyone and the special physician's duty not to kill one of his patients. (III, 14)

Obviously enough, one of the things Baier does in this passage is to bring in consideration of the physician's various special duties to his different patients. Yet, although they are not exactly irrelevant, I think it something of a distraction for Baier to do this. For Baier would presumably think it forbidden to kill Bill even in the absence of such special duties. Indeed, in the very next sentence, Baier asserts that "No one, especially no physician, has the right to terminate . . . one person's desirable life simply in order to lengthen another's," and I take this to mean that it would be forbidden for *anyone* to kill Bill in this case. So suppose we put aside whatever special duties the physician may have; what exactly explains why it is forbidden for anyone at all to kill Bill? As far as I can see, all that's left of Baier's initial account is this: killing Bill violates the general duty not to kill.

Now were Baier a simple-minded friend of ordinary morality, he might have thought this an adequate explanation. But Baier is not among the simple-minded. Indeed, in the very passage quoted, Baier himself insists that the explanation of the impermissibility of killing Bill does not lie in the mere fact that killing is worse than letting die. And yet it seems to me that what remains of Baier's initial account—the observation that killing Bill violates the duty not to kill—only serves to recycle this admittedly inadequate explanation. It is, after all, only a *prima facie* duty not to kill that has been established. For all that has been shown so far, it might be permissible to "violate" this prima facie duty, if this is the only way to avoid letting someone else die. And this means that, for all that has been shown so far, it may be permissible to kill Bill so as to save Anne.

Baier seems to sense that his initial account is inadequate, for in the next paragraph he goes on to articulate his reasons further. Why, he asks, can we let Anne die? Now strictly, I think this is the wrong question to ask. After all, according to Baier, it is not merely *permissible* to let Anne die (for that would be compatible with also believing it permissible to kill Bill instead), rather, it is *required*. Still, Baier's answer is instructive.

> The answer is that he lets her die, but not *in order* to save Bill's life, but because he cannot save her life in a morally permissible way, that is, without violating Bill's or someone else's right to life. (III.14)

I think we can separate out three distinct answers suggested by this reply. First, Baier is clearly suggesting that it is permissible to let Anne die, since the only way to save her life is by impermissible means. (He goes on to emphasize the point that were there a morally acceptable way of saving Anne's life—were there a heart available, say, through the recent death of some third party—then we would certainly be morally obligated to help her. This further claim raises a number of interesting issues, one of which I'll touch upon below, but it isn't central to our present concerns.) Now this first suggestion is certainly relevant to the question Baier officially asks. Why is it permissible to let Anne die? Because the only available method of saving her is impermissible. But for *our* purposes, at any rate, it is pretty clearly of no use. For what we want to know is whether the available method of saving Anne—killing Bill, and transplanting his heart—is indeed impermissible. Obviously, nothing in this first strand of Baier's remark helps in this matter. It *presupposes* that it is forbidden to kill Bill, rather than explaining why this should be so.

But Baier is also clearly suggesting, second, that the reason why it is impermissible to kill Bill is that this violates Bill's right to life. This is, perhaps, only implied in the sentence I have quoted, but later in the same paragraph Baier is more explicit: The physician "cannot save Anne's life without violating Bill's right to life, but he can let Anne die without violating her right to life" (III, 15).

Now the obvious question to ask about this last claim is what reason we have to believe it true. Why think that killing Bill violates his right to life, while letting Anne die does not violate *her* right to life? Unfortunately, Baier says nothing directly in defense of this claim. But some earlier remarks about the concept of a right (II, 12) suggest the following. For the most part, talk of a "right to life" is simply another way of talking about the duty not to kill. Since agents have a general duty not to kill anyone, each of us has a *right* not to be killed, that is, a right "to life." (Baier also thinks that rights-talk introduces the notion of a right holder being able to waive the protection afforded by the right; but this complication is unimportant for our purposes.) Similarly, were there a duty not to let die, no doubt it would be plausible to include this as well under the rubric of a "right to life." But we are assuming that there is no such duty not to let die. Accordingly, on this basic approach, once we have decided that there is a duty not to kill, but no similar duty not to let die, we can say that killing Bill would violate his right to life, but letting Anne die would not constitute a violation of *her* right.

But even if we do now grant this claim to Baier, it still won't follow—as Baier clearly seems to think it should—that killing Bill is impermissible. For if the right to life is simply a correlate of the duty not to kill, then given that the duty not to kill is only a prima facie duty, the right to life will itself only be what we might call a *prima facie* right. If so, then it might be permissible *all things considered* to "violate" someone's right to life, if this were the only way to save someone else. And so it might be permissible to kill Bill to save Anne.

It is possible, of course, that when Baier claims that Bill's right to life would be violated were we to kill him to save Anne, Baier intends a "stronger" notion of right than the merely prima facie notion that we have just identified, so that to violate a right of this stronger kind trivially entails that one has acted impermissibly all things considered. But if this is what Baier intends, then we can only note that nothing at all in Baier's argument would justify the assumption that Bill *has* a right to life of this sort, or that killing Bill to save Anne violates it. (Alternatively, it might be that Baier is happy to conceive of rights as prima facie rights, but wants to reserve talk of *violating* duties or rights for situations where one acts impermissibly all things considered. But on this construal, it would beg the question for

Baier to assume that killing Bill so as to save Anne's life does indeed *violate* Bill's right to life. For all that Baier has shown, it might rather be a case of permissible "infringement" of that right.)

There still remains a third possible line of argument that is suggested by Baier's remarks. Baier seems to be saying that part of the reason why it is permissible to let Anne die is that we do not let her die "*in order* to save Bill's life." He clearly thinks this point an important one—the italics are his—although he nowhere explains its significance. But there is, at any rate, an implicit contrast being drawn here with what would be the case were we to kill Bill. For only a few sentences earlier, in a passage already partially quoted, Baier asserts that "no one . . . has the right to terminate . . . one person's desirable life simply in order to lengthen another's. Hence this doctor may not kill Bill and then save Anne's life with Bill's kidneys" (III, 14).

All of this suggests that the distinction Baier has in mind is this. If we kill Bill, we presumably kill him *as a means* of saving Anne. (We kill him "in order to" save Anne, by transplanting his kidneys; were there no possibility of saving Anne in this way, there would be no reason to kill Bill.) In contrast, if we let Anne die, then even though it is true that we will eventually be able to use her heart to save Bill, nonetheless we do not let her die as a *means* of saving Bill. (We do not let her die "in order to" save Bill; even if there were no possibility of saving Bill in this way we would still let her die, since the only way to save her involves intending the death of another as a means.) Suppose then that there were a duty not to intend death as a means (or more generally, a duty not to intend harm as a means). Apparently, killing Bill (in order to save Anne's life) would violate this duty; but letting Anne die would not. And this might then explain why it is forbidden to kill Bill in order to save Anne.

There is some further textual evidence in support of this interpretation. As I have already noted parenthetically, Baier goes on to claim that were there a heart available due to the recent death of some third party, we *would be* obligated to save Anne, even though the result, of course, is that it would no longer be possible to save Bill. (If Anne is thus saved, her kidneys won't become available for transplant into Bill.) But why, exactly, would we now be obligated to save Anne? Whatever the explanation, as Baier himself notes, it presumably has nothing to do with the relative significance of killing versus letting die, since if we refuse to save Anne, despite the available heart, we are only letting her die. But if Baier is implicitly assuming that there is a general duty not to intend death as a means, then it is easier to see why he makes the judgments that he does. For if a heart is already available, then the only reason for refusing to save Anne is that we want to let her die as a *means* of saving Bill. Thus in the revised example, unlike the original, we would be letting Anne die "in order to" save another. So if there is a duty not to intend death as a means, then—just as Baier claims—in the revised example, but not the original, letting Anne die involves violating a duty.

What's more, if there is a duty not to intend death as a means, then we can also make sense of Baier's insistence that the impermissibility of killing Bill (in the original example) has nothing to do with the distinction between killing and letting die. What would be crucial would be the fact that killing Bill involves intending his death as a means, not the fact that it involves a killing. (After all, as Baier argues, it would be equally wrong to *let* Anne die—in the revised example—as a means of saving Bill.)

It seems likely, then, that Baier *is* assuming that there is a general duty not to intend death as a means, and that he believes that appeal to this duty can justify his claim that it is impermissible to kill Bill, even though this is the only way to save Anne. Unfortunately, it seems to me that this final strand of Baier's position is no more successful than the earlier ones. To begin with, it is obvious that this entire line of thought presupposes that there is a morally relevant distinction between intending death as a means, and merely permitting avoidable—but "unintended"—deaths. Yet Baier offers nothing by way of argument for the relevance of this distinction.

One imagines—though this is only conjecture—that were Baier to try to argue for this claim, he would adopt a strategy parallel to that adopted in arguing for the relevance of the distinction between killing and letting die. That is, I presume that Baier would first argue for the claim that a sound morality would contain a prima facie duty against intending death as a means, and that he would then argue for the claim that there would be no similar prima facie duty against permitting avoidable but unintended deaths. As before, the crucial step would be the second, and I doubt that Baier could succeed in defending it adequately. (Absent specific arguments, there is not much more that can be said on this point; but to the extent that these arguments would be similar to Baier's attempts to argue against the duty not to let die, I think they would be subject to corresponding objections.)

But even if Baier were successful in establishing that a sound morality would contain a duty not to intend death as a means, while lacking any corresponding duty regarding "unintended" deaths, this would still leave Baier far from his desired conclusion that it is impermissible to kill Bill. For presumably the duty not to intend death as a means would only be a *prima facie* duty. Thus, in certain situations, despite this prima facie duty, intending death as a means would still be permissible *all things considered*. Indeed, since Baier is committed to the permissibility of active euthanasia, and killing in self-defense, it seems clear that he will have to insist on this point himself. But this means that even if there is a prima facie duty not to intend death as a means, and even though in killing Bill to save Anne we "violate" this duty, it still might be the case—for all that would have been shown—that killing Bill is permissible all things considered. And so Baier's argument would still be inadequate. In short, appeal to a prima facie duty not to intend death as a means would not be sufficient for Baier's purposes. Establishing Baier's claim—that killing Bill is impermissible all things considered—would require further argument, argument that goes well beyond anything Baier himself offers, or even hints at. For myself, I see no reason to believe that any such further arguments would be successful.

I conclude therefore that Baier's attempt to "draw the line" is unsuccessful. As we have seen, as a sophisticated friend of ordinary morality Baier believes that at times it is permissible to kill. But like all true friends of ordinary morality, he also believes it *impermissible* to kill an innocent person so as to use his organs to save the life of another. I have argued, however, that Baier is unable to *defend* this judgment. It simply does not follow—not even if we grant Baier his initial claim that killing is worse than letting die.

Of course, I have also argued that Baier is unsuccessful in his attempt to defend that basic principle as well. Thus I think Baier is in error when he claims that his general approach to the foundations of ethics is able to yield normative results congenial to ordinary morality. At any rate, this doesn't seem to be true with regard to some central judgments concerning killing and letting die. (Somewhat more cautiously, perhaps I should say that Baier's attempts to show how his general approach yields the normative judgments of ordinary morality in this area are unsuccessful, and that I don't see any promising suggestions that he overlooks.)

Assuming my arguments are correct, Baier's general approach fails to support the normative judgments concerning killing and letting die that Baier wants to endorse. As a friend of ordinary morality, this conclusion will of course disappoint Baier. But Baier had also hoped to provide "indirect support" (II, 13) for his general approach itself—by demonstrating how it generated the normative judgments that he took to be independently plausible. Baier's failure may thus go deeper than meets the eye. If—as I have argued—his general approach is incapable of supporting the normative judgments of ordinary morality, this may argue against the adequacy of that general approach. Or rather, this may be the conclusion that some of the friends of ordinary morality will feel compelled to draw.

On the other hand, for those of us who reject the intrinsic moral significance of the distinction between killing and letting die, and who want to allow for the permissibility of killing in a range of cases where this is ruled out by common-sense morality, Baier's failure is doubly welcome. Had Baier's general approach actually generated the normative results he claimed it would, I—and all those who reject those normative judgments—would have had to conclude that Baier's general approach was itself flawed. As it is, however, the possibility remains that although some of Baier's specific normative conclusions are unsound, his overall approach to the foundations of ethics is valid. But whether this is indeed so—that is, whether Baier's *foundational* views are correct—is a discussion that I must leave for another day.

Returning to the normative claims themselves, what are we to conclude? As I have already indicated, I believe we should conclude that the distinction between killing and letting die is simply without intrinsic moral significance. (Recognizing this, I think, would also go some way toward freeing us of the thought that there is some morally significant asymmetry in the case of Bill and Anne.) Of course, Baier's inability to establish the relevance of the distinction does not by itself show that the distinction truly lacks moral significance. But his failure is instructive. For unlike many who simply assume the relevance of the distinction uncritically (or who apply it uncritically) Baier is a sophisticate. He sees the need for argument here, and he tries to offer it. This makes his ultimate failure more significant. Perhaps, as I think, the reason why people like Baier and other friends of ordinary morality regularly fail to justify the intrinsic moral relevance of the distinction between killing and letting die is that this distinction simply has no intrinsic moral significance. Becoming a sophisticated friend of ordinary morality is not enough. In this area, and in this regard (at the very least) we must cease to be friends of ordinary morality altogether.

Yale University

NOTES

1. In Kagan 1989, chap. 3.

2. In writing this paper, I follow the argument of Baier's 1990 Carus Lectures, "Three Linked Tasks for Ethics," which—unfortunately—have not been published. Baier's *The Rational and the Moral Order* covers the same material, in considerably greater detail; but the relevant portions of that work (mostly in book two) were not yet available when this paper was being written.

3. When referring to Baier's manuscript, I first give the lecture number, and then the page number within that lecture. This quotation is thus taken from the third lecture, pages 7 and 8.

4. The concept of an option is examined at length in Kagan 1989.

Baier's Carus Lectures on Killing and Letting Die

9

Judith Jarvis Thomson

I

Kurt Baier's three Carus Lectures[1] consist, as he says, of "two parts of ethical theory for one part of moral practice" (I, 1). I am going to focus primarily on the one part of moral practice, but I will also attend to some of the proposals he makes in the two parts of ethical theory, since my main concern is whether what he says in the theory parts supports what he says in the practice part. I wholly agree with the main thesis of the practice part, and think that the theory parts do supply an interesting and indeed promising way of looking at the issue addressed in the practice part; the question I raise is only whether they can be taken to lay it to rest without more ado.

The practice part aims "to settle a controversy over an issue in casuistry, namely, whether killing is morally worse than letting die" (III, 1). And what exactly is that controversy? Baier draws attention to the fact that it is not all that easy to say exactly what it is. Some instances of killing do seem markedly worse than some instances of letting die; Baier gives by way of example that it seems to us worse "to kill the child next door by giving it poisoned chocolates than to let a child in some distant place die by not giving more to famine relief than one is already giving" (III, 1). But so also do some instances of killing seem no worse than some instances of letting die; Baier gives by way of example that it seems to us no worse "to kill one's baby brother in the bath tub by holding his head under water to inherit all, than to let him drown for the same purpose" (III, 1). And finally, some instances of killing seem better than some instances of letting die; Baier mentions mercy-killing, and cases in which a villain is aggressing against an innocent person who can save her life only by killing the villain (II, 14). So what do the philosophers have in mind who express—or anyway summarize—their view in the words "Killing is worse than letting die"? Baier offers the following way of reexpressing their view: killing is prima facie worse than letting die. But what does *that* locution mean?

Let us begin with non-comparatives, that is, with locutions of the form "Doing such and such is prima facie wrong." Baier describes the meanings of such locutions in one of the theory parts (II, 14–15) as follows. Acting in such and such way is prima facie wrong where "there is a (not very well understood) quasi-logical relationship between the nature of the act and its being wrong" which has the following feature: the fact that an act is an instance of doing such and such does not entail, but generates a defeasible presumption, that it is wrong.

Then we should presumably take comparative locutions of the form "Doing so and so is prima facie worse than doing such and such" to mean: the fact that one act is an instance of doing so and so and a second an instance of doing such and such generates a defeasible presumption that the first is worse than the second.[2] And our philosophers are then to be understood to be saying: the fact that one act is a killing and a second an instance of letting die generates a defeasible presumption that the first is worse than the second. A defeasible presumption is, by definition, defeasible, so an act that is a killing may not in fact be worse than an act that is a letting die; still, there is a presumption that it is worse, which presumption needs defeating if the killing is not to be worse than the letting die.

Baier himself believes that this thesis is true and argues for it.

Now, like Baier, I am not going to try to give an account of the notion 'defeasible presumption'. While it appears everywhere in a certain style of moral theorizing, it is, as Baier says, not very well understood. However, those of us who make use of it take its not being very well understood to constitute a problem, not an incoherence; and I do think that it is sufficiently clear for Baier's purposes in his Carus Lectures, and for my purposes here.

What needs asking, then, is whether the theoretical claims Baier makes in his two parts of ethical theory support the thesis that the fact that one act is a killing and a second an instance of letting die generates a defeasible presumption that the first is worse than the second. So let us look at the relevant theoretical claims.

II

They can be seen as an effort to solve the following problem, which is at the heart of moral theory. The problem issues from the conjunction of three very plausible-looking ideas.[3] (i) There are occasions on which it would be to my own on-balance advantage to do a thing, which morality really does forbid me to do. (ii) I have reason to do a thing if and only if it is to my own on-balance advantage to do it, and *a fortiori* I have reason to refrain from doing a thing if and only if it is to my own on-balance advantage to refrain from doing it. From (i) and (ii) there follows: on those occasions, I have no reason to refrain from doing the thing. Now consider the third idea: (iii) a true moral proscription (or prescription) supplies a person with a reason, indeed, a compelling or overriding reason, to comply with it. From (i) and (iii) there follows: on those occasions, I have overriding reason to refrain from doing the thing. Thus given all three ideas, there are occasions on which I both have no reason for refraining from doing a thing, while having overriding reason for refraining from doing it. Something plainly has to give, and a considerable amount of moral theorizing consists in an effort to work out what.

Baier's own solution in the Carus Lectures emerges from a particularly sensitive and interesting discussion of the notion 'having reason': he can be seen as recommending to us that we give up (ii), more precisely, that we opt for something like (ii), but weaker. My summary of his idea will perforce be abrupt, but I think it expresses what is essential. Suppose that what is in question for me here and now is whether or not to do alpha; and suppose it would be to my on-balance advantage to do alpha. The second idea (ii) says that I have reason to do alpha, and no reason to refrain from doing it. Baier proposes instead (I, 15) that I may have a reason, indeed, an overriding reason, to refrain from doing alpha: I do have an overriding reason to refrain from doing alpha if and only if the compound state of affairs in which I here and now refrain from doing alpha *and* other people generally refrain from doing alpha, is more to my on-balance advantage than the compound state of affairs in which I here and now do alpha *and* other people generally do not refrain from doing alpha. (Prisoner's Dilemmas are what he has in mind, and refers us to; these are situations in which "were people generally to follow self-anchored reasons, this would have suboptimal outcomes" for all of them.) Thus, for example, though it would be to my on-balance advantage that I here and now kill my grandfather (because he is planning to disinherit me tomorrow), I have an overriding reason not to kill him since it is more to my on-balance advantage that I not kill my grandfather here and now *and* people generally refrain from killing than that I kill my grandfather here and now *and* people generally do not refrain from killing—for if people kill others as they please, I am myself at risk of being killed at any time.

Thus my advantage remains central to my having reason for refraining, but my advantage need not issue from my particular act of refraining—it is enough if it would be to my advantage that people generally refrain.

There are difficulties here, most prominently, perhaps, what expresses itself in the question why that should be thought enough. Why should I care about the advantage to myself that issues from general self-restraint including my own? If what is central to my having reason for refraining is my own advantage, why fix on the advantage to me that issues from general self-restraint instead of the advantage to me that issues from my proceeding here and now, given that others are restraining themselves? Morality supplies an answer, lying in the unfairness of profiting from the self-restraint of others while exercising none oneself; but we have not yet reached morality—we are so far concerned only with what a person has reason to do. I am going to bypass this and other difficulties, however. What I want to focus on is what emerges about morality given this idea about having reason for doing a thing.

Baier accepts idea (iii), namely that a true moral proscription (or prescription) supplies a person—*every* person—with a reason, indeed, a compelling or overriding reason, to comply with it. In light of his conclusion about having a reason for doing a thing, this means that a moral guideline is true if and only if it is or would be more to everyone's advantage that people generally comply with it than that people generally do not comply with it. That supplies us with a very attractive and straightforward test for the truth of a moral guideline.

The proposal Baier here makes is one of a family of moral theories that might be called Generalist. The weakest Generalist theory is an idea Baier expresses as follows: "an individual's morality must be his preferred candidate for the position of group morality" (II, 3). That is, you cannot believe that such and such moral guidelines are true without believing that their proscriptions and prescriptions govern everyone's conduct, and not just your own. A second idea is that a moral code is true if and only if everyone would agree to be governed by it, under this or that set of conditions or constraints on the decision-making situation; contractualist theories fall under this heading. A third idea is Baier's, namely that a moral code is true if and only if it is to everyone's advantage that people generally comply with it. The second and third ideas are both stronger than the first, and are interestingly similar and different from each other. Since what people would agree to in such and such a situation is a function of what each would (in that situation) think it to his or her advantage to agree to, the idea of advantage is at work in the second just as centrally as it is in the third; but the second invites a person to ask himself or herself "Would it appear to me, if I were in the specified situation, to be to my advantage that we agree on thus and such code?" whereas the third invites a person to ask himself or herself "Is it to my advantage that we generally comply with thus and such code?" I think it possible, however, that this difference would turn out on closer examination to be less deep than it looks.

Let us in any case turn now to the question what are the contents of the true moral code. Baier's discussion of this matter in Lecture II is very rich, and the distinctions he makes are of great importance. I will unfortunately have to restrict myself to what he says there that bears directly on the issue to be dealt with in the practical part, Lecture III.[4]

III

Baier says: we can think of a true moral code as specifying what "we can *in reason* want of one another" (II, 4). That is because a true moral code supplies us all with overriding reasons for action, and you and I can each "in reason want"—that is, it is reasonable for each of us to want—that the other act in accordance with those overriding reasons for action. He then says; "According to our morality, we can in reason want of one another that each refrain from killing others. Our moral guideline, 'Thou shalt not kill' can be interpreted as telling each of us to refrain from killing other human beings" (II, 7). Is it true that we ought not kill other human beings? The test suggested by the theoretical claims we have looked at is this: the guideline that we ought not kill is true if and only if it is better for each of us that people generally refrain from killing than that they do not. Surely it *is* better for each of us that people generally refrain from killing than that they do not! If so, Baier's test yields that we ought not kill.

But one thing we do know is that Baier doesn't think it true that we may never kill: he thinks it is only prima facie wrong to kill other human beings. As I said at the outset, he thinks mercy-killing permissible, and he thinks it permissible for an innocent to kill a person who is villainously aggressing against her. So something has gone wrong.

Baier does deal with this difficulty (II, 15–16), but does not tell us exactly how his attractive and straightforward test is to be modified to have it permit mercy-killing and killing in self-defense. And it is not easy to see how it is most plausible to modify it.

The trouble arose, I suggest, because of the comparison the test invites us to make: we are to ask whether it is better for each of us that people generally refrain from killing than that they do not. More generally: we are to ask whether it is better for each of us that people generally refrain from doing alpha than that they do not. (This comparison was suggested to Baier by Prisoner's Dilemmas.) Perhaps the test should be so modified as to invite making a different comparison, between the state of affairs that obtains if people generally comply with thus and such candidate moral guideline and the state of affairs that obtains if people generally comply with thus and such competing candidate moral guideline. Killings come in any number of kinds; which moral guideline should we take to govern them? One candidate is: one ought not kill. A competing candidate is: one ought not kill except where the killing would be a mercy-killing. Another is: one ought not kill except where the killing would be a mercy-killing *or* an instance of killing in self-defense. Since we may at any time come to be suffering so severely as to prefer being killed to continuing to live, and since also we may at any time be threatened with death by villains, the state of affairs in which people generally comply with the guideline that allows of both of those exceptions is better for us than the state of affairs in which people generally comply with a guideline that does not allow of either of them. And perhaps we should take it that *that* selects the rule containing the exceptions instead of the rule that does not.

Perhaps this, or anyway something like it, would bypass the difficulty, while yet remaining within the spirit of Baier's form of Generalist theory. For his purposes, it or something like it is attractive in another way too, in that beginning with a blunt candidate guideline and comparing the state of affairs in which it is generally complied with, with the states of affairs in which progressively narrower guidelines—containing exceptions—are generally complied with, expresses what is for him the heart of the notion of a kind of act's being prima facie wrong. He thinks it clear that we should "regard the wrongness of killing as *the normal case* and its not being wrong *as the exception*" (II, 15); and exceptions are precisely what the narrower guidelines specify.

Let us in any case now turn to the practice part, and look at the bearing of these ideas on the controversy about killing and letting die.

IV

Baier accepts the thesis that killing is prima facie worse than letting die, that is, that the fact that one act is a killing and a second an instance of letting die generates a defeasible presumption that the first is worse than the second.

Now this thesis is not itself a moral guideline in the sense I take Baier to have in mind, since it is not itself a "directive" (II, 4), and does not itself "regulate" behavior (II, 6): it neither proscribes nor prescribes. But it may be presumed to yield a guideline in that sense, for it may be presumed to yield (among other things) that when we must choose between killing a person and letting a person die, there is a defeasible presumption that we ought to let the person die.[5] So, anyway, I will suppose; and it is that guideline I will focus on in what follows.

Is it true? Baier's test for the truth of a moral guideline invites us to ask whether it is more to our advantage that people generally comply with this guideline than that they do not. Or, as emended in the preceding section, the test invites us to ask whether it is more to our advantage that people generally comply with this guideline than that they generally comply with a competing guideline. Which competing guideline? There are any number of possibilities, of course. But I postpone mention of them for the moment, since Baier does not in fact invite us to attend directly to the guideline governing choice in Lecture III. What he does is rather to draw attention to two considerations in support of saying that while there is good reason for adopting a guideline making it prima facie a duty not to kill, there is good reason not to adopt a guideline making it prima facie a duty to save lives.

The first of the two considerations is this: all of us who have an opportunity to kill a person can comply with the guideline declaring it a duty not to kill the person, but all of us who have an opportunity to save a person's life cannot comply with the (putative) guideline declaring it a duty to save the person's life—there would be conflict, confusion, and mutual interference among the competing rescuers if we all tried to.[6] He says: "This alone, I think, adequately explains and justifies why our morality imposes a general prima facie moral prohibition on killing human beings, but makes saving life only something morally desirable for everybody" (III, 8).

Something interesting is at work here. Suppose that A is drowning, and here are B, C, and D, about whom we are to suppose that each can save A's life. But the following cannot be true: B saves A's life, and C does, and D does. Does it follow that they do not each have a duty to save A's life? It is a familiar idea that a person does not have a duty to do a thing if he cannot do it; what is at work here is a different idea, namely that people (each of whom can do a thing) do not have a duty to do the thing if it cannot be the case that all do it. Should we agree to this? Consider the two possibilities. In the first place, nobody saves A's life. Isn't it in order for me to say to B later "You failed to do what you had a duty to do"? If B asks "Why me? What about C and D?" why can't I reply that I'll get to them next—I'm going in alphabetical order. The more interesting possibility is the second, in which (as it might be) D saves A's life. Does that mean I can't say to B later "You failed to do what you had a duty to do"? I don't find it obvious that I can't. I suppose we would have to grant that once it was fixed that D was going to save A, B ceased to have a duty to do so; and if you are a determinist, and therefore think of D's future saving of A as fixed from all time, you would conclude that B never did have a duty to save A. But why shouldn't we suppose that that is because from then on (when D jumps in, or from the beginning of time) A was in fact fixed to be saved, and why shouldn't we therefore appeal, for excusing B, to the quite different general principle that no one has a duty to bring about an outcome fixed to come about anyway? Perhaps there is nothing in the idea I point to here. I suspect in any case that the source of Baier's idea that it has to be possible for all to do a thing if all are to have a duty to do it lies in what leads him to adopt his form of Generalist theory.

But a further reply is also available, namely that this argument shows (if it does) only that we cannot be thought to have a duty to save lives, leaving entirely open that we have a duty to save lives when no one else will do so. *That* is something we can all do.[7] So something more needs to be said if that narrower guideline is to be rejected too.

Baier's second consideration in favor of rejecting a duty to save can be brought to bear against the narrower as well as against the broader guideline. He says it is easy enough to say what we all have to do to discharge the duty not to kill: don't kill. But he says it is not clear "what a person who is not a member of certain special classes [charged with saving lives by virtue of his or her position or role, as, for example, a lifeguard is] would have to do to discharge a duty not to let die" (III, 10). And he says that "we cannot justifiably regard something as a duty which it is seldom or never possible to say whether a person has or has not done it" (III, 10).

Now we are going to need to reput this consideration, for it really is just as easy to say what we have to do to discharge the duty to save (or to save when others won't) as it is to say what we have to do to discharge the duty not to kill. What we have to do is: save (or save when others won't). Nor can the point be put like this: we can 'complete' our duty not to kill, but can't 'complete' our duty to save (henceforth I omit the qualifier)—there is always someone else to save. After all, there is always someone else not to kill. What his discussion suggests is that he has in mind instead this: it is plain unreasonable to suppose that people have that duty. It would be too costly in money, time, energy, risk, and so on. He says that while there is a "natural duty to rescue" it is limited; it is "restricted to those in the best position to perform the rescue, and is limited by the cost to the rescuer" (III, 8).

This is a consideration I am very much in sympathy with. But how is the point to be got to go in firmly? Many people have complained that the rationale for excusing from a duty to save because of its costliness is unclear. Shelly Kagan, for example, asks why it should not as well be concluded that we are excused from a duty not to kill when it would be very costly to refrain, as where refraining from killing my grandfather tonight will mean he will disinherit me tomorrow.[8]

The theoretical parts of Baier's Lectures do suggest an answer: the cost to be considered is not the cost on the occasion, at the time, but rather the cost of general compliance with the guideline. Let us focus on two possible guidelines, (1) that we have a duty to save when others won't, and (2) that we have a duty to save when others won't ***and*** where it is not costly to save. Which guideline is such that it is more to my advantage that there be general compliance with it?

General compliance with (1) gives me a higher probability of being saved than general compliance with (2) does; that makes general compliance with (1) seem more to my advantage than general compliance with (2). But my complying with (1) is more costly to me than my complying with (2), and unless I think of myself as an exception to the guideline, general compliance with the guideline includes my compliance with the guideline; that makes general compliance with (2) seem more to my advantage than general compliance with (1). How does the balance of advantage come out? It depends on my preferences. If I am willing to forgo the increased probability of being saved in exchange for not having to pay the costs of costly saving, then I will prefer general compliance with (2). I suspect that this is true of (all? most?) of us.

Compare now the guidelines (1') that we have a duty not to kill, and (2') that we have a duty not to kill except where it would be costly to refrain from killing. General compliance with (1') gives me a higher probability of not being killed than general compliance with (2') does; that makes general compliance with (1') seem more to my advantage than general compliance with (2'). But my complying with (1') is more costly to me than my complying with (2'); that makes general compliance with (2') seem more to my advantage than general compliance with (1). How does the balance of advantage come out *here*? If I am unwilling to forgo the increased probability of not being killed in exchange for not having to pay the costs of costly refraining from killing, then I will prefer general compliance with (1'). I suspect that this is also true of (all? most?) of us.

If we all have those preferences—and if, also, having them is not irrational—then it really is more to our advantage that there be only a duty to save where saving would not be costly, but a duty not to kill even though refraining from killing might be costly. And if so, the theoretical parts of Baier's Lectures therefore do yield the wanted asymmetry.

I am sure there is more to be said about this issue. Let us instead suppose the argument here succeeds, and return, then, to the guideline governing choice.

V

The guideline governing choice was this: when we must choose between killing a person and letting a person die, there is a defeasible presumption that we ought to let the person die. Given the asymmetry pointed to in the preceding section, it follows that the duty not to kill is more stringent than the duty to save; and it might therefore be thought to follow from the asymmetry alone that the guideline governing choice is true. Does this conclusion follow from the asymmetry? I don't see clearly how it should be thought to do so. For it should be remembered what the asymmetry—and therefore the difference in stringency—pointed to consists in: there is a duty not to kill, but only a duty to save when it would not be costly to do the saving. Suppose, then, that A must choose between killing B and letting C die; thus the only way in which A can save C is by killing B. Suppose also that it would not be at all costly to A to save C. (Killing B would, we are supposing, be easy for A.) Then it looks as if, whichever A chooses, he violates a duty. And isn't the presumption, then, that what A ought to do is to flip a coin? In short, there is a gap between the asymmetry and the guideline governing choice.[9]

But there really is no need within Baier's theory to get to the guideline governing choice from the asymmetry; why not instead bring the theoretical apparatus to bear directly on the guideline governing choice? Doing that requires us to ask: is it more to our advantage that people generally comply with that guideline than that they do not? Or, as emended in section 3: is it more to our advantage that people generally comply with that guideline than that they comply with any other competing guideline? One competing guideline is: when we must choose between killing a person and letting a person die, there is a defeasible presumption that we ought to kill the person. Another is: when we must choose between killing a person and letting a person die, there is a defeasible presumption that we ought to flip a coin. Which of these three guidelines is such that general compliance with it is most to our advantage?

It is hard to get a grip on this question because it is hard to see how advantage would be affected by general compliance with guidelines declaring only that there are defeasible presumptions that one ought to do this or that—indeed, it is hard to see what general compliance with a guideline declaring only that there are defeasible presumptions that one ought to do this or that would itself consist in. (Don't we need to be told, first, what the defeaters are?) But perhaps we can get a firm enough grip to be going on with.

Let us focus on the difference between what I have been calling the guideline governing choice, which I will call the "let die guideline," and the first of the competing guidelines I mentioned, which I will call the "kill guideline." If we assume that the probability of "I will need saving, and will be savable only by A's killing B" is the same as the probability of "B will need saving, and will be savable only by A's killing me," then from the point of view of the advantage that consists in increased probability of survival, there is no advantage to me, whichever of the two guidelines A complies with. For suppose A complies with the let die guideline. Then it is probable to degree p (let us say) that there will be occasions on which I will live because A's saving B would require killing me; but it is also probable to degree p that there will be occasions on which I will die because A's saving me would require killing B. Similarly if A complies with the kill guideline.

Similarly for the more complicated guideline prescribing coin-flipping.

There are three ways in which Baier can go in face of this result. First, he can lean on the fact that the guidelines we are considering only say that there are defeasible presumptions that we should make these choices, and appeal to that notion to justify selection of the let die guideline.

Second, he can point to the fact that we don't think the probabilities are equal all round. I think that *is* a fact. Each of us does think he or she is more careful than others are; each of us does think that he or she is less likely to need the death of another for survival than the others are to need his or her death.

But I think that the third way in which Baier can go is more interesting: he can say that probability of survival is not the only thing that matters to us, and hence probability of survival is not the only thing that is to be weighed in assessing advantage. What I have in mind is this. Most of us do not wander about in fear of natural threats descending on us from out of the blue, whether the threat consists in a crashing meteor or the sudden onset of an ailment. We know those things can happen to us at any time, but do not normally worry about them. What of the prospect of being snatched off the street at any time for use as a resource to save the life of another? General compliance with the kill guideline (or the coin-flipping guideline) would generate fear of exactly that.

It seems to me, moreover, not merely that Baier can go this way, but that he had better. For he is going to have need of it when dealing with cases in which there is a difference in the numbers, as, for example, where killing one would enable A to save not merely one person but more than one. Baier does not discuss such cases, but they are crucial to the controversy about killing and letting die. Many (most? all?) of those who think that we may not kill one to save one also think that we may not kill one even to save five; and Baier, I am sure, would agree. But how is that to be made out in his theory? Probability of survival does look to be increased by allowing the killing of one to save five; unless the third route is taken, I see no outweighing disadvantage of a guideline that permits it.

But why *not* take the third route?[10] Whatever the foundations of one's moral theory, it just isn't an attractive idea that we be morally permitted to kill one to save five. We don't like the idea. And hadn't there therefore be something unattractive in it, something to our positive disadvantage in there being a guideline in force that permits it?

But I leave the question open, since Baier does not make clear in Lecture III which route he would take. My own inclination is to think that the theoretical theses he sets before us in Lectures I and II *are* helpful in thinking about the controversy dealt with in Lecture III; indeed, I know of no more promising way of thinking about it.

Massachusetts Institute of Technology

Notes

1. The pairs of numbers in parentheses following quotations from the lectures refer as follows: the roman number to one of the three lectures, the arabic number or numbers to a page or pages.

2. I say only "presumably," since there is another way of analyzing the comparatives: "Doing so and so is prima facie worse than doing such and such" means "The fact that an act is an instance of doing so and so generates a stronger presumption against it than does the fact that an act is an instance of doing such and such."

Under this analysis, by contrast with that of the text above, we must contrast the strengths of presumptions. So under this analysis we need the notion 'strength of a presumption' as well as the notion 'presumption'. But perhaps in the end, understanding the analysis of the text above would also require understanding both of these notions.

3. I here paraphrase Baier's introductory remarks in I, 1–2.

4. However I cannot resist pointing to a distinction Baier makes in Lecture II that I think wants closer study than he had space to give it there. What I have in mind is his distinction between "the optional and the non-optional." He says, "We think the choice between lying and not lying is non-optional: lying is *wrong;* we *must not* lie, *not* lying is a *duty,* is *obligatory.* The choice between doing and not doing someone a favor is optional: we *ought* to do him that favor, but don't have to; doing it is *desirable* but not *obligatory;* not doing it is undesirable but not wrong." (II, 8) This is often said, and no doubt there is something right in the offing. But what, exactly? For in the first place, what marks an act as (merely) "doing someone a favor"? If a man is drowning, and I throw him a life preserver, is that my doing him a favor? If that is doing him a favor, then there surely are favors it is not merely undesirable to fail to do but wrong to fail to do. Or is my throwing the life preserver marked as not a favor since the man's life turns on whether he gets the life preserver? So that what we do is a (mere) favor only if what we do supplies only a relatively minor benefit? (And how minor is minor enough?) If so, it appears that the reason why doing favors is not required is merely that nothing much turns on whether they are done, and that it is for that reason alone that it is undesirable though not wrong to refuse to do them. But then, second, what if a relatively minor benefit could be produced for a person at no or utterly trivial cost? A man asks me courteously "Could you tell me the time?" I have just looked at my watch, and the cost to me of telling him the time is the cost to me of saying (as it might be) the words "Five past ten." Is it wrong for me to say "I can't, because I don't have a watch" (a lie), but merely undesirable for me to say "I can, but I won't" (a refusal to do a favor)? My own feeling is that morality governs the small as well as the large, and that the small needs more attention than it usually gets.

5. Baier denies that his thesis yields this guideline (III, 2). I find that puzzling, for it seems to me undeniable that if there is a presumption that alpha-ing is worse than beta-ing, then when we must choose between alpha-ing and beta-ing, there is a presumption that we ought to choose beta-ing. (Baier's ground for rejecting this step from thesis to guideline lies in his view—see III, 11–12—that wherever one has a choice between killing someone and letting her die one also has the option of saving her life, for [he thinks] one cannot let a person die unless one also has the option of saving her life. That seems to me implausible, for it seems to me a doctor might truly say to himself of his dying patient, whom he has no way of saving; "I can either kill her now, or let her die naturally." In any case, Baier's idea here would, if true, mean, not that the guideline is false, but at most that we are never so situated that its guidance is relevant.)

6. I bypass, as Baier does, the possibility that there is only one possible rescuer.

7. This is a point made by Shelly Kagan in his contribution to this volume. (I am indebted to him for showing me an early draft of his paper.)

8. See his contribution to the present volume—as also his discussion of this matter in *The Limits of Morality* (Kagan 1989).

9. One way of crossing it is to assume this: when A must choose between killing B and letting C die, there is a presumption that A's saving C would be costly. If that assumption is true, then—given the asymmetry—when A must choose between killing B and letting C die, there is a presumption that A ought to let C die. But that assumption is not particularly plausible. And moreover, what if it is defeated? (That is, what if, as in the text above, it would not be costly for A to save C?) Should we agree that A ought to flip a coin? Or even that there is a presumption that A ought to flip a coin? Baier would surely not agree; nor would most of the rest of us.

10. My own account of the Trolley Problem in *The Realm of Rights* takes the third route. See also the symposium on that book in *Philosophy and Phenomenological Research* (1993).

Self-Anchored Morality

10

T. M. Scanlon

I. Introduction

As has been evident at least since Prichard,[1] attempts to answer the question, Why be moral? face an acute dilemma. Anything that looks like a moral reason for taking morality seriously will be unsatisfactory, since it seems to presuppose the very concerns whose justification is in question. On the other hand, most answers that are clearly nonmoral are also unsatisfactory. In particular, attempts to show that being moral is in one's self-interest face a double burden. First, they advance a claim that is implausible on its face in view of the evident conflicts between self-interest and the demands of morality. Second, if they were to succeed they would appear to provide the wrong sort of reason for being moral. A person who accepted morality only because of its supposed contributions to his or her self-interest would strike us as more expedient than virtuous.

In *The Moral Point of View,* and then again in somewhat different forms in the last section of his APA Presidential Address, in "Moral Reasons and Reasons to be Moral," and now in chapter 5 of his newest book, Kurt Baier has set out a strategy for answering the question in a way that seems to have a good chance of avoiding this dilemma. Put simply, the strategy is this: We should accept a system of reason which counts moral guidelines as expressing normally overriding practical reasons (at least in circumstances in which most others do likewise), because following such a system will leave each of us better off than we would be under a system that did not have this property. Put the other way around: if we all accepted a system of reasons according to which moral guidelines had no intrinsic reason-giving force, then we would all, as a result, be worse off than we would be had we accepted a system of reasons supporting morality. Moreover, leading to this kind of mutual disadvantage would be a cardinal fault in a system of reasons, a deficiency that the very idea of being rational requires us to avoid.[2]

This strategy holds out the possibility of avoiding Prichard's dilemma since, on the one hand, the reason that is ultimately appealed to does not seem to be explicitly moral but rather has to do with the idea of rationality and its link with doing what conduces to our advantage. On the other hand, what is invoked is the idea of mutual advantage, an idea which seems much more relevant to morality than self-interest is. It is not implausible (even if, as I will argue, it is not the whole story) to claim that this is what morality is about, what gives it its point and rationale, and undergirds its reason-giving authority.

I am not going to discuss directly the question of whether this strategy succeeds. My interest is rather in whether and how we should be concerned at all with the question, Why be moral? In the next section I want to say something about the various ways in which this question might be taken. In subsequent sections I will be more concerned with the categories in which Baier discusses the question in his most recent work, in particular with his ideas of self-anchored and society-anchored reasons.

II. Why Be Moral?

Why ask, "Why be moral?" One answer takes the question to be asked from the perspective of someone who already regards moral considerations as normally overriding practical reasons, and who wishes to understand better what kind of reasons they are. The question is not asked out of doubt, or as a demand for justification. The enterprise, rather, is one of self-understanding. And while a negative outcome of this investigation is not excluded—since it might turn out that none of the available accounts of morality supports its presumed authority—such an outcome is not presupposed, so the aim is not to forestall it by providing a justification. Nor is it presupposed that the question must have a single answer: it may be that what we call "morality" involves a plurality of considerations with different kinds of importance for us.

This relatively unambitious view of the enterprise does not make it trivial. In particular, Prichard's dilemma still retains its bite: our answer (or answers) must be manifestly connected to morality but must not appeal to its authority. It is no answer simply to say that we have reason not to do what is wrong because wrongness is something it is important to avoid. On the other hand, the description of our reason for avoiding wrong action must have some recognizable connection with wrongness. Splitting this difference is not easy, but it may seem more feasible than the task of justification.

On this interpretation, the question "Why be moral?" is asked with the aim of self-understanding. This is the interpretation of the question that I take most seriously. Others, however, may regard it as insufficiently ambitious, on at least two related grounds. First, even from the first person point of view, a mere portrait of the reasons we have for caring about morality may seem to give us less than what we want: what we want to know is not merely what we care about when we care about morality but why morality is something we must care about. And this concern is magnified when we turn to consider others: an account of morality that is adequate to its claims must explain not merely what those who care about it are moved by but why this is something that everyone has reason to recognize as of great (normally overriding) importance. On this second interpretation, then, the question, "Why be moral?" is asked with the aim of justification.

As I have indicated, I am inclined to regard this more ambitious project (at least as it is frequently understood) as probably impossible but, fortunately, unnecessary. The first project is enough for me. But I think that a certain amount of the appeal of Baier's argument lies in the fact that it holds out hope of accomplishing this more difficult aim. I do not think, in the end, that it does, but that is not, for me, a reason to think less of it.

There are points in Baier's writing where a third, and to some degree intermediate, aim is suggested.[3] Even if one has a clear and fully satisfactory understanding of the appeal of moral reasons, and even if one felt no need for a further justification of those reasons, one might still be troubled by the conflict between moral reasons and other reasons, such as those based on self-interest or other personal concerns. This worry could be addressed in at least two ways. One would be by, as it were, bolstering the reason-giving force of moral reasons—making it clearer why they are of such distinct importance as to take priority over all other reasons. (This strategy leads back to the need for justification.) Alternatively, one might look for a better understanding of the relation between moral and other reasons, not with the aim of finding more power behind moral reasons but rather with the aim of gaining a clearer understanding of the conflict, perhaps showing that on a proper understanding of the two kinds of reasons, especially of the nonmoral ones, they do not conflict as sharply as one might at first think. On this interpretation, the question "Why be moral?" raises what I will call the question of compatibility.

Whether "Why be moral?" is asked as a question about self-interpretation, justification, or compatibility, this question is understood against the background of some class of (usually nonmoral) reasons. In Baier's case this is the class of "self-anchored" reasons. In the next section I will examine his characterization of this class. In section 5 I will return to the various interpretations of "Why be moral?" that I have just distinguished, and in particular to the relation between these different interpretations.

III. Self-anchored Reasons

I find myself somewhat confused about the distinction between self-anchored and society-anchored reasons. The idea is not that reasons of the latter kind are inculcated in us by society while reasons of the former kind are ones we might have had "on our own." Baier makes clear that in both cases it is an important function of "society" to help individuals to acquire guidelines and standards of choice which represent the collective wisdom of our predecessors and fellow citizens. The distinction, rather, concerns the content of these reasons and, especially, their grounds—what it is that makes them reasons. On this view, a consideration is a self-anchored reason for me if its being a reason depends on its direct contribution to "my life." Whereas in the case of society-anchored reasons this connection is only indirect. This, at least, is my hypothesis. My uncertainty about the distinction is, first and foremost, uncertainty about the idea of self-anchored reasons, so let me begin with this idea.

Baier characterizes what I might call the target of his analysis in three successively less abstract ways. First, he is interested in finding what it is that "ultimately grounds practical reasons" (RMO, 119), the practical analog of truth (at least, one might add, from the personal point of view.) That is, (this is still a version of what I am calling the first characterization), he wants to know "whether there is a privileged point of view from which the world must be judged if any improvement in the world brought about by someone's action constitutes a reason for him to do it, and if so what that point of view is" (RMO, 132). This point of view, he says, is the point of view of self-anchored reason, called "self-anchored" because it involves reasons "based on the individual's preferences and motivational patterns and the most complete relevant information available, but [not] guidelines developed by the society for the purposes of remotivating them for some purpose or other" (RMO, 132).

In another characterization (RMO, 129–30) Baier says that self-anchored reasons are self-anchored in four ways: (1) "their ground is some agent-favoring property of the action for which they are reasons, as for instance prudential reasons or those favoring the agent's loved ones"; (2) they are independent of other people because they are reasons for doing something that the agent can do without the help of others, the doing of which confers a benefit on him; (3) "they are independent of others following the same reason in the same circumstances"; and (4) their motivating force is not normally backed up by social sanctions.

Baier then proceeds, if I understand his argument correctly, to characterize the point of view in question more fully by specifying more exactly the "ground" mentioned in the first of these conditions. When I ask, from the point of view of self-anchored reason, "What do I have most reason to do?" what question am I actually asking? I might, for example be asking, "What would be most to my benefit?" Alternatively, I might be asking, "What would make my life best (as judged by an unflawed conception of a good life for me)?" Baier concludes that the latter answer offers the correct characterization of this privileged point of view.

The basis for this conclusion is provided by the example of Fred and Frieda, a two-career couple who are deciding which jobs to take. Each has been offered a job in Texas and one in the Northeast. Fred prefers the job in the Northeast, so there is a clear sense in which, by accepting the job in Texas because the job there is better for Frieda, he is making a sacrifice (choosing the smaller benefit to him.) But this does not mean, Baier maintains, that it would be contrary to self-anchored reason for him to take this job. This is because, given the importance in his conception of a good life of his being near Frieda and of her life going well, in choosing the job in Texas Fred is also following the course of action that leads to the best life for him.

Now someone might reply that, if going to Texas so that Frieda can have a better job is what leads to a better life for Fred, then it is also the course of action that benefits him more. But surely we want to preserve the common-sense idea that in going to Texas Fred is making a sacrifice. We might try to preserve this idea by speaking simply of particular goods (not "points of view") since we can say that in going to Texas Fred would be giving up something he has reason to value, namely the difference between the two jobs. But if he took the Texas job because they offered him more money he would still be giving this up, and would we be as willing in that case to say he is "making a sacrifice"? Perhaps not, or at least not "on balance." Our tendency to say this indicates that there is a "point of view" from which the money makes up what Fred loses in other ways so that he is not, on balance, worse off, judged from this "point of view." This indicates one thing that a "point of view" is: what might be called a sphere of compensation, a range of gains and losses which counterbalance one another because they are all counted as gains or as losses with respect to the same thing: the agent's good.

Baier wants to say, not implausibly, that the point of view we have just defined, or gestured toward, the point of view of "one's own good," cannot be the privileged point of view of self-anchored reason, since it could be true that (1) Fred's decision to go to Texas is, from this point of view, a sacrifice, even on balance; and (2) his doing so is nonetheless not "contrary to reason," provided at least that (3) doing so is in accord with his conception of what makes for the best life for him (or perhaps, what is somewhat different, that doing so is required by concerns that he must have in order to live what he regards as the best life.)

Baier concludes (RMO, 153) that the preferred characterization of the privileged point of view, the point of view of self-anchored reason, is this: the point of view of self-anchored practical reason is the point of view defined by the agent's conception of the good life, provided that that conception is not internally flawed.

I want now to raise a few questions about this point of view. Basically, my questions are these: to what degree does the idea of "a good life" actually circumscribe this point of view? What reasons does it rule out other than those deriving from social norms? To the degree that it does rule out some reasons, in what sense are these less "privileged" than self-anchored reasons? How does the idea of "a good life" account for this difference in status?

The passages I have quoted suggest two possible interpretations of the idea of self-anchored reasons. The first takes quite literally the idea that these reasons are grounded in some "self-favoring property of the action of which they are reasons," and hence that the criterion of relevance, from the point of view of self-anchored reason, is whether an action "favorably or unfavorably affects the excellence of the agent's life." I will call reasons that meet this criterion "self-grounded."

It is commonly recognized that not only our de facto preferences but also what might be called our "rational aims" (those desires and preferences that we would ideally have) include preferences for things other than benefits to ourselves. Benefits to loved ones, as in the Fred and Frieda case, provide one example, and Baier clearly means to include these within the sphere of self-anchored reasons. But there are many other such concerns. Highly altruistic aims, such as saving the rain forest or relieving the plight of the homeless are obvious examples, but also slightly misleading ones. For while such aims are clearly not irrational they may strike us as rare exceptions to the general rule that most aims are grounded in some envisaged benefit to ourselves or to others near and dear to us. But we all in fact recognize many more mundane reasons which are counter-examples to this "rule." People make sacrifices in order to make their firms or associations or departments more successful, even when this is not directly beneficial to them; they write books and give lectures at least in part because they think it is important for people to understand the subjects in question (not only because they like being in the limelight); and they help to foster recycling schemes in hopes of alleviating the problem of solid waste even though they do not think that waste is likely to be buried "in their backyard."

Suppose, for example, that one of my aims is for a certain way of looking at questions of freedom and responsibility to be more widely understood and accepted. I might believe that this would not only constitute an intellectual advance but that it would also lead to clearer understanding of important issues of social policy ranging from punishment to health care. Given that this is one of my professional aims, accomplishing it would make my life better, because more successful. So I have two sorts of reasons for undertaking actions directed to this end: they make it more likely that I will succeed in my aims, and they make it more likely that a result that I regard as important and desirable may be accomplished. Reasons of the first sort are self-grounded, while those of the second are not. It is quite conceivable, even natural, for a person to be motivated by both sorts of reasons at the same time, but it does not seem plausible, to me at least, to say that in order for reasons of the second kind to be reasons they must be grounded in reasons of the first kind.

This seems even clearer when we consider objectives of a more clearly altruistic character, such as saving the rain forest or preventing Venice from sinking beneath the waves. Here again one can have reasons of two kinds: some self-grounded (since it makes for a better life to have accomplished some important goal) others not (those that derive from the agent's belief in the value of the goal itself; and even though a given agent might be moved by reasons of both kinds it does not seem that those of the latter sort must be grounded in the former.

Whatever the aim, suppose the sacrifice required is very great. Suppose that, in order to accomplish my aim I have to move to a boring place where the cost of living is very low, and take a very boring night job to leave the days free for writing, or work day and night at the telephone banks, raising money for Venice by interrupting people's dinners in various time zones. This would surely be, in one clear sense, a miserable life. In order, then, to decide whether it is rational to make these sacrifices (or rational from the point of view of self-anchored reason) do we first need to decide whether the attainment of the goal is such as to make my *life* better despite the sacrifice? It does not seem to me that we do. I think we could be convinced that my sacrifice could be worthwhile—that I was not acting contrary to reason—even if we were in doubt about whether the result was a worse life, overall, for me, as measured by my conception of such a life. It would not be nonsensical, I think, to say that I (quite rationally) chose a life that was worse overall for me in order to accomplish something important.

Insofar as it involves sacrifice of "one's own good" for the sake of some other goal, this example may seem to have the same structure as the case of Fred and Frieda. But I believe that it in fact differs in an important way, which we can bring out by considering another example involving the good of a loved one. Imagine a mother who, in order for her children to have the chance at a better life, has to take two hard and demeaning jobs so that she hardly ever sees her children until they are grown. In the Fred and Frieda example, we supposed that being together with Frieda and caring about her good was part of Fred's conception of a good life. But suppose, in the present case, that the mother is not convinced that this life of sacrifice is the best life available to her, and may even think that this is not so. Couldn't she still be convinced that making this sacrifice is what she has most reason to do—that the improvement in her children's lives is an "improvement in the world" that she has reason to bring about? In order to be rational, she need not say to herself, "This involves sacrifice, but it is still the best life I can live." She can say instead, "This will not lead to the best life for me, but under the circumstances, the best life for me is not what matters most to me."

The Fred and Frieda example was instructive in showing that the point of view of "one's own good" is not the privileged point of view of practical reason. But it is a slightly misleading example because the act Fred winds up choosing is one that contributes directly to his having the kind of life he wants (a life with Frieda that is also satisfying for her). His reason for going to Texas is thus "self-grounded." The examples I have given show, however, that there are many other reasons which seem as well grounded as Fred's even though they are not grounded in any "agent-favoring property of the actions for which they are reasons."

Now it might be answered that the reasons that the agents have in the examples I have mentioned are not self-anchored in the sense that Baier has in mind. One ground for saying this, which I will mention only to set it aside, is that these reasons may fail to satisfy the "independence" conditions stated in the second clause of the original characterization of "self-anchored reasons." The ends in question are not ones that the agent could accomplish independently of what others do. Indeed, my reasons for writing a book about responsibility would not make sense outside of a quite specific social setting, and the idea that a certain course of action will *benefit* one's children also depends on assumptions about what other people will do, in particular on the maintenance of a social system in which certain opportunities will be available to them provided that they have the resources I am trying to provide. If we take this independence condition literally then the class of self-anchored reasons will shrink to almost nothing. My conclusion is that this cannot be the way it was intended.[4]

This brings me to a second interpretation of self-anchored reasons. In discussing the example of Fred and Frieda. Baier observes that the point of view of one's own good cannot be the point of view of self-anchored reasons "because for many people a life that contains such other-regarding concerns [as Fred and Frieda's concern for one another] comes closer to a good life as they conceive it than one without such concerns" (RMO, 140–41). This suggests that X is a better world than Y from the point of view of self-anchored reason if one would prefer X to Y all things considered if one were well informed and had those desires which, if one had them, would bring one closest to the good life, as defined by one's unflawed conception of such a life.

Reasons that are self-anchored in this broader sense need not be grounded in any agent-favoring property of the actions for which they are reasons. Even when they are not self-grounded, however, they may still be connected in other, less direct, ways with the agent's conception of a good life. First, being the kind of person who is moved by such reasons may be part of the agent's conception of a good life. The self-sacrificing mother in my last example may well believe that a life in which she was not moved by a willingness to sacrifice for the good of her children would be for that reason seriously flawed. Second, it may be true, as in my earlier examples, that the actions that the agent is moved to perform have "agent-favoring properties"—for example, that they lead to a more successful life for the agent—

even though it is not true that all of the agent's reasons for choosing those actions are grounded in these properties.

It seems then that Baier's various remarks about self-anchored reasons in fact suggest two different classes of reasons, each of which defines a point of view. The first is that of reasons that are self-grounded in the sense I defined above; the second is that of reasons that are self-anchored in the broader sense I have just discussed. Which of these constitutes a "privileged point of view from which the world must be judged if any improvement in the world brought about by someone's action constitutes a reason for him to do it"?

The point of view of self-grounded reasons seems too narrow for this task. Examples likes the ones I have given, which are only slightly different from the case of Fred and Frieda, show that an agent need not give weight only to reasons that are directly self-grounded in this sense. The point of view of reasons that are self-anchored in the broader sense is a much more plausible candidate to be the privileged point of view that Baier is seeking. But it gains this plausibility by giving the idea of a good reason or "something worth caring about" priority over the idea of a good life for the agent, thereby diminishing the grounding role of the quality of the agent's life that seemed to give the point of view of self-anchored reasons its distinctive content.

The requirements of a good life for the agent still do some work in determining what can and what cannot be counted as a self-anchored reason. There may, for example, be considerations which are in general well worth caring about but which nonetheless do not figure in a particular agent's unflawed conception of a good life (and hence not in his or her self-anchored reasons.) This may simply be because there is not enough room for them (one can't after all, include every worthwhile pursuit in even the best life) or because the agent is less suited to that aim than to some others. So the agent's conception of a good life may serve to exclude some considerations from the sphere of self-anchored reasons and include others. On the other hand, as I have argued above, many of the reasons that are included in this sphere will be grounded in the first instance in the value of certain aims and only secondarily, if at all, in the contribution that these aims make to the agent's life.

IV. Society-Anchored Reasons and Morality

Let me turn now from this somewhat expanded interpretation of self-anchored reasons to consider the idea of society-anchored reasons and the question of whether moral reasons are self-anchored or society-anchored.

Fred's choice of a job in Texas was supported by a preference for a situation in which Frieda's job preferences were satisfied even though his were not. This is an example of what Baier calls a self-distributive (SD) preference: a preference regarding the degree to which one's own and others' preferences are satisfied. In chapter 5 of *The Rational and the Moral Order* Baier argues that reason requires us to modify our SD preferences so that we have overall reason to follow certain coordinating guidelines whenever the following conditions are fulfilled: (1) Universal adoption of these guidelines would make everyone better off (as measured by his or her self-anchored reasons). (2) We know or have reason to believe that most others have modified or are willing to modify their SD preferences in this way. (3) Some measures will be taken to insure that those who do not so modify their preferences will be treated in a way designed to motivate them to comply with the guidelines nonetheless. The willingness to change one's SD preferences under such conditions is called Limited Conditional Good Will.

An agent who has undergone the change that Limited Conditional Good Will mandates (when the conditions appear to be fulfilled) has acquired new reasons for action—reasons to act in the way the guidelines require. Unlike "self-anchored reasons" these reasons are conditional upon the assumption that others are similarly motivated and that certain social institutions of punishment are in place. For this reason, Baier calls them "society-anchored reasons." He notes, however (RMO, 190), that even if these reasons differ from (most) self-anchored ones in these respects, they are nonetheless "indirectly self-anchored." This for two reasons. First, their primary appeal lies in the fact that by following them (and, I would add, by being the kind of person who is motivated by them) we make our life better as judged by the self-anchored standard. (We make it likely that in Prisoner's Dilemma situations our first-order preferences will be better satisfied.) Second, their content (what they require us to do) is guided by the aim of giving us all better lives as measured by this standard. Indeed, these reasons are "self-favoring" in one of the ways that Fred's reasons for going to Texas with Frieda were, since in his case one could also say, parallel with the first of the points just made, that having a disposition to take Frieda's welfare into account made Fred's life better, by opening up the possibility of a relationship of this kind with her.

I want now to inquire, however, following in part the parallel with the case of Fred and Frieda, whether the "society-anchored" reasons that Limited Conditional Good Will leads to might not be self-anchored in a further, less instrumental, way. When I said that Fred's life was made better by his being moved to take Frieda's welfare into account even when it conflicts with his own interests, narrowly construed, this claim was not meant in a purely instrumental sense. The claim was not that by recognizing this new reason Fred will be able to lead a better life as measured by his degree of success in achieving his other self-anchored aims (getting his laundry done, finishing his book, and so on). This claim may well be true—if Fred and

Frieda love one another they will help each other and the result may be that their lives will go better in many ways. But these benefits are consequences of their love, not its raison d'etre or their reason for feeling or fostering it. If Fred were examining the question "Why care about Frieda's good?" with what I called earlier the aim of self-understanding he would not cite these advantages as part of his answer.

Similarly one might ask, in the case of Limited Conditional Good Will, whether the case for it is purely instrumental, based on the contribution that this transformation makes to the likely fulfillment of one's other aims, or whether, like Fred and Frieda's love for one another, it has another basis even though it confers these benefits as a result of what it is. As you might guess, I believe that the latter is true: that something very much like Limited Conditional Good Will is, for most of us, directly self-anchored.

There are many accounts of moral motivation that would give moral reasons this self-anchored character, but I will use my own version of contractualism as an example. My view is that for those of us who are moved by the morality of duty and obligation its demands are "anchored" in our recognition that we have reason to treat others in ways that they could not reasonably reject insofar as they too are moved by this reason. Like the reason someone might have to work to save the rain forest and the reason Fred has to take Frieda's welfare into account, this reason does not present itself as one I should recognize because doing so makes my life better. Nonetheless, recognizing it does make my life better, just as Fred's concern for Frieda improves his life.

It does so in several ways. First, a concern to act in ways that others could not reasonably reject establishes a relation with them that is desirable in itself. Second, the content of the principles that this motive supports will benefit us in other ways. Given that each of us is reasonably concerned with the satisfactions of our first-order preferences, in particular with doing better, if we can, in Prisoner's Dilemma situations, principles that leave us free to be "free riders" are ones that we could all reasonably reject. So if we are all "mutual justifiers" we will also be better off in these other ways. But, like the advantages of Fred and Frieda's love, these benefits are consequences of the motivation to be moral, not, I would say, its basis.

This basic reason for being concerned with morality is independent of what others do in at least one sense: I take it as having force for me whether others recognize it or not, even though what it gives me reason to do may vary, depending on what others around me are like and what they do. For example, treating others in ways required by principles they could not reasonably reject (if they were similarly motivated) does not require me to behave "cooperatively" even when there is every reason to think others will not reciprocate. This kind of self-sacrifice is not reasonably required. If this kind of independence and contribution to my life are sufficient to make a reason self-anchored, then this one is. It has, I would say, as much claim as Fred's love for Frieda to be self-anchored in the broader sense I described in the previous section.

This alternative account of moral motivation also provides an easier way around a difficulty that Baier confronts at the end of chapter 5 of *The Rational and the Moral Order*, where he considers the possibility of a social arrangement that is much better for everyone than the alternative of noncooperation, but which nonetheless benefits some vastly more than others. If Limited Conditional Good Will is understood in the purely instrumental sense, then it might seem to give people reason to go along with this inequitable scheme even if more equitable arrangements are equally feasible. Yet the more equitable scheme is clearly morally preferable. Baier explains how Limited Conditional Good Will exerts pressure toward the more equitable alternative as follows: "For why should any fully rational person welcome a transition from a system of merely self-anchored reasons to one in which self-anchored ones are defeated by society anchored ones unless the contribution to other people's lives they require of him is no greater than that they require of others and that general conformity to them equally improves other people's lives?" (RMO, 192).

This explanation invokes the concern with *mutual* advantage which, as I said earlier, helps to make Baier's account of moral motivation a plausible response to Prichard's dilemma. But in invoking this concern, Baier seems to go beyond the outlook of individuals who are merely seeking means to advance their self-anchored reasons as far as possible, and to covertly introduce some less instrumental idea, such as mutual justifiability. How is the comparison with how much others benefit relevant if all I am interested in is making my share as large as possible? It might be relevant simply because a glaringly unequal scheme is likely to be an unstable one. This explanation would keep the account a purely instrumental one, but Baier does not, as far as I can see, rely upon it. Appealing to the independent desirability of arrangements that others can also accept makes the account more plausible, but it also makes moral reasons (directly) self-anchored, at least in the broad sense I have described.

V. Conclusion

Let me return to the question, "Why be moral?" and to the three aims I distinguished in my opening section. It may well be true that we make ourselves better off in other terms by adopting a new SD preference for Limited Conditional Good Will. But this claim is not a plausible response to the question "Why be moral?" when that question is asked with the aim of self-understanding. It falls too clearly on the nonmoral side of Prichard's dilemma. For a related reason, I do not think that this claim, by itself, can serve as a response to that question when it is asked as a request for justification, since it fails to account for the full range of moral concerns (such as a concern with equity). Of course, the alternative I have proposed may not satisfy that request either, since it may not be plausible to argue that every rational agent must be moved by the desire to justify his or her actions to others on grounds they could not reasonably reject. My response is that I do not consider justification in this sense to be a reasonable theoretical aim.

What remains is the question of compatibility, and it is here that Baier's argument seems to me to have its greatest force. I have argued that the importance that morality has for us is not adequately captured by the instrumental argument that being moral (having Limited Conditional Good Will) enables us, collectively, to do better in other terms. Even if this is so, this argument does show that the cost of being moral, measured in these terms, is much less than we might have supposed; indeed, that over time it is not a cost at all. This is a powerful response to the objection that it is foolishly self-sacrificing to be moral. I might add here that if Baier's argument is understood as addressed to this question of compatibility, then what Schneewind called the problem of opacity is not such a serious objection.[5] If almost anyone can be expected to see what morality is really about, then while it might be useful for them all to understand why it does not conflict sharply with self-anchored reasons, there is no moral objection to a situation in which only game theorists have a full understanding of exactly why this is so.

Harvard University

Notes

1. H. A. Prichard, "Does Moral Philosophy Rest on a Mistake?" (1949). The essay first appeared in 1912.

2. See, for example, pp. 721–22 of "The Social Source of Reasons" (Baier 61). In understanding Baier's argument I have been helped by Steve Darwall's discussion on pp. 180–91 of *Impartial Reason* (1983.)

3. See, for example, the first few pages of section 1 of chapter 4 of RMO.

4. I assume that what this condition is intended to rule out is not just any dependence on what others do but rather the kind of dependence that is crucial in Prisoners' Dilemma cases: dependence on the assumption that others will in general behave in the very way that is in question.

5. See Schneewind's essay in the present volume, p. 000.

Comments

11

Kurt Baier

I. Introduction

When I first read the papers now published in this volume, and appreciated the wide range and degree of their excellence, their toughness of mind as well as the empathy in their interpretations, their insightfulness as well as the cogency of their arguments, their originality as well as their scholarliness, their brilliance as well as their fairness, I realized that I would not be able to respond adequately to any, let alone all of them. But then Jerome Schneewind, the editor of this volume, convinced me that it would be preferable, because more helpful to the readers and the contributors, if I commented at least on those about which I felt I had something helpful to say rather than, even-handedly, comment on none. So I wrote down the thoughts that occurred to me on reflecting about these papers and then selected for publication those that I thought combined well with one another to throw light on topics in the essays and in my own work. I hope that I shall one day think of something helpful to say also about those other challenging papers on which I thought it wiser to keep silent for now.

The papers in this book fall naturally into four groups roughly paralleling the structure of mine: those, namely Gauthier's, Hampton's, and Railton's, that take up, with more or less explicit reference to it, the whole or an important aspect of my theory of reason; those, namely Raz's and Scanlon's, that take up in a similar way the theory of morality; those, namely, Darwall's and Schneewind's, that examine, summarize, and scrutinize my handling of all three of these matters, each raising an acute problem for me; and finally those, namely, Kagan's, Thomas's, and Thomson's, that take up the problems connected with applying moral theory to the solution of concrete moral problems.

If someone wanted to have a clear, brief, accurate, completely fair, and insightful introduction to my work, and also wanted to locate it in the vast territory of the history of moral theory as seen through the eyes of friendly but not uncritical interpreters, they could do no better than begin with the paper by Schneewind (who does me the honor of sketching my philosophical development from the beginning to the present), and then continue with

Darwall's who travels over some of the same ground but with a different aim.

In my comments, I do not, however, follow this natural sequence. I comment earlier on a paper when doing so appears helpful for making and understanding subsequent comments. The length of my comments is normally determined by two subjective factors. One is my concern to clarify, in my own mind, as well as the contributors' and the readers', the relevant issues and my position on them. The other is what I came up with as I grappled with these essays. So, if a comment is long, this means that I both thought the points made in the paper important and difficult and that I managed to think of several things I considered helpful. If my comments are short or none at all is published, the reason is that nothing much or nothing at all that linked with the other comments and seemed to me worth publishing had risen to the surface.

II. T. M. Scanlon: "Why Be Moral?"

I begin with Professor Scanlon's paper because it takes up one of the fundamental questions about the moral enterprise and deals with it in a new and illuminating way. It also convinced me that I was wrong on an important point which therefore requires a reformulation of my view that will have to be borne in mind in my subsequent comments.

Section A

Scanlon starts by reminding us of the dilemma which, according to Prichard, is generated by the question 'Why be moral?'. The dilemma is, of course, that in answering this why-question we must offer reasons and they must either be moral or nonmoral, but neither seems appropriate: relying on moral reasons "seems to presuppose the very concerns whose justification is in question" (p. 197) and so seems to be *logically* inappropriate because circular; but relying on nonmoral ones would seem to turn the person relying on them into something less "than virtuous" (ibid.) and so this answer would seem to be *morally* inappropriate.[1]

Scanlon's central concern in this paper is whether and how this dilemma can best be circumvented. As part of this investigation, he examines whether my distinction between self-anchored and society-anchored reasons would be helpful, but he finds both unclarity and error in my way of drawing the distinction. As he notes, the question 'Why be moral?' "is understood against the background of some class of (usually nonmoral) reasons. In Baier's case this is the class of 'self-anchored' reasons"(p. 199). Scanlon correctly says that I was looking for a privileged point of view—the practical analog of truth—considerations derived from which count as one kind of practical reason. This kind resembles prudential or self-interested ones in the two following respects: they are "other-things-equal," that is, "defeasible" when in conflict with some other types of practical reason, such as moral ones, and they are of what might be called "restricted universality": every person has them, but what I call their "scope" is person-relative; they are like self-interested reasons in being reasons *only for* the person the promotion or protection of whose preferred life is their ground. Thus their ground is wider than that of self-interested or prudential reasons and they may conflict with the latter and defeat them.

It is my positive characterization of this ground which was not only unclear—though it was that too—but was wrong or at least seriously misleading. I gave as the ground of this type of reason and as the end of this privileged point of view, a person's internally unflawed conception of the good life for herself.[2] Scanlon allows that there is or may be such a privileged point of view, considerations derived from which amount to a certain important kind of reason, but he claims that it cannot be what I said it was, for one thing because, as he puts it, "it would not be nonsensical, I think, to say that I (quite rationally) chose a life that was worse overall for me in order to accomplish something important" (p. 203). To substantiate this claim, he offers the example of a mother who for the sake of her children makes what she herself regards as an important sacrifice and who thinks "that this life of sacrifice is not the best life available to her" (ibid.). There is no reason to think that this mother must have an internally flawed conception of the good (or best) life for her, as she would if, for instance, she wanted to become a concert pianist although she is quite unmusical. I entirely agree with this constructive critical point,[3] and think I can accommodate it in my account.

How did I come to make this mistake? Here is my explanation with which, however, Scanlon may not agree. I think I failed to notice that the idea of a good life, as we ordinarily understand it, is, in certain contexts, tied quite closely to the sorts of things that ground what Scanlon felicitously calls "self-grounded" reasons. I was not unaware of the fact that these reasons are only an (important) subclass of self-anchored reasons as I conceive of them[4] but, because I did not notice the association of the idea of a good life with self-grounded reasons, I wrongly used the expression "a person's internally unflawed conception of the *good* life for her" to refer to the aim of the privileged point of view from which the whole class of self-anchored reasons is derived. This misdescription of that aim committed me to an implausible conclusion. Thus, in Scanlon's example, the mother's internally unflawed conception of the good life for her gave her no adequate self-anchored reason to choose to do something that made her life a less good one by her own criteria of a good life than another also available to her at that point, although she was rightly convinced she had adequate (nonmoral!) reason to choose this "less good" life.

Thus, it would appear that we ordinarily employ criteria for judging someone's life a good one, or a better (or less good) one than another life accessible to her, which are different from the criteria I had in mind when I spoke of a person's internally unflawed conception of a good life for one. More generally, I thus allowed (unnecessarily, it seems to me now) the possibility that, by one's internally unflawed conception of a *preferred* (or choiceworthy) *life* for one, one sometimes both should and should not make what one rightly judges to be a certain sacrifice.

Is it possible to reformulate the aim of the privileged point of view that I (and it appears Scanlon) have in mind? Of course, it may well be that there is no simple unmisleading characterization available in the language, but in the absence of a detailed characterization of it, which I could not attempt to give here, I shall try out another simple term to see whether it is, and in the hope that it is not, similarly flawed or misleading. My revised formulation of this aim now is, ***a person's internally unflawed conception of the preferred life for her***. Perhaps it will give greater clarity to this idea if I say that the life I have in mind is not the sort one may *have or have had* (as in, 'she had a good (or wonderful) life'), but the life she *led* (as in, 'she led a solitary life dedicated to her research in the archives') with the emphasis not on what befell her as the criterion of evaluation but on how she conducted herself, as judged by her overall preference of what to *make of* her life as her abilities and opportunities allowed. Of course, this still leaves much unclear about what may be included in this preference. But it should be clear at least that it includes more than the protection and promotion of her own good, and that it does not include the things she makes her ends only because morality requires that she do.

As I said, I have found illuminating, and am in agreement with, Scanlon's claim that what he calls "self-grounded reasons" (p. 202), delineate only a narrow sense of self-anchored reasons, namely, those in conformity with what does not require the agent to make a genuine sacrifice, because the point of view from which self-grounded reasons are derived defines "a sphere of compensation, a range of gains and losses which counterbalance one another because they are all counted as gains or as losses with respect to the same thing: the agent's good" (p. 201). We can thus construe self-anchored reasons as having two subclasses: self-grounded (self-interested, self-regarding) and other-grounded. Although other-grounded reasons are not self-interested or self-regarding, they resemble them in being directly self-favoring in the sense that following them protects or promotes one's chances to lead one's internally unflawed conception of the preferred life for one. Both subclasses are agent-relative: only those for whom following is directly self-favoring have them. If I am right, then, by contrast, moral reasons, while also other-grounded, are not, as such, directly self-favoring nor are they agent-relative.

I am, however, less clear about, and persuaded by, Scanlon's account of what he calls the broader sense of self-anchored reasons which, in addition to self-grounded ones, also includes reasons grounded in "objectives of a more clearly altruistic character, such as saving the rain forest or preventing Venice from sinking beneath the waves" (p. 203). I can accept this as it stands,[5] but am doubtful about the "objectivist" interpretation of it that, I suspect, Scanlon has in mind. Thus, in one place, Scanlon allows that reasons that are not self-grounded "may still be connected in other, less direct, ways with the agent's conception of a good life. First, being the kind of person who is moved by such reasons may be part of the agent's conception of a good life" (pp. 205f.). I can accept this if "the agent's conception of *a good life*" is replaced by "the agent's internally unflawed conception of *the preferred life* for her" in conformity with my new description of the aim of the privileged point of view I am looking for. I do not see how being the kind of person who is moved by such reasons can be part of her conception of a *good* life for her if she must not, because it makes no sense, say "'This involves sacrifice, but it is still the best life I can live'" (p. 203) but must say instead "'This will not lead to the best life for me, but under the circumstances, the best life for me is not what matters most to me'" (ibid.).[6]

However, although I can agree with this if 'preferred life' is substituted for 'good life', I am much less sure about Scanlon's suggestion that some objective whose realization is not even likely to be, as such, agent-favoring can ground self-anchored reasons, whether or not being moved by such reasons is part of an agent's internally unflawed conception of the preferred life for himself, simply because the objective is objectively important or worth caring about. On the account I suggested, an objective could ground an agent's self-anchored reasons in Scanlon's broader sense (which includes both self-grounded and other-grounded reasons) only if pursuing or attaining it was at least likely to be agent-favoring in a broad sense that does not involve the agent's own good, while it could ground them in the narrower sense only if pursuing or attaining it was at least likely to be agent-favoring in the narrow sense of promoting or protecting the agent's own good.

In other places, Scanlon distinguishes the broader sense from the narrower (to which my use of the expression "the good life" had wrongly confined it) in a negative and in a positive way. The negative way helps to bring out what is *not* the aim of this privileged point of view in the broader sense by stressing that one may have self-anchored reason to do something "even though they are not grounded in any 'agent-favoring property of the *actions* for which they are reasons'" (p. 204) or "'a privileged point of view from which the world must be judged if any improvement in the world brought about by someone's action constitutes a reason for him to do it'"

(p. 205). In these remarks, the expressions 'agent-favoring' and 'world-improving'[7] appear to imply that the excellence (or as I would say, 'the preferred character') of the agent's life as he conceives of it is *not* the defining aim of this privileged point of view when understood in the broad sense.[8]

The positive way indicates more explicitly what that aim is. Thus, he specifies the direction of the shift away from that excellence of the agent's life by saying that it gives "the idea of a good reason or 'something worth caring about' priority over the idea of a good life for the agent, thereby diminishing the grounding role of the quality of the agent's life that seemed to give the point of view of self-anchored reasons its distinctive content" (p. 205), and again "So the agent's conception of a good life may serve to exclude some considerations from the sphere of self-anchored reasons and include others. On the other hand . . . , many others that are included in this sphere will be grounded in the first instance *in the value of certain aims* and only secondarily, if at all, in the contribution that these aims make to the agent's life" (ibid.).

What I am not persuaded of in these formulations is the need to reject, as Scanlon apparently does, my underlying more general thesis that the ground of self-anchored reasons (in both the narrower and the broader senses) is some agent-favoring (or if that is thought to smack too much of the agent's good) some agent-life-favoring property (as judged by the criterion of the agent's internally unflawed conception of the preferred life for her) of the actions for which they are such reasons. For all that Scanlon has said, it still seems to me that what grounds self-anchored reasons, whether in the narrow self-grounded or the broader sense, is the agent's preferred life for him, as he himself conceives it, when his conception is not internally flawed.

Scanlon appears to suggest that the pursuit or attainment of these self-anchored reasons need not be even likely to favor the agent or his life. Do the differences between self-grounded self-anchored reasons, that is, those grounded in the agent's good and good life and those not so grounded, show that the latter are not grounded in what favors the agent or his life? Are the latter grounded in something that is important, valuable, or worth caring about, even when its pursuit is not likely to promote its attainment and its attainment does not favor, or actually disfavors, the agent or his life? Here the crucial question would seem to be whether only what contributes to a person's good, favorably affects him or his life, or whether there are other objectives than those subsumable under the agent's good whose pursuit and attainment also do so. The answer to this would seem to depend, at least in part, on whether an aim is such that its pursuit and attainment grounds a self-anchored reason because its attainment constitutes the realization of something objectively important, worth caring about or valuable, or whether what makes it so is that it is one of the objectives included in an agent's internally unflawed conception of the preferred life for him. It seems that Scanlon accepts the first, call it the "objectivist" answer, while I accept the second, call it the "subjectivist" answer. As everyone knows, this is an ancient and difficult controversy which I cannot hope to settle here (if indeed anywhere). But I would like to offer one very small and somewhat peripheral point that may appeal to some. My point is that (1) the notion of a person's good seems strongly to support the objectivist answer, but it really does not and (2) even if it did, the special features of the good that give the appearance of objectivity are absent when reasons are self-anchored in the broader sense, so that the parallel to the good life does not hold.

(1) I take a person's good, what is for his good, to be roughly things such as health, wealth, power, longevity, having friends, about which experience strongly suggests that they are a good thing from anyone's point of view. Of course, my health is a good thing from my point of view, not necessarily from yours: anyone's health a good thing from that person's. The appearance that I have self-anchored reason to protect and promote my health because health is an objectively good thing is generated by the fact that we say that my conception of the preferred life for me would be internally flawed if it failed to include among its objectives the protection and promotion of my health. We are quite confident in saying that everyone prefers being healthy to being sick, that everyone is better able to attain his other objectives whatever they may be if he is healthy rather than sick and so on. Nevertheless, even in the case of health what makes it important, really worth caring about, being of value to one, is the central and almost indispensable role it plays in virtually everything one wants to do. The objectivity of the value of health is made more plausible by the fact that its value is independent of the peculiarities of people's conceptions of the preferred life for them, by the fact that that conception would rightly be judged internally flawed if it had no place for the protection and promotion of health, and by the plausibility of the belief that one would have self-anchored reason to do those things which actually protect and promote, and to refrain from those that undermine it, even if one did not know or believe this or believed the opposite. But, of course, the fact that it is one's unflawed conception of the preferred life for one which gives importance and so on to health is not undermined by these facts, for it would not be *important to* anyone unless it played that virtually indispensable role in his life, and it would not be *important, period*, if it did not play that role in *everyone's* life.

(2) By contrast, objectives such as saving the rain forest or preventing Venice from sinking beneath the waves, lack the features that give that appearance of objectivity.

The capacity of these objectives to ground self-anchored reasons is not independent of the particularities of the agent's conception of the preferred life for him, nor would his conception of the preferred life for him be flawed on account of not including this objective, nor would he have reason to do those things which helped save the rain forest when the objective of saving them is not included in his unflawed conception of the preferred life for him.[9]

How does all this affect the main question now before us, namely, whether following self-anchored reasons in the broader sense at least tends to affect the agent's life favorably from the point of view of his internally unflawed conception of the preferred life for him, even if it affects it unfavorably from the self-interested, or prudential, point of view, the point of view that grounds merely self-grounded reasons? Well, if I am right, then what makes these objectives reason-grounding ones is not that their attainment is objectively important, has objective value, or is truly worth caring about, whether or not a given person regards it as for him important, valuable, or worth caring about. And this makes it more plausible to think that what makes these objectives reason-grounding for a person is that he regards them as important to him, valuable to him, or worth caring about. But in that case, it is more plausible that even self-anchored reasons in the broader sense are grounded in something the attainment of which would be regarded by the agent as having had a favorable impact on his life. And at the time of acting he would not be justified in thinking that he had self-anchored reasons to pursue this objective, unless he had reason to think that the particular course of action, to which the reason directed him, was at least likely to contribute to his attaining that objective.

What would the favorable impact on his life consist in? Would it simply be that he would then be *successful* in respect of the objective he had chosen? I think the answer is No. Success is neither a sufficient nor a necessary condition of the impact on the agent or his life being favorable. If my aim is to cut off my ears, success may not amount to a favorable impact: it all depends on whether my ultimate objective in cutting them off could be included in my internally unflawed conception of the preferred life for me. If the answer is No—and it is hard to find an objective that would require and so justify an alternative answer—then success in attaining that objective would be just as flawed as cutting them off for its own sake would be.

But neither is success a necessary condition. The rain-forest savers would think of their lives as favorably affected even if its preservation came about, not through their own or any human endeavor, but through natural causes. What inclines them to regard this outcome as a favorable impact on their lives, is not that they *succeeded* in bringing about something they were aiming to bring about, but that, what came about either through their own efforts or in other ways, is something they want or would welcome in their lives. They want to live, or would welcome living, in a world in which there are rain forests.

We can further support this view by considering the opponents of the forest-savers who, in their conception of the preferred life for them, include the objective of cutting down the rain forest or certain major parts of it to prepare the ground for crops. Suppose the forest-savers succeed in their objective, would we not want to say that this has had a favorable impact on their lives, and not because they have achieved their objective or because preservation of the rain forest is an objectively important thing, but because it is important to them and because they would be seriously distressed if the rain forests disappeared from this earth, even if that disappearance had no other impact on their and other people's lives. Of course, if they battle for the forests' preservation because they think that their health will suffer if the forests go, then they think they have self-grounded reason to try to preserve them.

Section B

Grant me, then, at least for argument's sake, that I have found an acceptable characterization of the aim of that privileged point of view we were looking for. The question, then, is whether my account of self-anchored reasons and the answer to 'Why be moral?' in terms of these reasons can escape the dilemma Prichard extracts from it. As a preliminary to answering this question, Scanlon opens section 2 of his paper by asking why one would want to raise the question "Why be moral?" at all. His answer is that there are three aims with which one may ask this question (pp. 198–99), namely, "as a question about self-interpretation, justification, or compatibility" (p. 199), and he suggests that my strategy for answering is helpful when understood in the third, requires considerable modifications in the first (pp. 208–9), and will not work at all in the second way, though the last failure is not a weakness of my strategy because, when understood in this second way, the project is "probably impossible, but fortunately, unnecessary" (p. 199), for it does not have "a reasonable theoretical aim" (p. 209).

The main difficulty I have with these three aims is to understand how one can answer 'Why be moral?' as a question of self-understanding without also answering it as one of justification. When I ask it with the first aim, I already regard "moral considerations as normally overriding practical reasons" and wish merely "to understand better what kind of reasons they are" (p. 198). I take this to mean that my question is, 'What kind of reasons are these moral reasons that override other nonmoral, including self-anchored practical reasons?' But in asking 'Why be moral?' in this way either I already know (or take myself to know) what being moral is or I don't. If I do, then presumably I know two things: *what* they direct me to do in particular situations—for if I don't know that, then I would seem not to know what it is to be moral in the sense of this question—and *that* they override other reasons, say, self-anchored, ones, when these, as they may, conflict with them. But then, it seems, I must also accept the view that whatever else moral reasons are, they are of a kind that is rightly taken to override these other practical reasons. But then does not my question about what kind of reason these moral reasons are, inquire into the relation between my knowledge (or my assumed knowledge) of what they direct me to do and their being such as to be rightly taken to override other practical reasons? Does it not raise either the question of whether what I take to be moral reasons really are, or the question whether what I take to be moral reasons really override these other practical reasons, even if I do not doubt that what are *rightly* regarded as moral reasons are *rightly* taken to override these other moral reasons? Does not my, non-skeptically, regarding moral considerations as overriding other practical reasons raise the justificatory question of whether what for me are moral *considerations* really are moral *reasons*, that is, whether the considerations I accept as moral are rightly taken to override other practical reasons? And does not that in turn raise the more general justificatory question how any kind of reason can be such as to override these other, especially self-anchored, reasons in the narrow sense, those Scanlon felicitously called self-grounded?

The other horn of this dilemma seems to raise the same justificatory matters. For if I do not yet know what moral reasons direct me to do, but regard moral reasons—whatever they may direct me to do—as overriding other practical reasons, then presumably I also want to know what they direct me to do, so that I at least know what I would have to do in particular situations if I want to be moral. But then, again, I must wish to derive from "the fact" I accept, namely, that moral reasons override other practical ones when the two kinds conflict, an answer to the question of what *sound* moral reasons—those that are *rightly* taken to override other practical ones—direct me to do in particular situations. But, again, it would seem I cannot begin such a derivation until I have an adequate account why everyone, and therefore I, should regard a certain kind, and why that kind, as overriding other practical reasons, and especially self-anchored ones, the flouting of which will sometimes, possibly often, require painful sacrifices.

When Scanlon says that the self-interpretive version of 'Why be moral?' "is not asked out of doubt, or as a demand for justification" (p. 198) I presume he must mean doubt about the overridingness of moral reasons and justification of why they are overriding. For if he means doubt about what moral reasons direct, or justification of why there have to be any reasons that override self-anchored ones, then we are back with our dilemma. But if this questioner does not doubt that moral reasons are overriding and does not ask for a justification of why they are, is he not thereby blocking the possibility of getting an answer to 'Why be moral?' Is he not merely raising the question 'Why follow this or that morality?' But that seems to me to be a very different question from 'Why be moral?' which I take to be about all moralities that are sound, rather than about this or that morality whether sound or unsound. We would not be surprised or dismayed to discover that in answer to 'Why conform to Nazi morality?' the answer would be 'No reason.' But many, if not most, of us would think it more likely that such a "skeptical" answer to 'why be moral?' must rest on a mistake about what the thinker took morality to be rather than that it was the profound and revolutionary discovery that the moral enterprise rested on an illusion, or worse, a systematic attempt to exploit the gullible.

I therefore have to admit that, as Scanlon suspects, I intended my answer to 'Why be moral? to include a rational justification of the moral enterprise. He may well be right that I failed to give one, but I am puzzled about his claim that the project of giving one, at least as frequently understood, lacks "a reasonable theoretical aim" (p. 209). But probably the explanation of my puzzlement is that my insufficiently thorough study of his paper has led me to misunderstand his point.

Section C

My last topic is Scanlon's probing and important treatment of the question whether moral reasons—which, in my view, are primarily society-anchored—are also *indirectly* self-anchored, as I believe, or whether they are, "for most of us, *directly* self-anchored" (p. 207; my emphasis). Scanlon thinks this depends on what is the central commitment of the moral enterprise. In his view, they are merely indirectly self-anchored if, as I say, that commitment is what I have called "Limited Conditional Good Will." For I make two points about that commitment. It is regarded by the members of a moral order as merely a means to make one's life better, as judged by the standard of self-anchored reasons. And, I claim, under certain conditions, no member of such a moral order has adequate self-anchored reason not to accept it (p. 206). But, he believes, it can be directly self-anchored if it is accepted, not in this purely "instrumental" (ibid.) way, not *because* it makes one's life better (though it does so), but for its own sake, because it "has force for" one (p. 207), because it has "independent desirablilty" (p. 208).

Scanlon offers this suggestion as an improvement on my account of moral motivation and, therefore, ipso facto as an improvement on my answer to the self-interpretive version of 'Why be moral?' I believe I agree with Scanlon (if I understand him correctly), as far as the nature of moral motivation is concerned. I agree that if a person adopts moral principles only as means to the end of improving his life by self-anchored, and especially self-grounded, standards, he will often find that he does better by these standards if he does not follow moral reasons, if he breaks moral principles, if he violates moral guidelines, and so on. A person who thinks of morality in this instrumental way, has not yet understood what it is.

Scanlon also seems to me completely right in his discussion of the kind of interpersonal relation sketched in my example of Fred and Frieda.[10] They would not truly love one another if they made their decisions about how to treat each other out of the expected gain from making them. Each member of a truly loving couple would decide on the same other-favoring behavior, even if he or she knew that, for some reasons, the other's behavior would not have the intended partner-favoring consequences which it normally or often has. A truly loving couple does not base its mutual interactions on what would, for people who do not truly love one another, be self-anchored reasons. What are self-anchored reasons for a truly loving couple is determined by a standard of mutual altruism higher than that which, as I see it, morality minimally requires for interactions between (people simply qua) members of the same moral order.[11] Hence I can completely agree with Scanlon's point that "[i]f Fred were examining the question 'Why care about Frieda's good?' with what I [that is, of course, Scanlon] called earlier the aim of self-understanding he would not cite these advantages as part of his answer" (p. 207). But this seems to lose its bite if different standards of altruism are appropriate in determining what are self-anchored reasons for people interacting with one another when they are lovers and when they are (merely) members of the same moral order, or not even that.

Furthermore, while it is true and important that "their reason for feeling or fostering [their love]" (p. 207) are not the direct and indirect self-favoring consequences of their partner-favoring behavior, it is misleading to say that these consequences are not the rationale of their love (ibid.) or even of that more or less enduring pattern of interaction, for it appears to imply that it has *a raison d'être* in the sense of *a rationale*. The explanation of it is that they are in love which is a condition in which people are strongly motivated to engage in such behavior. Love itself has no raison d'être or rationale nor does the behavior pattern that springs from it. We do not ask, "Why fall in love?" as we ask "Why be moral?" and, it seems to me that we are not normally seized with the desire to be moral as we are, when in love, to do things that would please our beloved. We can, of course, ask the general question whether, and if so why, one should do what one strongly desires to do when one is in love, and people give widely different answers from many different points of view, including the moral. I imagine that, concerning the desire love generates to engage in partner-favoring behavior, most would give it moral approval, perhaps with the warning that it tends to generate an "egoisme à deux" and so to cause the neglect of other moral requirements. But I am not sure what to make of the question, "Why care about Frieda's good?" Fred would not need to ask it himself and, if someone else asked him about it, he might take it as a request for an explanation and say simply "because I love her," or as a request for a justification and say things like, "She is a good sort and she is fun to be with" and so on. To continue with this would be to flog the wrong horse, though probably not one that is safely dead.

Finally, there appears to be a sharper difference between reasons and motives than Scanlon's argumentation suggests. In asking 'Why be moral?' we are, I believe, asking for *reasons* to be moral, in the sense of reasons to be disposed to do *whatever* moral considerations direct us to do—call that the "reason-interpretation"—not for *motives* from which we must follow these considerations, if we are to "be moral," in the sense of acting from motives on account of which one is judged (highly) moral, that is, morally praiseworthy.[12] As I understand the reason-interpretation of 'Why be moral?', it inquires into what self-anchored reasons there are for one to follow moral considerations, even when they conflict with one's self-anchored reasons.[13] If I am right in this, then, it would seem, Scanlon's very interesting discussion of whether "something . . . like Limited Conditional Good Will is, for most of us, directly self-anchored" (p. 207) is not strictly relevant to what is an acceptable answer to 'Why be moral?' On my conception of morality, the motive-interpretation presupposes the reason-interpretation and so the disputes over the motive-question presuppose at least an understanding, perhaps even an agreed answer, to the reasons-question.

At this point, a different problem arises: how can the advantageousness of the general recognition, in a moral order, of the overridingness of moral reasons be separated from the motive from which we follow moral reasons? Does not the reason for being moral unpack into, or at least involve, the motive for being moral? Could a person have a reason to be moral without that reason being *his* reason and so his *motive* for it?

Let me first return briefly to the case of Fred and Frieda. As I suggested, Fred must do the loving thing whether or not it has the normally expectable self-favoring consequences, but the members of a moral order need not be that indifferent to these consequences. For whereas, in Fred's case, the self-favoring consequences are not *his reason for* nor the *rationale of* his Frieda-favoring behavior, they are the rationale of the other-favoring behavior patterns of moral members of a well-functioning moral order. But that rationale is not necessarily identical with the reasons for which the members acted; the members may have, in the sense of there being for them, self-anchored reasons to be moral, but these reasons may not be the ones for which, and so not the motives from which, they acted. The rationale of a moral enterprise may be the maximization of its members' chances of leading lives as close as possible to their conception of the preferred life for them and so these members may have self-anchored reasons to be committed to moral principles, but they may act from these principles rather than for self-anchored reasons. For, as we have learned from Hobbes and the discussions of Prisoner's Dilemma, everyone's directly following the self-anchored reasons will have suboptimal outcomes. Thus, there is not, in my view, a conceptually necessary connection between someone following a moral reason to do something and his thereby directly contributing to leading his preferred life, whereas there is such a connection between someone acting in an other-favoring way out of love for that other and his thereby directly contributing to leading his own preferred life.[14]

Thus, genuinely moral members of a moral order, as I conceive of it, do not follow moral reasons in order to benefit from the reciprocation of other moral members. The Hidden Hand in the moral order works in the opposite way from that of Adam Smith. The moral guidelines every member is required or encouraged to follow work out in such a way that every member benefits. The benefits accruing to the members are not the result of their own efforts to maximize their own utilities nor is it the consequence of everyone's trying to benefit others and others gratefully reciprocating, nor is it the doing of things one knows will benefit others which ipso facto benefits oneself, as in the case of lovers. The general mutual (rather than reciprocal or self-generated) beneficiality is the overall consequence of everyone following guidelines suitably designed to override individual self-anchored behavior when general conformity to it would have suboptimal outcomes. This is the rationale of the moral order, but the generally beneficial results depend on the members not treating their conformity with moral guidelines as conditional on being effective individual means to the end which is the rationale of the collective moral enterprise.[15] Thus, a moral order so understood requires its members to adopt the general moral directives (such as principles, rules, and reasons) in a noninstrumental way, and as overriding self-anchored reasons.

For these reasons, I can agree with the spirit of Scanlon's claim, "I take it [i.e., morality] as having force for me whether others recognize it or not, *even though what it gives me reason to do may vary, depending on what others around me are like and what they do*" (p. 207; my emphasis). As I interpret the emphasized passage (along roughly Hobbesian lines), the principle of Limited Conditional Good Will having force for me means that there are certain conditions, including for instance a sufficient number of members being committed to Limited Conditional Good Will, in which I am morally required or recommended to follow optimally mutually beneficial guidelines, and I am morally required to do what I can to maintain or bring about these conditions: Where these conditions are completely satisfied, every member of a moral order is morally required to follow them; where they fall widely short of being completely satisfied, the force they have for me is merely to do what I can to bring things closer to a state in which these conditions are completely satisfied; where, though not completely satisfied, they are close to it, members are morally required to do what they can to move them even closer to complete satisfaction and, depending on the circumstances, to follow the optimal guidelines or some suitable modification of them.[16]

If this is on the right track, then 'Why be moral?' can be answered by providing a suitable rationale for a moral order. Providing such a rationale would be a rational justification of the existence of a moral order with all that this involves, including, for instance, a system of moral education which helps to develop a moral sense (analogous to Rawls's sense of justice, but covering the whole of morality), a system of social pressures motivating members to follow the ideal moral guidelines, the practice of moral criticism of oneself and others and the practice of moral reform. In my view, only in the context of such moral orders can the question of the overridingness of moral reasons be understood and justified.[17]

One last point. Is it true, then, that "something very much like Limited Conditional Good Will is, for most of us, directly self-anchored"? If what I have said is roughly on the right track, it might well be a good thing, other things equal, if it were so. For then, being moral might well be, for those for whom moral reasons are directly self-anchored, less of a sacrifice than for those for whom they are only indirectly and so less reliably self-anchored. But whether or not they are seems to me to depend, to a very great extent, on the efficacy in the various dimensions of the moral order to which one belongs. It is in any case an empirical question, though I would not wish to have to design a questionnaire for arriving at an answer. If 'most of us' means 'most of mankind', I would be surprised if it were true. If it means, 'most contemporary residents of the USA' I would not be much surprised either way. But, whether it is or is not does not seem to me to affect the answer to 'Why be moral?', at least when asked with Scanlon's first or second aim.

There are a great many important and interesting things in Scanlon's paper which merit close attention, but I hope I have said enough to indicate some of the important things on which we agree or disagree and why.

III. Joseph Raz: The Moral Point of View

Introduction

I next turn to the paper by Professor Raz, which challenges not just a major thesis in my book, but the very approach to morality and the moral distinctions on which it rests. Although he modestly characterizes his paper as "inconclusive reflections on the existence and nature of a moral point of view" (p. 58), his effort to bring greater rigor into the delineation of the various things that might be understood by that expression, his outline of one such conception which he apparently thinks plausible at least at first blush, his construction of what he calls "one common and powerful case for a distinct moral point of view" (p. 70), his ingenious attempt to refute it, (sections 5 and 6, pp. 70–76), and his treatment of the many important preliminary issues required by this powerful case and its refutation amount, in my opinion, to a significant contribution to our thinking about morality on a grand scale.

Raz distinguishes two rival approaches, the "context-dependent" and the "context-independent," to arriving at a satisfactory understanding of the distinction between "the moral" and "the nonmoral" in general, and that between moral and nonmoral considerations in particular. However, he says very little about the context-dependent, and I shall follow him in concentrating on the context-independent approach. In my comments, I offer reflections on three topics: In my section A, I discuss Raz' centerpiece, the development (in section 4 of his paper) of the powerful argument already mentioned, call it RA, and its two versions which I shall call "RA1" and "RA2" respectively, and his refutation of them (in his sections 5 and 6); in my section B, I offer a tentative typology of points of view, including the moral; and in my section C, I examine several distinctions one might draw between "the moral and the nonmoral," including Raz's and mine.

Despite the length of my comments, there is a great deal in Raz's fascinating, deep-cutting, rich, and far-ranging investigation that I had to leave for another occasion; for instance, his insightful and suggestive distinction between those things, such as cars, for which other things, such as regular servicing, can be good only if they (are likely to) make cars better (or in better condition) for being thus serviced, and those things, such as humans and cats, for whom things can be good without thereby making them better humans or cats, and his suggestion that this is so because the good of the latter kind of thing "matters in itself," and so is perhaps good "*tout court*" or "*simpliciter*" or "in itself" (pp. 63–64).[18]

Section A

Raz singles out for examination all those conceptions that are committed to two theses: "(1) there is a philosophically deep [i.e., context-independent] way of dividing considerations into moral and nonmoral such that even though other, context-dependent uses of the terms are legitimate, it marks the correct or the significant delineation of morality" (p. 58); and "(2) moral considerations are a distinct type, distinct either in how we find out about them or in what makes them into considerations with a call on our attention" (ibid.) or, as he puts it further on, there is an "ontic, metaphysical, or epistemic significance to the distinction between moral and nonmoral considerations" (p. 61). The opposing context-dependent approach, apparently favored by Raz, rejects both these contentions.

For an understanding of RA, at least four further ideas must be borne in mind. The first is the value-dependence of practical reasons which, in essence, asserts "a one-way dependence. Reasons [for action] . . . are rooted in values" (p. 63); values give rise to reason but, I take it, not conversely.

The second idea is the distinction between relational and nonrelational goods or values. He approaches it by way of the less problematic, language-based distinction between "relational and nonrelational judgments about goods or values" (ibid.). Relational judgments "have the form 'X is good (has value) for Y', nonrelational ones the form 'X is good (or valuable)' or 'something is a good (or valuable) X'" (ibid.). For an important, but rather complex, reason we need not now consider, Raz then "stipulate(s) that a good is relational if and only if it is good solely because it is good for someone, i.e., if it can be stated by a true relational value judgment the reason for which, or explanation of the truth of which, is exhausted on showing that it is good for someone" (p. 65). By contrast, "a good or a value [is] nonrelational if what makes it good is (or depends in part on) something other than that it is good for someone" (ibid.).

Although this account of the distinction contrasts the grounds on which things have one or the other of these two kinds of value,[19] it does not exclude the possibility that the same thing can possess both kinds of value or be a good of both kinds. One of the points at issue between, on the one hand, Raz and, on the other, the supporters of RA and of certain versions of the moral point of view, is whether nonrelational goods ground universal reasons, that is, practical reasons for everyone. That nonrelational goods ground universal reasons does not seem to follow from Raz's definition of 'nonrelational good', hence it may have to be argued for independently, say, on the grounds that the characteristics of a thing that make it a nonrelational good also ground a reason for everyone to act in a certain identical way.

But it seems that Raz is in fact simply assuming it. For he speaks of "the common understanding," and that is the third idea, to wit, "that universal reasons arise either from what is good for everyone or from what is good *simpliciter*" (p. 67). Thus, "if everyone has reason to protect and promote what is good for John regardless of whether what is good for John is good for everyone, then what is good for John is also good *simpliciter*" (ibid.). In other words, if moral reasons are universal reasons, as they are often taken to be, and if their being universal does not depend on their being followed (by someone? everyone?) being good for everyone, then they must arise from things that are good *simpliciter*, that is, not good because they are good for the people who have the moral reason to act in the way they direct, hence not relationally good, hence nonrelationally good, hence good *simpliciter*.

The fourth idea is that "[t]wo obvious ways in which moral reasons can be distinct suggest themselves: the values (the moral goods) which give rise to moral reasons may be distinct, or they may be related to moral reasons in a way which is distinct and unlike the usual relations between goods and reasons" (pp. 67–68). Accordingly RA relies on "two priority theses: The priority of relational goods over nonrelational ones and the priority of relational reasons" over nonrelational ones (p. 68).

This last idea is what distinguishes RA1 and RA2. The former rests on the priority of relational goods, the latter on the priority of relational reasons. Although the two versions are thus closely parallel, for various reasons that I hope will become apparent eventually, it will be helpful to look at them separately. I begin with RA1, whose main steps I take to be something like the following (pp. 67f.)

(1) "[U]niversal reasons arise either from what is good for everyone or from what is good *simpliciter*" (p. 67).

(2) The way in which moral reasons are distinct from other reasons is that "the values (the moral goods) which give rise to moral reasons [are] distinct" (ibid.).

(3) Therefore, if moral reasons are universal reasons grounded in what is good *simpliciter*, and "if everyone has [moral] reason to protect and promote what is good for John, regardless of whether what is good for John is good for everyone, then what is good for John is also good *simpliciter*" (ibid.).

(4) Only considerations related to the character and the well-being of people are moral reasons, but morality regards—that is to say, from the moral point of view, one rightly regards—"the well-being of all humans and the virtue of their characters as nonrelationally valuable," that is, as good *simpliciter*, "and thus as a source of universal reasons for action" (ibid.).

(5) But the good or "well-being of people is nonrelationally valuable only because it is relationally valuable, only because it is, tautologically, good for the people whose well-being it is" (p. 68).

(6) Furthermore, one's own "well-being is good for one independently of whether it is good for anyone else, or just good *simpliciter*" (p. 68).

(7) This one-way dependence of nonrelational on relational, this priority of relational to nonrelational goods, holds for all relational and nonrelational goods, hence the good or well-being of a person is no exception to it.

(8) Thus, "the normal way to show why it is good [nonrelationally] *that* John," say, "shall not be homeless," must rely on showing that not to be homeless is good *for* John, "but one can show that it is good for John without presupposing in any way that it is good in a nonrelational way" (ibid., my emphases).

Raz attempts to refute this argument by attacking (7), the thesis of "the priority" of relational goods. He offers, as a counter-example to this priority claim, goods that are intrinsically valuable, that is, *things* such as, "health, money, adequate temperature, etc.," the having of which would "*enable* people to have a better life," and activities, such as, "reading poetry, climbing, skiing, disco-dancing, being with friends" that "*make* the life of the person engaged in them better" (p. 70). These intrinsic goods, he says, "constitute his life and their goodness makes his life good. These are good for the agent. They are also good *simpliciter*." The reason why they are both is that, in reply to the question, "are they good [i.e., relationally] because they are good for their agents or are they good for the agent because they are good [i.e., *simpliciter*]? . . . both answers are correct, and therefore the priority thesis is mistaken in that it denies this reciprocity" (p. 70).

On the basis of several arguments (on pp. 70–72) Raz arrives at three conclusions[20]: "that (i) understanding the concept of a relational good requires understanding the notion of nonrelational goods, (ii) there are no relational goods unless there are also nonrelational ones, and (iii) if anything is intrinsically good for a valuer (and I am assuming that the good of valuers is good in itself) then it is also good *simpliciter*" (p. 72). It seems to me that for Raz's refutation of (7), conclusion (iii) alone is crucial, for (i) is compatible with (7), hence does not undermine it, and (ii) rests on (iii). However, there are problems with (iii) for Raz confusingly fails to draw the crucial distinction between what he means by 'good nonrelationally', 'intrinsically', and 'simpliciter', and he explicitly offers only the following reason for (iii):

> [I]n justifying that anything is good for any agent we show (a) that the thing is good and (b) that the agent has the ability and the opportunity to have that good. I can think of no other way to account for why what is *intrinsically* good for some person or other (*or for other things whose good matters in itself*) is good for them. If this is so then relational goods *presuppose* nonrelational goods. (p. 70, my emphases)

It seems to me that the very condensed reasoning in the above argument from intrinsic goods goes something like this, though I may well have misunderstood it. When we try to justify that something is good for someone, we begin by showing that it is good, in a certain sense. To clarify that sense, let us take Raz's case in which we try to justify that "engaging with music" is intrinsically good for Johnny. Then, it appears, the sense of 'good' in which we must show that it is good, is that it is intrinsically good, period. For it could not mean we must show that it is *intrinsically good for Johnny*, since that is the conclusion of our justification, not its premises. Neither could it mean we must show that it is extrinsically good for Johnny, for that is irrelevant. And there does not seem to be anything else it could mean. The question, then, is what is meant by 'intrinsically good, period', as opposed to 'intrinsically good for Johnny'.

It seems that Raz favors one or other of two likely interpretations. The first is that he construes the connection between its being intrinsically good and its being intrinsically good for Johnny, in the following way: the answer to the question of whether it is intrinsically good for Johnny rests on whether it is intrinsically good, period. Thus, he says "I know that going to see good films would be (intrinsically) good for me . . . because that is a valuable activity which it is within my imaginative, emotional, and intellectual capacity to benefit from" (p. 72). And again, "[a]ppreciating art is intrinsically good, and is good for those animals (so far as we know, all of them human) who can appreciate art" (p. 72).

But if that is his interpretation, might not a defender of RA1 argue that the connection between what is intrinsically good and what is intrinsically good for someone really runs the other way? Don't we try, he might say, to improve our life by leading it in such a way that it contains a certain proportion of certain experiences, activities, and relations to other beings, while not containing certain others whose respective presence in, or absence from, our life would bring it closer to our unflawed[21] conception of the preferred life for us? Thus, what we judge to be intrinsically or extrinsically good *for us* would seem to be those experiences, activities, and so on, that fit into that conception in this way.[22] And we call them *intrinsic goods* if but only if we think that by possessing them the lives of all or most people are improved, by the standard of their own unflawed conception of the preferred life for them.[23] If this is correct, then we would expect to find more agreement on whether or not something is intrinsically good for someone—say, *his* having won *his* tennis match—than that winning *one's* tennis match *is* an intrinsic good. And if this is correct, then the case of intrinsic goods appears not to show that nonrelational goods are prior to relational ones. For in order to determine what are intrinsic goods, we must first know what is good, though not as a means, for *all* or *most* people.

Of course, there may be some intrinsic goods, and there certainly are intrinsic bads, concerning which we may indeed seem to proceed in the way Raz's remarks suggest we do. Take a simple case, say, having a headache. We appear to know it is an intrinsic bad quite independently of knowing that it is bad for a given sufferer. And we appear to know that the sufferer's life is a worse life for having it and would be a better one for being free of headaches altogether. We would not accept—or would look for a pathological explanation of—someone's claim that his life had greatly improved since he had come to have migraines twice a week. It seems that our understanding of what a headache is includes this evaluation of the experience. This is not so with our understanding of many other experiences, activities, and relations, such as, listening to rock and roll, exchanging gossip, getting drunk, rock-climbing, or feeding the hungry, concerning which the question of whether they are intrinsic goods, intrinsic evils, or neither, cannot be answered because whether they are intrinsic goods (or evils or neither) *for people* varies from person to person: they may be intrinsic goods for some, intrinsic evils for others, and neither to a third group. For these experiences, activities, and relations, it would seem, we have no expressions that have universal evaluative connotations, as 'pain' does, and coining such expressions would not be a help, since it might mislead people into thinking that these things are intrinsically valuable *for everyone*. In their cases, at any rate, it seems clear that something's being intrinsically good for someone does not presuppose its being intrinsically good, period.

But suppose we accept what I have taken to be Raz's construal of the relation between what is an intrinsic good and what is intrinsically good for someone. There still seems to be a major gap between intrinsic and nonrelational goods (or evils), if one understands the latter to imply, as Raz seems to do in RA1, that nonrelational goods ground universal practical reasons. For even if all intrinsic goods are the positive counterparts of intrinsic evils, such as pains, the universality of the practical reasons they ground amounts only to this, that possessing them is good for everyone who possesses them, so that everyone has reason to try and possess them. But they do not ground universal reasons in the sense, it seems, so avidly sought after in ethics, namely, that everyone has reason to promote and protect everyone's possessing nonrelational goods. If, let us say, an orgasm is an intrinsic good in the sense in which a pain is an intrinsic evil, and so is good for everyone who has one, it does not seem to follow that everyone has reason to promote everyone else's having one, or perhaps two or three, or as many as they would like. This incidentally may reveal an asymmetry between pleasures and pains, and I think, more generally, between goods and evils, in respect of their capacity to ground reasons for one to promote the former and prevent the latter for other people.[24]

Consider, then, the second interpretation of 'intrinsically good' that may well be favored by Raz. Suppose he and supporters of RA1 hold that his argument from intrinsic goods *presupposes* that what is intrinsically good for a person and so is part of a person's good, is ipso facto a nonrelational good. Thus, the fact that something is intrinsically good for someone must not be taken to *entail* that it is a nonrelational good; we are simply taking it for granted without argument that what is intrinsically good for someone is, because it is part of his good, a nonrelational good, but we can then *infer* from this assumed fact that something being intrinsically good for someone grounds universal, including moral, reasons. Thus, he says, "[m]ost commonly it is assumed that morality regards the well-being of all human beings . . . as nonrelationally valuable and thus a source of reasons for action for all human beings" (p. 68; see also the paragraph from p. 70 and conclusion (c) from p. 72, both already quoted above on p. 228).

But does not this leave, between being a nonrelational good and grounding universal reasons, a gap similar to that we noted before, between being an intrinsic good and being a universal reason? Even if it is true that a person's good is a nonrelational good, this does not entail that it grounds universal reasons. Raz' "stipulative" definition of 'a nonrelational good' says only that it is not a relational one, that "what makes it good is (or depends in part on) something other than that it is good for someone" (p. 65). But this does not seem to me to entail that it grounds universal reasons. I can agree that the fact that something is good for someone, and that it therefore would make his life better if he possessed it, and therefore is a relational good, grounds a reason for him to want to possess it, but I do not find the same plausibility in the claim that something's being a nonrelational good, i.e., a good grounded in some fact other than that it is good for someone, grounds a universal reason for action.

Indeed, it may well have been the wish to explain moral as universal practical reasons and the felt difficulty of finding a plausible ground for them that gave G. E. Moore the idea of laying it down that 'intrinsic goods' are things of which it is true to say that they (i) are "intrinsically good," that is, possess a certain "simple, indefinable, non-natural quality," and (ii) therefore ought to exist.[25] This stipulation enables him to claim that things that are intrinsically good ought to exist, which he took to imply that everyone has reason (other things equal) to bring them into, or maintain them in, existence; but it also prevents and so excuses him from producing any evidence that the possession of a given "natural" (roughly, an empirically discoverable) property by a thing constitutes a fact that grounds such universal reasons. Some moral philosophers (myself included) have found this maneuver, despite its ingenuity, unsuccessful.

The same weakness, it seems to me, fells the various revivals of this Moorean idea—beginning with Thomas Nagel's brilliant *The Possibility of Altruism*—which introduce predicates closely similar to Raz's ". . . grounds universal reasons." For they seem no more able than Moore to describe a way (other than intuition, which comes to much the same as no describable way) in which an empirically detectable property can be plausibly portrayed as grounding such universal reasons.

I conclude that neither of these two interpretations constitute a proof of, or indeed any support for, thesis (c) which is the heart of Raz's attempt to refute RA1. This ends my brief reflections on Raz's attempt to refute the first priority thesis, that of relational *goods* to nonrelational ones. Instead of making what, from the nature of the case, would have to be analogous remarks also about the second priority thesis, that of relational *reasons* to nonrelational ones, I briefly sketch a way in which RA2 could be strengthened by dropping the assumption that nonrelational goods ground universal reasons. This is not as radical a step as might be thought, for it does not imply what I would regard as implausible as well as radical, namely, that "all reasons are agent-relative, and that they all derive from what is good for the agent or for her life, or from goals which he happens to have" (p. 67) or, in other words, that all are what Scanlon felicitously called "self-grounded." If I am right in this, then one also need not accept Raz's claim that, by retaining the assumption that nonrelational goods ground universal reasons, his conception of the moral point of view approach is "a much weaker, and therefore more plausible, thesis" (p. 67).[26] For one may well think, as many would, that the assumption of nonrelational goods and their grounding of universal reasons actually weakens RA.

Dropping these assumptions will enable us to construe RA2 as aiming to show, as Raz puts it, "that moral reasons are distinct" because "the values (the moral goods) which give rise to moral reasons . . . are related to moral reasons in a way which is distinct and unlike the usual relations between goods and reasons" (pp. 67–68). Thus reformulated without reliance on nonrelational goods that ground universal reasons, RA2 then argues that the distinctness of moral reasons lies, not in the distinctness of the relation between the specifically moral nonrelational values and the reasons to which they give rise, but in the distinctness of the relation that holds between certain relational values and the reasons, with their wider (though not universal) scope, to which they give rise and of which we think as moral reasons. If moral values are nonrelational and so goods *simpliciter*, then the reasons to which they give rise unconditionally have universal scope. If, as unreconstructed RA2 appears to assume, we can tell, without the assistance of the moral point of view, that certain values[27] are nonrelational, then the refutation of either of the two priority theses would indeed dispose of RA. But if there are no nonrelational values, then the moral point of view can do the job which was assigned to nonrelational values by their inventors. But then the specific characteristics of that point of view are needed to tell us which relational values do and which do not give rise to "agent-transcending" (as opposed to agent-relative) reasons, that is, reasons with a wider (though not universal) scope than the person(s) for whom acting on them is good, and just whom that scope includes.

This reconstructed version of RA2 can bypass the difficulty, not to say impossibility, of finding goods *simpliciter* that give rise to reasons whose scope (that is, the number and identity of the beings for whom they are reasons) is as wide as is often ascribed to moral reasons (e.g., all normal human adults, or all humans or all sentient beings, and the like). Instead, that version relies on a conception of the moral point of view able to explain why, and to justify the claim (if suitably reduced) that—as Raz puts it—"from the moral point of view, we may say, people have reason to protect and promote the good of all" (p. 67), even though the people who have reason to do so may include some for whom doing so is not good. At the same time, it can deny that relational goods can ground only agent-relative reasons—that is, reasons whose scope includes only those for whom it is good to do what they direct be done. Such a conception of the moral point of view enables us to see that, if interaction between people takes place under certain conditions, then *everyone* interacting with others *under these conditions* has adequate reasons, grounded in relational goods, to regard certain practical principles designed to protect and promote the good of those with whom she interacts as reasons that defeat any agent-relative reasons that conflict with them. This is so because, to be sound, these overriding (i.e., moral) principles must be formulated in such a way that under these conditions she will have a better chance to lead the preferred life as she conceives of it than if everyone always followed agent-relative reasons. On this view, then, one of the main tasks for moral philosophy is to make clear exactly what these conditions and these principles are.

This is not the place to spell all this out,[28] but it may be worth mentioning one of these conditions and a well-known difficulty that comes with it. The condition is that everyone recognize and follow the same overriding principles.[29] The difficulty, of course, is that this condition will not always be satisfied, if indeed ever. Hence, if this approach is to be of any practical use, one must still have adequate reason to conform to these principles, even when the circumstances of interaction constitute, not indeed a full satisfaction of these conditions, but only a certain degree of approximation to them. In other words, the situation must be such that people would still have a better chance to lead a life closer to their conception of the preferred life for them if they followed these principles and worked for the further improvement of the conditions under which they interact with one another than if they acted in the way which, in their judgment, would best protect or promote their own good and/or that of those near and dear to them.[30]

But is not the dropping of nonrelational goods, goods *simpliciter*, a very implausible move? Surely, it may be said, what is good for a person, say, John, generates reason to protect and promote it, not merely for John for whom, or from whose point of view, it is a good thing to do so, but for other people as well; but how can that be so unless this good is a good *simpliciter*, a nonrelational good? This is a complex and difficult question a satisfactory answer to which would go beyond the scope of these comments. I hope that what little I can say is not entirely without merit. I accept something close to Raz's assumption (p. 67), that doing something which is good for another can be a reason for John to do it only either if it is good also for him or if it is good from the moral point of view.[31] Raz takes it that the latter can be so only if, from that point of view, we can see that "what is good for John is also good *simpliciter*." Against this, I have suggested another possibility which requires only relational goods and a distinct relation between them and reasons. We can think of moral reasons as based on what we can "in reason" *want of one another*, that is what, *in certain circumstances*, we have relational reasons to want of one another; we therefore have reason to do for one another what will satisfy this want and not do to one another what will frustrate it. This recognizes that we do not have reason to satisfy what any and every person wants us to do for her, but that we may have such reason on a basis of mutuality and within certain specified and reasonable limits.[32]

I conclude, very tentatively, that if my reflections are on the right track, then the two versions of RA, especially the reconstructed RA2, which does not rely on nonrelational values, are more persuasive than Raz's attempted refutations of the two "priorities" (his sections 5 and 6) might lead one to believe.

Section B

Perhaps a few words are now in order about two matters: how points of view are, or might usefully be, classified into certain types and to which of these types the moral point of view—if there is one—should be ascribed.

There are, of course, many different points of view and they appear to be of different types, though we may not agree on the best way of arranging them in a perspicuous order. We speak, for instance, of (i) a person's own and that of his family's, friends' and enemies'; (ii) the parents', teachers', students', and Administration's; (iii) the educational, pedagogical, theological, juridical, legislative, and judicial; or (iv) the prudential, legal, moral, religious, and economic points of view, and so on and on.

All these points of view, and indeed all those I am here concerned with, are or can be "normative" in one of two different senses. A point of view is "independently normative" if and only if it is such that it ought, from its very nature, to be adopted by everybody (as we think is true, for instance, of the points of view of consistency, the law, and morality) and that "its" considerations—those that are derived from it—ought to weigh with everyone. A point of view is "dependently normative"—if and only if there is some other independently normative one *from which* everyone or a certain class of people ought to adopt it. Thus, the farmer's point of view, for example, is not independently normative, and I can think of no independently normative one from which everybody ought to adopt it; but it may be dependently normative for some classes of people, such as farmers, if it is so from another point of view, say, that of self-interest, and if that one is, as many seem to believe, nonderivatively normative.

But whether or not it is dependently normative for some people, the farmer's point of view can and is likely to be adopted by at least some farmers and probably by others, but it is conceivable though unlikely that no one has actually adopted it. By 'adopting a point of view' I mean an intentional way of coming to have a point of view, and not just taking it temporarily and exploratorily to see what those who have it would judge and do in certain matters, as when a legislator or politician tries to judge a piece of legislation from the farmer's point of view to see what his farmer constituents are likely to think about it, and about him if he votes for it. There are, of course, other ways of coming to have a point of view. One may come by it less self-consciously and deliberately; some farmers, for instance, as it were, "slide into" having the farmer's point of view because they are farmers, and they judge and act from it,[33] perhaps even without being aware of doing so or of having it. Thus, those politicians and legislators I just imagined do not necessarily take, let alone acquire, or have, the farmer's point of view. They merely, as it were, slip it on experimentally, like trying on a suit in a department store, not necessarily with a view to, let alone a way of, acquiring it.

How, then, is a point of view, such as the farmer's, related to the considerations that derive from it, and how does it thus normally weigh with one who has it? Clearly, such a point of view is *defined by* certain ends and interests—in the present case, those that people occupying that role typically come to have. The considerations that are derived from it are derived from those ends and interests; they are those which recommend behavior that protects and promotes those ends and interests. One can know what the farmer's point of view is without being or having been a farmer, or even without having the ends and interests characteristic of farmers, but not without knowing what interests a person occupying that role typically develops. And the same is true for adopting it. I call this type "role-interest points of view."

Those who, on a particular occasion, take such a point of view, can derive, from the ends and interest that define it, various considerations that will then enable them to guide their judgments about what to do and about what they have done. If they adopt one, they normally adopt its considerations as principles and so are set to follow them. Of course, they adopt these principles with the provisos built into all principles, the most important being that it may sometimes be appropriate to act contrary to them, namely, when and because they then conflict with other more important principles. But although adopting such a point of view normally means that these considerations will weigh with one, it does not mean that they *ought* to do so, even other things equal. Thus, if someone adopts the burglar's point of view, the considerations that go with it may well weigh with him, but that does not imply that they ought. There will also be points of view, such as the farmer's, of which it is neither true that one ought nor that one ought not to adopt it, since it is neither contrary to, nor required by, reason to do so.

However, there are points of view, such as that of consistency which, it seems, everyone ought to adopt and from which it can be seen that one ought not both to adopt—or at least claim to have adopted—the farmer's point of view and at the same time not be motivated to act in accordance with its considerations. If this is right, then from the point of view of consistency, any person who has adopted the farmer's point of view ought either to be motivated (disposed) to act on its considerations, or else abandon it.[34]

That a point of view is independently normative does not imply that it is so *unconditionally*, or, what comes to the same thing, that its considerations are *reasons all things considered.*[35] Thus, many think of the self-interested point of view as independently normative, because they think that it is not contrary to reason to adopt and act from it and that it is contrary to reason not to do so; they think of people as foolish or misguided, that is, as behaving contrary to reason, if they don't adopt it and don't regard its considerations as reasons for them, as directing them to do what they ought to do. At the same time, they think that reasons of self-interest are so only *other-things-equal*, and they believe that other things often are not equal, as when moral considerations conflict with those of self-interest. Hence, as we noted above, although the farmer's point of view is only dependently normative and only for certain classes of people, it may well be that farmers ought to adopt it because it is in their interest to do so and because everyone ought to adopt the self-interested point of view and so regard its considerations as other-things-equal reasons.

Next, we must distinguish a person's self-interested point of view, call it "SI," from another so similar to it that it is seldom recognized as distinct. Its defining aim and interest is to be able to lead a life as close as possible to the preferred life for one—call it 'a person's "preferred life" point of view', or "PL" for short.[36] It differs from SI in that it often generates considerations favoring the interests of others in their own right—that is, not just as a means to protecting or promoting one's own—and from role-interest points of view, in that it is not based on the interests of the role(s) the person plays. The interest or end defining it is indicated explicitly by incorporation in its name, as in the case of SI, rather than indirectly by reference to the sorts of people or roles whose typical interest or end is its defining interest or end, as in the case of the farmer's point of view.[37]

To derive the considerations of PL, we need criteria of relevance and soundness. The criterion of relevance makes relevant those facts about a person's actions which indicate that they affect his life, either favorably or unfavorably, as judged by his unflawed conception of the preferred life for him. The criterion of soundness makes such facts pros for him if they indicate that those actions affect his life favorably, cons if they affect it unfavorably.

Is PL independently normative, as SI seems to be, or is it only dependently so, as are role-interest points of view? The question is difficult and my answer[38] is (a somewhat puzzled and diffident) "Yes." The conflicting considerations will become clearer, as we examine the relation between SI and PL. I have already noted that SI appears to be independently normative, but further reflection on the relation between SI and PL calls that in question. On the one hand, SI considerations are reasons for a particular person if and to the extent that they protect and promote the preferred life as she conceives it. One has a reason to protect and promote one's own good or interest if and only if that is included in one's conception of the preferred life for one. At the same time, it is hard to imagine a conception of such a preferred life which is both internally unflawed and does not include the promotion and protection of the person's own interest. Indeed, one might be inclined to argue that the total absence of that concern from a conception of the preferred life for one would itself be a strong reason to think, if not a proof, that this conception is internally flawed.

I conclude that we can characterize the relation between SI and PL in two different ways either of which seems correct. We can say, in the first place, that SI is not an independently normative point of view and that the ultimate ground on which self-interested reasons rest is a person's unflawed conception of the preferred life for her, because one has to take PL in order to determine the proper range of self-interested reasons, that is, the circumstances which must prevail, if self-interested considerations are to amount to reasons for her. And there are such circumstances limiting the range of SI reasons because a person's own interest may, and at times is likely to, conflict with that of other people, and because the preferred life as she conceives it may, and is bound to, put certain interests of certain others, say loved ones, ahead of certain interests of her own. Hence, in such a case it would be contrary to reason always to follow self-interested considerations rather than considerations favoring those interests of those others. Hence SI considerations are reasons only to the extent to which they conform to PL considerations.

However, we could, perhaps with equal justification, say that SI is an independently normative point of view because no internally unflawed conception of the preferred life for a person can lack a place for her interest. Hence one's conception of the preferred life for one would be flawed, and acting on considerations derived from it contrary to reason, if it had no place for the protection and promotion of one's interest. But then self-interested considerations are reasons nonderivatively. At the same time, it has to be admitted that what may be called "the target" of these reasons—what they are reasons for—will be determined by the details of that person's internally unflawed conception of the preferred life for herself. Call these two ways of conceiving the nature of the relationship between SI and PL reasons, the derivative and the nonderivative relationship, respectively.

Thus, it makes little practical difference which of these relationships we subscribe to, for on both versions we allow that self-interested considerations are other-things-equal reasons, where the questions of when other things are not equal, and the question of the exact target of these reasons, is determined from PL. What is crucial, in other words, is the delimitation, from PL, of what SI considerations count as reasons.

The distinction between the derivative and the nonderivative relationship between SI and PL can throw light on the slightly different relationship between PL and the moral point of view, call it MPV. In one respect, the relationship between SI and PL (call it R1) is like, and in another unlike, the relationship between PL and MPV (call it R2). R1 and R2 are similar in this respect: in both of them, one of the two points of view is "higher"—in R1 it is PL and in R2 it is MPV—in the sense that the "higher" point of view delimits which of the considerations belonging to the "lower" are reasons.

However, the justifications for saying that, in both R1 and R2, the "higher" points of view impose such restrictions on what are reasons from the "lower," can with roughly equal plausibility be described as the same or as different. We can think of these justifications as the same in R1 and R2, because, without the imposition of these limitations, the ends of the two "higher" points of view—PL and MPV—would not be attained. What is more, in both cases, the end is one and the same, namely, that of PL: leading a life as close as possible to one's unflawed conception of the preferred life for one. For the function of MPV with its paramount considerations is to limit what counts as reasons from PL, and to do so with a view to increasing everyone's chances to lead a life as close as possible to his internally unflawed conception of the preferred life, which is also the end of PL. At the same time, the considerations of MPV amount to reasons *only* because they are designed so as to attain the end of PL, and this can be achieved only by allowing moral reasons (considerations from MPV) to delimit what considerations from PL can constitute reasons.

On the other hand, the sense in which the justification for the delimitations imposed on the "lower" considerations is not the same in R1 and R2, is that in R1 the end to be promoted is that of the "higher," the limitation-imposing, point of view, whereas in R2 the end to be promoted is that of the "lower," i.e., the one on whose considerations the limitations are imposed. But, of course, in both cases, the point of view whose end is to be promoted is PL.

Perhaps the most important aspect of MPV, at any rate as I conceive it, is that it is invented to improve the chances of those recognizing it, to lead the preferred life by the criteria they themselves subscribe to. The reflections leading to this conception center on the insight that one's chances to lead such a life depend at least as much on what others do as on what one can do oneself. Hence the importance of a social order which points to worthwhile ends in life and to reliable ways of attaining them, erects barriers to *mutual interference*, builds avenues of *mutual aid*, and sets up fruitful *forms of cooperation*.

This adds a further aspect to moral considerations not present in those we have so far examined: members of a society are not "free" to ignore moral reasons, as they are to ignore those of SI, PL, and role-interest points of view. Other things equal, they are free to act contrary to reason by being foolish, but not by doing evil. The former is solely their own business, the latter is not. The former reasons tell them to do things to attain ends *they themselves* may be presumed to want to attain; if they do not try to attain them, that is solely their own business. The latter reasons tell them to do things that there is reason for them to *want one another* to aim at attaining, whether or not they already want to. This account of a widespread conviction of common-sense morality is closer to Mill's than to Kant's, whose categorical imperative seems to me to make an unnecessary metaphysical mystery out of a relatively straightforward social relationship, and whose hypothetical imperative seems incapable of giving mere counsel or advice, as it is supposed to.

Thus, if I am right, the hub of the many points of view and their respective ends and considerations would seem to be PL. It determines for all considerations which of them are to be regarded as reasons, and which not. Even MPV, from which the rational limits of PL considerations are determined, is itself designed to protect and promote, within a moral order, every member's end determined by PL.

However, this central position of PL in the system of practical reasons seems to generate a paradox when we want to ask whether it is contrary to reason for someone not to adopt PL. On the one hand, it seems we cannot raise that question for, if PL really is the hub of the enterprise of practical reason, as I am arguing, then whether doing anything is according or contrary to reason depends on whether it protects and promotes, or hampers and frustrates attaining the end of PL, but that seems to preclude asking whether adopting PL is according to reason, and not adopting it contrary to it. By assigning to PL this central place in the system of practical reasons we have closed a question which, it seems, should remain open.

I am convinced this Moorean kind of problem can be dissolved, but I am unsure about how best to do it. One approach would be to ask whether accepting PL as the hub of the enterprise of practical reason would have implications in some domain of the enterprise of reason, including the practical one, that are contrary to reason. This would enable us to make sense of the question seemingly made senseless by the acceptance of PL as the hub, and to answer it by another method than the one precluded by that acceptance. Of course, this gives rise to the possibility that, by using this method, we will discover such damaging implications. But that could be construed as the analog of an empirical test of acceptability.

We could extend this approach by examining rival candidates for the central role I assigned to PL. I can think of two candidates that have found favor in the past. One is SI, but it seems easy to demonstrate the superiority of PL over SI;[39] the other is "the point of view of the world or the universe" favored by, among others, Sidgwick.[40] An important remark by Raz encourages me to think he might agree with me that the end of improving the world would not be an anchor for the enterprise of practical reason that is superior to the end of attaining the preferred life as one conceives it. As he puts it firmly, "While it makes sense to say that someone wants a good holiday in order to have a good life it seems absurd to suggest that someone desires a good life, for himself or for another, *in order* to make the world into a better world" (p. 66). Some philosophers, no doubt, would wish to replace the end of PL by some other end they take to be that of the moral enterprise, some *summum bonum*, but it is hard to find one that has both the appeal and the accessibility of PL.[41]

I have spoken mainly about the three central and most general points of view, SI, PL, and MPV, and their intricate hierarchical relationship. We employ them mostly in evaluating the more specific points of view from which we actually deliberate about what to do on particular occasions and judge the various kinds of merit and demerit of what we ourselves or others have done. This is not the place to give a detailed discussion of all these other points of view and the considerations derived from them. But it may be helpful to give one example of the many that are relevant. Suppose I am asked to review a book on philosophy. I will normally decide from PL whether or not to do it. When people judge my life, to the extent that I have made it what it is, and me as the one who is leading it, they may take into account whether my conception of the preferred life for me generates considerations favoring my doing the sorts of thing I have done, including my decision about reviewing books in general and this book in particular. If I decide to review the book, I shall, and I think I ought to, judge its merits and demerits from a number of points of view that are generally thought relevant to this type of activity: the stylistic, logical, metaphysical, religious, epistemological, and perhaps other points of view. These, too, are normative points of view. That is to say, we may or ought to adopt these points of view, and may or ought to judge or act in accordance with the considerations they generate by the various appropriate criteria of relevance and soundness. But these points of view differ from PL in that they are not related specifically to my life, but to a widely practiced activity, that of reviewing books. There are well worked-out criteria of relevance and soundness, as there are in many cases of judging the merit of things of a certain kind, such as knives, cars, and books. People who are interested in such judgments, and perhaps study them in consumer reports or literary reviews, know these criteria and take other people to be judging by them also. In these contexts, the standardization of criteria and standards is as much a condition of communication as in all other areas in which individuals have to rely on judgments made by others.

Judgments of lives can also be made by these person-neutral points of view and considerations. We may say that someone had or led a good or a miserable life, meaning thereby that we might not call, say, Wittgenstein's life a good one, either because he too frequently suffered deep anguish and despair, or because he did things one should condemn from the moral point of view. But he himself said, I assume sincerely, that his had been a good life, perhaps meaning thereby, not that it was a good life by the criteria and standards most people would apply, but one he ranked (fairly or even very) high from what I have called PL; that he had ample opportunity to do the things, have the experiences, and establish the relationships that brought his life close enough to his conception of the preferred life for him.

When we judge a person or his life from a moral point of view, we do something similar to what we do when we judge it from a prudential, religious, or aesthetic point of view. That is, we judge him or it on the basis of whether and to what extent he or it satisfied the requirements of morality, prudence, religion, or art, usually as the judges, not the judged, think they are rightly understood; the concern is whether something was moral or immoral, wise or foolish, pious or impious, beautiful or ugly. But this sort of judgment, it seems to me, presupposes another, namely, how these basic moral, prudential, religious, or aesthetic distinctions are to be drawn. In the earlier book, to which Raz refers, I thought of the moral point of view as one that enables us to distinguish between the moral and the *im*moral in the broadest sense, that is, (in keeping with what Hume called "our moral distinctions") to make such distinctions as virtue/vice, right/wrong, and justice/injustice (Hume included many more, some of which I myself would not have included). I was not then, I seem to remember, much concerned about the distinction Raz relates to the moral point of view, namely, that between the moral and the nonmoral. However, for some time now, I have been very much interested in the latter distinction because I have concluded that, in at least one of its senses, it bears on the other distinction about which I was then and still am primarily concerned. Raz's interesting remarks encourage me to add, in the following section, a few more words about these two distinctions.

Section C

The moral point of view as conceived by Raz implies, it will be remembered, that "there is a coherent, context-independent way of *separating the moral from the nonmoral*, on which a correct understanding of morality depends" (p. 61; my emphasis). It will also be recalled that in his view, "we are not compelled by the facts on the surface of our discourse . . . [to believe] that there is [a] common basis for all our (correct) classification of actions or of considerations into moral and nonmoral" (p. 62). Nor, on the other hand, are we compelled to believe "that there is no common basis" for such a classification (ibid.).

It seems to me that, in order to get clearer about what we should believe on this matter, it would help to be clearer about exactly how Raz conceives of this distinction. Does he subscribe to the now widely accepted difference between the moral/nonmoral and the moral/immoral distinctions? It seems not, for in the first of his two examples, apparently illustrating "how the distinction between the moral and the nonmoral could be context-dependent" (p. 61), someone says, "What I did may have been tactless, but it was not *immoral.* I'm not saying that it was a *moral* act. Rather that it was neither *moral* nor *immoral*, but merely tactless" (ibid., my emphases). And in the second example, involving Peter and Butrus, which classifies their "actions as moral or nonmoral . . . Peter's act is moral because of a combination of his motivation and of the disruption to his normal life that his action will—if successful—bring about . . . To the extent that we feel some ambivalence about calling Butrus' action moral, that is because it involves no disruption to his normal life" (pp. 61–62).

The first example seems ambiguous between whether 'moral' and 'immoral' are contraries like 'ugly' and 'beautiful', or contradictories like 'dead' and 'alive'. If they are contraries, then 'tactless' and 'neither *moral* nor *immoral*' may lie somewhere in between 'moral' and 'immoral', as 'homely' may lie between 'ugly' and 'beautiful'. But if it is like 'dead' and 'alive', then 'tactless' and 'neither *moral* nor *immoral*' must lie outside this little universe of discourse, must be 'nonmoral', just as 'inorganic' cannot lie between 'dead' and 'alive', but must be 'non-living'. Is tactlessness in the same "ball game" as morality and immorality, the ascription of a *morally* evaluative quality intermediate between the two? Or is it in a different ball game altogether, one that places the behavior on a scale different from that which registers the moral and the immoral?

The second example suggests quite strongly that, by the 'nonmoral', Raz means a quality based on the same type of considerations as would, in some cases, result in judgments ascribing morality or immorality to an action, but in Butrus' case only "nonmorality," that is, something falling short of morality, on account of there being "no disruption to his normal life." Presumably, 'disruption' and 'nondisruption' bear on whether something is moral (in the sense of praiseworthy or meritorious) or nonmoral (in the sense of falling short of being praiseworthy).

I am confused by these examples. Is the moral point of view as he conceives it a point of view from which to draw a sharp distinction between what is moral in the sense of having moral merit and falling short of having it? I doubt it, but have failed to find another plausible account that fits in with his examples. Perhaps I should mention here that I, myself, do not now think, and have never thought, of it in this narrow way.

There are two other distinctions between the moral and the nonmoral which are worth examining briefly. The first is the distinction I have used in the past, the second is one in which I have become interested only in relatively recent years.

Suppose we can single out at least some distinctions, such as those between virtues and vices, right and wrong, or justice and injustice, that we agree on their being *moral distinctions*, and that we can discover or construct ways for applying them correctly, as, for instance, utilitarians and contractarians are trying to do. Then there would seem to be a *moral domain*, namely, that of these moral distinctions and what they apply to. And there would also seem to be the various domains of comparable such distinctions we would agree are not moral ones, and what they apply to. These latter, I imagine, might quite naturally be called the nonmoral domain(s) or the domain(s) of the nonmoral. Some of them, such as the religious, the rational, the legal, the political, and the prudential, have often been used as models for, or rivals of, the moral domain, while the aesthetic and economic domains have been so used less often.

What belongs in each of these domains is not an unimportant question, for exactly which distinctions we take to be or not to be moral ones, has a strong influence on what we work out to be the appropriate ways for correctly applying them. Hence the distinction between the moral and the nonmoral domains would seem to be *morally* (or if you prefer, *ethically*) important. As is well known, Hume, while recognizing that "we refuse to natural abilities the title of virtues" (1978, 607) nevertheless thought it worth arguing that some of them, such as a good memory (1978, 612) or being "a good *women's man*" (1978, 614; Hume's emphasis; what a wag he could be!) should be included among the natural virtues. He based his argument for this inclusion on his account of the distinction between virtue and vice, while others regard this as evidence of the inadequacy of that account. This apparent connection between the way in which we draw these domains and the distinctions we draw within them would seem to call for a general scheme by which an underlying coherent relationship between these domains with one another could be brought to light or constructed. I have tried to do that, in RMO, for a few domains—in some detail for those of morality and practical reason, and less fully for certain forms of theistic religion and for law. I hope that this topic will attract the attention of others with wider knowledge and deeper insights than I was able to bring to it.

Contrasting with this synchronic distinction between the moral and the extramoral is another, diachronic one, between the premoral and the moral stages of our thinking and acting. The distinction has similarities with Hume's and Rawls's account and use of the circumstances of justice.[42] I have tried to bring out some of the societal presuppositions of our having what Hume calls the moral distinctions and those other distinctions that, at least in the *Treatise*, he tried so vigorously to disentangle from them, namely, those we draw with terms from the concept of reason.

IV. David Gauthier: Individual Reason

Gauthier propounds two main theses, both in opposition to ideas advanced in RMO. The first rejects my claim that reason has "social roots" and insists that on the contrary "an individual['s] . . . exercise of reason and rationality are characterized without reference to society . . . and . . . that their ascription is strictly individualistic" (p. 39). The second rejects my claim that morality involves a kind of what I call society-anchored reasons. In section A of these comments, I try to clear up merely verbal disagreements and other misunderstandings, while in section B I examine some of what seem to be our real disagreements, defending my views on some issues and revising them on others.

Section A

Gauthier seems to begin section 1 of his paper in what used to be called "the material mode." Thus, he writes, "I want to propound a very different thesis; that the roots of human morality and society are to be found in reason" and that "the ascription of both reason and rationality to individuals is quite independent of any social context, much less that peculiar social context that Baier characterizes as 'an order of reason'" and that "Rationality is a socially subversive characteristic of individuals" (p. 39).

But then, in section 2, he seems to switch to the "formal mode," for he there offers definitions of key terms such as 'reason', 'reasons', 'rationality', and 'acting for reasons'; but he seems to offer them, not by way of trying to capture what they actually do mean, but stipulatively, perhaps to sharpen their meaning or by way of reform. Thus, he "identifies" or "proposes to identify" what some of them refer to with certain capacities, while of course knowing full well that others, including myself, have not chosen so to identify them and obviously do not think it best to do so. For these and other reasons, it is not clear to me exactly what our disagreements in these matters come to. Are they all merely verbal, cases of misunderstanding, of talking past each other? It would certainly seem that some are. But are there also real, substantial disagreements? I shall shortly try to translate our, plainly divergent, terminologies into each other and try to disentangle the real issues, if any, from the merely verbal ones.

Even where terminological discrepancies from the domain of reason do not seem to be involved, Gauthier claims opposition where I can find none. Thus, the original title (now subtitle) of my book, *The Social Roots of Reason and Morality*, prompts Gauthier to ask "Why suppose that *the* roots of reason and morality are social?" (p. 39; my emphasis). The answer is that I supposed no such thing and the subtitle does not imply it nor, by my lights, does the text. In any case, what I supposed was that some of the roots are social, and it is these, in my view somewhat neglected ones, to which I allude. I did not mean to deny, indeed I emphasized, that there are equally important individual roots as well.[43]

Again, he claims, as if I was in disagreement on this point, that "[r]ationality is a socially subversive characteristic of individuals . . . Baier is right to speak of a society that is 'an order of reason', but this order must be created and its creation presupposes and depends on individual reflective rationality. And this order of reason proves to include some, if not all, of what we traditionally consider morality" (p. 39). I could not agree more and indeed much of my book is an attempt to show just this. Some of Gauthier's opposition to my quite central views may therefore rest on a misunderstanding of them, probably due, at least in part, to the opacity of my formulation of them.

At this point, a well-meaning pacifier may want to suggest that our disagreements are no more than differences in emphasis: While I am concerned to give an account of the structure of reason in its most fully developed form, Gauthier is concerned to show what is necessarily involved in all its stages, even the first and least developed ones. Now, I think there is something in this, but it does not seem to me the whole or even the most important part of the story. Unfortunately, to get to the bottom of our disagreement, it will be necessary to find out whether we can agree, in language not involving any terms from the concept of reason, what are the presuppositions a being must satisfy before we can say of it any of the things we say with some term or all the terms from the concept of reason, and what role society plays at each of the stages in the development of reason.

Section B

Perhaps Gauthier and I can agree on the following. Animate beings[44] have widely differing organic structures on account of which they engage in a wide range of "behaviors" the suitable explanations for which vary with these structures. Unsurprisingly, there are significant similarities in the organic structures of human beings and the higher mammals which correlate with and explain corresponding similarities in some of the types of behavior these beings engage in, and in the suitable types of explanations of these similar behaviors. We can perhaps agree that human beings and some of these mammals are capable of the following importantly different types of behaviors. The first are those, such as reflex actions,[45] whose explanations require neither any knowledge nor motivation on the part of the creature engaging in it. Secondly, there are those, such as yieldings to urges, which require motivation but not knowledge. Thirdly, there are those that require motivation, such as desiring something, and the relevant knowledge, say, what it is one wants and how one goes about satisfying it. Thus, the pubescent child may not know what she longs for or how to get it, so her behavior when she has these longings may not be capable of the usual means-end and belief-desire explanation. Fourthly, the creature may have the capacity to be motivated or moved by a semantic "representation of some part of the present state of the world, and one or more representations of those parts of the world, each as it would or might be, were she to perform an action that she consider possible for her. We explain the agent's action, then, by reference to the content of some or all of these representations" (p. 40).[46]

Next, we may agree, such a creature may have the ability to "assess" (p. 40) his capacity, that is, "the mechanism built into it," of being thus moved. Here, assessing it means judging the merit or demerit of this type of mechanism or of this or that particular instance of it. Lastly, such a creature may have the capacity (the mechanism, the tendency, the propensity) of being moved by such judgments.[47]

Supposing, then, that we agree on these matters, how does Gauthier's use of the terms from the concept of reason differ from mine? Gauthier, it will be remembered, defines 'reasons' as "representations of some part of the world, as it is or might be" (p. 40) and he defines 'reason' itself as "the capacity that human beings, and perhaps certain other animals, have, to act for reasons" (p. 39), that is, as the capacity "to be moved by the content of these representations" (p. 40) Thus, by 'explaining an agent's actions in terms of her reasons,' he means a causal explanation "by reference to the content of all of these representations" (ibid.). The causally operative factor of this explanation thus is the content of these representations.

However, in his view, beings who "possess [reason], at least in a rudimentary way," (p. 40) and can act for reasons, need not be rational. For they may lack the second capacity, that for "assessing reasons" (ibid.), that is, for assessing (semantic) representations of the world. Of course, this second capacity presupposes the first, while the first is independent of the second. Gauthier identifies the second with *rationality* or being *capable of rationality* (ibid.). Thus, to have reason, to have reasons, and to be capable of acting for them does not require the second capacity, that of assessing reasons. One can act for reasons without being able to assess whether it is a good thing for one to be moved in the way one is by these representations.

From this it would seem to follow that if, as it would not be implausible to assume, Koehler's ape has "the capacity to form at least some representations of the world as it is and might be, and to be moved by the content of these representations" (p. 40) then, according to Gauthier, he may be able to act for reasons and so to have acted for a certain reason on some occasion or, in other words, to have had that very reason *for* acting the way he did, and therefore also to have had that very reason *to* act in these ways. However, he or his behavior can be rational—and so presumably also irrational—if, but only if, he has the capacity for being rational, that is the capacity to determine by reflection whether or not it is, in general or on a particular occasion, a good thing, for him and/or for others, that he is moved in the way he is by his (semantic) representations of the world as it is and as it might be.

It should be clear to readers of my book that my use of the expressions 'reason', 'reasons', 'acting for a reason', and 'rationality' differs from Gauthier's in two general ways (among others). In the first place, my use of these terms extends beyond the domain of *practical* reason, reasons, and rationality, but I can ignore this point here and confine myself to the realm of the practical, to which Gauthier's definitions confine reason and rationality. But I must confess I find Gauthier's apparent restriction of reason to the realm of the practical no more palatable than Hume's exclusion of it from that realm.

The second general way is that whereas, according to Gauthier, even nonrational beings can possess reason, can have reasons to do things, and can act for reasons, I have closely tied these capacities to the possession of rationality. I agree that rationality requires capacities (and abilities, that is, developed—or actualized—capacities) that go beyond the capacity to be motivated by certain semantic representations, but I do not ascribe to beings (such as, let us say, Koehler's ape) who have the capacity to be moved by such representations, the possession of reason, the possession of reasons to do things, and the ability to act for reasons. I recognize the possibility that beings such as Koehler's ape have the capacity to be moved by such semantic representations[48] but I ascribe to them, on that account, at most the capacity to act from "considerations."[49] For each such being, some such representation—of course, not necessarily the same for all—is a consideration in favor of doing a certain thing—again, not necessarily the same thing for each.

Thus, the main difference I see between us is that, on my view, for such beings, as we may assume Koehler's ape to be, certain semantic representations could perhaps be considerations in favor of doing certain things, but could not be reasons for them to do them, whereas in Gauthier's view they could and would be such reasons. In my view, such beings can wonder about what to do only if certain semantic representation can motivate them to bring about a certain state of affairs and, if they do not know how, try to find out, as when Koehler's ape apparently was motivated to reflect about how to get hold of the bananas outside his cage. However, such reflection does not amount to deliberating about *what* state of the world *to* bring about. For the only capacity relevant to deliberating that such beings have is that of being motivated or moved to act in certain specific ways by certain semantic representations. *Ex hypothesi*, they lack the capacity to be *motivated* to bring about alternative states of affairs without being *moved* to bring about one rather than another; they lack the capacity to weigh, in this state of "suspended motivation," the merits of acting in one of these ways against the merits of acting in another; and they lack the capacity of being motivated to act according to their comparative evaluative judgments of these alternative motivations and actions. But, in my view, these additional capacities are presupposed not only by rationality but also by being able to act for reasons.

I hold, in other words, that a being *can* act for a reason only if something *can* be a reason for him *to* do what he does. But this means that there can be a fact about his acting in that way on account of which it would, from the appropriate point of view, *be a good thing* if he did act in that way and that he therefore ought to do so. By contrast, the fact that a being was moved by a representation of the world as it is and another as it would be if he acted in a certain way, merely amounts to his having acted not for a reason but merely from a certain consideration or motive. That one has acted for a reason requires, in addition, that one should have believed that the representations were sound, i.e., that the world really was and really would be as they represented it, *and* that one also believed that acting in the way in which these representations move one to act would be a good thing from the appropriate point of view, and that it is *therefore*, at least, other things equal, according to reason for one to act in this way.

Thus, if a creature is capable of being motivated by semantic representations, we can *explain* his behavior in terms of these representations, but this does not imply that we can *justify* his behavior on the grounds that it had been, was, or would be action in accordance with, and for (or on), a reason, at least other things being equal. And I take an explanation of a person's behavior in terms of *her* reasons for it to be a step also in its justification. Of course, it is only a first step. If her reason was a bad one, the justification fails.

Might one not argue, though, that this is an arbitrary regimentation of the use of 'acting for a reason'? Do we not often say of a person that he acted for a reason which was not a good one? Is not the evaluation of the reason for which a person acted a higher-level judgment, which is not presupposed by her having acted for a reason? Can we not tell what reason a person acted for, quite independently of the higher-level evaluative judgment that that reason was a good or a bad one?

The claim that someone acted for a certain reason is not, it seems to me, independent of this higher-level evaluative judgment. For, although others can claim that he acted for a certain reason, without having to make the judgment that his reason was a good or a bad one, they cannot claim this without thereby implying that he acted from two beliefs, namely, that something was a fact and that that fact was a reason for him to act in that way. And this implies that he acted in a way he *thought* was, from some relevant point of view, a good thing, a way of acting that was in accordance with, rather than contrary to, reason. Of course, he has acted for a reason even if either or both of these beliefs are mistaken, although then his reason was a bad one. The truth or falsity of these beliefs is one of the criteria of the goodness or badness of the reasons for which someone acts. Thus, although one can act for bad reasons, one cannot act for reasons without believing that they *are* reasons, and that seems to me to require, in Gauthier's terminology, that one at best believes the representations that move one to be true. This would, I think, normally be granted. In my view it also requires that the agent think the generated motivation to be a good one from the appropriate point of view, the one indicated when calling the reason a prudential or a moral one. If that is not so, then there was nothing the agent *took* to be a reason for him to act in this way, hence nothing that was *his reason* for acting, and so his behavior was not a case of his acting *for a reason*, though of course he may have acted from a motive or from a consideration.

Admittedly, my argument relies on the way we ordinarily use these expressions. I have also offered a general theory of the concept of reason that encompasses in a connected and coherent way the way in which terms rooted in this concept are used. Gauthier's *proposing* to identify a certain capacity with reason, and another with rationality, may signal that he is dissatisfied with what we ordinarily mean by these expressions. But I would have to know what he thinks is wrong with the way we use these terms and in what way his revisionary use is an improvement over the ordinary, before I fall in with his proposal.

Gauthier makes many other important and interesting points that deserve close attention, but I must postpone this pleasure for another occasion.

V. Jean Hampton: On Instrumental Rationality

Introduction

Professor Hampton, in her wide-ranging paper, distinguishes two types of theory of rationality, the instrumental and the noninstrumental. The former, exemplified by Hobbes and Hume, is a view according to which, in Hume's famous words, reason is and ought only to be the slave of the passions (or, she adds, of God, or of some other master, who determines our ends). The latter, exemplified by Plato and Kant, is a view according to which reason is the master that does and ought to set our goals in life and permits or excludes the pursuit of goals "proposed" by our desires or other such tentative goal-setters. Her main aim in the present article is to "challenge both the idea that the normative form of the instrumental conception of reason is acceptable to the naturalist, and the claim that only this theory is motivationally plausible" (p. 92).

There is little in her searching and illuminating paper with which I strongly disagree and very much with which I agree. Thus, I have myself embraced what she calls "the authority" and "the motivational efficacy" (p. 94) of reasons.[50] I take the ground of this authority and the source of its motivational efficacy to be the evaluative meaning or normative implication of there being a reason for one to do a certain thing.[51] I hold, in other words, that it would, from a suitable point of view, be a good thing if one followed that reason rather than some other conflicting extra-rational motivation, such as an inclination or desire. In my terminology, "fully rational beings"[52] (e.g., normal human adults) must be motivated by what they take to be a reason (or combination of reasons) for them to do a certain thing and must normally be moved to do it even when doing so runs counter to their then most strongly felt desires or other motivators.

However, despite this and other important agreements, I must take up two specific matters. Discussion of the first may dispel certain misunderstandings of my own account of reason, and discussion of the second should clarify some reasons for my discomfort with certain aspects of the Kantian theory of practical reason, which Hampton clearly takes herself to be following.

Section A

Concerning the first matter, Hampton includes me among the exponents of an instrumental theory of reason (p. 87). And, of course, I have myself characterized my theory as a version of Instrumentalism.[53] Still, my Instrumentalism does not fit her conception of instrumental theories. I do not believe or claim, as her instrumentalists do, that reason is and ought only to be a servant, and that this "servitude can involve obeying orders from the master (e.g., our desires, or our God) to take efficient means to achieving the end(s) set by the master; or it can also involve at least on occasion, finding out who its master is" (pp. 88–89). In my view, reason ought always to be, often can be, and sometimes is, the master, as her non-instrumentalists think (p. 90). I hold this to be true for reason not only in its so-called "theoretical" but in every employment, including the moral. Of course, as we all know, reason does not always *achieve* mastery and, in some persons, it does so only rarely.

But this authority of reason, which implies that it ought to be the master, and this motivational efficacy (p. 94), which implies that it can be the master, is perfectly compatible with my version of Instrumentalism. For what one must or ought to do for the attainment of the high-level aims which I believe the various branches of the enterprise of reason to have,[54] may, of course, conflict, on particular occasions, with one's then most strongly felt desires or other motives. Thus, on my view, one's practical reasons can, on particular occasions, have normative supremacy and motivational efficacy over the specific desires one then has, even though the ground of their being reasons is that following them is the best (known) *means* to attaining the relevant specific high-level *end* of the relevant branch of the enterprise of practical reason. Furthermore, the fact that following certain practical reasons (say, those based on health) rather than other conflicting ones (say, those based on avoiding a certain pain) is more effective in attaining this high-level end, is also the ground of the paramountcy of the former reasons over the latter and of the authority that practical reason as such has over fully rational beings. Finally, whether those who have these reasons may or ought to do what their desires or other motivations prompt them to do or whether they ought instead to resist these promptings, or whether they may or ought to adopt the ends that their desires and other motives incline them to adopt and choose the appropriate means to them, depends on whether following these promptings would help attain the relevant high-level ends of the enterprise of reason. Thus, my Instrumentalism seems to me to differ from Hampton's (and Kant's) conception of reason much less than does what she calls instrumentalism. But this is not the proper occasion to trace these similarities and differences in detail.

Section B

The second matter I wish to comment on is more important in itself and seems central to Hampton's paper. As I mentioned before, she says that naturalists[55] favor the instrumental theory of reason because they believe (mistakenly) that it and it alone is compatible with naturalism. She makes her antiinstrumentalist and antinaturalist point about the authority and motivational efficacy of practical reasons by way of a close examination of four theories, the Kantian, the Millian, the Humean, and the Gibbardian (which latter she regards as "a 'naturalized' version of the Kantian view" (p. 102). But, in her opinion, naturalists are not helped by espousing instrumentalism, for the only tenable theory of instrumental reason is Kant's theory of the hypothetical imperative, and that is as incompatible with naturalism as is, undeniably, that of his categorical imperative (pp. 102–3).

I cannot here take up her account of these four theories of instrumental reason, but should say that I have found it fair, perceptive, and illuminating. My more limited concern springs from the fact that I am less persuaded than she is that Kant's theory of imperatives is an adequate basis for a conception of the structure of practical, including means-end, reasoning. I begin by noting a few differences between her account and Kant's, then treat in more detail a problem about finding a coherent interpretation of Kant's account of the hypothetical imperative in the *Foundations of the Metaphysics of Morals*, and conclude with some remarks about whether her modifications of Kant are radical enough. Since I am quite diffident about my reading of Kant, especially my understanding of Kant's distinction between analytic and synthetic propositions, my remarks should be taken primarily as an appeal to Hampton (and, hopefully, other interested Kant scholars) to revisit the problem that has bothered me.[56]

Hampton has this to say about Kant's theory of the hypothetical imperative:

> Although predicated on a desire, Kant maintains that hypothetical imperatives "present the *practical necessity* of a possible action as a means to achieving something else which one desires." This "necessity" is the substance of the authority of the imperatives, and it is *in virtue of that authority* that it has motivational effect on the agent: "Whoever wills the end, so far as *reason has decisive influence on his action*, wills also the indispensably necessary means to it that lie in his power." I have emphasized the phrase that shows that Kant believes, when we act from a hypothetical imperative, that it is not desire but (instrumental) reason that moves us, just as, when we act morally, it is not desire but reason (in this case, moral reason, not instrumental reason) that moves us by virtue of its authority. (That is, these imperatives command us with "practical necessity.") And while Kant is aware that many human beings resist the means they ought to take to achieve their ends, his position is that in virtue of the fact that we *ought* to will means appropriate to our ends, we will do so for as long as "reason has decisive influence" on our actions. (pp. 95–96, Hampton's emphases.)

In Hampton's view, then, the hypothetical imperative is a normative principle of practical reason that *tells* us that we *ought*[57] to will means *appropriate* (rather than *indispensably necessary*) to our ends and, that, therefore, we will *necessarily* choose such means when *"reason has decisive influence"* on our actions, but not necessarily if reason lacks that influence. She seems to include among "our ends" not only those we (fully) *will* but also those we merely *desire*; she does not limit the hypothetical imperative to *requiring* us to choose the indispensably necessary means to "our ends"; nor does she seem to base the authority of the hypothetical imperative on the *necessity* of an analytic proposition that, given certain conditions, connects one's willing of an end to one's willing of the indispensably necessary means to that end. It seems to me that these claims constitute moves away from Kant and in the right direction, but I think these departures are hard to combine with Kant's proof of what he calls "the possibility"—which I take to mean the rational bindingness of the hypothetical imperative. At the same time, they seem insufficient to sidestep the problem I have with Kant's account to which I now turn.

Section C

I assume that Kant's hypothetical imperative is a normative principle of practical reason that has the form, "Whoever wills A, also must (or ought to) will B." My problem can be put as a dilemma: If Kant succeeds in proving that this imperative is possible, then the imperative cannot be a principle of *practical* reason, but if it can be such a principle, then Kant's proof of its possibility fails. In short, my suspicion is that Kant cannot, as he sets out to, show the possibility of the hypothetical imperative as a principle of practical reason. Let me elaborate.

As every reader of the *Foundations*[58] knows, Kant's theory of practical reason rests on his theory of "imperatives," that is, formulae expressing objective laws and necessary principles of reason guiding and binding the will of all imperfectly rational beings, including, of course, humans. Such imperfectly rational beings do not from their nature always follow these guides, but are nevertheless subject to and bound, constrained, or necessitated ('genoetigt') by them. Thus, that a person is "bound" by these imperatives does not imply that she cannot but choose or decide to act as they require of her; she may even *decide* not to act as she knows or believes they require of her.

Kant himself explains the "bindingness" ('Noetigung')[59] of imperatives as follows: "Since every practical law presents a possible action as good and thus as necessary ['notwendig'] for a subject practically determinable by reason, all imperatives are formulas of the determination of action which is necessary by the principle of a will which is in any way good" (1959, 414). Hence, this bindingness of imperatives does not necessarily generate the corresponding practical judgments, decisions, and overall motivation.

What factors transform the necessity of the necessary objective principles into bindingnesses of apparently varying force, namely, imposition, counsel, advice? It can hardly be the different degrees of resistance imperfectly rational beings experience in conforming with these different kinds of principle. For would not that resistance tend to vary with the psychological make-up of the person rather than with the function of the principle? Nor, it seems, can the explanation be that particular hypothetical imperatives bind merely conditionally upon the particular end of the agent in question. For the principle of the hypothetical imperative "as such" (1959, 420) appears to be as unconditional as that of the categorical imperative. Furthermore, even what a particular hypothetical imperative "tells" an imperfectly rational agent, namely, either to take what he knows to be the indispensably necessary step in his power or to give up his end, presumably would seem to be not merely counsel or advice, but command. And since the hypothetical imperative appears not to direct us to choose one rather than the other of the alternatives, one of which it commands us to choose, it is not clear when it merely counsels us to do one thing rather than another both of which we could do. But I need not pursue this question here.[60]

With these preliminaries out of the way, I can return to my central problem which is generated by Kant's own answer to his question of how imperatives are possible. "This question," he explains, "does not require an answer as to how the action which the imperative commands *can be performed*, but only an answer as to how the constraint ['Noetigung,' "bindingness"] of the will, which the imperative expresses in setting the problem, *can be conceived*" (1959, 417). I take his question to be an inquiry into how it can be shown that the principles underlying these two imperatives as such are objective laws, that is, necessary practical principles unconditionally binding on all imperfectly rational beings. Kant thinks that this question raises great difficulties for the categorical (1959, 419), but none for the hypothetical imperative (ibid.).[61] Why not the latter? Because, although to be a law governing the will, the hypothetical imperative as such must be unconditionally binding, that bindingness is unproblematically explained by the "analyticity" of a certain proposition. Indeed, the explanation may be wholly unproblematic, for Kant explicitly ascribes this analyticity to the hypothetical imperative itself, rather than to some other proposition relevantly related to it (1959, 417, 419). By contrast, "in the case of the categorical imperative or law of morality, the cause of the difficulty in discerning its possibility is very weighty. This imperative is an a priori synthetic proposition and since to discern the possibility of propositions of this sort is so difficult in theoretical knowledge it may well be gathered that it will be no less difficult in practical knowledge" (1959, 420).

Thus, Kant's answer to how an imperative is possible seems to be that it is possible if and only if its principle has the force of law, for then it is necessary and so binding on imperfectly rational beings. But an imperative has that force if (and it seems only if) the content of its principle can be expressed in a proposition that can be known a priori. Such knowledge is unproblematic if that proposition is analytic, but problematic if it is synthetic.

These preliminaries appear to raise two main questions: (i) If the hypothetical imperative itself is an analytic proposition, can it be a principle of practical reason? (ii) If the analytic proposition is not the hypothetical imperative itself, how can the analyticity of that other proposition be proved?

Question (i): As we have seen, Kant appears to think that what he proved to be an analytic proposition is the (principle of the) hypothetical imperative itself. For he says, "If it were only easy to give a definite concept of happiness, the imperatives of prudence would perfectly correspond to those of skill and would likewise be analytical" (1959, 417). And he concludes the discussion of that problem with the claim that, "[s]ince both . . . command the means to that which one presupposes as a willed purpose, the imperative which commands the willing of the means to him who wills the end is in both cases analytical" (1959, 419). This seems to be confirmed by the proof itself which Kant offers of the analyticity of the crucial proposition, namely, "Whoever wills the end, so far as reason has decisive influence on his actions, wills also the indispensably necessary steps to it that he can take" (1959, 417).

Much seems to depend on the exact role of the qualifying clause, "so far as reason has decisive influence on his action." For it seems that the principle of the hypothetical imperative itself cannot be "Whoever wills an end ought, as far as reason has decisive influence on his action, to will also the indispensably necessary steps to it that he knows he can take." For Kant leaves no doubt that imperatives *bind* all imperfectly rational beings, and does so always even when reason does not have that decisive influence, although, of course, they do not always *motivate* them.

It would seem, then, that the principle of the hypothetical imperative itself is "Whoever wills an end ought also to will what he knows[62] to be the indispensably necessary steps he can take." And when we examine in greater detail Kant's proof of the analyticity of the relevant proposition, we find that it appears not to incorporate the qualifier, "so far as reason has decisive influence on the agent's actions." For Kant's argument tries to establish that two apparently different willings of the same person, namely, willing an end and willing the necessary means to it, are, under certain knowledge and ability conditions, *one and the same thing*.

Kant uses two seemingly equivalent formulations.[63] One is: "if I know that the proposed result can be obtained only by such an action, then it is an analytical proposition that, if I fully [vollstaendig] will the effect, I must also will the action necessary to produce it. For *it is one and the same thing* to conceive of something as an effect which is in a certain way possible through me, and to conceive of myself as acting in this way" (1959, 417). The other is this: "in the willing of an object as an effect, my causality, as an acting cause of that effect shown in my use of the means to it, is already thought, and the imperative derives the concept of actions necessary to this purpose from the concept of willing this purpose" (ibid.).

Kant's thought here appears to be this. If the proposition that someone who wills an end and also wills what he knows to be the indispensably necessary steps he can take to that end, is analytic, then these seemingly different willings are only two formulations of one and the same thing. But then, under these knowledge and ability conditions, when the seemingly two willings are one and the same thing, the agent who wills the end ipso facto wills the means. There is no logical space for the agent to will the one without willing the other. But then, if the hypothetical imperative is possible because that proposition is analytic, then the hypothetical imperative cannot be a principle of practical reason since no one could possibly fail to act contrary to it.

This, then, is the first horn of the dilemma I had in mind. In order to prove the possibility (the bindingness) of the hypothetical imperative, Kant must, and appears to try to, prove that the principle of the hypothetical imperative is an analytic proposition. But if that principle is the proposition, "whoever wills the end, wills also what he knows to be the indispensably necessary steps to it that he can take," then we may perhaps grant that Kant has indeed established that the hypothetical imperative is possible, but he has at the same time demonstrated that it cannot be a principle of practical reason.

One response to this would be to admit this, but to claim that it could be a sound principle of theoretical reason, and one that can be flouted. For since its analyticity may come to light only through (correct) analysis, some people who have not analyzed this proposition may not notice its analyticity. Thus, some people who are imperfectly rational also in the field of theoretical reason, may be in a position to know, and under certain conditions should know, but conceivably may not, that this proposition is analytic. They may therefore think, wrongly, and under these conditions, contrary to reason, that one can will the end without willing what one knows to be the necessary means in one's power. Thus, it is perhaps not implausible to hold that only in so far as someone's theoretical reason has decisive influence on what she believes, will she necessarily *believe* that one cannot will an end without willing what one knows to be the necessary means to it in one's power.

This interpretation seems to be least forced, perhaps even invited, by Kant's third formulation: "whoever wills the end wills also (necessarily according to reason [der Vernunft gemaess notwendig]) the only means to it which are in his power" (1959, 417–18). This formulation appears to fit in best (or should I say, least badly?) with Kant's argument trying to show that although the seemingly two different willings are one and the same, a person whose beliefs are not necessarily according to reason, may believe in such case that she can will the end without willing the means.

But can this principle of theoretical reason have any practical significance? Is there practical significance to the fact (if it is a fact) that it is conceivable that someone believes, irrationally, that he can will (attain) his end without willing what he *knows* to be the indispensably necessary means in his power? It seems not, if we grant Kant the proof that for a person who knows that doing A is the indispensably necessary means in his power to attaining his end, willing the end and willing these means are one and the same thing. If they are one and the same thing, they are not separable, hence the fact that someone conceivably may *believe* that they are separable, is beside the point. If he wills the end, he ipso facto wills the means. If he does not will the means, he ipso facto does not will the end.

Of course such a person could will the end and the means, yet not actually employ the means, as when he is prevented from doing so by someone else or because he is immobilized by paralysis. Such cases, presumably, are irrelevant. Cases of so-called weakness of will do not seem to me counter-examples: they are cases, it seems to me, of someone not "fully willing," not willing in the relevant sense, but only pretending to will, wrongly thinking that she is willing, because she mistakes her desire for a willing and so on. Since, in such cases, there is no breakdown of the connection between willing and acting, their failure to act must be taken as their failure to have willed, not a breakdown of the efficacy of their will.

Can one know both these things, yet will the end without *willing* what one knows to be the indispensably necessary means? Presumably not, if under these knowledge and ability conditions willing the end and willing the means are one and the same thing. If he can will the end without willing the means, then there are two separable willings, so they are not one and the same thing. And if the analyticity of the proposition that he who wills the end wills the means entails that the willings are one and the same thing, they cannot be separable. So the fact that a person may not know or believe that the relevant proposition is analytic, does not make it possible for anyone under these conditions to will the end without willing the means.

Admittedly, a person could, falsely and contrary to reason, believe that taking a cab is not the indispensably necessary means to his end of catching the train and so could will the end but not employ the means. But this only shows that the proposition that taking a cab is an indispensable necessary means etc., is not analytic. So this case is irrelevant. What is analytic is only that if someone *knows* that in his circumstances taking a cab is an indispensably necessary means to his end, he cannot will the end without willing the means. And we have already shown that in these circumstances nothing would *be* willing the end without willing the means.

I conclude that, as one would expect, this principle of theoretical reason cannot open up the logical space needed for a practical principle that is floutable.

Hampton seems well aware of the problem illustrated by the preceding answer to question (i), for she warns against the sort of "enthusiasm," what might be called "the overkill," with which I am charging Kant in his attempt to prove the bindingness of certain principles of reason by proving their analytic necessity. Her warning (p. 96) is directed against one possible interpretation of Kant's ascription of necessity to the proposition, 'If I fully will the effect, I also will the action required for it', namely, that it "is a kind of psychological thesis, to the effect that, *in fact*, one cannot desire the end without desiring the means to it" (p. 96, my italics). And then she rightly warns, "one must not argue too enthusiastically for the correctness of a normative thesis, lest one make it impossible for human beings to act contrary to it" (p. 96). If my reading of Kant's account of the hypothetical imperative is on the right track, then, although what he has in mind is not this psychological necessity, yet his answer to the question of how that imperative is possible seems to be to just such overkill, though by different means.

I suspect that, to avoid this "enthusiasm," Hampton, though presumably still taking herself to be following Kant, substitutes "desiring the end" (e.g., p. 96), for Kant's "(fully) willing the end." Of course, if she meant, 'both desiring *and (fully) willing* that end', this would not avoid the sort of overkill against which she warns. I therefore take her to mean merely, 'desiring something which, however, one has not, at least as yet, *made* one's end'. Thus, Jones, for example, may want or desire to catch the three o'clock train, but may not yet have settled in his mind whether or not actually to do what he knows are the indispensably necessary steps, namely, to take a cab, which he can take to reach that desired end.

However, Hampton's 'desiring an end' appears to move away from Kant's 'willing an end' ('einen Zweck wollen'),[64] for it introduces three points not implied or suggested by Kant's claims about willing ends. The first is that there is not even a prima facie case for saying that 'who desires something also wills or even desires what he knows is a necessary means in his power to satisfy the desire'. By contrast, it really does seem, at least prima facie, plausible to hold that someone who (fully) wills, and therefore has, an end, must either will and so do what he knows to be a necessary means[65] in his power to attain it or else give it up. Suppose I desire a drink before dinner. Must I, therefore, either do what I know to be the necessary means in my power, say, buy a bottle of whiskey if I have run out of it, or else give up my desire?

Kant, at any rate, cannot make a plausible case for Hampton's version. For whereas, it seems, one can, at will, cease or continue to have an end, one cannot cease, at will, to have just any occurrent desire, though perhaps one can, over a period of time, root out some dispositional ones, such as that for a drink before dinner. Of course, some desires such as hunger, and perhaps the desire for happiness, seem not under this sort of control.

The second difference follows from the first. Whereas, if Kant is right, we cannot will an end without ipso facto willing what we know to be the indispensable means to it in our power, we can have occurrent desires we may not choose to satisfy, and for good reasons.[66] We may even cultivate the dispositional desire, even though we know or believe that we shall sometimes, perhaps often, have excellent reasons for frustrating it when it becomes occurrent. Extirpating a dispositional desire may impoverish our life even if we sometimes, perhaps often, have to frustrate it when it becomes occurrent. This does not seem to make sense with regard to willing our ends.[67]

The third point (perhaps less clearly implied by Hampton's substitution of 'desired' for Kant's 'willed' ends) is a suggestion or assumption that, if one desires something, one has a reason for doing what one knows is a necessary means in one's power to do what would satisfy the desire. Kant himself does not appear to extract this sort of reason from the hypothetical imperative, for he says it prescribes "what is *necessary merely for the attainment of some chosen end*" (1959, 420), and implies that questions about the rationality or irrationality, and so possible nonoptionality, of an end are not in the domain, not of the hypothetical, but exclusively of the categorical imperative, "which alone implies the necessity which we require of a law" (ibid.).[68] One might have thought that the prudential imperative also answered such questions but, in Kant's view, it, too, is a merely hypothetical (albeit assertoric) imperative. At the same time, as we have seen, he says of all hypothetical imperatives that they "*command* [gebieten] the means to that which one presupposes as a willed purpose" (1959, 419).[69]

Thus Kant's and Hampton's versions of the hypothetical imperative seem different also in this last respect, for hers would seem to direct (though not command) one to do what is an appropriate (rather than a necessary) means to satisfying one's desire unless one has reason not to. It does not seem to direct one (let alone apprise one of the *necessity*) to choose between either (trying to) satisfy one's desire or else giving it up.

I conclude that, if Hampton rejects these differences between willing and desiring an end, then her switch from 'willing' to 'desiring' does not avoid the problem of overkill she rightly warns us against. But if she allows these differences, then, it seems to me, her argument for the possibility of the principle of the hypothetical imperative would have to be very different from Kant's.

Question (*ii*): It is clear, however, that Hampton rejects the interpretation which assumes that Kant's analytic proposition is the hypothetical imperative itself. She appears to think, on the contrary, that that imperative is a synthetic proposition and that the analytic proposition is one *about* the imperative. The analytic proposition connects the willing of an end and the willing of what is known to be the necessary means in the power of a person *in whom reason has decisive influence on his actions.* Of course, such a person is not a holy will, but only an imperfectly rational being; but for the examination of Kant's problem, he can be regarded as exactly like a holy will because, as far as the particular action under consideration is concerned, reason has decisive influence on his action.

Let us remind ourselves of the proposition Hampton and other commentators have thought to be the relevant analytic one: "Whoever wills the end, *so far as reason has decisive influence on his action*, wills also the indispensably necessary steps to it that he can take" (1959, 417). Let us also bear in mind the links in the chain that connects a person's willing an end and what he knows to be the necessary means to it that are in his power, and what role reason's decisive influence on his action plays at each link in that chain.

Starting from the action end, the first link seems to be between the agent's decision or choice and his action. If reason has decisive influence on his action, this must mean at this point that the agent must carry out his *decision* to the extent that he is not prevented by physical factors or by "exonerating" psychological factors (such as duress) from doing so; he must, in other words, not be afflicted by weakness of will. Moving in the same direction, the next link is that between his decision and his *judgment* of what reason, through (the principle of) the hypothetical imperative, requires of him. If reason has decisive influence on him, his decision will conform to his judgment. If Jones judges that he must either give up his end of catching his train at three o'clock or take a cab, then his decision will either be to take a cab or give up his end to catch the three o'clock. The next link will be that between his judgment and what reason, through the hypothetical imperative, requires of him. If reason has decisive influence on his action, then this will, at this point, mean that his judgment will be in accordance with what he takes that imperative to be and how it applies to his choice situation. The last link will be that between what the objective principle is and what he takes it to be. If reason has decisive influence on his action, then what he takes the principle to be will be what it is.

Thus, to get an analytic proposition, we must suppose that in a certain imperfectly rational agent whom we are considering, reason has decisive influence on his action in the situation he is in. In other words, in the case envisaged, the imperfectly rational agent acts like a holy will. Then, unsurprisingly, the analytic proposition is that in such a case, if the agent wills an end, then he also necessarily wills what he knows to be the indispensably necessary steps he can take to attain the end he wills. For in inserting the clause about reason having decisive influence on his action, we have postulated that he *does* what theoretical and practical reason requires of him and does so because reason requires it, and so we find that he does what reason requires of him. But this does not reveal what the employed principle of reason is. It does not show that, if it is a principle the agent could have flouted,[70] it is a necessarily binding one, as Kant thinks he has shown independently, by showing the principle to be analytic and so necessary and so binding. I suggest that, on this interpretation, the proposition whose analyticity was supposed to demonstrate the bindingness of the hypothetical imperative, cannot be shown to be analytic unless the bindingness of that imperative is *presupposed*. If it is not presupposed, we cannot infer from the supposition that reason has decisive influence on his actions, that, if he wills an end, he will necessarily also will what he knows to be the indispensable steps he can take to attain his end. Thus, instead of anwering Kant's question, this interpretation seems to me to beg it.

Put more abstractly, my argument has been that Kant can show the analytic necessity of a related principle of theoretical reason, but he cannot show the analytic necessity of the principle of the hypothetical imperative. I took it that Kant assumed that if X willed an end, E, at a certain time t, then, under certain conditions c, X also willed the means, M, to E, at t. From this it would seem to follow that if, under c, X did not will M at t, X also did not will E at t. If X had willed E prior to t but did not will M at t, then, by t, X had given up (willing) E.

Kant's various formulations seem to leave open the possibility that the qualification, "so far as reason has decisive influence on [X's] actions" may or may not be included among the conditions on which this implication between willing an end and willing the necessary means depends. I mentioned that Kant says in so many words that it is the hypothetical imperative itself that is analytic and that, in his attempted proof of the possibility (i.e., bindingness) of the hypothetical imperative, he implies that X's willing an end and X's willing the means are one and the same thing. I concluded from this that Kant's proof left no logical space for a certain normative principle of practical reason, namely, that, whoever willed E, ought to will M, since his proof showed that it is inconceivable that X should be willing E without willing M, and since a normative principle of practical reason implies that this is at least conceivable. I also accepted, at least for argument's sake, that there was some plausibility in Kant's claim that under the conditions he mentioned—that X knew what were the indispensably necessary steps he could take to attain E—the proposition really was analytic, irrespective of whether or not reason had decisive influence on X's actions.

I then entertained the supposition that Kant did not mean what he said when he declared that the hypothetical imperative was an analytic proposition and when he implied that he was trying to prove that it was, but that what he really proved and wanted to prove to be analytic was a proposition *about* that imperative, namely, 'that if X wills E, so far as reason has decisive influence on his action, X also wills M'. I argued that this proposition is analytic *only if* the principle of the hypothetical imperative—i.e., whoever wills E, ought to will M—is possible (i.e., binding). This supposition—which I think Hampton takes to be the correct reading of Kant—indeed frees Kant from the objection of enthusiasm or overkill, against which she rightly warns—but her reading seems to leave Kant without a proof of the analytic necessity of the principle of the hypothetical imperative.[71]

The last suggestion for a way out for Kant that I shall consider in this paper[72] is the idea that Kant relies on a distinction between 'willing' and 'fully [vollstaendig] willing' and that the connection between willing E and willing M holds only for fully willing E. It seems to me, however, that the problem remains the same. If the analyticity of the connection between willing E and M holds only for fully willing, and if, when one fully wills E, one necessarily wills M but, when one merely wills E, one does not necessarily will M, then the practical principle, 'whoever wills E, wills M' is shown to be binding only for fully willing and not for mere willing. But then, again, there is no room for a practical principle in the case of fully willing, and there is no proof of bindingness in the case of merely willing.

Finally, a disclaimer. I am not, of course, arguing that there is no such thing as means-end reasoning at all. I am arguing only that Kant's account of it appears to be incoherent. Perhaps the situations closest to those Kant had in mind as governed by the hypothetical imperative are the following two:

(1) Smith tells Jones that, if he wants to catch the three o'clock train, he *must* take a cab. We may think of this as a case of Smith (a) giving Jones a reason to take a cab or of (b) telling him that he must choose between taking a cab and giving up his end of catching that train. If one holds (a), one is committed to the view that having an end is itself an other-things-equal reason to take what one knows, or has reason to believe, is the indispensably necessary means one can take. If I am right, Kant cannot hold this view because he thinks the hypothetical imperative does not provide reasons for one's ends. If one holds (b), then Smith's remark does not amount to giving Jones a reason for doing anything, but simply purports to inform him that he has only two options, either to take a cab or give up on catching his train. This information can do no more than enable Jones to bring to bear whatever reasons beyond the hypothetical imperative he has on the choice he is told he has to make. If I am right, then Kant's account of the hypothetical imperative does not fit this interpretation either, for that account commits him to the view that Smith's information provides Jones with a reason, not indeed to choose one rather than the other of these alternatives, but to choose one or other of them. But if I am right and if what Smith tells Jones is not misinformation, then Jones has no third alternative he might also be tempted to choose: whatever he does will amount to a choice of one or other of these alternatives; there is simply nothing he could do that would amount to any other choice: he either wills (chooses) the means or he does not; if he does, he also wills (and attains) the end; if he does not, he does not will (i.e., gives up) the end. Thus, Jones has no need and no use for a reason to choose between these alternatives, since he can neither ignore it nor therefore follow it either. If I am right, then Kant seems to have confused the *necessity* of making what amounts to a choice *between* two

alternatives, and having a reason for choosing one or the other of them *rather than some third or fourth* . . . and so on. If Jones has a third alternative, say, to run, then there may be a reason why he should choose between taking a cab and running, say, because it is very important for him to catch that train, rather than between taking a cab and giving up his end, as might be the case if he just had by-pass surgery. But, of course, Kant's hypothetical imperative does not provide such a reason.

(2) Jones has adopted the farmer's point of view[73] and subscribes to the principle of consistency. On the basis of these two principles he arrives at the conclusion that he *ought* to vote for Smith, a candidate for reelection to the House of Representatives who has consistently voted for legislation supporting farm interests. Of course, this is not (and Jones does not believe it is) the indispensably necessary means in his power to promote farmers' interests but it may well be *a* means of promoting the farmers' interests (although it may not be since, unbeknownst to Jones, Smith has been won over to the anti-farm block). Nor is it a case of following Kant's principle of the hypothetical imperative or a principle derivable from it, since the bindingness of the practical principles involved is not based on their analytic necessity nor derived from the analytic necessity of any other proposition.

There is, of course, a great deal more to be said, but perhaps I have said enough to raise the suspicion that Kant's unproblematic demonstration of the possibilty of the hypothetical imperative is more problematic than he leads us to believe. In any case, surely, I have said enough.

VI. Stephen Darwall: Reason, Norm, and Value, and J. B. Schneewind: Baier's Theory of Morality: A Historical Introduction

I turn now to two papers, largely historical, whose authors, while advancing different arguments against my position and exposing different shortcomings in it, identify more or less the same philosophical ancestors for my views and suggest somewhat similar remedies for these shortcomings. These similarities and overlaps and their affinities in meta-ethics make some of my comments relevant to both, and I shall therefore comment on them together. However, since I have already discussed the main problem raised by the first paper, most of my attention will be focused on the second. The papers are both concerned to pinpoint "the problematic" of my book, to locate, in the history of ethics, earlier versions of it and of the various proposed solutions, and to draw attention to an important problem that arises out of my way of trying to solve it. Both find striking similarities between my work and that of Grotius (Schneewind also between it and that of others). I am, alas, insufficiently familiar with the details of the work of

Grotius and some of the others in whose problematic and solution they detect similarities with mine, to offer scholarly comments on their comparisons. I would like to think, however, that these similarities in problematic show that these "forerunners" of mine and I have fastened on real problems rather than merely pseudo-problems spawned by the misconceptions and blinkers thrown up by the spirit of the times enmeshing us all and bound to vanish with that spirit. It seems to me that both Darwall and Schneewind take the problematic seriously, but consider my resolution vitiated by the apparently insuperable new problems it generates.

Section A

Darwall's complex and formidable argument culminates in the conclusion that "a good-based account of practical reason [i.e., such as mine] cannot vindicate moral reasons, and thereby enable Baier to resolve his problematic" (p. 35). He therefore suggests that "perhaps there is some reason to reconsider a principle-based, Kantian approach" (ibid.) I cannot at this point—and it seems to me I need not—answer Darwall's argument in detail, for in my comments on Raz I have tried to provide adequate reasons to think that a good-based account of practical reason can vindicate moral reasons, and in my comments on Hampton's paper I have tried to explain why a purely principle-based Kantian approach to practical reasons is unpromising. However, I should emphasize, just in case it has been overlooked, that I have not denied the importance, indeed the indispensability, of principles, especially in morality. I have, on the contrary, insisted that a good-based approach can accommodate and must assign pride of place to principles in practical reasoning, but that the good is needed for the rational choice between rival principles that have found favor.[74] I have, furthermore, in my comments on Raz' paper, made some suggestions about how the problem of whether the good is prior to principles or principles are prior to the good dissolves on closer inspection.[75]

Section B

Schneewind begins his article with a lucid, illuminating, careful, and more than generous summary of those of my papers (beginning with my very first publication in 1948!) whose main theses I later incorporated in my first book, *The Moral Point of View*. He goes on to sketch, with admirable succinctness, the differences, both overall (not many) and in detail (a lot) between it and my new book (RMO), to which the present book is a companion volume. As I said, Darwall's paper and this part of Schneewind's would be a very clear, knowledgeable, and fair summary of my views which would, I think, be helpful even for readers who are quite unfamiliar with my work.

Concerning the summary of my views, I wish to suggest only two minor modifications. The first concerns what I say in the introduction to RMO. Basing himself on my remarks there, Schneewind says "[t]he first part of the book naturally begins with a diagnosis of the issues that prevent us from having a firmly grounded science of morality" (p. 1). Actually, what I meant to suggest was something slightly (but not insignificantly) different. I alluded to the fact that when we want answers to important questions, such as what would enable us to explain and predict certain phenomena—for instance, the motions of heavenly and other bodies or the occurrence of rainbows and other optical phenomena—we try to develop reliable methods for doing so. I then suggested that getting the right answers to moral questions is also thought to be important and that we have been engaged in trying to find such a method for a very long time. Despite all this, despite the widespread belief that wrong answers and action on the basis of wrong answers can do great harm to a great many people, and despite what seems to be a fervent wish by many to be able to use such methods to find such answers, we still find a great deal of often passionate disagreement about what are the right answers and the appropriate and reliable methods for finding them.[76] I then raised the question of why we have not succeeded in developing a discipline which, like a science or logic—and I could and should have added, 'like jurisprudence or grammar (even before it [grammar] became a science)'—has become independent of philosophy, a discipline with its own competent practitioners and with a body of answers generally accepted as sound and with a method of investigation that is generally recognized as the best currently available for improving accepted answers and finding new ones to hitherto unanswered questions. I mentioned that one possible answer to my question is, of course, that the nature of the moral enterprise is such that it does not call for, and in any case does not permit, the development of such a discipline. I did not pursue this radically skeptical view—largely because it does not seem to me any more profitable in ethics than it is in epistemology: it seems to be undeniable that we have made progress in both domains, at least in theory if not in practice. But I nowhere ruled out the possibility that we shall not succeed in doing much better in the future than we have done so far. My own account of the nature of the moral enterprise—the frequent conflicts between reason and passion (such as hatred or jealousy) and desire (such as ambition or greed), the dependence of the general beneficiality of the moral life on a sufficient number doing their bit, the lure for many of counting on doing doubly well for themselves by relying on others doing their bit while being free riders themselves, and the genuine difficulties in reforming a society's way of life to conform to the requirements of morality—might well encourage such pessimism, at least in practice if not in theory.

However, in the introduction, I did suggest that one reason for our failure to succeed in putting ethics, the theory of morality, on a sound foundation (as, by many accounts, we have done in the field of the natural sciences) may be certain external and internal obstacles peculiar to the moral enterprise. Among the latter I mentioned three that seemed to imply an internal conflict in the demands we make on the moral enterprise, a conflict I thought needed to be resolved if a discipline of ethics capable of making real progress was ever to get going.

At the same time, I never meant to suggest that the obstacles I listed were the only ones that need to be removed nor that if such a well-founded independent discipline could ever be developed, it would be something exactly like what we now call science. Nor did I mean to suggest that such a discipline would be able to find or work out the right answers to ever more detailed and controversial moral questions, in the sense that all those competent in the discipline would have to recognize them as right answers. I shall return to this question in my main comment.

The second modification concerns his ascription to me of the view that "we need not and cannot answer the question 'what sort of person should I be?' in order to answer the question 'What should I do?'. *The latter question is fundamental!*" (p. 1; my emphasis). I think the last sentence in this quotation could be misleading. For, as I put it in my comment on Raz's paper, the hub of the enterprise of practical reason is a person's unflawed conception of the preferred life for her. But it seems to me that that conception must also be a conception of the sort of person she ideally would want to be. She may, as a child, come to think of the preferred life for her as, say, that of a professional entomologist. But that will involve both a certain range of behavior and a certain sort of personality. She must think of herself as a person who enjoys, seeks, and spends much time and effort in close contact with insects. As she grows older, she may add other features to the conception of the preferred life and these in turn will involve both certain kinds of behavior and certain aspects of personality. For the sort of behavior implied by such a conception of the preferred life is, of course, motivated behavior, and the sort of person one wants ideally to be implies having the appropriate motivation. Hence my hub concept does not imply the priority of action over personality, nor the other way around. The unflawed conception of a preferred life for oneself implies an appropriate conception of a personality that fits into that sort of life. One may find that one would not want to be the sort of person one would have to be to lead that sort of life.

Again, my account of doing the morally required or recommended thing as conforming to principles which, when generally conformed to in a moral community, would give all its members an equal chance to lead a life according to their unflawed conception of the preferred life for them, requires of them a personality trait, what I have called Limited Conditional Good Will, which is at the same time a very general principle of behavior, roughly similar to the Golden Rule. Thus, the most general moral requirement about what sort of a person one ought to be is identical with the most general behavioral principle one morally ought to conform to. There is, therefore, no priority of one of these questions over the other.

I want to raise one further point, this time about a similarity Schneewind finds between my moral theory and that of Leibniz. This comment is perhaps as much a call for future clarification as it is an expression of disagreement. Schneewind takes "Leibniz . . . to be Baier's forerunner" (p. 12) because Leibniz thought that "reason would lead us from self-centered concerns to a direct interest in the good of everyone alike that we would otherwise not have" (p. 12), and "he sought, as Baier does, a way of explaining action that allows the possibilityof not acting from the most strongly felt desire one happens to have" (p. 13). Further, "[h]is philosophical ground for imposing this constraint was the same as Baier's," namely, "[h]e thought he could show that *the differing perfections of things in the universe provide an objective order of reasons for action, that we can come to know this order, and that the knowledge can be effective in guiding action.* Consequently, like Baier, he is an externalist about practical reason" (ibid., my emphasis).

My uncertainty concerns the italicized sentence. I do indeed hold that there is an order of practical reason in which various kinds of reasons are ordered in a complex hierarchical way that determines their relative force when they conflict with one another, an order in which these different kinds of reasons have objectivity and force in various senses. Thus, self-interested (and more generally, self-anchored) reasons are objective in the sense that there is a formulation of the aim of the point of view—the promotion and protection of the agent's best interest—from which the criteria of relevance and soundness can be derived: anything that affects the agent's best interest favorably or unfavorably is relevant; what affects it favorably is a pro, and what affects it unfavorably, a con. But, of course, it is not objective in the sense that, if X's doing A (whether in general or on a particular occasion) is favored by a reason of self-interest, Y's doing A (whether in general or on the same particular occasion) must also be favored by a reason of self-interest. For, notoriously, different people's self-interested (and, more generally, self-anchored) reasons can conflict with one another: one man's meat may be another's poison, or it may be also the other's meat (the only meat they could lay their hands on).

Moral reasons are objective in a different sense: they hold for more agents than self-interested ones, but their validity for, or bindingness on, those for whom they are reasons, depends on the existence of a moral order, whereas the validity of the merely agent-relative self-interested reasons does not depend on the existence of a moral or some other order. In a given moral order, the criteria of relevance and soundness are determined by the same end, and members of the same appropriately differentiated classes (e.g., children/ adults, children/parents, sick/healthy) are subject to the same moral requirements and recommendations. At the same time, their validity or bindingness does not necessarily extend beyond their moral order. I doubt whether the sense or senses of 'objectivity' in which practical reasons in my theory may be thought to be objective is the same as Leibniz's.

Be that as it may, there seems to be nothing in my conceptual framework that corresponds to Leibniz's idea of "the differing perfections of things in the universe" which "provide an objective order of reasons for action." I take it that by 'the differing perfections of things in the universe' Leibniz did not mean that the objective order of reasons for humans was determined by the differing perfections of the many nonhuman kinds of things that existed in the universe; if he did, that conception would be entirely alien to mine. I take it he means that what are reasons for a being of a given kind is objectively determined by the perfection peculiar to that kind of being. There is indeed a certain resemblance between this view and mine for, on my view, what grounds practical reasons, whether self-anchored or society-anchored, is each individual's unflawed conception of the preferred life for herself, though this conception grounds these reasons in quite different ways.[77] However, my conception of the aim that grounds practical reason seems to me different from what I take to be Leibniz's, for on my view, that aim need not be, and often is not, the aim of attaining the perfection of humanity, whether that means a single ideal condition for the race as a whole or a single ideal of the person to be aimed at by each person, or the aim of each individual to transform her more or less imperfect peculiarities in the direction of greater perfection. The aim is merely to bring about conditions in which everyone is in the best possible position, compatible with everyone else being equally well positioned, to come as close as possible to leading a life according to her conception of the preferred life for herself. But this unflawed conception of the preferred life for oneself is not a perfectionist ideal.

Section C

With these minor points out of the way, I can now turn to the deep and worrisome problem that Schneewind poses for me: "If morality is to function as an effective means of guiding action, then it must somehow be effective in each moral agent. It must motivate us all alike. And if its motivational power depends on each agent's knowing the reasons for the requirements morality imposes and not simply the requirements, then a full reply to the moral skeptic must include an account of how awareness of the rationale for morality can be equally available to everyone alike" (p. 15). On this view, a sound moral theory, one that has a satisfactory answer to the moral skeptic, must do two things: (i) it must develop a method which enables every normal adult member of a moral order to find a correct answer to all (or perhaps at least most) moral questions that he may confront (or perhaps at least those that do not constitute impossibly "hard" cases) and (ii) it must provide reasons for the guidelines it offers the members for use in the method it recommends for answering the moral questions they confront, and these reasons must be accessible to every member alike to provide the necessary motivation for the actions they require or recommend. If I have understood him correctly, what Schneewind calls an "opaque" theory (p. 15) is one that satisfies (i) but not (ii). In the discussion that follows, I shall call a theory "unusable" if it does not satisfy (i). Furthermore, I shall apply these terms, 'opaqueness' and 'unusability', not only to theories but (mutatis mutandis) also to moralities, whether those of a person or a society.

I realize that my brief and tentative comments may not satisfy Schneewind, for although I plead guilty to the charge that my theory is opaque, or at least not completely transparent, the thrust of my comments is that, at this point in the development of moral theory, the demand for complete transparency would be unreasonable. Roughly, my excuses for the opaqueness of my theory are these three: (1) no moral theory other than intuitionism is transparent, and I regard intuitionism as a refusal to ask the question which, it seems to me, moral theory sets out to answer; (2) there are degrees of opaqueness and transparency and my theory is as transparent as can, at this point, be expected; and (3) even the development of merely imperfectly transparent theories may help to remedy the first and worst evil generated by the opaqueness of moral theories and moralities.

(1) Is Kant's theory transparent? Schneewind says, plausibly, that "one of the philosophical motivations for Kant's radical revolution in moral theory was the aim . . . of showing how moral knowledge and motivation to act on it are equally available to everyone alike" (p. 17), but Schneewind also appears to believe that Kant has succeded in accomplishing his aim of constructing such a moral theory. I do not find that plausible. The continuing disagreements over the deduction of the categorical imperative strongly suggest that the theory is opaque, even to the experts. Hence I find it hard to believe that the person in the street could understand, remember, and apply, say, Kant's distinctions, in the *Metaphysics of Morals*, between the various types of duty and obligation.

Schneewind seems to agree with Kant "that categorical duties can be known to everyone in part because their consequences are not what ground their binding force" (p. 17). I am not sure whether this is a point about why Kant's theory is transparent or why it is usable. In any case, I doubt whether Kant's categorical imperative can be applied without drawing on the agent's knowledge of the causal consequences of the types of action he and others engage in. Admittedly, we think killing someone wrong, not because of the consequences of killing her, but because of what killing a human being is, though even that does not mean that its actual or foreseeable or intended consequences are morally irrelevant, as when someone kills the President or a single mother of five. And if we could not draw on our extensive causal knowledge of what actions cause other people's death, we could not kill someone intentionally or with malice aforethought nor take care to avoid killing her, nor be guilty of killing her carelessly or recklessly, nor could anyone find out whether someone, and if so who, killed a certain person, or even that he himself did.

That people can usefully apply moral principles (such as, never kill an innocent human being, do punish people who do so, and do try to deter them from killing others by the punishment of killers), is due to the fact that, for a large number of our activities, fairly reliable knowledge of the harmful consequences of our "intrinsically" harmless behavior is already available. If we could not draw on such knowledge, we would not have words such as 'killing' which have death as their internal object; death would occur in our thinking only as something that befalls someone at some time, something we can deplore or rejoice in, but not something that raises moral questions, such as 'who is responsible for this death?', 'who killed this person?', 'who let this person die?', and so on.

As it happens, our increasing knowledge of the consequences of our actions continually extends the domain of morality. In learning about the consequences of passive smoking, for instance, we learn that we are causing cancer in others and must bear this in mind when we examine the question of whether we ought not to smoke in their presence or whether they ought to put up with our smoking. For these and other reasons, I think Kant's belief (if he believed it) in the irrelevance of the consequences of our actions to the determination of their moral properties must be treated cautiously. In any case, it seems to me that a person must, as far as possible, work out the consequences of his action if he is to be able to give a correct description of his action, say, "a deliberate killing of a person," under which it can be claimed to be wrong *as such*, quite apart from its consequences.

It seems, therefore, that we should keep apart two different issues: (i) whether a moral theory can be maximally usable if (ia) it allows or requires societies in the formulations of their various middle-level moral principles or precepts or judgments (such as 'never to kill an innocent human being' or 'one must not kill an innocent human being' or 'killing an innocent human being is wrong'), to use "causally loaded" action descriptions (such as 'killing', 'deceiving', or 'hurting') which allow the (other-things-equal) moral assessment of *actions as such*, that is, independently of their consequences; and if (ib) it allows or requires individuals using such "causally loaded" action-descriptions to make (all-things-considered) moral assessments of contemplated or past actions by taking into account also their expected, foreseeable, or actual consequences; and (ii) whether a moral theory can be completely transparent if (iia) it allows or requires a society in the formulations of its various middle-level precepts or principles to employ "causally-loaded" action descriptions; or if (iib) it allows or requires of individuals using such "causally loaded" action descriptions to make (all-things-considered) moral assessments of contemplated or past actions by taking into account also the expected, foreseeable, or actual consequences of such actions.

It seems to me, therefore—although I cannot argue this here—that a moral theory would be only minimally usable if it did not allow a society to use "causally loaded" action descriptions and that, for the same reason, its moral assessments of actions, though perhaps transparent, would be limited to very few if any actions. More seriously, if a moral theory did not require individuals using "causally loaded" action descriptions to take into account also their consequences, but to rely solely on the assessment of the actions as such, these assessments, while perhaps completely transparent, could not be regarded as properly grounded all-things-considered judgments.

(2) Why are opaque moral theories unsatisfactory? There seem to be two rather different main objections. The first is that, if people are taught to accept opaque moralities or moral theories, they may come to take it for granted that they ought to accept and respect precepts and principles without finding out whether they deserve to be respected and followed. Such a (opaque) method of socialization or teaching may more easily inculcate in them behavior that amounts to, or tends to cause, the unjustified exploitation or oppression of others or the infliction on them of other kinds of harm. The "conscientiousness" in respect of these principles of individuals thus socialized or morally educated, say, a Nazi's conscientiousness in carrying out his genocidal role duties, makes his behavior the more devastating, some would say the more morally obnoxious.

Such reflections about opaque theories and moralities may lead one to hope or expect that a transparent moral theory, by its addition of reasons why the theory's principles ought to be respected and followed, would enable moral agents to detect the soundness or unsoundness of the moral principles their socialization or explicit moral teaching had inculcated in them. And it might be thought that this availability to people of generally graspable methods for detecting the soundness or unsoundness of recommended or taught principles would increase the probability that only sound principles would come to be respected, adopted, and followed.

I cannot here examine the reasonableness of this hope or expectation, but I should say that, in the form stated, it would seem to beg the very question at issue, namely, whether we can devise a system of reasoning that is both transparent to and usable by everybody. I shall, however, shortly return to this point for a few additional comments.

The second objection is that opaque theories and moralities tend to be elitist: an elite invents and imposes the principles, the rest is subjected to and forced to follow them. If the moral order is embedded in a reasonably free social order and if a good many rival transparent theories are freely available, this may enable members to choose the principles that really are supported by the best known reasons. Under such conditions, transparent moral theories and moralities fit in better than opaque ones with the Kantian—and indeed widely accepted—ideal of autonomy. If every moral agent adopts the principles that are supported by what she regards as the best reasons, then these principles are voluntarily adopted and also followed, at least by and large. This might well tend to reduce the need for external sanctions which, surely, are intrinsically undesirable. But note that this commitment and freedom to adopt and follow only such moral principles as one finds acceptable may conflict with another desideratum, that the principles adopted and followed by all the members of a moral order be the same. We know only too well how undesirable it is when half the community thinks abortion is often morally permissible or even desirable, while the other half thinks the opposite. However, to simplify this discussion, I shall suppose, for argument's sake, that such a divergence, as far as it is undesirable, can be overcome by continued discussion.

(3) Can theories improve in respect of transparency? In light of my remarks in (1), I shall now assume that Kant's theory is not completely transparent and that no other theories in the field do much better, mine included. But might we not now assume, in light of my discussion in (2), that there are degrees of transparency and opaqueness, so that theories and moralities may gradually become less opaque and ipso facto more nearly transparent? I envisage a scale stretching from complete opaqueness to complete transparency, with the points in between marking degrees of decreasing opaqueness and increasing transparency. How is progress along this scale to be conceived?

Consider the morality of the Jews when Moses descended from Mt. Sinai with the Ten Commandments, as it is often portrayed. Did Moses or the Ten Commandments offer reasons why the Jews ought to follow these commandments? Well, he is usually thought to have said that they were *God's* commandments. If one believes that, then one believes something that may well be reason enough. Nevertheless, this reason may be thought weak because cognitively obscure. There certainly does not seem to be a method for discovering whether a supposed divine commandment really is one. Nor has much been revealed about why these rather than other commandments have been issued, nor much by way of *reason* that would help "to motivate us all alike." This, then, would seem to be fairly close to a completely opaque moral theory or morality.

Consider, next, the Golden Rule, given by Schneewind as his first example, perhaps his paradigm of an opaque moral theory or morality. I think that it can, nevertheless, be regarded as an advance over the Ten Commandments on the opaqueness/transparency scale. It may be less easily usable than the more specific Ten Commandments, but it amounts to a general principle of how people ought to treat one another. It is similar to the test of "reversibility" ("what if that were done to you?") which implies the principle of treating others in a way we would find acceptable even if the roles of agent and patient were reversed. Since it is a principle that is intended to be used by everyone, there is even a suggestion of "universalizability" ("What if everyone did that?") and that it may be subject to a "condition of mutuality" (that one is required to treat another in this way only as long as the other treats one in the same way). This does not itself clearly spell out a reason for the principle, but it does hint at one, namely, that if everyone follows this principle then everyone is likely to have done for and to him what he wants. Indeed, we can think of quite a few of the Ten Commandments that deal with interactions between humans as applications of the Golden Rule to more specific situations, and of it as the reason for these specific commandments.

There are, of course, well known difficulties with this spelling out of these hints contained in the Golden Rule, but it seems quite plausible that this Rule at least suggests something like a reason with great and almost universal appeal. It seems to enable us to see, though we may not be able to say in so many words, why we should and might want to follow this principle, even in the absence of external sanctions for it. And this is important since in the absence of such an explanation, external sanctions strike us as morally objectionable.

Consider, next, Plato's moral and political theory in the *Republic*, including his "Noble Lie," and Hobbes' moral and political theory in *Leviathan*, with its nineteen or twenty specific Laws of Nature. Hobbes, of course, arrives at these Laws by a long and complex argument still vigorously argued over by commentators even today. It may, therefore, be presumed too difficult for the average person to grasp. At the end of his list of Laws, Hobbes offers, perhaps primarily to those who cannot follow his derivation of the more specific laws of nature, a version of the Golden Rule, as a snappy summation of his earthly life-preserving counterpart of the Ten Commandments.

These last two cases differ from the earlier ones in that these theorists advance certain specific moral principles with whose help the person-in-the-street is supposed to be able to solve his moral problems, and also certain reasons why he should respect and follow these principles rather than others supported by other reasons in other theories. Plato adds (somewhat condescendingly) a metaphorical summary of the reasons for his moral and political principles—his Noble Lie of the three metals. Hobbes adds only his simplified version of his principles in his version of the Golden Rule, but does not provide an abridged edition intended only for the hoi polloi.

Thus Plato's and Hobbes' theories are less opaque than the Ten Commandments and the Golden Rule by itself, because they are not opaque to everybody, though their authors seem to assume that they will be opaque to the average person. Hobbes' theory seems less elitist, less patronizing about the uneducated than Plato's, whose "theory of the three metals" is only a persuasive myth to sway the classes destined to be ruled. Its characterization as a 'Noble Lie' is only for the ears of the ruling class. By contrast, Hobbes' Golden Rule is in no way a lie and, although it may be an oversimplification, it is offered as an aid for anyone who wants help. At any rate, Hobbes does not exclude anyone, who has the ability and the wish to do so, from examining his reasons in support of his principles.

In such a "free" social order, more and more people may start constructing rival moral theories, and as they do so, more people are likely to become able to compare them critically with one another, and so more theories become more transparent to more people. This could be the beginning of a development that would eventually end the first, and in my opinion worse, of the two faults (described in [2] of this section) of the opaqueness of moralities and moral theories.

This hoped-for development is twofold. The first is a double convergence: one in the content of the middle-level moral principles on which moral agents must rely in answering moral questions and the other in the alternative systems of reasons on which these rival theories base their rival middle-level principles. The second hoped-for development, which can only occur as the first progresses, is a growing social and political influence of moral theories on the mores (including the law) of the social order that encourages theorists to produce their (rival) theories.[78]

If these two developments occur, then even those to whom these moral theories and the morality of their moral order remain opaque and who still follow the principles of the morality of their moral order either from "second nature" inculcated in the course of their socialization or from fear of the external sanctions, are now less likely to become one anothers' victims. For, if the theorists have done their work well and their findings have influenced the legislators and the judges, then following the morality of their group from ingrained habit and/or fear of punishment is less likely to result in mutual harming.

Of course, even if these hoped-for developments actually occur and the first fault of opaque moral orders can be eliminated, those insufficiently educated or intelligent to be able to understand the reasons for the moral principles and laws accepted in the society, will probably still suffer the other undesirable consequence of the opaqueness of moralities and moral theories: they will not be properly autonomous. But, if I am right, the worst objectionable consequence of the opaqueness of a morality is not that its members can follow its principles only for external reasons, whether fear of punishment or hope of reward; it is rather that such opaque moralities make it easier for those who try to shape the moral beliefs of its members, to skew those beliefs (as Thrasymachus and Marx suggest they will) in the direction of their advantage and of the disadvantage of those unable to get themselves to disregard these supposedly moral rules, even when they are not supported by adequate reasons. Suppose, then, that as a result of this hoped-for development, an elite of moral thinkers has succeeded in changing the mores of their social order in the direction of a sound morality. Then, the opaqueness to many of the morality and of the available moral theories would seem to be much less objectionable. For, at least, being motivated by external reason (through the sanctions attached to the law and the social morality) now motivates them to do what really is morally required or permitted.

The situation would then be analogous to that in which it is thought by some that they know the will of God, but there are still some who have doubts about what the will of God is and who, in any case do not love God enough always to obey even what they think they know are his commandments. Nevertheless, even in this group some or most are frightened enough by the prospect of punishment for disobedience always to obey what are generally accepted to be God's commandments. Suppose, then, that it is the case that God's will really is what these people say they know it is, then it is not objectionable for there to be adequate external sanctions to provide the needed additional motivation than it would be if God's will is quite different. In the development I have envisaged, moral theory has advanced to a stage such that it has what a significant proportion of the community, by the highest available standards, regard as adequate reasons for accepting a certain set of middle-level principles. In such a situation, it is presumably not as objectionable if the available moral theories and moral education are not completely transparent, and if there are external sanctions imposed on those who act contrary to these middle-level principles, even if the moral teaching they received, though correct, was opaque to them.

(4) Can any more be done to diminish the opacity of moral theories and moralities? Clearly, moral theories and moralities opaque to any of its normal adult members (the young, the senile, the retarded, and the insane presumably are not included) are inconsistent with the requirements of the ideal of autonomy. I admit I cannot think of any way to remove this last obstacle to achieving the highly desirable ideal of autonomy for all normal adults, before the above hoped-for development (described in [3] in this section) is much further advanced than it seems to be anywhere in the world today and, I fear, is likely to be in the near future. To the extent that this is true, complete transparency and with it universal autonomy may be utopian ideals.

However, if that development gathers momentum, if, let us say, some moral theorist or movement achieves the eminence in ethics that Newton achieved in physics or Darwin in biology, then we may hope to advance further on the road to complete transparency by greatly intensifying our efforts at moral education. We may never achieve complete unanimity on what are the sound principles of morality; it might even be dangerous to achieve it, as J. S. Mill suggested, but I do not think it is needed before moral education can be introduced in the schools. We can now teach the theory of evolution, the heliocentric theory of the solar system, and the "big-bang" theory of the origin of the universe, although some schools insist on also teaching "creation science."

In any case, it seems doubtful that any moral theory already deserves to have the prestige of any of these scientific theories and at this point it is not clear (certainly not to me) that it even makes sense to hope, let alone expect, that one day some moral theory will be constructed that will deserve to have and will have that prestige. Until then, I fear, the demand for completely transparent moral theories and moralities will remain unreasonable.

In light of these very sketchy remarks, I want now to offer two suggestion to alleviate Schneewind's deep and troublesome problem. My first is the suggestion that the problem is less acute in personal than in institutional morality. Those who have read my remarks on applied ethics in chapter 9 of RMO perhaps agree when I say that my theory is much closer to being transparent in personal morality than it would be in institutional morality. The derivation of the principles involved in the former is much more accessible to everybody than those, say, in the assessment of economic institutions. And my central moral principle, that of conditional limited good will, has a certain intuitive plausibility which may suffice to provide some motivation, though, of course, not always enough to overcome the pull of other motives. Even if this intuitive plausibility comes from indoctrination rather than from genuine moral education, this is less objectionable if the indoctrination has been designed by an elite who have been genuinely educated and who inculcate the sound principles of morality.

As far as institutional morality is concerned, the spread and improvement of democracy perhaps raises the hope that voters will become better at distinguishing between more and less nearly just party platforms and individual candidates and will vote for the more nearly just. As long as there is progress in that direction, members of the moral community should perhaps trust their government to pass legislation that is as nearly just as can be expected in the circumstances, and satisfy the requirements of institutional morality by the appropriate analog of Bradley's principle, 'My Station and its Duties', namely, 'My Institutional Roles and their Duties'. Of course, those who feel they know better what morality requires than their representatives, may take whatever democratic methods are available to them to advance reform.

My second suggestion is a wave of the hands in the direction of moral education. As democracy is an advance in the direction of transparency where political morality is concerned, so moral education would be an advance in the direction of transparency in the field of morality. However, to hope for that would require that we can distinguish between education and indoctrination, and that would require agreement at least among the experts, and there is no such development in sight. And even if it were, the general public is not even persuaded by the fairly general agreement among scientists that so-called creation science is not a science, so why would they be willing to accept an agreement among the experts in ethical theory—and how would "moral experts" establish their credentials—to let moral education be guided by them? But if moral education is politically unthinkable, could we reasonably hope to move in the direction of greater transparency in the field of moral theory?

University of Pittsburgh

Notes

1. I think the second horn of this dilemma is the less menacing one, since its menace depends on a questionable assumption: that an explanation of why being moral is always in accordance with reason and not being moral contrary to it, presupposes that one cannot be moral unless one always follows what one takes to be the best reasons, even if one does so for, or only for, the purpose of obtaining the goods that acting in accordance with reason assures for one. Of course, this assumption conceivably may be true, but it is not plainly so, for there seem to be cases in which one can show that what someone is doing is in accordance with reason for her to do because doing it makes her happy, although that is not *a* reason, *let alone the only reason why* she is doing it, as when she likes cuddling her child or listening to Brahms. One may learn about certain practices one engages in for their own sakes and not for the sake of some further pay-off, that engaging in these practices also makes one happy or satisfied with one's life, or the opposite. Thus, a logically and morally appropriate, though not necessarily true, answer to "why cuddle one's child?" or "Why listen to Brahms?" may be "partly because it will make you (one) happy." But this answer does not seem to imply that you (one) must or ought to be doing it only for the sake of the happiness it brings. But neither does it imply—though it may well be true—that doing these things *cannot* make one happy if one does them only in order to be happy. Here, questions concerning the different implications and presuppositions of being happy and being moral need to be taken into consideration.

2. A person's conception of the good life for her can also be externally flawed when the way she wants to lead her life conflicts with society-anchored reasons.

3. I have given a very similar example to make the same point in the paper listed as #88 in the bibliography at the end of this book.

4. I am encouraged by the fact that Scanlon saw this more clearly than I did, because this suggests that at least people who have thought about these matters can sense what this privileged point of view is and how it should be characterized. This is an important starting point for the work that needs to be done if we are to reach a point where, as Scanlon puts it, "we have defined" and not just "gestured toward" that privileged point of view we are looking for.

5. Apart from not wishing to characterize these objectives as altruistic; they indeed seem not to be self-regarding, but they are not even other-regarding, let alone altruistic. See RMO, chap. 5, sec. 4.

6. The clause, "under the circumstances, the best life for me is not what matters most to me" must be interpreted with care, for the reason the mother has for saying it may not be a self-anchored one, but another, say, a moral one, that overrides her self-anchored ones whether in the narrow or the broad sense. To test our intuitions about self-anchored reasons, we must eliminate moral reasons, so that we do not assume the presence of agent-non-favoring self-anchored reasons when there are only agent-non-favoring moral reasons. Scanlon might explain that 'a *good* life' is different from 'the *best* life', but that would require him to argue that the point of view from which practical reasons are determined is that of one's internally unflawed conception of the good life for one, in the sense in which the good is the enemy of the best, and includes the second-best or some other life inferior to the best of the lives accessible to him. It seems that something other than the goodness of a life is here invoked as what makes it choice worthy and so preferred. If one is not bothered by this, then, it seems to me, one should not be bothered, as Scanlon is, by my view, on the grounds that it implies the inconsistency that doing a certain thing involves a sacrifice, but doing it is still required by the best life one can live.

7. My own use of the world-improvement terminology was not intended to introduce a change in the ground of self-anchored reasons. For the criterion that I (and I think most people) have in mind, when they think of a change in the world as a world improvement, is of a person's life or people's lives generally getting better, or getting closer to their internally unflawed conception of a life for them. It is hard to think of a plausible criterion of world-improvement that is not in this way tied to human life improvement. We may think that a world in which there was less suffering would be a better world even if there were no human beings in it, but then this would not help us define that privileged point of view from which self-anchored reasons are defined.

8. The word 'agent-favoring' is not intended to mean 'favoring over another agent' or 'favoring the agent to the detriment of another'. I mention this only to ensure that readers will not reject the idea that the ground of self-anchored reasons is that following them at least tends to favor the follower.

9. There is, of course, a good deal more to be said about this, and I do in fact make a few pertinent points in section B of my comments on Raz's paper.

10. See RMO, chap. 4, sec. 4.

11. Of course, morality requires more of members when they stand in certain special relations to one another, say, parents and children, and it *recommends* more than it *requires,* as in acts of so-called supererogation.

12. Here I agree with what I take to be Kant's view, that if there are certain things that moral reasons direct us to do, we may do the morally *right* thing from a variety of motives, and it depends on the motive from which we do it whether what we do has "moral worth," which I take to mean moral merit, desert, or praiseworthiness. As is well known, there is disagreement among scholars about exactly what Kant thought was the motive or range of motives that gave one's morally right action moral worth. Leaving aside the question of what Kant actually meant, what he should have meant is not, I believe, "for the sake of duty," (as 'aus Pflicht' is often translated), because that seems to imply that he thought a person's morally right action had moral worth only if he did not act from any motive other than a sense of duty or reverence for the moral law; not, for instance from love, benevolence, friendship, and so on, even though he would not have been moved by these motives if they motivated him to do something morally wrong, as when from parental love, a father hid his son who had escaped from prison. What he should have meant, I believe, is something like, "with due attention to the requirements imposed by duty," as would be true of a loving father if, from parental love, he did things to benefit his son, but not when duty forbade it.

13. As I suggested in section B, because the question has this paradoxical structure, it calls for an answer that explains how this apparent impossibility is possible. At the same time, this would amount to a justification of the widespread belief that moral reasons defeat or override self-anchored ones.

14. For a more detailed discussion of this behavior pattern, see RMO, chap. 7, esp. sec. 4.

15. I have developed this at greater length in RMO, chap. 7, esp. secs. 3.6 and 4.

16. I have discussed this question in greater detail in RMO; for references, see fn. 14.

17. I shall not here outline the rationale of a moral order because I have done so more fully in RMO, chap. 7, and because Scanlon has not objected to it qua rationale, but as an account of moral reasons.

18. I have said a few things that are relevant to these matters in my comments on Scanlon, in II, section A.

19. Or is it goodness? Does what is good for me and so is *a* relational *good, have* a different kind of good*ness* (or value) from what *is* a nonrelational good (or value)?

20. To avoid confusion in the comparison between the reasons labeled (a) and (b) (on p. 70) and those labelled (a), (b), and (c) (on p. 72), I have labeled the latter (i), (ii), and (iii).

21. By 'unflawed' I here mean something satisfying conditions such as Raz's (b) in the quotation from p. 70. I have discussed this in greater detail in chapter 1 of

RMO. I assume that this could be done and that arguments undermining any of its premises would undermine this argument.

22. In the widest sense. I have said more about this in #88, also #29 and #36 in the bibliography; and in my RMO, chap. 4, esp. secs. 4–6.

23. Rawls' first account of what he calls "primary goods" would seem to be of this sort, although only some of them appear to be intrinsic goods, e.g., self-respect, but not income. See John Rawls, *A Theory of Justice* (henceforth TJ) (Cambridge, Mass.: The Belknap Press of Harvard University Press, 1971), 62f.

24. I once heard Professor Anscombe argue, with great vigor and candor, that whereas one acted contrary to an other-things-equal reason if one failed to do what one knew would prevent, terminate, or lessen a pain, this was not so for a pleasure.

25. G. E. Moore, *Principia Ethica* (Cambridge University Press, 1903), viii.

26. I give a fuller account of this point in RMO, chaps. 4 and 5.

27. Including moral ones; see Raz, p. 69.

28. I have done some of the spelling out in RMO, chaps. 6 and 7.

29. In other words, a broadened version of what Rawls called "a well-ordered society." See Rawls, p. 4f., sec. 69.

30. I have discussed this in RMO, chaps. 5, 6, and 7.

31. For some differences, see below, III, section B.

32. I am here suggesting an extension of Hume's idea—one he presumably would not accept—that certain virtues, which he called artificial, especially the virtue he called 'justice'—presuppose the satisfaction of certain conditions, which he called "the circumstances (or conditions) of justice." My suggestion is that, at a higher level of abstraction, the whole of morality presupposes the satisfaction of such conditions, despite the undeniable differences he noted between what he called the natural and the artificial virtues. I think he may have overlooked the fact that, although each naturally virtuous act confers a benefit on someone else, the distribution of the motivation to do what confers these benefits and the cost of following it are determined by natural endowments present in different degrees in different individuals and by the varying social conditions helping to reinforce or undermine that motivation in certain individuals or classes of individuals, and that there is, therefore, a danger of a one-sided exploitation of such naturally skewed motivational endowments.

33. Here, I do not use 'from' in the sense employed in 'from duty' in translations of Kant's 'aus Pflicht', which implies that the agent thinks that what he does is his duty and does it because of that. However, it does not quite mean the same as Kant's 'in accordance with that point of view' either, for it certainly excludes the case where the "accordance" is accidental. Any form of acquiring the point of view means that the considerations derivable from it *weigh* with one.

34. Of course, if by not being thus motivated, he has already abandoned that point of view anyway, then he ought to cease claiming that he has it. I examine the question of whether one can have an end and fail to do something that one can do, that one knows how to do, and that one believes is a necessary means to attaining

that end, in my comments on Hampton's discussion of Kant's hypothetical imperative.

35. Although Raz seems to use reasons and considerations interchangeably, I here draw a sharp distinction between them, as in RMO, chap. 3, sec. 4. As I use the terms, a fact is for someone a consideration for doing something, if knowing or believing that it is a fact, motivates him to do it. By contrast, a fact is a reason for someone to do it, if knowing or believing that it is a fact, ought to motivate him to do it.

36. I have discussed this conception in RMO, chap. 4, esp. secs. 5 and 6.

37. For a fuller discussion, see RMO, chap. 4, esp. secs. 3 and 4.

38. Which is based on my discussion in RMO, chap. 4.

39. My example of Fred and Frieda, in RMO, chap. 4, sec. 4, illustrates such an approach.

40. I have discussed Sidgwick's version in RMO, chap. 4, sec. 1.

41. I have tried to show, in RMO, chaps. 6 and 7, how this limitation on reasons of self-interest can be accomplished without abandoning PL as the hub of the enterprise of practical reason.

42. For Hume, see *Treatise,* 494–95; *Enquiry,* sec. III, pt. I, 149. For Rawls, see TJ, p. 126.

43. I state this quite clearly in RMO, chap. 1, esp. secs. 11 and 12.

44. I think for our purposes here we can ignore others.

45. We need not here examine the question of what we understand by 'behavior' as opposed to, on the one hand, conduct, actions, activity, action, inaction, reaction, and the like, and on the other, doings, doing-nothings, undergoings, unconscious and semi-conscious processes, such as digesting, temperature-maintenance, sleeping, dreaming, and so on. We can here rely on a rough understanding of what things are behavior.

46. At this point, we need not examine when or why we would pick out that representation as the cause of the motivation to act or of acting in this way, when, as may often be the case, there are also other conditions that must be satisfied, if that representation is to move the agent. Often, one of the important other conditions will be a preexisting desire, as when a person is hungry and sees in front of her some food she likes and also has the appropriate semantic representations, although when she is not hungry, these representations would not motivate or move her to eat that food. Hume and many others thought that such desire-based motivation would always have to be present.

47. I have discussed these stages in RMO, chap. 1, esp. sec. 5, and chap. 3, sec. 2, esp. 2.4–2.6, and sec. 3. I have given a more complicated account of the last capacity which seemed to me necessary to explain why we think of it as a capacity rather than a mechanism to which we are subject. I should also mention that Gauthier's emphasis on the capacity to be moved by semantic representations of the sort he describes is superior to the way I put it: the capacity to be moved by the belief that something is a fact. The advantage is that my account presupposes that the

creature has a language, but I think it is better to allow the possibility that a creature, such as Koehler's ape, who has no language, could conceivably have this capacity; of course, as Gauthier says, "a great many representations of the world as it might be are clearly quite impossible without a language" (p. 40).

48. And so may have capacities that go beyond mere intelligence, as Gauthier rightly points out against what I say.

49. These motivating representations would be, for one, a consideration in favor of acting as they motivate one to act if one took them to be sound, and if one's taking them to be sound was a condition of these motivating one. If Koehler's ape is incapable of "taking these representations to be sound or unsound," they are considerations, but merely motivating representations.

50. I am here in contrast with Gauthier; see my comments on his paper in this volume, and RMO, chap. 3, esp. secs. 2.5, 2.6, and 4.

51. And here she may disagree with me, for she thinks this authority cannot be explained along naturalist lines, whereas I rather think it can.

52. For an account of this term, see RMO, chap. 1, sec. 7. Roughly, it means the level of mastery in the skills of reason that normally comes with maturity. It is compatible with a good deal of irrationality.

53. RMO, chap. 1, p. 64.

54. See RMO, chap. 1, esp. secs. 10 and 12.

55. In a sense of 'naturalism' which she does not define, but which I trust I am not misunderstanding.

56. I have greatly profited from the papers on Kant's ethics by Thomas Hill, Jr., especially "The Hypothetical Imperative," all reprinted in Hill's *Dignity and Practical Reason in Kant's Moral Theory* (Ithaca, NY: Cornell University Press, 1992), 17–37. I have also benefitted from several discussions with my colleague, Nicholas Rescher, and from his paper "The Unity of Kant's Categorical Imperative," *Akten des Siebenten Internationalen Kant-Kongresses* (Kurfurstliches Schloss zu Mainz, 1990, hrsg. Von G. Funke, Bonn: Bouvier, 1991). All my references to Kant are to his *Foundations of the Metaphysics of Morals,* trans. Lewis White Beck (reprinted in *Kant Selections,* ed. Lewis White Beck, New York: Scribner/Macmillan, 1988), 245–98. I have, very occasionally, relied on my own understanding of the German text. I have also profited from reading H. J. Paton's *The Categorical Imperative. A Study in Kant's Moral Philosophy* (Chicago, Ill.: University of Chicago Press, 1948); Robert Paul Wolff's *The Autonomy of Reason* (New York: Harper Torchbooks, 1971); and Onora Nell's (now O'Neill) *Acting on Principle: An Essay in Kantian Ethics* (New York: Columbia University Press, 1975).

57. Presumably, it would be odd to say, 'it commanded us that we ought to . . . etc.' The German 'Du sollst' is closer to the biblical 'Thou shalt' and, therefore, to a commandment, command, or 'you must', which indicate that there is only one possible option, than to advice, counsel, or 'you ought', which indicate the best among at least two possibilities. Kant wanted an account in terms of necessity for both commands and counsels. Hampton is not tying the necessity of the hypothetical impera-

tive to the indispensably necessary means, but applies it also to the appropriate means, which provide a better fit than does Kant's necessity and necessitation for the supposedly merely advisory force of that imperative.

58. It is interesting that Kant does not discuss the hypothetical imperative in the second *Critique,* but I have not seen any suggestion that he abandoned it or modified his proof in later writings.

59. Like the English 'compulsion' or 'being obliged' and unlike the English 'obligation' or 'bindingness' and the German 'Verpflichtung' or 'Verbindlichkeilt', the German word 'Noetigung' implies "success": one cannot have been 'genoetigt', i.e., compelled, to do something if one did not do it. It seems clear, however, that Kant did not think of 'Noetigung' as implying success in this sense. I take it that the necessity of objective practical principles of laws yields, for imperfectly rational beings, something corresponding roughly to the English 'ought' or 'must', as in 'You ought to—or must—visit your mother in hospital'. I use the word 'bindingness' to convey what Kant is referring to, although 'necessitation' is a more literal translation and may well render more accurately not only what Kant said but what he thought he was referring to and explicating.

60. This supposed difference between the categorical and the hypothetical imperative may mislead Kant's readers into thinking that the principle of *the* hypothetical imperative, "the hypothetical imperative as such" (1959, 420), that is, the principle of which we do not "know what it will contain until the condition is stated [under which it is an imperative]" (ibid.), lacks the unconditional bindingness of a law. They may be misled in the same way by Kant's remark "There is only one categorical imperative" (1959, 421), which may seem to imply that there are no specific categorical imperatives and that there is no hypothetical imperative as such. But this inference would appear to be false for, when considered *as such, the* imperative of either type is a law, even though more specific hypothetical imperatives are said to be merely principles, whereas more specific categorical imperatives (e.g., 'one ought not to make lying promises') are also laws (that is, unconditionally binding principles). The difference between these two types of law would seem to lie, rather, in the different logical structures of what they command. The unconditionally binding law of a categorical imperative (e.g., not to make lying promises) leaves rational beings "no freedom to choose the opposite" (1959, 420). By contrast, the no less unconditionally binding law of the hypothetical imperative as such, commands a disjunction, thus leaving rational beings free to choose between two alternatives though not, of course, free to choose the opposite of what this disjunctive imperative commands. For what it commands, equally unconditionally, is either to will the necessary means to one's end or to give up that end; or, to put this negatively, it unconditionally forbids one both to will the end and not to will the necessary means. And this disjunction is equally unconditionally commanded in a particular hypothetical imperative when the indispensably necessary means in one's power is known to one. But, of course, it still leaves open the choice between giving up the means and giving up the end. I can here also ignore a second dimension of impera-

tives, their degree of permissiveness. Thus, a specific categorical imperative is, of course, unconditional, but it may be permissive, for it may generate imperfect duties or duties of wide obligation. For an illuminating discussion of the various ways in which categorical imperatives may differ from one another in this dimension, see Onora Nell, *Acting on Principle.*

61. Kant draws several important distinctions between the two subclasses of hypothetical imperatives, those of skill and those of prudence, but these differences are irrelevant to my concerns. For, as Kant puts it, "Since both, however, command the means to that which one presupposes as a willed purpose, the imperative which commands the willing of the means to him who wills the end is in both cases analytic" (1959, 419).

62. I ignore the question whether 'believes' or 'justifiably believes' could justifiably be added as alternatives to 'knows'.

63. I leave aside the third formulation (Kant 1959, 417–18) until I consider the question of whether the analytic principle could be one of theoretical reason. See below pp. 255–57.

64. But I have to admit that Kant's terminology is also confusing. 'Einen Zweck wollen' is almost as odd as 'willing an end' or 'willing a purpose'. It is less so only because 'Er will etwas' is not odd at all, whereas 'He wills something' is. What is odd in both languages is the fusion of the language of being disposed or motivated to do what one believes or knows to be a way of bringing about or preventing an event or state or state of affairs, with the language of events or states or states of affairs itself. The ingestion of food is an event, the having of a full stomach a state or state of affairs, depending on whether it is the outcome of a single ingestion of a certain amount of food or the outcome of sufficient ingestions of food, whether by eating or by intravenous feeding, that will maintain that state over time. To have a desire, such as hunger or desire for food, is to be disposed or motivated to do something, say ingest food, which one believes or knows would satisfy that desire. To have an end or purpose is to be *set on* doing these things. One can have many desires one knows cannot all be satisfied by one at a given time, even when one knows one can do what will satisfy any one of them. One cannot *have* such ends or purposes, even when one knows, and knows that one can do, what will attain any one of them, though one can believe and sincerely say one has them all. It is therefore odd, because pleonastic, to speak of 'desiring an end' or even 'willing a purpose', because 'end' and 'purpose' already imply the motivational element over and above the reference to an event or state or state of affairs. In Hampton's use of 'desiring an end' the oddness therefore seems increased because she does not mean 'having and desiring an end', which means being set on bringing about something one desires to bring about. She means merely desiring it, but that suggests the wrong motivation. I believe an end that one has is something (e.g., an event) that one is *set on* bringing about or preventing, not something one merely desires to bring about or prevent.

65. I take a means to be an action in one's power which, in the relevant circumstances, is a sufficient condition of attaining one's end. I take a necessary means to be the sole such action in the situation one is in.

66. I take it Kant is committed to the view that we cannot root out the dispositional desire to be happy, but that we can and sometimes ought to resist the desire to take what we believe (know?) to be the indispensably necessary means in our power to satisfy an occurrence of that desire.

67. Hampton could avoid this objection by construing the reason provided by the hypothetical imperative not as an unconditional disjunctive one, but as an other-things-equal reason for taking what one knows to be the indispensably necessary steps one can take for attaining the end one desires. But see what I call "the third point" in the next paragraph.

68. I have taken this to mean that whereas both the hypothetical and the categorical imperative as such imply ('bei sich fuehrt') the necessity of law, only particular categorical, but not particular hypothetical, imperatives imply that necessity.

69. It is perhaps not crystal clear how one can reconcile what Kant says about each of the two types of hypothetical imperative with what he says about the hypothetical imperative as such. How, for instance, can the hypothetical imperative as such command us to choose the necessary means to our chosen end or give up the end in view, if happiness is a "purpose which [all imperfectly rational beings] not only *can* have but which we can presuppose they all do have by a necessity of nature" (1959, 415), and how is it they have an option to give up that end; or how can the imperative command them either to give up that end or choose the indispensably necessary means to that end, if "the task of determining infallibly and universally what action will promote the happiness of a rational being is completely unsolvable" (1959, 418)—as the task of "bisect[ing] a line according to an infallible principle" (1959, 417) is not; or how, if the directives of the "imperatives of prudence cannot, in the strict sense command (i.e., present actions objectively as practically necessary)" (1959, 418), can the analyticity of any proposition explain how the prudential imperative is possible? But I shall simplify matters by ignoring these further complications.

70. Hampton suggests that "the analytic proposition is a kind of principle of 'practical logic', analogous to other principles of logic (like, say, DeMorgan's law) which people can violate, but which they ought not to violate" (p. 96). This is an interesting suggestion, but what is at issue here is precisely whether what Kant says about why the proposition he seems to be talking about is analytic, allows him to say that (the principle of) the hypothetical imperative is a principle of practical logic. For if, as Kant's remarks seem to imply, the principle is at best one of theoretical logic, then the only way in which one can violate this principle is by believing something the principle deprives one of adequate reason to believe.

71. In his ground-breaking paper, "The Hypothetical Imperative," from which I have profited greatly, Thomas Hill suggests a slightly different way out. He takes the first two steps of Kant's argument to be these: "(1) Whoever wills an end also wills the sole means which are in his power if he is rational. (2) Whoever wills an end ought to will the sole means which are within his power. Or, in other words, if a person wills an end and certain means are necessary to achieve that end and are within his power, then he ought to will those means" (pp. 19f.). The problem with

premise (1) is how to show, along the lines chosen by Kant, that this is analytic. If the agent does not know that a certain M is necessary and in his power, he may not choose M when he wills E even when reason has decisive influence on his actions. Another person who knows it can tell him that, if he wants E, he *must* do M. Even if he accepts the information and so believes a certain M to be necessary and in his power, the proposition is not analytic, for what he gets may even be misinformation. It is only if he *knows* that a certain M is an indispensably necessary means in his power that it is even plausible that the proposition is analytic. But then we are back with the question how (1), now modified to read '. . . wills what he knows to be the sole means in his power . . .' and so analytic, can show the bindingness of the practical principle that one ought to will M, if one wills E, and M is the necessary means to E. For in the first place, Kant's principle is supposed to tell us only that we ought to will M *or* give up E. However, in its now modified (analytic) form, (1) does not leave room for a practical principle: whatever X chooses to do under these knowledge and ability conditions will *be* either a willing of M or a not-willing of E. If we turn from X under these conditions of knowledge and ability, when (1) is analytic, to X not under these conditions when (1) is not analytic, then how does the analyticity of the former render the latter binding? Does Kant want to say that the person, who does not will M when he does not know it is an indispensably necessary means in his power, behaves irrationally or contrary to reason, in the sense that reason does not have decisive influence on his actions? But, surely, ignorance is not necessarily irrationality. And if this is not what Kant wants to say, what is his proof of the possibility of the hypothetical imperative?

72. This suggestion is also made by Thomas Hill in the same article, pp. 20ff. It may also have been in Hampton's mind when she substituted 'desiring' for 'willing' an end.

73. See my comments on Raz, above, III, sec. B.

74. For a relevant discussion, see my comments on Scanlon's objection based on the wrongness of the motivation that is generated by a good-based (consequentialist) justification of principles. See above, II, sec. C.

75. See above, III, sec. B.

76. Such passionate disagreement is not, of course, wholly absent from the history of other disciplines either. Still, the venerable age of ethics and its painfully slow progress, if indeed there is any, suggests that there are special difficulties here.

77. I have discussed this point in my comments on Raz; see above, III, sec. B.

78. One might interpret the developments in medical ethics, or the popularity of Rawls's work among social scientists, as small signs of the growing influence of moral theory.

Bibliography of the Works of Kurt Baier

BOOKS

1. *The Moral Point of View.* Ithaca, NY: Cornell University Press, 1958. (This book has been translated into German and Urdu.)
2. *The Moral Point of View,* abridged and revised edition, with a new introductory article. New York: Random House, 1965.
3. *Values and the Future.* Edited together with Nicholas Rescher. New York: The Free Press, 1969.
4. *The Rational and the Moral Order.* Chicago and La Salle: Open Court, 1995.

TRANSLATION

Der Begriff Des Geistes. Reclam Verlag. Stuttgart, 1969. (Translation into German of Gilbert Ryle's *The Concept of Mind.*)

ARTICLES AND ESSAYS

1. "Objectivity in Ethics." *Australasian Journal of Philosophy* 26; no. 3 (December 1948): 147–65.
2. "S. Hampshire: Fallacies in Moral Philosophy. A Note." *Mind* 59, no. 234 (April 1950): 223–29.
3. "Decisions and Descriptions." *Mind* 60, no. 238 (April 1951): 181–204.
4. "Doing My Duty." *Philosophy* 26, no. 98 (July 1951): 253–60.
5. "On Describing." With S.E. Toulmin. *Mind* 61, no. 241 (January 1952): 13–38. Translated into German.
6. "The Ordinary Use of Words." *Proceedings of the Aristotelian Society* 52 (1952): 47–70.
7. "Good Reasons." *Philosophical Studies* 4, no. 1 (January 1953): 1–15.
8. "Proving a Moral Judgment." *Philosophical Studies* 4, no. 3 (April 1953): 33–48.
9. "Contradiction and Absurdity." *Analysis* (1954): 31–40.
10. "Good Reasons: A Reply to Mr. Terrell & Mr. Sachs." *Philosophical Studies* (June 1954).

11. "The Point of View of Morality." *Australasian Journal of Philosophy* 32, no. 2 (August 1954): 104–35.
12. "Is Punishment Retributive?" *Analysis* 16, no. 2 (December 1955): 25–32.
13. "The Meaning of Life." Inaugural Lecture, Canberra University College (October 1957).
14. "Existence." *Proceedings of the Aristotelian Society* (1960): 19–40.
15. "Smart on Sensations." *Australasian Journal of Philosophy* (1962): 57–67.
16. "Pains." *Australasian Journal of Philosophy* 40, no. 1 (May 1962): 1–23.
17. "Could and Would." *Analysis,* supplement (1963): 19–29.
18. Review of Georg Henrik von Wright, *The Varieties of Goodness* (New York: Humanities Press, 1963). *Journal of Philosophy* (1963): 17–28.
19. "The Place of a Pain." *Philosophical Quarterly* (1964): 138–50.
20. "Reasons for Doing Something." *Journal of Philosophy* (March 1964).
21. "Action and Agent." *The Monist* 49, no. 2 (April 1965): 183–95.
22. "Acting and Producing." *Journal of Philosophy* 62, no. 21 (November 1965): 645–48.
23. "Responsibility and Freedom." *Ethics and Society* (1965): 49–84.
24. "Moral Obligation." *American Philosophical Quarterly* 3, no. 3 (July 1966): 1–17.
25. "Fact, Value, and Norm in Stevenson's Ethics." *nou[td]s* (May 1967).
26. "The Concept of Value." *Journal of Value Inquiry* 1, no. 1 (1967): 1–11.
27. Review of R.S. Peters, *Ethics and Education* (Chicago: Scott, Foresman and Company, 1967). *Harvard Educational Review* 37, no. 4 (Fall 1967): 700–3.
28. "Welfare and Preference." *In Human Value and Economic Policy,* ed. Sidney Hook. New York: New York University Press, 1967.
29. "What is Value: An Analysis of the Concept." *In Values and the Future,* ed. Kurt Baier and Nicholas Rescher, 33–67. New York: The Free Press, 1969.
30. "Meaning and Morals." *In Moral Problems in Contemporary Society,* ed. Paul Kurtz, 33–47. Englewood Cliffs, N.J.: Prentice-Hall, 1969.
31. "Responsibility and Action." In *The Nature of Human Action,* ed. Myles Brand, 100–15. Illinois: Scott, Foresman & Co., 1970.
32. Review of Robert J. Fogelin, *Evidence and Meaning. Studies in Analytic Philosophy* (New York: Routledge & Kegan Paul, Humanities Press, 1967). *Journal of Value Inquiry* 4, no. 1 (Spring 1970): 77–80.
33. "Obligation: Political and Moral." *In Political Obligation, Nomos,* ed. R. Pennock & J. Chapman, 116–41. 1970.
34. "Ethical Pluralism and Moral Education." *In Moral Education. Interdisciplinary Approaches.* Proceedings of the Conference on Philosophy and Education held at Toronto in 1968, ed. C. M. Beck, S. Crittenden, and E. V. Sullivan, 93–112. Toronto: University of Toronto Press, 1971.
35. "Moral Value and Moral Worth." *The Monist* 54, no. 1 (January 1970): 18–30.
36. "Value and Fact." *In Ethical and Social Justice,* Vol. 4 of *Contemporary Philosophic Thought,* ed. Howard Kiefer & Milton K. Munitz, 93–121. Albany, NY:

State University of New York Press, 1968, 1970.

37. "Could and Would" (revised version). In *New Readings in Philosophical Analysis,* 2d ed., ed. Herbert Feigl, Wilfrid Sellars, and Keith Lehrer. New York: Appleton-Century-Crofts, 1973.
38. "The Justification of Governmental Authority." Lead paper in APA Symposium entitled Authority and Autonomy, APA Eastern Division Meetings, December, 1972. Published in *Journal of Philosophy* 69, no. 20 (November 1972): 700–15.
39. "Guilt and Responsibility." In *Individual and Collective Responsibility: My-Lai,* ed. Peter French, 37–61. Cambridge, Mass.: Schenkman, 1972.
40. "Indoctrination and Justification." *In Educational Judgments,* ed. James F. Doyle, 74–89. London: Routledge & Kegan Paul, 1973.
41. "Reason and Experience." Lead paper in Symposium, Western Division Meeting of APA (with Hector Neri Castaneda), *Noûs* 7, no. 1 (March 1973): 56–67.
42. Review of G. J. Warnock, *The Object of Morality* (New York: Barnes & Noble; London: Methuen & Co. Ltd., 1971). *Philosophical Review* 80, no. 2 (April 1973): 269–73.
43. "Moral Autonomy as an Aim of Moral Education." In *New Essays in the Philosophy of Education,* ed. D. J. O'Connor and G. Langford, 96–113. London and Boston: Routledge & Kegan Paul, 1973.
44. "Individual Moral Development and Social Moral Advance." Symposium with Lawrence Kohlberg on moral education, Eastern Division Meeting of the APA, December 1973. Abstract in *The Journal of Philosophy* 70, no. 18 (October 1973): 646–48.
45. "Ethical Egoism and Interpersonal Compatibility." *Philosophical Studies* 24 (1973): 357–68.
46. "Towards a Definition of 'Quality of Life'." Paper read at a Symposium on Economic Growth and the Quality of Life, held at Oregon State University, sponsored by the National Endowment for the Humanities, May 1973. Published in *Environmental Spectrum,* ed. R. O. Clarke & Peter C. List, 58–81. New York: D. Van Nostrand Company, 1974.
47. "The Sanctity of Life." Paper for the Fifth International Herceg Novi Conference, Scientific, Technological and Social Development—Goals and Values, July 1973. Sponsored by the Board for Coordination of Science and Technology in Yugoslavia. Published in Vol. 1 of *Proceedings of the Fifth International Conference,* "Science and Society," 1974.
48. "The Sanctity of Life." *Journal of Social Philosophy* 5, no. 2 (April 1974): 1–6.
49. "Moral Development." *The Monist* 58, no. 4 (October 1974): 601–15.
50. "The Practice of Justification." Paper read at the Ripon Conference on Political Justification, 1971. Published together with comments by David Lyons in *Journal of Value Inquiry* 9, no. 1 (Spring 1975): 34–41.
51. "Deontological Ethics." *Encyclopedia of Bio-ethics* (1975): 413–17.
52. "Teleological Ethics." *Encyclopedia of Bio-ethics* (1975): 417–21.

53. Review of M. R. Kadish & S. H. Kadish, *Discretion to Disobey* (Stanford, Calif.: Stanford University Press, 1973). *Pennsylvania Law Review* 124, no. 2 (December 1975): 561–85.
54. "Ethical Principles and Their Validity." Invited monograph-length paper for the National Commission for the Protection of Human Subjects of Biomedical and Behavioral Research. *The Belmont Report,* Appendix. Vol. 1, no. 5(1975): 1–55.
55. "The Ethics of Passive Euthanasia." *Critical Care Medicine* 4, no. 6 (1976): 317–19.
56. "Rationality and Morality," with a reply by A.K. Sen. *Erkenntnis* 11 (Summer 1977): 197–223.
57. "The Strengths and Limits of the Retributive Theory of Punishment." Invited paper read at Brockport Center for Philosophic Exchange. *Philosophic Exchange* 2, no. 3 (Summer 1977): 37–54.
58. Review of G.H. von Wright, *Erklären und Verstehen.* German translation of *Explanation and Understanding,* trans. Gunther Grewendorf and Georg Meggle (Frankfurt: Athenaeum, 1974). *Grazer Philosophische Studien* 3 (1977): 137–53.
59. "Moral Reasons." Paper read at the Third Annual Midwest Philosophy Colloquium. *Midwest Studies in Philosophy* 3 (1978): 62–74.
60. "Moral Reasons and Reasons to be Moral." Invited paper for the Festschrift for Professors Stevenson, Frankena, and Brandt. *In Values and Morals,* ed. A.I. Goldman and J. Kim, 231–56. Dordrecht & Boston: D. Reidel Publishing Co., 1978.
61. "The Social Source of Reason." Presidential Address, APA Eastern Division, 1977. *Proceedings and Addresses of the American Philosophical Association* 51, no. 6 (August 1978): 707–33.
62. "Merit and Race." *Philosophia* 8, nos. 2–3 (November 1978): 121–51.
63. "The Liberal Approach to Pornography." Paper presented in a Symposium on the 1st Amendment, Pittsburgh, March 1979. *Pittsburgh Law Review* 40, no. 4 (Summer 1979): 619–25.
64. "Technology and the Sanctity of Life." In *Ethics and Problems of the 21st Century,* ed. K. M. Sayre & K. E. Goodpaster, 160–74. Notre Dame, In.: University of Notre Dame Press, 1979.
65. Essay length review discussion of Friedrich Kaulbach, *Ethik und Metaethik. Darstellung und Kritik metaethischer Argumente.* In *Contemporary German Philosophy,* 285–99. Atlantic Highlands, N.J.: Humanities Press, 1979.
66. "Freedom, Obligation, and Responsibility." In *Humanist Ethics, Dialogue on Basics,* ed. M. B. Storer, 75–97. Buffalo, N.Y.: Prometheus Books, 1980.
67. Review of William K. Frankena, *Thinking About Morality. Michigan Academician* 13, no. 3 (Winter 1981).
68. "The Ethics of Behavior Modification." *Ethics* 91 (April 1981): 499–509.
69. "Maximization and the Good Life." Paper read in Plenary Session of Conference on Ethics held by Wittgenstein Society, Kirchberg, Austria. *Akten Des 5. Internationalen Wittgenstein Symposiums* 25. Bis 31. August 1980, 33–42. Wien: Holder-Pichler-Tempsky, 1981.

70. "When Does the Right to Life Begin?" *Human Rights, Nomos* 23, ed. J. R. Pennock & J. W. Chapman, 201–29. New York: New York University Press, 1981.
71. "Defining Morality Without Prejudice." *The Monist* 64, no. 3 (July 1981): 325–41.
72. "The Conceptual Link Between Morality and Rationality." Invited lead paper in Symposium: Moral Rationality, for Western Division, APA, Spring 1982. *Noûs* 16, no. 1 (March 1982): 78–88.
73. "Virtue Ethics." *Philosophic Exchange,* Proceedings of Addresses to Philosophical Exchange, 3, no. 3 (1982): 57–70.
74. Review of B. C. Johnson, *The Atheist Debater's Handbook. Teaching Philosophy* 5, no. 4 (October 1982): 363–66.
75. "Duties to One's Employer." In *Just Business: New Introductory Essays in Business Ethics,* ed. Tom Regan, 60–99. New York: Random House, 1983.
76. Review of N. J. H. Dent, *The Moral Psychology of the Virtues* (New York: Cambridge University Press, 1984). *Philosophy and Phenomenological Research* (1984): 757–60.
77. "Rationality, Reason, and the Good." In *Morality, Reason, and Truth: New Essays on the Foundations of Ethics,* ed. D. Copp and D. Zimmerman, 193–211. Totowa, N.J.: Rowman and Allanheld, 1985.
78. "Maximization and Fairness." Reply to a paper by James Griffin on Utilitarianism and the Free Rider Problem, read at a Conference at Oberlin in April 1984. Published as part of the Conference Proceedings in *Ethics* 96 (October 1985): 119–29.
79. Review article on T. Nagel, *Ueber das Leben, die Seele, und den Tod.* German translation of *Mortal Questions* (Cambridge University Press, 1979). *Grazer Philosophische Studien,* Graz, Austria (1985) 135–57.
80. "Justification in Ethics." *Nomos* 28, ed. J. R. Pennock and J. W. Chapman, 3–27: 1986.
81. Foreword to *Ought, Reasons, and Morality: The Collected Essays of W. D. Falk.* Ithaca, N.Y.: Cornell University Press, 1986.
82. "Individual and Collective Responsibility." In *Views on Individualism: Presentations by I. M. Kirzner, W. J. Ong, M. Olson, and K. Baier.* Published by the St. Louis Humanities Forum of the Charron Institute, 1986.
83. "Moral, Legal and Social Responsibility." In *Shame, Responsibility and the Corporation,* ed. Hugh Curtler, 185–95. New York: Haven Publishing Corp, 1986.
84. "Moral and Legal Responsibility." In *Medical Innovations and Bad Outcomes,* ed. M. Siegler, S. Toulmin, F. E. Zimring, K. F. Schaffner, 101–29. Ann Arbor, Mich.: Health Administration Press, 1987.
85. "Rationality, Value and Preference." Comment on D. Gauthier, *Morals by Agreement. Social Philosophy & Policy* 5 (Spring 1988): 17–45.
86. "Radical Virtue Ethics." *Midwest Studies in Philosophy* 13 (1988): 126–35.
87. "Threats of Futility: Is Life Worth Living?" *Free Inquiry* 8 (Summer 1988): 47–52.

88. "Preference and the Good of Man." Invited paper, written in 1973, for *The Philosophy of Georg Henrik von Wright*. Library of Living Philosophers, vol. 19, ed. P. A. Schilpp and L. E. Hahn, 233–70. La Salle, Ill,: Open Court Publishers, 1989.
89. "Zeitzeuge" (Philosophical Witness). In *Vertriebene Vernunft II. Emigration und Exil österreichischer Wissenschaft,* ed. Friedrich Stadler, 125–31. Jugend und Volk Wien Munchen, 1988. Published in Polish as "Rozum Wygnany." Znak 1988: 129–40.
90. "Justice and the Aims of Political Philosophy." *Ethics* 99, no. 4 (1989): 771–90.
91. "Autarchy, Reason and Commitment." *Ethics* 100, no. 1 (1989): 93–107.
92. "Moral Reasoning." In *Encyclopedia of Ethics,* vol. 2, ed. Lawrence C. Becker and Charlotte B. Becker. New York & London: Garland Publishing Inc., 1992: 852–56.
93. "Egoism." In *A Companion to Ethics,* ed. Peter Singer. Oxford: Blackwell, 1992: 197–204.
94. Review of Judith Jarvis Thomson, *The Realm of Rights.* Forthcoming in *Dialogue.*
95. "Justice and Procreation." Paper for a symposium on James Sterba. Forthcoming in *Journal of Social Philosophy.*

Bibliography of Works Cited

Alexander, H.G., ed. 1956. *The Leibniz-Clarke Correspondence.* Manchester: Manchester University Press.

Anderson, Elizabeth. 1993. *Value in Ethics and Economics.* Cambridge, Mass.: Harvard University Press.

Aquinas, St. Thomas. 1945. *Basic Writings of Saint Thomas Aquinas.* Vol. 2. Ed. Anton C. Pegis. New York: Random House.

Balguy, John. 1734. *A Collection of Tracts.* London.

Bond, Edward J. 1983. *Reasons and Value.* New York: Cambridge University Press.

Brandt, Richard. 1979. *A Theory of the Right and the Good.* New York: Oxford University Press.

Brink, David. 1989. *Moral Realism and the Foundations of Ethics.* Cambridge: Cambridge University Press.

Christman, John. 1991. "Autonomy and Personal History." *Canadian Journal of Philosophy* 21 (March): 1–24.

Cudworth, Ralph. 1838. *A Treatise of Freewill.* Ed. John Allen. London: John W. Parker.

Cumberland, Richard. 1727 (1978). *A Treatise of the Law of Nature.* Trans. John Maxwell. London. Reprint, Garland Publishing.

Dancy, Jonathan. 1993. *Moral Reasons.* Oxford: Oxford University Press.

Darwall, Stephen. 1983. *Impartial Reason.* Ithaca: Cornell University Press.

______. 1986. "Rational Agent, Rational Act." *Philosophical Topics* 14: 33–57.

Dretske, Fred. 1988. *Explaining Behavior: Reasons in a World of Causes.* Cambridge, Mass.: MIT Press.

Fischer, John Martin, and Mark Ravizza. 1993. *Introduction to Perspectives on Moral Responsibility.* Ithaca: Cornell University Press.

Foot, Philippa. 1978. "Morality as a System of Hypothetical Imperatives." In *Virtues and Vices.* Berkeley: University of California Press.

Frankfurt, Harry. 1988. *The Importance of What We Care About.* Cambridge: Cambridge University Press.

Friedman, Michael. 1979. "Truth and Confirmation." *Journal of Philosophy* 76: 361–82.

Gauthier, David. 1986. *Morals by Agreement.* New York: Oxford University Press.

______. 1995. "Public Reason." *Social Philosophy & Policy* 12: 19–42.

Gibbard, Allan. 1990. *Wise Choices, Apt Feelings.* Cambridge, Mass.: Harvard University Press.

Grotius, Hugo. 1925. *The Law of War and Peace.* Trans. Francis W. Kelsey. New York: Carnegie Endowment for International Peace.

Gruyer, Frederique, et. al. 1991. *La Violence Impensable.* Paris: Nathan.

Hampton, Jean. 1992. "Rethinking Reason." *American Philosophical Quarterly* 29 (July): 219–36.

______. 1994. "The Failure of Expected Utility Theory as a Theory of Reason." *Economics and Philosophy* 10: 195–242.

Harman, Gilbert. 1977. *The Nature of Morality.* Oxford: Oxford University Press.

______. 1983. "Human Flourishing, Ethics and Liberty." *Philosophy and Public Affairs* 12 (Fall): 307–22.

Herman, Barbara. 1993. "Obligation and Performance." In *The Practice of Moral Judgment.* Cambridge, Mass.: Harvard University Press.

Herman, Judith Lewis. 1992. *Trauma and Recovery: The Aftermath of Violence—from Domestic Abuse to Political Terror.* New York: Basic Books.

Hill, Thomas. 1992. *Dignity and Practical Reason in Kant's Moral Theory.* Ithaca, N.Y.: Cornell University Press.

Hobbes, Thomas. 1991. *Leviathan.* Ed. Richard Tuck. Cambridge: Cambridge University Press.

Hume, David. 1975. *Enquiries Concerning Human Understanding and Concerning the Principles of Morals.* Ed. L.A. Selby-Bigge, revised by P.H. Nidditch. Oxford: Clarendon Press.

______. 1978. *A Treatise of Human Nature.* 2d ed. Ed. L.A. Selby- Bigge. New York: Oxford University Press.

Hurley, Paul. 1990. "The Many Appetites of Thomas Hobbes." *History of Philosophy Quarterly* 7, no. 4 (October): 391–407.

Kagan, Shelly. 1989. *The Limits of Morality.* Oxford: Oxford University Press.

Kant, Immanuel. 1956. *Critique of Practical Reason.* Trans. Lewis White Beck. Indianapolis: Bobbs-Merrill.

______. 1959. *Foundation of the Metaphysics of Morals.* Trans. Lewis White Beck. Indianapolis: Bobbs-Merrill.

______. 1964. *Groundwork of the Metaphysics of Morals.* Trans. H.J. Paton. New York: Harper Torchbooks.

______. 1988. *Selections.* Ed. Lewis White Beck. New York: Scribner/Macmillan.

Kenny, A. J. P. 1963. *Action, Emotion, and Will.*

Korsgaard, Christine. 1986. "Skepticism About Practical Reason." *Journal of Philosophy* 83, no. 1 (January): 5–25.

Leibniz, G. W. F. 1956. *Leibniz-Clarke Correspondence,* ed. H.G. Alexander. Manchester: Manchester University Press.

______. 1981. *New Essays on Human Understanding.* Trans. and ed. Peter Remnant and Jonathan Bennett. Cambridge: Cambridge University Press.

Lobel, Arnold. 1980. *Fables.* New York: Harper and Row.

Locke, John. 1954. *Essays on the Law of Nature.* Trans. and ed. W. von Leyden. Oxford: Clarendon Press.

______. 1985. *An Essay Concerning Human Understanding.* Ed. P. H. Nidditch. Oxford: Oxford University Press.

______. 1990. *Questions Concerning the Law of Nature.* Trans. and ed. Robert Horwitz, Jenny Strauss Clay, and Diskin Clay. Ithaca: Cornell University Press.

Mackie, J.L. 1977. *Ethics: Inventing Right and Wrong.* Harmondsworth: Penguin.

McDowell, John. 1978. "Are Moral Requirements Hypothetical Imperatives?" *Proceedings of the Aristotelian Society* 52: 13–29.

Mill. J.S. 1972. *Utilitarianism, On Liberty, and Considerations on Representative Government.* Ed. H.B. Acton. New York: E.P. Dutton.

______. 1979. *Utilitarianism.* Ed. George Sher. Indianapolis: Hackett.

G.E. Moore. 1903. *Principia Ethica.* Cambridge: Cambridge University Press.

Nagel, Thomas. 1970. *The Possibility of Altruism.* Princeton: Princeton University Press.

Nell, Onora (O'Neill). 1975. *Acting on Principle: An Essay in Kantian Ethics.* New York: Columbia University Press.

Nelson, Alan. 1990. "Are Economic Kinds Natural?" *Minnesota Studies in the Philosophy* of Science 14.

Parfit, Derek. 1984. *Reasons and Persons.* Oxford: Oxford University Press.

Paton, H.J. 1948. *The Categorical Imperative: A Study in Kant's Moral Philosophy.* Chicago: University of Chicago Press.

Prichard, H. A. 1949. "Does Moral Philosophy Rest on a Mistake?" In *Moral Obligation.* Oxford: Clarendon Press.

Putnam, Frank W. 1989. *Diagnosis and Treatment of Multiple Personality Disorder.* New York: The Guilford Press.

Putnam, Hilary. 1983. "Why Reason Can't Be Naturalized." *In Realism and Reason.* Vol. 3. Cambridge: Cambridge University Press.

Quine, W. V. 1977. "Facts of the Matter." *In American Philosophy from Edwards to Quine,* ed. R. W. Shahan and A. R. Merrill. Norman: University of Oklahoma Press.

Rawls, John. 1971. *A Theory of Justice.* Cambridge, Mass.: Harvard University Press.

______. 1993. *Political Liberalism.* New York: Columbia University Press.

Raz, Joseph. 1989. "Facing Up." *Southern California Law Review* 62:1153.

______. 1988. *The Morality of Freedom.* New York: Oxford University Press.

______. 1990. *Practical Reasons and Norms,* 2d ed. Princeton: Princeton University Press.

Rescher, Nicholas. 1991. "The Unity of Kant's Categorical Imperative." *Akten des Siebenten Internationalen Kant-Kongresses.* Kurfurstliches Schloss zu Mainz, 1990, hrsg. Von G. Funke, Bonn: Bouvier.

Ross, Colin A. 1989. *Multiple Personality Disorder: Diagnosis, Clinical Features, and Treatment.* New York: John Wiley & Sons.

Rousseau, Jean-Jacques. 1964. *Oeuvres complètes* III. Eds. B. Gagnebin and M. Raymond. Paris: Gallimard.

Scheffler, Samuel. 1992. *Human Morality.* Oxford: Oxford University Press.

Schneewind, J.B. 1991. "Natural Law, Skepticism, and Methods of Ethics." *Journal of the History of Ideas* 52, no. 2 (April-June): 289–308.

———. 1993a. "Kant and Natural Law Ethics." *Ethics* 104 (October): 53–74.

———. 1993b. "Modern Moral Philosophy: From Beginning to End?" *In Philosophical Imagination and Cultural Memory,* ed. Patricia Cross. Durham, N.C.: Duke University Press.

Shaftesbury, Lord. 1900. *Characteristics.* Ed. J.M. Robertson. London.

Simon, H.A. 1955. "A Behavioral Model of Rational Choice." *Quarterly Journal of Economics* 69: 99–118.

———. 1956. "Rational Choice and the Structure of the Environment." *Psychological Review* 63: 129–38.

Sugden, Robert. 1991. "Rational Choice: A Survey of Contributions from Economics and Philosophy." *Economic Journal* 101, no. 407 (July): 751–85.

Thomas, Laurence. 1989. "Doing Justice to Egoism." *Journal of Philosophy* 86 (October): 551–2.

———. 1992–93. "Moral Deference." *Philosophical Forum* 24: 233–500.

———. 1993. "The Reality of the Moral Self." *Monist* 76 (January): 3–21.

———. 1996. "Evil and the Concept of a Human Person." *Midwest Studies in Philosophy* 20. Notre Dame, Ind.: University of Notre Dame Press, in press.

Thomson, Judith Jarvis. 1971. "A Defense of Abortion." *Philosophy and Public Affairs* 1: 47–66.

———. 1990. *The Realm of Rights.* Cambridge: Harvard University Press.

———. 1993. Symposium on Realm of Rights, *Philosophy and Phenomenological Research* 53, no. 1 (March): 151–94.

Tuck, Richard. 1987. "The 'modern' theory of natural law." In *The Languages of Political Theory in Early-Modern Europe,* ed. Anthony Pagden. Cambridge: Cambridge University Press.

Watson, Gary. 1987. "Responsibility and the Limits of Evil." In *Responsibility, Character, and the Emotions,* ed. Ferdinand Schoeman. New York: Cambridge University Press.

White, Robert W. 1963. *Ego and Reality in Psychanalytic Theory.* New York: International Universities Press.

Williams, Bernard. 1985. *Ethics and the Limits of Philosophy.* Cambridge: Harvard University Press.

———. 1991. "Internal and External Reasons." In *Moral Luck.* Cambridge: Cambridge University Press.

Wolff, Robert Paul. 1971. *The Autonomy of Reason.* New York: Harper Torchbooks.

Van Fraassen, Bas. 1980. *The Scientific Image.* Oxford: Oxford University Press.

Velleman, J. David. 1989. *Practical Reflection.* Princeton: Princeton University Press.

Von Wright, G.H. 1963. *Norm and Action.* London: Routledge and Kegan Paul.

Index